DESIGN AND THE PUBLIC GOOD

DESIGN AND THE PUBLIC GOOD

SELECTED WRITINGS
1930–1980
BY SERGE CHERMAYEFF

EDITED BY
RICHARD PLUNZ

THE MIT PRESS
CAMBRIDGE, MASSACHUSETTS
LONDON, ENGLAND

This book was set in Bodoni Book and Spartan by Achorn Graphic Services and printed and bound by Halliday Lithograph in the United States of America.

Library of Congress Cataloging in Publication Data

Chermayeff, Serge, 1900—
Design and the public good.

Bibliography: p.
Includes index.
1. Architectural design. 2. Architecture and society.
3. Modernism (Art) I. Plunz, Richard.
II. Title.
NA2750.C445 1982   729   82-48164
ISBN 0-262-16088-9

CONTENTS

PART II
THE PROFESSIONAL CONDITION   **101**

FOREWORD

John Ruskin suggests that a professional be defined by the fact that it is his duty "on due occasion" to die for the cause to which he is committed. According to Ruskin, the test for the true professional is to die rather than be delinquent:

The Soldier, rather than leave his post in battle.
The Physician, rather than leave his post in plague.
The Pastor, rather than teach Falsehood.
The Lawyer, rather than countenance Injustice.

Ruskin adds "for truly, the man who does not know when to die, does not know how to live."

This statement suggests that professionals ought to have moral commitment, passion, and valiant, even heroic, devotion to service as well as to a body of knowledge. It suggests righteous practice as well as informed practice. It suggests articulate pursuit of perfection as well as the exercise of skill. It suggests proselytizing as well as transmitting specialized knowledge. It suggests that the self be identified with principle.

When I think of Serge Chermayeff, I think of Ruskin's words. Serge is a committed teacher-designer-intellectual, and it is his passion that captivates me. I do not know what Serge was like in his youth in Russia and England. I know him from his life in America, first in Chicago, where he headed the Institute of Design, but most intensively when we were colleagues at Harvard. And I know that every word, every look, every stroke of his pen, inside the studio or out, was a tool for teaching. His students were his pupils of course; but his friends, his professional peers (and few equal him), his family, his university colleagues were also privileged to be his students. He is one of the rare architects of distinction who also edified through his writing and his oral precision as well as eloquence. I shall not forget the brilliance with which, in mid-1951 at the Institute of Contemporary Art in London, he sketched the character of postwar Britain as a framework for its art, architecture, and urban design.

Serge wants to instill new ways of seeing, thinking, and relating architecture to the world. He has been more interested in process than in a particular product. He has been concerned with the design of individual buildings and even more with the relationships of those buildings to the social and political as well as physical environment. He wants to know and have others be aware for whom they are building, for what purposes, and with what effects. For him, as his writings in this volume indicate, society is the client and not an individual, perhaps idiosyncratic, patron.

Serge has never been stereotyped. He can be a devastating critic in detecting flaws, false reasoning, the hypocritical, the fawning, and in routing out the inferior. But he always has been a loving teacher, even when devastating, because he cares about his students, he cares about architecture and design, and he cares enough about standards to insist that all do their best. Serge never lets students be content with the half-good when they are capable of more, even when they themselves do not realize their potential. Studying with Serge might at times be painful; but studying with Serge has always been stimulating and memorable and often exalting.

Serge is one of the few teachers of architecture and design in this country who is aware of the larger world of the economic, political, cultural, historic setting in which the built environment takes shape. And few in the visual arts are as articulate with language as he. He has not scorned the trivial. He has sought his friends among artists, writers, intellectuals, political thinkers. And he has carried to his students this excitement and curiosity about fields other than their chosen profession. As a many-gifted individual, his talents have been revealed to his students as well as his friends. He has been interested in the interior of buildings as well as the public scale and form of design; he has been interested in the interior of thought as revealed by his poetry and paintings; he has loved language as revealed by his incisive speech and writing. He loves nature as well as cities. Although an elitist in standards, he has not been an elitist in social outlook.

Whenever I see Serge, after a gap of several years, I find him as I did when I saw him daily. He remains brilliant and charming, impatient and discontent, teaching with passion through his writings as well as his designs and painting. He is still accessible to the young and responds to their call for advice in all ways. He pretends that he does not like his contemplative life to be interrupted, but both he and the young know better. I find it an enormous tribute to Serge that perhaps his chief protégés are his own sons, Ivan and Peter, both of whom are immensely gifted; each son found his way to the same general profession as his father, a man of strong opinions, high standards, and great love.

Serge Chermayeff is a creative force, a professor who never stops professing, as this book reveals.

Martin Meyerson

ACKNOWLEDGMENTS

The editor is indebted to Raniero Corbelletti, chairman of the Department of Architecture at the Pennsylvania State University, who first supported this effort in 1971, helping to obtain a small grant from the Central Fund for Research of the College of Arts and Architecture. In 1974, with the substantial support of Dean James Stewart Polshek, funding was obtained from the Center for Advanced Research in Urban and Environmental Affairs of the Columbia University Graduate School of Architecture and Planning; and other support was obtained through the efforts of Ivan Chermayeff. In the same year, the Serge Chermayeff papers and documents were deposited in the Avery Architectural Library, Columbia University, through the efforts of Adolf Placzek, Avery librarian. The editor is most indebted to the following students in the Graduate School of Architecture and Planning who assisted in numerous ways toward completion of this volume: Linda Yowell, Robert Dean, Thaleia Christidis, Ann Kaufman, Robert Woods, Graham Wyatt; and especially to Wiebke Noack, who completed much of the graphic material, and Marta Gutman, who was invaluable for her assistance in all aspects of the final preparation of the manuscript.

All illustrations are courtesy of the Avery Architectural Library, Columbia University, with the exception of the illustration on page 186 from the Frances Loeb Library, Harvard University; and the illustration on page 326 from the New York Public Library.

INTRODUCTION:
CHERMAYEFF AND HIS CIRCLE

Serge Chermayeff occupies a unique position in the evolution of twentieth-century architecture. His legacy is complex, and time will serve to reinforce his importance. His contribution is a composite of several periods and preoccupations, each with its own consciousness. Included must be his role in British design innovation in the thirties, extended in a limited but significant way later in the United States. Also included must be his initiatives in design education and research in the United States: his curriculum for a Department of Design at Brooklyn College; his further pedagogical development of the Lazlo Moholy-Nagy curriculum at the Institute of Design in Chicago; and finally, his extended involvement with teaching and research at Harvard and Yale. Also included must be Chermayeff's position as critic, in the most profound sense, involving both architectural and social commentary that reached beyond popular journalism. Above all, he has been an architect, but an architect who is also a literary person. In 1940, when Chermayeff sailed from England for America, he left behind original drawings and documentation of his architectural projects, and they were destroyed in the war. He did, however, bring his Left Book Club volumes with him.

Chermayeff's critical constancy has been as apostate to both mainstream professionalism and academism. Very early, in Britain, he joined the company of a previous generation of skeptics, his clearest polemical antecedent probably being Wyndham Lewis and his "vorticism." In *The Caliph's Design,* first published in 1919, Lewis noted the lack of participation of English architects in the modern movement to that date. He asked the question, "Architects! Where is your vortex?", which Chermayeff would quote many years later.[1] And when the architectural revolution finally arrived in England in the thirties, Chermayeff would have to be considered a principal "vortex." The vorticist critique argued that the "ramshackle empire of architecture" might be replaced by a collaboration of painters and engineers unless architecture could be challenged to respond to modern life. Lewis argued that architecture must respond "by building a new arena," or else "the Architect, as he drags out his miserable, if well-paid life" would be placed "into the dustbin."[2] For Chermayeff, an important precedent to the range of concern that comprised the "new arena" was the work of Patrick Geddes and his concern with the physical environment as a social organism.[3]

Chermayeff's informal mentor, Eric Gill, was another important influence, and Gill's writings culminated a philosophical lineage that can be traced back through William Lethaby, William Morris, and Thomas Carlyle. Chermayeff often repeats the phrase from Gill that "beauty would look after herself." In his book of the same title, Gill argues that "architecture, more than any of the other arts of man, is a social art" and that "what is done by several or many men working in collaboration is necessarily different in kind from what is done by an individual working by himself, and what is necessarily used and enjoyed by many is different in kind from what is made for private use." Gill also dealt with the myriad new realities of technology, arguing for a new intelligence, for an "intelligent building . . . facing the facts of men and materials and construction" with "proper consideration of the purpose for which the building is required."[4] This purpose, essentially social in emphasis, combined with rejection of stylistic or programmatic precedent, became an important basis for Chermayeff's own design innovation and theoretical stance.

The political dimension of Chermayeff's thinking must be placed within the tradition of reform socialism in England dating back to the late nineteenth century, most specifically within the realm of the Fabian Society and Labor Party. Both organizations were concerned with pragmatic goals of immediate political reform rather than with struggles to achieve utopia. Both focused more on the inequities of capitalism than on promoting a holistic new vision. They were not revolutionary. By the twenties, they had become the "loyal opposition" of the left. This stance, while by no means cohesive, did tend to bar the Marxists, although by the thirties, even those differences had become somewhat blurred in relation to actual alliances. The English modernism of the thirties cannot be separated from these left political ideals that nurtured it. The sudden prominence of the modernist architects received the notice and support of the older generation from the left. Such figures as Eric Gill or George Bernard Shaw were often in attendance at architectural talks and discussions, including Chermayeff's.

Chermayeff's political circle broadened through acquaintances made while completing the interiors for the British Broadcasting Corporation in the early thirties. Chermayeff himself contributed to the BBC programming in architecture in the following years, and he encountered many of the most prominent personalities involved in left causes; his acquaintance with Bertrand Russell, for one, developed at this time and continued over many years. The list is long, but one BBC association of extreme importance to Chermayeff's development was the "scientific socialists"—the so-called "Cambridge Scientists," who launched a critical revolution in thinking related to the boundaries between science and society and to the issue of the social responsibility of the scientist.[5] Within this group, J. B. S. Haldane, the biologist, and J. Desmond Bernal, the crystallographer and pioneer in the field of molecular biology, were Chermayeff's closest acquaintances. Bernal, especially, maintained a profound interest in the relationship between science and culture. He argued that "the present situation, where a highly developed science stands almost isolated from a traditional literary culture, is altogether anomalous and cannot last." He saw the assimilation requiring "very serious modifications in the structure of science itself," and he was fascinated with intuition and the process of "discovery."[6] These interests contributed to the attention he gave architects. On many occasions, he participated with Chermayeff and others in talks and debates about modernism.[7]

The public forum was an extensive one. From the beginning, Chermayeff's input was literary. It was also good theatre, with Chermayeff playing the "brilliant talker and wit, not too austere in his conceptions of the artist's role," as he has been described by Noel Carrington.[8] His visibility to the public led to difficulties with the political right, however. At its worst, in Britain, he became the quarry of anti-Semitic and nationalistic sentiments, which still linger almost five decades later, although within the subtleties of more academic scrutiny.[9] These difficulties first surfaced around 1934, concurrent with the appearance of the public face of fascism in Britain, largely through the effectiveness of Sir Oswald Moseley's British Union of Fascists organized two years earlier.[10] Chermayeff and Mendelsohn's winning entry to the Bexhill competition sparked the first such reaction, with objections raised to the architects' national origins in the architectural press and elsewhere. Public reaction to Chermayeff's influence peaked after the 1935 publication of his article "A Hundred Years Ahead," coauthored with J. M. Richards, for *The Architects' Journal*.[11] It was an ingenious and witty provocation that might well have incited both modernists and traditionalists, but as Chermayeff and Richards admitted, it gave the clear impression that they were "on the side of socialism and internationalism."[12] The ensuing controversy dominated the letters to the editor of *The Architects' Journal* for many subsequent issues, with extraordinarily vicious attacks from both traditionalists and fascists.

The voice of the right was eclipsed as Hitler's power became more ominous and as economic and political uncertainty throughout the world pointed ever more certainly toward war. By 1938, the preoccupations of the left in architecture broadened in response to the obvious crisis at hand, with attention directed toward the architectural consequences of war. Much of this activity was related to the civilian threat posed by the technological advancements in aerial bombardment, which, at that point, represented an unprecedented advance in the practice of war. By 1938, "Air Raid Precaution" involved a range of issues, from design of refugee camps to bomb shelters, and this agenda promoted concrete collaborations between architect and "scientific socialist." Chermayeff's study, *Plan for Air Raid Precaution,* published in 1939 contributed an architectural development of J. B. S. Haldane's book on the same subject published in the previous year.[13] Both authors criticized contradictions in government policy emanating from the ARP Act of 1937. Chermayeff's work also coincided with many others, involving formal or informal collaborations, through the ARP Coordinating Committee or otherwise. For example, Chermayeff worked with TECTON on a graphic system for signage for their ARP plan for the Borough of Finsbury.[14]

Ultimately, the war led to Chermayeff's removal to the United States. After immigration he extended his involvement with ARP, publishing a series of articles and otherwise attempting to promote discussion. In general, he transferred his political sensibilities from the British to American context, connecting with the network of progressive architects and organizations that had been fostered by the Depression years or that had originated with the crisis of war. In San Francisco he supported the formation of "Telesis,"[15] and in New York the Federation of Architects, Engineers, Chemists, and Technicians (FAECT), the most powerful of the several labor unions for architects and draftsmen.[16] He participated in forming the American chapter of the International Congress for Modern Architecture (CIAM), the American Society of Planners and Architects (ASPA),[17] and the Architects Committee of the National Council of Soviet-American Friendship.[18] In New York, he could be found lecturing to the ILGWU[19] or auctioning artwork for the benefit of *Task* magazine.[20] He briefly assisted Bertrand Russell in his attempt to gain employment in the United States.[21]

As in England, Chermayeff's activity in the United States was controversial, especially in New York. The protest in 1941 against his nomination to the chairmanship at Brooklyn College brought his foreign origins to issue once again.[22] In 1944, the new Chermayeff curriculum for a Department of Design also became the object of outside censure, as political reaction against the New Deal and progressivism of the thirties were beginning.[23] Charges against Chermayeff ranged from alleged communism (belief in social purpose) to fascism (the Bauhaus was German). As the McCarthy era unfolded, the dilemmas that it presented to architects are an important, if neglected, segment of the history of the profession. For liberal architects within a profession that represents a quite fragile public art subservient to the sources of economic and political power, the period forced difficult choices. As Victor Navasky relates, there was ample evidence "of how deep were the divisions that beset the liberal community in the third great cold war conflict—the war between those who thought of themselves as progressives and those who inhabited what they like to call the vital center."[24] Consistent with tradition, the compromises of the "vital center" were paramount to commercial survival for architects, leaving the progressives adrift. An interesting indication is the conservative stance taken by the American Institute of Architects (AIA) toward public housing after the close of World War II.[25]

For Chermayeff's circle, difficulties did arise. For example, the Architect's Committee of the National Council of Soviet-American Friendship, which was active between 1944 and 1946, found itself listed by the U.S. attorney general as a subversive organization in 1952. Those on the leadership roster, almost entirely AIA members, were thus prevented from gaining approval for certain government work. Ultimately some of the membership renounced their affiliation with the National Council in order to obtain clearance for work.[26] By

1949, when Chermayeff gave his talk to the famous Cultural and Scientific Conference for World Peace ("Waldorf Conference") sponsored by the National Council of the Arts, Sciences, and Professions,[27] most architects were back to work—and silent.

By the close of the forties, even the politically ecumenical American Society of Planners and Architects (ASPA) had long since disappeared. Between 1944 and 1946 it had pursued a wide range of concerns in relation to urban problems and modern architecture. Its almost eighty members included a cross section of architects who would mold the direction of United States architecture in the next two decades: Chermayeff and Louis Kahn, whose commitments crossed, as Kahn pursued the social architecture of housing and hospitals; Marcel Breuer, Walter Gropius, and José Luis Sert, of CIAM and Bauhaus formation; Siegfried Giedion and Henry Russell-Hitchcock, with their ideological strictures in place for the next wave; Gordon Bunshaft, John Johansen, Philip Johnson, I. M. Pei, Eero Saarinen, Hugh Stebbins, and other newly trained Americans waiting to launch their careers. The ASPA coalition quickly ceased after the war. It was against the backdrop of professional ambiguities toward social commitments that, in 1954, Chermayeff finally resigned from the AIA, which was all that remained of the professional organizations of the previous decade. The only professional affiliation that he retained was his first, with the Royal Institute of British Architects (RIBA), which he joined in 1932. Chermayeff's censure of the mainstream architectural profession in the United States is consistent with a critical position that found its origins in England, but by comparison, the American context for architectural practice in the fifties would only serve to heighten that critique.

In contrast to the AIA, the RIBA existed within a tradition of liberal discourse in which, for example, differences between the modernists and traditionalists remained a dialogue. In 1933, older traditionalists like H. S. Goodhardt-Rendel would support Chermayeff's nomination as Fellow in spite of his youth and scanty building to that date—perhaps even because of his well-articulated critique of the profession. Traditionalists and modernists converged on certain moral commitments. A comparison of Chermayeff's talk "New Materials and New Methods," given at the RIBA in December 1933, with the newly elected President Giles Gilbert Scott's inaugural address given in November 1933 indicates a substantial agreement on the superficiality of modernism—its desire for "striking effect rather than functionalism" with "materials still largely misunderstood"—or agreement that "mechanical science has rendered this age obsolete" while also mandating a responsibility "to put the machine in its proper place." Scott even protested that traditional architecture had become "largely divorced from the practical side of modern life," and as a consequence of "too much superficial style and too little real architectural building," architects were left with "only a miserable fraction of the building activities of the country."[28] Other RIBA members of the same generation actively supported Chermayeff and the new work in general. By comparison, the postwar AIA was far from a forum; rather, it fulfilled a function of commercial expediency.

The patronage for a postwar practice in New York also contrasted with the situation of the thirties in Britain. In London, Chermayeff's patrons, like many others who supported the modern movement, prevailed on the edge of the commercial marketplace. They tended to embrace the left political philosophies, were intellectuals, and were permitted a free rein. There was an abundance of work within the small modernist constituency. As Chermayeff recalls, "none of us, it seems, sought commissions. They simply came."[29] Chermayeff's Harrow associations served him quite well, from his first decorating job in 1924, with the firm of Ernest Williams, Ltd., to his commissions for W. and A. Gilbey, Ltd., and the Imperial Chemical Industries. His father-in-law's association with the immense construction firm, Holland, Hannen, and Cubitts, Ltd., also proved to be very helpful. He introduced Chermayeff to Lord Waring, leading to the modern exhibition at Waring and Gillow organized in 1929.[30] Unlike in New York, obtaining commissions in London was not so much a matter of commercial enterprise as of intellectual and social connection. This euphoria, which persisted in spite of international political and economic turmoil, ended abruptly in 1939, when, like many others, Chermayeff's office was forced into bankruptcy, precipitated by the bank crisis and the lack of new work.[31]

Chermayeff's dislocation to America could only be reconciled by the same promise that it held for Gropius and Breuer. But he waited longer before leaving, having established irrevocable British ties. In some ways, his circumstances recast the personal crisis of the Russian Revolution two decades earlier. After less than a year at his Bentley

Wood, located along the flight path of the war planes, belongings were auctioned off to friends and acquaintances.[32] Within weeks Chermayeff was a nomad. At the outset, the United States held out the promise of renewed practice, especially in California, which attracted Chermayeff as it had compelled Schindler or Neutra. In spite of war, he received commissions in California in quick succession—the Mayhew House and the Horn House—but by this time the desire to practice was no longer paramount.

In 1941, consistent with his activities of the previous year in Britain, Chermayeff explored alternatives to private practice. He unsuccessfully tried to cultivate the possibility of public work with the Pacific Northwest Regional Planning Commission. He also prepared curricula proposals for architectural studies at Stanford and Berkeley,[33] and he taught a course at the San Francisco Art Institute. Teaching became more and more a preoccupation. Opportunity to teach emerged only in New York, however, resulting in his move in late 1941. In New York, he also briefly pursued practice, obtaining his license in 1943 and opening the office on East 37th Street in 1946 in anticipation of postwar commissions. But work did not come easily, and commercial practice in postwar America would obviously entail the kind of compromise of intellectual involvement that bordered on dereliction.[34] Chermayeff demurred. Design activity became, like his painting, a pleasurable activity rather than a livelihood.

Community and Privacy was one of the few important books to emerge from the fifties wasteland of architectural theory and criticism in the United States. Almost two decades after its publication it remains in print, now of interest as much to students of sociology as architecture. For the architect in 1963 its appearance was exciting. Apart from the importance of the social and architectural critique, the clarity of organization and the innovative design of the book was without precedent—the latter the accomplishment of Peter Chermayeff, then a student at the Graduate School of Design. In certain ways the book is almost reminiscent of the French Enlightenment—of J. N. L. Durand's *Précis*. It also takes its rightful place within the proliferation of cultural criticism in the fifties—Marshall McLuhan's *The Mechanical Bride*, C. Wright Mill's *White Collar*, or John Kenneth Galbraith's *The Affluent Society*.

Community and Privacy, published in 1963, was the culmination of a decade's work toward development of a critical position on the deurbanization of the postwar American city and toward development of design prototypes for an alternative to the detached single-family suburban house. The latter design investigations centered primarily around projects at Harvard University's Graduate School of Design, with the first sophisticated versions of the "Harvard Urban Family House" produced in 1956. They were pioneering work in "low-rise, high-density housing." The prototypes were intended to be a hybrid form for a new kind of development between city and suburb, retaining the long, narrow lots of traditional nineteenth-century gridiron planning while placing the yard space within the house itself in the form of small courtyards. A wide range of house plans evolved, with differing lot dimensions and numbers of patios and with one or two stories. Some plans integrated the automobile; others segregated it into concentrations at the periphery of the house clusters.

The analytic method used in *Community and Privacy* represented a kind of "neo-functionalism," addressing one of the dilemmas of modernism that had concerned Chermayeff for over two decades, namely that the functional basis of form involved more than a proclamation. This preoccupation had been represented in Chermayeff's teaching methods dating at least from the studio projects at the Chicago Institute of Design. As a conscious process, the design problems would be decomposed into subproblems, which would be interrelated, but each with its own set of design criteria. Gradually, the design would emerge in a process of reconstruction. The most developed such studio was the first-year course at the Graduate School of Design, which Chermayeff created beginning in 1954. The generic problem was design of a neighborhood. The student would begin by analyzing an existing neighborhood, breaking it down into its physical components in extreme analytic detail, and then redesigning each. In such fashion, the community would be reassembled over the period of a year by the entire class.[35]

The analysis employed in *Community and Privacy* decomposed the problem of house and its grouping into subcomponents whose functional requirements were individually addressed in a series of idealized quasi-architectural patterns and then combined to define an ideal prototype. The statistical method of structuring the interrelationships between requirements was developed by Christopher Alexander, a doctoral candidate at the Graduate School of Design who was working under Chermayeff and the psychologist Jerome Bruner. Applying pioneering work, such as Ross Ashby's *Design for a Brain,* Alexander produced the program that could cluster the interactions between the various requirements for the house and its grouping. The potential for such an application was well known among design behaviorists, but the key lay in Chermayeff's intermediate diagram, which bridged the gap between the verbal functional requirement and the final design. This realm of intermediate language had long fascinated Chermayeff, dating back to diagrams used to describe the organization of Bentley Wood in 1938. Alexander continued to develop the method in his doctoral thesis, *Notes on the Synthesis of Form,* and in subsequent studies.[36]

Critical reaction to *Community and Privacy* ranged from that of scandalized aesthetes, who were enraged by what they considered to be computerized creativity, to the neophytes who saw the methodology as the savior of the design profession. In retrospect, the real power of the book cannot be categorized so easily. The methodology now seems less important as a working method than as a kind of manifesto that creativity and rationality in design might both reach new heights. Of significance was the attempt to obtain a deeper understanding of the enduring problem of "form and function." Function was described in terms of private *activity* and communal *activity* rather than private and communal *space.* Thus, *activity* and form were correlated in a manner that broadened considerably for architects the possibilities of a behavior-oriented understanding of design.

Community and Privacy posited the Hegelian notion that a rational urban ideal might be a state of equilibrium rather than a frozen formal vision. The proposition defied traditional architectural criticism. The fledgling Charles Jencks was steadfast in his defense of art.[37] Alan Colquhoun seemed to have difficulty with the dialectic in which a paradigm for "community" included "privacy."[38] Allen Temko traced his reservations to excessive functionalism or, more precisely, the separation of functions. Yet Temko was obliged to admire the book for having broken new ground among "environmental humanists," from Ruskin to Mumford, through "recasting this longstanding humanist tradition . . . in a specific design program."

And he saw the attempt as charting "the most forbidding terrain. . . providing a glimpse of a distant city in golden light which rational men can build."[39]

After completion of *Community and Privacy*, Chermayeff continued to develop the dialectic, primarily in relation to urban scale studies. This work centered around his master's studio in environmental design at Yale. Apart from their abstract pedagogic value, these studies served as a forceful critique of CIAM planning principles and their application in the fifties-era "urban renewal" initiatives in the United States, which were characterized by "city-in-the-park" formalism, with rote application of undefined open space and nonintegration of the existing urban context. Chermayeff emphasized the importance of a more direct response of urban form to underlying patterns of use, and in this respect, his strong interest lay in movement as a generator at all scales. His first environmental design studio at Yale dealt with this issue in relation to the design of an idealized urban movement hierarchy in which the dialectic shifted from "community and privacy" to "mobility and tranquility."[40] This work stood quite apart from the revisionist CIAM urbanism of the same period—for example, the work of Team 10 in Europe or of José Luis Sert or Colin Rowe in the United States, all tending toward a CIAM vernacular, although each with somewhat differing formal sensibilities.

In 1966, with the assistance of Alexander Tzonis, a student from the original Yale studio, the dialectic was considerably expanded and developed as the "Yale Model," which became the basis for a seminar supported by the United States Bureau of Standards and was published as *Advanced Studies in Urban Environments*. This document was one of few efforts of lasting interest from that era which attempted to integrate the concerns of environmental disciplines with those of urban design in a school of architecture. The dialogue between Chermayeff and the biologist Edward Deevey, the lawyer Charles Haar, the philosopher Paul Weiss, the naturalist A. D. Parr, and others was interesting. A number of hypothetical and built urban projects, typical of the decade, became the principal focus of much of the discussion. Similar but more modest seminars were organized for subsequent studios, most notably for the fall of 1968.[41] The dialectic continued to develop, becoming, at this point, the "urban yardstick."

The book *Shape of Community*, which had been tentatively titled *Mobility and Tranquility*, represented a summary of the studies and discourse at Yale. It reflected quite precisely the particular confluence of political and environmental issues that directed much architectural thought toward the end of the sixties: misuse of technology, destruction of urban centers, and threats to natural and human ecology. Some of its foresight would require the crises of the seventies for verification to a populist constituency. Yet the book was caught between architecture and something else, and by 1971, when it appeared, architectural criticism was already experiencing the resurgence of more conservative concerns. To be sure, the book suffered from other problems, most notably a lack of visual and textural clarity. In the United States, *Shape of Community* was greeted with the strongest possible critical reaction, which was silence. There was notable interest in Europe, however, in Britain and especially in West Germany.

In his youth Chermayeff was preoccupied with the most populist aspects of twenties modernity: jazz, dance, and digression into surrealist painting. Ballroom dancing was a serious activity for several years, reflecting his fascination with the great American bands and his penchant for performance in the milieu of the Barclay or Savoy. Lacking a formal education in architecture, he is not a product of nineteenth-century eclectic academicism or its antidote in Teutonic functionalism. He is, instead, a product of twentieth-century eclecticism—an original, and eccentric in the best sense. His initiation into architecture was gradual, with his early formation aligned as much with the *deco moderne* of the 1925 Paris Exhibition as with anything else. As late as 1929, he chose Paul Follot, a French romantic, as his collaborator for the Waring and Gillow exhibition. He designed drawing room sets for Gerald du Maurier before he designed interiors. As late as 1930, he did some of the sets for the premier revue at the Cambridge Theatre. It was a gregarious period, which imparted to his later design an openness to embellishment—almost flamboyance, in contrast to the work of many others in Britain.

If there is a common purpose that links all of Chermayeff's design, it must be innovation in program and in the application of new technology. This "design without precedent" rendered style without precedent. He exploited a myriad of "new materials and new methods" to their fullest in terms of impact on both program and aesthetic. By 1930, with the completion of his house interior on Abbey Road and the interior for the Cambridge Theatre, his disposition toward design had already achieved a certain maturity. Abbey Road was a virtual catalogue of his furnishing innovation. The Cambridge Theatre represented his first totally designed large-scale interior in which no detail was unconsidered. Its most notable innovations included the use of color in the floor surfaces to codify circulation and the lighting of the auditorium, which dimmed from rear to proscenium along the great continuous gilded arches of the auditorium shell. Samuel Rothafel ("Roxy"), who visited the Cambridge Theatre in 1931, adapted the idea for the lighting at his Radio City Music Hall in New York.[42]

In subsequent years, as Chermayeff obtained larger commissions, his collaboration with the German émigré engineer Felix Sammuely was extremely effective in furthering technological innovation. This collaboration included the Entertainment Hall at Bexhill, Gilbey House, the laboratories for the Imperial Chemical Industries, and Bentley Wood. In Berlin, Sammuely had produced the first welded steel-frame building, and he set the same precedent for Mendelsohn and Chermayeff at Bexhill. Chermayeff's most individual contribution to Bexhill was the auditorium, designed to be easily transformed from theatre to all-purpose space. The form of the stage was flexible, adjusting to the needs of each performance. The spatial shell pioneered an acoustical treatment, including the ceiling disks designed for sound diffusion. External noise abatement was a major consideration at Gilbey House, with footings set on cork pads and cork placed between some columns and girders to eliminate vibration and sound transmission. Ceilings were treated acoustically, and the teak windows were sealed, within the concrete frame. The building was air-conditioned with naturally cooled air.[43]

The laboratories for the Imperial Chemical Industries were a definitive twentieth-century precedent for that particular building type, rejecting completely any predisposition to nineteenth-century design assumptions for the organization. The linear form met the complex modern supply requirements for air-conditioning, chemicals, etc., and responded to the need for flexibility. The laboratory and office space was adaptable to change without structural modification, and the building organization permitted side lighting and views rather than top lighting typical of traditional laboratory buildings.

Bentley Wood, while reverting to more traditional materials, also represented significant technological innovation. For example, the timber structural grid, designed for spatial flexibility, was constructed in a manner not dissimilar to steel. Prefabricated timber sections were assembled on the site using special connectors at the joints that could be tightened over the life of the building to compensate for shrinkage.

In general, Chermayeff's design has exhibited a devoted willingness to experiment, without undue compulsion for aesthetic strictures. Chermayeff's first house, the Shann House, completed only a few years before Bentley Wood, represented very different concerns. An in situ concrete box, it was a significant precedent in the English climate, and to this day it is in excellent condition. His experimentation with wood continued in the United States, especially in the series of structures built on Cope Cod in the early fifties that were constructed of standard timber framing adapted to new structural forms incorporating new materials, principally "Homosote." Of course, in microcosm much of Chermayeff's prodigious production of furnishings and product designs evidences concerns kindred to those of his buildings: the numerous chairs[44]—for example, the Plan Armchair W-5, with its removable upholstery, or the early experiments with plastics—the radio cabinets for E. K. Cole, Ltd.; or the pianos that slightly adjusted the traditional idiom. Much later, in a totally different context, the new technology of the computer was embraced as a design tool in *Community and Privacy* and indirectly contributed to the design for his own house on Lincoln Street in New Haven, in many ways his most remarkable house.

Chermayeff was not afraid of craft. In fact, "design without precedent" frequently had to be hand-produced before it could be mass-produced, even door and window hardware. A large part of his early design schooling involved reapplication of the venerable techniques of Waring and Gillow craftsmen in the transformation from Chippendale and Sheraton to *deco moderne*. There was also the realm of visual art, represented, for example, in fabric design or in the large number of carpets designed for Wilton. In New York he again took up the interest of his youth in painting. So strong was his visual curiosity that he could copy a Picasso or Léger with great exactitude. In the late forties, he played a considerable role in shaping the identity of the "Chicago School" of abstraction, exhibiting extensively during this period. He still paints, and his language is still partially reminiscent of the artist friends from London—Paul Nash, John Piper, Barbara Hepworth, Ben Nicholson, and Henry Moore.

In Britain, Chermayeff's circle among artists and critics shared both politics and projects. Collaboration was frequent, with no project of any consequence lacking the input of an artist colleague, especially in the early years, from Paul Nash at Bath House to A. C. Gibbons Grinling at Cambridge Theatre. Around 1930, the ill-fated European Mediterranean Academy was organized with Wijdeveld, Chermayeff, Mendelsohn, Gill, and the painter Amedee Ozenfant, the sculptor Pablo Gargallo, the ceramicist Paul Bonifas, and the composer Paul Hindemith.[45] At Bexhill, Edward Wadsworth executed a mural and Frank Dobson proposed a sculpture that was never realized. Together Moholy-Nagy and Chermayeff photographed the finished building. Bentley Wood was a repository for the work of many friends, the most prominent being Henry Moore's *Recumbent Figure,* placed at the intersection of the terrace and lawn, intended to organize "a kind of focal point of all the horizontals."[46] It was also a turning point in Moore's outdoor work and his first collaboration with an architect in which his sculpture was not "on a building, but outside it, in a spatial relationship to it." Bentley Wood was also a turning point for Chermayeff and represented a "new wealth" for British modernism, as Charles Reilly expressed it.[47]

Among the architects in Chermayeff's circle in Britain and the United States, the early alliance of the "three musketeers"— Chermayeff, Wells Coates, and Raymond McGrath—was perhaps the strongest and certainly the most infamous. They collaborated in minor ways, but more importantly they learned together through their separate commissions. Their work was not as didactic as some of their contemporaries', such as the founders of MARS. On the other hand, they held little patience for others who plunged too far into the realm of "pure" decoration. Gropius enjoyed Chermayeff's unswerving allegiance to the end, but Chermayeff's most important single architect-mentor was Mendelsohn. They had become personal friends long before Mendelsohn left Germany. Their projects together understandably reflect Mendelsohn's influence, and to this day Chermayeff's architectural sketches still evoke certain memories of Mendelsohn. Chermayeff's own projects are clearly his own, however.

History will reveal misconceptions, complexities, and ironies about Chermayeff's life and career. For example, Leonardo Benevolo's implication that Chermayeff's contribution to the Mendelsohn partnership could be discounted is without basis.[48] One has only to reflect on the mastery of the auditorium at Bexhill, which was Chermayeff's execution. Ironically, Bentley Wood, one of the most accomplished buildings of the decade of "social revolution" in Britain, was identified much later by John Summerson as "the most aristocratic building of the decade."[49] It probably was. Certainly it is a minor masterpiece and is in its own right very much a sequel (if unintentional) to the legacy of Lutyens. Chermayeff's buildings have a significance far beyond their small number. Even the Gilbey House has captured renewed interest today. Hugh Casson praised it at the time of its completion as "sound vernacular design—a city building [that] is primarily an element of the street"[50] It was nonmonumental urban infill, which responded through a new language to the nineteenth-century urbanism of its surroundings—"contextualism" with base, middle, and top, the latter cornice composed of covered terrace and repetitive skylights. Three decades later, Chermayeff described Venturi's winning entry to the Yale Mathematics Building competition as déjà vu,[51] and it was, considering the similarities (if unintentional) to Gilbey House. The ironies of this century and its architectural elaboration will be many, and for all sides. Herewith, another portion of that legacy.

Richard Plunz

DESIGN AND THE
PUBLIC GOOD

The issue of "pathology," which was woven into the fundamental precepts of "modernism," is very much in evidence from Chermayeff's earliest declarations. He saw the modern movement much more as a response to untenable conflicts in society and the environment than as a conscious stylistic development. Modernism was felt as an explosive force, emerging first on the Continent, where the destruction of war catalyzed new economic and political realities to produce unprecedented building problems and solutions. In Britain, the new realities were catalyzed rather belatedly and were tied more directly to wider political movements. Modernism was a response to scientific and technological advances, which were nonetheless believed to possess a potential for cataclysm equal to war.

Chermayeff's early writing exhibits an optimism for the prospects of the humane use of science and technology and the general prospect for the resolution of environmental conflict. Over time, however, the optimism faded, and his warnings became more and more prophetic. The promise of modernism as a social force degenerated with the triumph of aestheticism. The turning point was the end of the Second World War, after which the balance between forces of technological change and environmental stability began to shift. Simultaneously, architects' concerns became more and more insular, and the language of modernism was reduced to questions of style, which ultimately led to "mannerism." As the latter phase progressed, Chermayeff was one of the few of his architectural circle in the thirties and forties who was to find a coherent and consistent path along which he pursued the original social commitments of the modern movement long after other concerns eclipsed them.

By the beginning of the decade of the thirties, Chermayeff had embraced his particular polemic in relation to modern design (Modernism). He looks to France and Germany for relatively populist precedents like the Paris Exhibition of 1925. He mentions El Greco, Beardsley, and Art Nouveau as precursors to "modernism," but he neglects the theories of Walter Gropius and the Bauhaus and Le Corbusier's *Towards a New Architecture*, which was published in Britain three years earlier. Though the origins of his own thinking were quite eclectic, he notes that "functionalism" was spreading "all over Europe" and that the "immediate future of modernism is undoubtedly towards the continued development of function," with a tendency "more and more consciously to examine function."

Within a very short period, by 1932, he elaborates the concept of "functionalism," sets it apart from both "sham modern" and "simplified classicism," and cautions against the danger of letting modernism degenerate into yet another style, making a "vicious circle of evolution" (Snobbery, Sentiment, and Stupidity). He argues that the question to be posed is neither of "elimination" nor "elaboration" but of a fundamentally different approach to form-making—one without precedent. For Chermayeff, the most important pretext for "functionalism" had much more to do with social purpose than with aesthetic expression, and his ideas quickly moved toward that concern. By 1934, in his seminal address to the Royal Institute of British Architects, he attempted to place the stylistic issues associated with modernism within the larger context of a broadly-based social program, and he found a sympathetic audience (New Materials and New Methods).

Chermayeff's RIBA address, appears to have made a considerable impact, which was heightened undoubtedly by his great talents for the delivery. It was a formidable frontal assault in which he played out a role he always enjoyed. The talk was widely published. Using the theme of the need for an understanding of "new materials and new methods" rather than "new art," he argues, by way of analogy with science, that they would be the "chemicals of a new science of living." He also argues that to have new form, one must have new purpose, and at the most fundamental level he urges the application of new technique to thinking. The architectural program which Chermayeff outlines also shows his connection to socialist politics in England in the thirties through the influence, by 1934, of acquaintances such as J. Desmond Bernal, J. B. S. Haldane, and Bertrand Russell. He calls for applying the resources of the architectural profession to the problems of mass society rather than the individual—"mass dwelling," "mass travel," "mass shopping," and "mass entertainment." He also argues that the economies of mass production should be used to enhance "convenience, appearance, and quality" and not simply to enhance profits. This view identifies some basic contradictions between the goals of "functionalism" and capitalism.

The intervention of the war led to Chermayeff's dislocation to the United States, where, in 1941, he cites American "youth," "courage," and "technology" because they hold great promise in addressing issues which the modern movement in Europe had left unresolved (Architecture and a New World). After only a year in the United States, he realized that the great potential was not without compromise, and he found that even the one country which more than any other possessed the resources and imagination to create a "new world" in fact had many of the same obstructions and afflictions as Europe. He also notes that the American view of the new European architecture was distorted by such representations as the International Style, which he found to lack recognition of the "philosophy behind the facade," and a "travesty of the truth" in that any "international" basis for the new architecture should in fact grow "out of needs and means, a principle of ever-increasing universality," rather than from fashion.

Chermayeff questioned the regressive purposes of the Beaux Arts and "commercial classic" of the East Coast. It was the regional architecture of the West Coast with its origins in the American tradition of social functionalism which attracted Chermayeff's interest. California probably showed more clearly than elsewhere the possibilities for new technology to generate new building types, and he notes the influence of the automobile in that regard. He criticizes, however, the lack of architects' involvement in building projects other than costly private houses. The intervention of the war restrained his criticism, but the priorities of the postwar period would only serve to confirm his suspicions. The architectural establishment's dramatic shift to the right put the progressives and their earlier modernist ideals in disarray.

Chermayeff remained a member of the National Council of Arts, Sciences, and Professions until it was decimated by the harassments of the McCarthy period in the early fifties. It made a major initiative in 1949 with the Cultural and Scientific Conference for World Peace of the Committee for American-Soviet Friendship. Chermayeff's address was obviously counter to the prevailing national political tide (World Peace). He argues that cooperation with the Soviet Union would benefit the United States more than cultivation of confict. The "scientific and technical control of the environment" is recognized at a world scale, beyond the realm of even the largest political powers. He urges the solution of world problems such as provision of adequate shelter through the application of new technical knowledge rather than through its use for purposes which would ultimately produce more deprivation and inequity. As for the United States, he warns that the new economic prosperity may simply support the inconsistency that the "world's highest standard of living" complements a lack of "at least ten million dwellings of decent standard."

As the decade of the fifties unfolded, short-term pleasures and profits helped transform the environment and culture of the United States. The most notable changes included the massive suburban displacement and the systematic destruction of urban centers, coupled with uncontrolled use of the automobile and the decline of public forms of transportation. Chermayeff's professional concerns shifted toward these issues and he began to explore them within the context of university research. By the mid-fifties he had already completed studies with Harvard Graduate School of Design students on alternatives to the detached suburban house. Development of the prototype urban patio houses at Harvard became the earliest step in a continuing research. The considerable publicity given these studies in the media, including television, presented the public with an alternative to the suburban house. In his 1956 NBC television presentation he explained in detail their characteristics, contrasting their amenities with the typical suburban tract house. He emphasized in particular the problem of providing adequate privacy (Problems of Privacy).

By 1957, Chermayeff developed in greater depth a more critical context for his research into the prototype house (Design and Transition). He comments on the existence of the "tremendous migratory patterns" related to economic and cultural transformation in the United States, which by then had become "quite obvious to anyone who looks around him." He extends the issue of "privacy" and "communality" to the largest scale—to the breakdown of "complementarity" between private and public interests, especially in relation to transportation. He identifies the automobile and the "huckster" corporations such as General Motors as major villains.

He condemns the corporations in particular because their enormous unbridled impact on United States culture involved potential negative consequences which could far outweigh the short-term considerations of the gratification of consumerism and the maximization of profits. He sees the suburb not only as an overextension of resources but as a threat to fundamental natural and human relationships associated with traditional urbanism. It is neither city nor country, and, like the new culture in general, he considers it temporal and illusory, involving more and more "vicarious" relationships and experience.

Within the postwar architectural establishment's intellectual milieu Chermayeff found little corroboration for his ideas from colleagues, so it is not surprising that by the end of the fifties he had begun to reach toward different disciplines. Others had also begun to step outside of traditional academic boundaries in relation to some of the same cultural transformations which concerned him. In his seminal talk of 1961 (Shape of Privacy), he mentions the anthropologist John Whiting, the psychologist Marshall McLuhan, the art historian Ernst Grombrich, and the biologist J. Z. Young. By then the infusion from other disciplines had made considerable impact on Chermayeff's thinking. The old dilemma of "functionalism"—of establishing relationships between architectural form and use which go beyond aesthetics—reasserted itself in new terms.

When discussing architectural form, Chermayeff emphasizes that "I am not speaking about these things either aesthetically or stylistically or structurally, but I am speaking about them as pure matters of organization"; and that "esthetics, problems of style and structure of the man-made, are but a piece, as far as I can see, of a great organic hierarchy of form." In relation to his concern about the erosion of privacy, he argues for a view which is both hierarchical and complementary, between the characteristics of "community and privacy." This theme dominated his book of the same title, published two years later. In his final theoretical elaboration for the patio-house prototypes, the issue of "noise" assumes greater importance, addressed through the clear separation of functional entities within the house. He criticizes the fad of the "open plan" as unlivable—from Philip Johnson's Miesian "single occupancy pavillion" to the vaguely Wrightian tract houses popular among suburban developers. He makes the most basic plan description of the patio-house prototypes in terms of "realms" and "joints" rather than spaces in an effort to define an intermediate architectural language between form and function and to more clearly understand the meaning of both.

In his 1964 article for *Punch*, Chermayeff discusses the issue of community and privacy on a global scale and characterizes it as a general conflict between public and private purpose in all of the technologically advanced nations of the west (Private Affluence and Public Squalor). The sixties, which were among the most affluent years in this century, produced the contradiction that "the careful programming and loving care given to the private realm are replaced by indifference and expediency in the public realm," at precisely the time when man-made intervention in the environment reached new limits, without adequate public controls. The balance between the natural and man-made appeared to be reaching a tipping point. From this period on, Chermayeff's attention focused more on large-scale problems of urbanism as well as architecture.

In 1966, urbanism is described as a "special fourth ecology," in addition to the "ecology of land, air, and water"—a "new stage in the development and deployment of man" (Environmental Design and Change). Chermayeff criticizes the view of urbanism which segregates out various purposes, and instead he suggests a descriptive language of "motion and interaction" rather than static zones of activity. He points to the need for a conception of the city that includes both historic core and region, governed by "a theory or system of principles." Mobility is seen as a major consideration toward development of theory, with public transportation as a "catalytic force" in urban restructuring. He questions the national priorities, which by the mid-sixties had "degraded" the historic cores of United States cities, relegating them to the poor. And he contrasts this cultivated pathology with the cultivation of the technological virtuosity required for the impending lunar landing. In 1967, the same theme is explored in a slightly different way (Shape of the Urban Community). Chermayeff contrasts the latest advances of science—for example, the extension of "the whole of our nervous system through new processes and methods of cybernetics"—with the increasing inability to control the consequences of technological development. He points to the possibility that it will be unnecessary "to wait for a nuclear holocaust to destroy our humanity."

Chermayeff further develops the question of mobility in relation to urban form in 1971. It is posed as fundamentally involving political "purpose" rather than technological "hardware" (Shape of Community). He notes a lack of government commitment to anything but private interests which results in the glaring cultural symptom of "automania." With "random movement so highly developed technically," "territorial anarchy" results, with only an imagined maximization of "individual choice," which, "scattered randomly over low density...can only support the stereotyped." The argument was given further credence in 1972 in an impressionistic description of an odyssey through megalopolis (Shape of Community: Realization of Human Potential). Once again he argues for placing the goal of "social betterment through politics reaching toward new systems of power" as a priority above "formal design."

In 1980, in London, on the anniversary of the founding of the Society of Industrial Artists and Designers in the Chermayeff office of fifty years before, he contrasts the optimism of that earlier period to the "near pessimism" of the present (The Third Ecology). In this partially autobiographical address, he describes some transformations in outlook over a half-century—for example, how conceptions of "functionalism," which figured so importantly in the earliest period, changed from the first definitions, which were "simplistic, largely mechanical in content, and materialist in cultural purpose," to a recognition that "functionalism is a complex composite which affects every aspect of our being." What remains unchanged, however, are Chermayeff's political commitments, making him one of the most important and consistent voices from the left in architecture in the last half-century.

Firescreen designed for
Waring and Gillow,
London, circa 1929.

While it is a little difficult to write about any period still with us and in process of evolution, one may usefully draw attention to the beginnings of what is now called modern art in furnishing by referring to periods long anterior to the Paris Exhibition of 1925, which is usually regarded as having been the inception of the new style. The fact is, of course, that styles never have their definite beginnings and endings. They continuously move like a stream which changes its course, alters its depth, meets and deals with many varying obstacles, and as it proceeds on its journey gradually assumes character in accordance with its environment.

Perhaps the roots of the modern style are as far away as the nineties of the last century, and the name of Aubrey Beardsley occurs to me as the one which is most significant to the beginnings of the movement. I must also refer to El Greco as another great artist who showed in his work suggestive form or symbolism instead of formulae. This symbolism was carried through by architects in many public and private buildings. Today furnishers may have some difficulty in realising the force of the ideas which thus began to appear in the last century, when they look upon what is known as the modern art of today. Because the Paris Exhibition of 1925 and following annual exhibitions of "Les Arts Decoratifs" were certainly the most emphatic concentration of effort in the new style, it is not surprising that these should be regarded as the original fount from which modernism sprang. But before 1925 many other exhibitions of the decorative arts had been held at various places on the Continent. In particular, those of Germany were important; in Darmstadt the new idea was embodied in much of the exhibited craftsmanship. There was about this time a series of exhibitions on the Continent inaugurated by the municipalities of various towns, and in all these one encountered the gradual appearance of the newer forms of art.

From an article, "Modernism," published in *The Cabinet Maker*, June 28, 1930.

It is a matter of history that a phase appeared known as Art Nouveau, which had a brief but hectic run towards the end of last century, and it is clear that our modernism found at least some of its inspiration from this half-forgotten movement. But how different! Whereas the old new art, if one may call it such, saw a wild growth of vegetable and animal forms, expressed in what became an extravaganza of ornamental detail, today ornamentation in this sense has entirely disappeared. Yet, at that time, the effort made was merely a sincere desire to get away from old historical and classical styles. The treatment which decorative art received at that time arose from revolt against a stereotyped tradition.

We have moved so rapidly in this matter of art development that the 1925 Exhibition and almost all it stood for is now obsolete. Those who visited this truly remarkable show will remember that the exhibition showed furniture, and of course other decorative productions, whose chief claim to recognition rested upon the amazing skill with which enrichment was carried out for enrichment's sake. The exhibition was a huge exemplification of fine and expert craftsmanship, and in every conceivable direction the idea was to express the maximum of impact with the utmost prodigality of material. No pains were spared to select the rarest woods. No pains were spared to use them in the most extravagant manner. Today all this has gone and function rules the roost. The French have realised the ephemeral nature of the work done in 1925, and have themselves cleaned up all the pretentiousness and artistic violence of that exhibition of five years ago. For the last two years all over Europe the spread of "functionalism" has been rapid and decoration as usually understood has been discarded by modernists. The form which furniture takes now is not dictated by artistic considerations alone, but by a realisation of the function which it will be called upon to perform; and its use in rooms is gauged by the blending of the piece with its surroundings. No piece of furniture lives by itself. The fact of its existence suggests two things: a human being to use it and a room in which it is to be used. A satisfactory piece of furniture should realise these two conditions, and if the designer resolutely keeps his mind attuned to the problems suggested by these conditions by rejecting the traditional, and refusing to be fascinated by ornament for its own sake, he will produce furniture which has perfect utility and in consequence a perfectly satisfactory appearance. . . .

. . . The immediate future of modernism is undoubtedly towards the continued development of function. We shall tend more and more consciously to examine function, to find it and strip it of the extraneous decorative details which have gradually grown around it through the centuries. Our furnishing will thus become simpler and clearer of expression, and the final elimination of fussy details should leave us, not with a skeleton, but with as pure a style as was finally achieved by the Greeks in the age of Pericles.

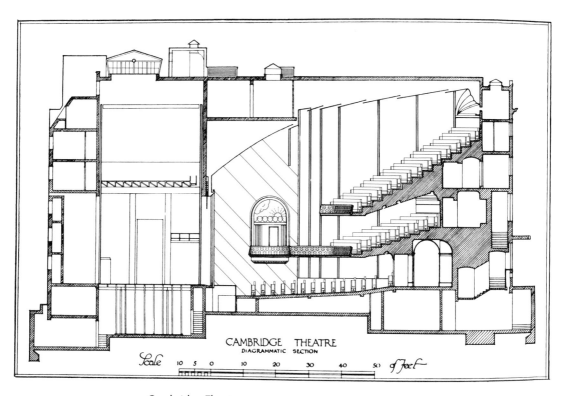

Cambridge Theatre
interior, London, 1930.

SNOBBERY, SENTIMENT, AND STUPIDITY

. . . Let us for a moment examine the designer's job and the knowledge which is necessary to produce these various things in order to fulfill our demands. We can now say that buildings and furniture have, first, definitely to do a job which is their only reason for existing, and second, if possible, must look at least pleasant, if not beautiful, in the course of their function.

The designer, no matter what his specialty, must fulfill the requirements of all demands made upon him. While having to be a cultured man and technical exponent, he has a third and most important function—that of the selector. It is this quality of selection which is the definable one of taste in the artist. There is no problem, however large or small, which has not as a rule more than one solution, and it is important to stress that the successful solutions to any problem are arrived at through the process of solving, and not from any preconceived idea that the whole should conform to this style or another. A choice of the various solutions has to be made. The selector must be a man who understands not only his job, but man, for obviously all things are created for man and not for themselves. We all have, or pretend to have, an aesthetic sense. We all react to beauty as well as to convenience. Mr. Aldous Huxley wrote a short time ago that tradition is the next best substitute for talent.[1] The modern designer, in seeking beautiful forms, has realized that a great many things which he is asked to create today are without a precedent. He has also realized that we must live up to the tradition of creation as this was realized by the craftsmen of other days, but it is obviously stupid to be content to copy and adapt where conditions demand entirely new things.

In the course of my own work I have evolved a few maxims to which I rigidly adhere—I will submit them to you for what they

From a BBC radio broadcast and discussion with John Gloag entitled "Design in Decoration and Furniture," September 14, 1932; published as "Away With Snobbery, Sentiment, and Stupidity" in *The Listener*, September 21, 1932.

are worth. First comes fitness of purpose, that is to say materials are for a purpose and not for an effect. For instance, there is something unsuitable about an entire sideboard in metal merely for effect. It would be logical, however, if the top was made of metal, which does not damage with hot dishes and spilt drinks.

Second, form and colour are of a thing and not on it. For example, if you desire to introduce a cheerful note of yellow into your bedroom, have a yellow chest of drawers, but don't paint on a mahogany chest a bunch of yellow daisies or a canary! Buildings and furniture are like ourselves—they have bodies and skins; unlike ourselves, they require no clothes.

Third, meaningless decoration as such is desecration. For example, we are all of us familiar with festoons of plaster vegetables crawling over the walls of buildings, inside and out. We have seen furniture with a Chinese landscape in the middle of an English walnut panel. Yet wood is a lovely thing in itself, and needs no enrichment. All that things like that succeed in doing is to destroy the purity and effect of the thing itself. If buildings and furniture require when finished the addition of ornament, this can only mean their failure in the first place.

Fourth, simplicity is essential in a scientific age if we are to retain our sanity. When we return home most of us feel pretty well jaded after the rush of our business life, the speed and noise of traffic, the complexity and variety of powerful lights, a medley of signs and colours which we encounter inevitably in our daily lives. We require a direct contrast to this bustle in order to give our nerves a well-earned rest.

. . . Designers of furniture, fabrics and fittings in the past were antagonistic to machinery, or shy of it. Machinery was supposed to be at war with craftsmanship. The result of their attitude was that machinery did without designers and its ghastly products ran amok over the face of the land. Some of these horrors are still to be encountered in various stores. This spuriousness encouraged designers to stage various period revivals and art-and-crafty movements which are all too familiar. All this must come to an end. . . .

. . . Equally today there has appeared a flood of the sham modern. To a large extent this can be explained by the work of conversion, of the so-called modernising of old buildings inside.

While such work was restricted to the improvement of sanitation, the building of bathrooms and the introduction of electric light, no great harm was done. Architects with sensibility preserved the completeness of the building as far as possible, with a sense of appropriateness and harmony. But there soon sprang up in the period of post-war prosperity a third denomination to those of architects and furniture designers—the so-called decorators who exploited new possibilities and vied with each other in producing interiors so novel as invariably to surprise and in some cases to succeed in positively shocking the unsuspecting visitor. Old and new materials alike have been and are being abused through ignorance and stupidity. So-called modern things began to be created by conceited and under-taught amateurs, and were collected by their idiotic friends.

Chairs designed for wood construction were made in metal. Glass and metal tables made their appearance in drawing-rooms before they had been tested in hospitals and offices where they properly belonged during the experimental stages. Foolish chat about Cubism scattered clumsy pieces with sharp and painful corners through all kinds of rooms. Floor linoleum was put on walls inside out to obtain some meaningless effect. Black glass floors were laid in expensive bedrooms for ladies to regret at leisure every time they put their foot down. Tiny electric heaters replaced the large fireplaces of logical design of the period, around which giants gathered like a herd of elephants around a glow-worm. The craze for change pickled and petrified old pieces and limed them, robbing them of the quality that time gives to wood, and forced a great indignity on old friends. Illiterate manufacturers dressed old forms in new clothes, borrowing decorative motifs from all sources regardless of any merit, and stuck them on their eternal suites, producing a sort of procession of Elgin marbles dressed in top hats and petticoats.

Equally, new design was not achieved any more successfully through elimination than it had been through elaboration. Nothing was contributed by simplifying some classic form in order to conform to the economic demand of today. This method seems to make a vicious circle of evolution.

The first wood chair made as a support for the human body developed by gradual processes to a very comfortable and beautiful thing within the limits of materials and construction and reached its most finished form in the eighteenth century. To take such a finished product and to begin to eliminate, for example, some carving or inlay, is merely walking backwards on the road of its evolution. It cannot produce a better article and robs the original of whatever merit it possesses. . . .

. . . By buying intelligently we can all help in the fight against snobbery, sentiment and stupidity, and range ourselves on the side of simplicity, directness and usefulness. We can then demand the best that modern designers can produce in the knowledge that these things are obtainable as cheaply or cheaper than the rubbish with which we have been content.

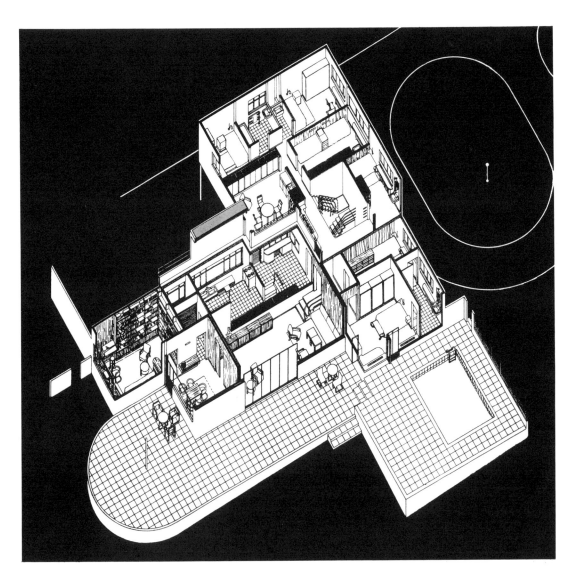

Chermayeff House
proposal, Puttenham,
Surrey, 1932.

NEW MATERIALS
AND NEW METHODS

When the Institute determined the title of this paper I presume
they required a discussion of contemporary materials and
methods which have made serious contribution to the art of building. At the same time, in spite of the implication, the adjective
"modern" has been avoided.

The terms "moderne" and "modernistic" have been discredited by all sorts of people as words, but I suspect that the
Institute's diffidence in employing the comprehensive "modern"
is caused, not by the desire to avoid confusion of words, but in
order to dissociate itself from executed work claiming this title.

The substitution of the adjective "new," however, brought
about another complication. It occurred to me that the lecturer
would be expected to produce novelties like rabbits out of a hat.
But what selected rabbit can *one* Maskelyn produce effectively
before a *crowd* of Devants?. . .[2]

. . . I will endeavour to examine generally what claim to be
contemporary materials and methods in order to distinguish in
the profusion between those which really contribute something
new and those others which simply complicate or directly clog the
machinery of progress in construction and architecture . . . between the legitimate and the illegitimate "new," particularly as
most new things are at first suspected of being the latter.

I would submit that nothing need occupy our serious attention
at this particular time in examining new materials other than
those which have a direct social significance. This is to say: those
problems in building which now require the architect's fullest
attention and best service are the practical and economic problems of housing, industry and transport; the problems of regional
and town planning, slum clearance and the erection of new buildings in a manner and with materials which will not saddle the

From a lecture, "New Materials and New Methods," delivered to the
Royal Institute of British Architects, London, December 18, 1933; published in full in the *RIBA Journal*, December 23, 1933.

obsoleteness of a bygone age on ourselves or on those who will come after.

We must examine materials and methods in relation to these principles and *not* in connection with details of secondary importance concerned with "artistic embroidery." The parallel ideal in industry is not to build bigger and better chimneys with the latest materials, but to eliminate them.

The state of emergency, as I see it, permits the "artistic architects" to comfort themselves by remembering Oscar Wilde's dictum, which began: "We can forgive a man for making a useful thing as long as he does not admire it". . . . Other architects who are less concerned with art can derive a pleasant feeling of warmth from the second half of the quotation, which you will remember, goes on: "The only excuse for making a useless thing is that one admires it intensely. All art is quite useless."[3]

It is my endeavour to show that *new* materials and *new* methods worth examining have nothing in common with "Art Nouveau," but are, as it were, the chemicals of a new science of living. At the same time it is not suggested that this may mean that engineers must replace architects, but rather, that this period so anxious to be governed by rationalism, may establish once more the proper place and value of both science and art, which have been so far confused. . . .

. . . Materials are still largely misunderstood and mishandled. Commercial variations, which are neither improvements in, or additions to, the science of building jostle each other for existence in advertisements, and worse still, in architects' waiting rooms. Grotesque new uses are discovered for old friends, which appear in periodicals for no better reason than that these whimsies "photograph well". . . .

Cottage competitions which set old riddles with conditions that these should be solved with new fountain pens contribute nothing to progress.

It is not progressive to disguise the commonplace to make it appear significant, or the obsolete to bring it up to date. It is essential to select for a specific purpose within the defined cost, the most adequate material and method; that is to say, that material which best solves the problems of purpose, money and time.

Problems require clear recognition, knowledge, and honest decision. Method, therefore, is far more than the technique of application of materials. It stands for the application of technique to thinking.

If such honesty of purpose were commonplace among architects, it would be handed down through them to all others concerned with building, particularly to the contractors and clients whom we have to educate, and thus remove some of the familiar obstacles to new method.

The contractor may find that there are other directions in constructional possibilities than the line of least resistance, and that fifty years' experience is too long a period in technical history to serve as a recommendation.

The client would value far more the perfectly functioning organism rather than the well-made-up facade and would demand of the architect to pay more attention to the realities of construction, to for instance, plumbing and heating, and less to the representational art.

The removal of such obstacles would effectively prevent the excesses of extravagance on the one hand and of moderation on the other, moderation which is more often than not another name for "misconception" or "complacency"—two of the children of abstract aesthetic education and discussions.

Professor Julian Huxley spoke in a recent broadcast on applied science of "Tradition and Prejudice" as synonymous terms.[4] Is it not prejudice, however watered down, which pleads to allow evolution to continue today at the measured pace of the past? A parallel in transport would be an invitation to the London Passenger Transport Board to run a few Roman chariots "for old time's sake."

It seems that immediate and urgent problems require immediate facing of realities, in spite of the fact that today the dislike of realism is, as in the nineteenth century, "the rage of Caliban not seeing his own face in a glass."[5]

. . . New methods and materials have grown naturally and inevitably, mutually stimulating, out of the beginnings of the scientific age to serve the changes of our social and building activities.

Scientific harnessing of power gave us industry and mechanical transport. Both helped to develop out of iron and the tool and inherent constructional possibilities of the material, which led to its recognition as an elastic, reliable building material. Industry's need of hand power close at hand and tranport's ability to bring materials to workers and factory called for greater concentration. These concentrated communities, and the necessity to house them and to provide for their simplest needs, inevitably brought about the *mass* conception with its entirely new structural symbols. . .

Mass dwelling. Flats and settlements, with the planning differences for the accommodation of space-devouring motor traffic, wider thoroughfares, higher buildings in proportion to their land occupancy, with their sanitation and other mechanical installation which differentiates the *considered* street of our day from the *slum* of the past. There came into being the large town and the necessity for greater and higher buildings to meet the requirements of restricted space and property speculation.

Mass Travel. Railway stations, roadways with tram and bus halts, garages, petrol pumps, hotels.

Mass Shopping. The multiple shop, the store which was not until quite recently, to quote Mr. [Erich] Mendelsohn, an ideal display of saleable goods, but a display of unsaleable architecture.

Mass Entertainment. The public swimming-bath, the cinema. The stadium of the race-course and the sports ground. We are, I think, all agreed that the modern stadium provides better protection and visibility for more people at less cost than the ancient coliseum did in Rome.

These forms are new, while the purpose is merely a revival. It would be interesting to take this mass building at one end of the scale, and say a small domestic unit at the other, and draw a graph on which an architect could indicate where the classic basis of form begins to preponderate or is weakened.

Such a mark could be accurately placed only if the architect were able to see formal expression as a consequence of material, constructional method, time and conditions of life, governed by their position in time.

Parallel to the mechanical and industrial development, the study of health and hygiene demanded of our mass structures maximum accommodation to fulfill to even a greater extent new requirements of better sanitation, greater cleanliness, more light, larger windows and improved artificial illumination. . . .

At the same time, while contributing to comfort, the increase of scientific apparatus complicated the accommodation of these new additional organs, and necessitates the calculated design of what Mr. Morton Shand calls "a negative skeleton" for the accommodation of equipment.[6] Complementary to the "positive" structural skeleton, leaving the best, uninterrupted, maximum usable space, this method is just beginning to oust the more common one of marking the wasted space on plan "duct." This points to the obvious economic duty of the architect to avoid the waste of space as well as of money.

Scientific economy, with its inherent profit-making, demands the minimum outlay of capital and subsequent maintenance, without sacrificing convenience, appearance and quality. This led [Hans] Poelzig to say humorously: "Architects have to build as cheaply as possible—at whatever cost."

Cost cutting is being effected in two ways. On the one hand, we have the natural evolutionary process of growth, which has achieved this object of cheapening through the machine or machine-components. The machine makes such components accurately and economically, in large quantities.

In fact, mass production which is the inevitable purpose for which the first power-driven machine, the modern tool, was invented, is complementary to the hand-operated tool of the craftsman.

We also find the deliberate elimination of the costly labour item to achieve a saving. This principle could be admirable where the benefits of saving are vested in the occupier, particularly in the case of the lower paid worker, instead of taking the shape of additional profit for the speculator.

This principle could consist in the prefabrication of all essential structural parts of the simplest dwelling. It has been attempted on the continent, in Russia and in America.

Mass production and maximum prefabrication are the good results of the machine.

On the other side we find that profit-making has been responsible for the commercial expedient of turning the machine into competing with the artist and craftsman by reproducing hand-work. This is a very widely spread result of mechanisation, in spite of the fact that the implication of machine-production in its final analysis is that of producing exclusively things which in form and cost could have been produced only by the machine. . . .

In conclusion, in case my intention is misunderstood, let me explain the conception of realities, science, the machine and mass production—expressions which apply at the same time to our business of architecture as well as the social and economic conditions of our time.

There is no suggestion that unbridled standardisation should replace individualism. On the contrary, there could be a time and place for everything, including individualism. The immediate present does not appear to be the time for individualism, because we are faced with the most urgent problems of reconstruction affecting the lives of millions.

The houses, streets and towns of the most cultured times have never been places where unbridled egotism could thrust itself on society as it is allowed to do today.

There has been much talk in recent years of *applied art*. There has been a singular dearth in *applied intelligence*.

If we were to employ immediately and intelligently the materials and methods of our machine age, to supply the physical and economic needs of humanity, we would release a society of sane individuals.

If benefits of technical developments could be broadcast to raise the general *standard of living* we should have less *standardised thinking*. . . .

A sense of physical and economic well-being would make the mass of released individuals once more sensitive to the graces of life.

Individualism would develop inwardly to find its outward expression in the philosophies and the arts, instead of mocking us from buildings which are rapidly becoming a procession of advertising hoardings.

There will come into being an orderliness and a stable art which will enable the architect once more to give the world a new expression of creation which it lost in the nineteenth century.

We have an abundance of new materials with which to build it. Now we require new methods to make the building possible.

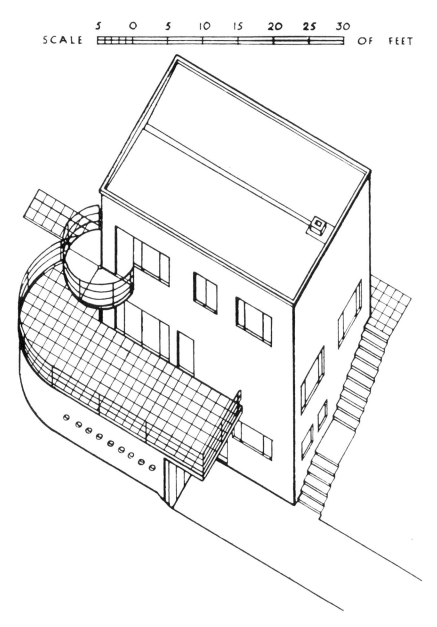

Shann House, Rugby,
1933.

All architects interested in contemporary work get the same feeling when they pick up a foreign publication: that the only place where modern design is really appreciated and understood, where an enlightened adminstration makes experiment and progress possible, is abroad. Only after many years of friendly contact with architects on the continent of Europe and long hunts over the face of it in search of their work, I learned the fallacy of this idea as applied to the Old World. In spite of this disillusionment I retained a half-wishful belief that America would realize the promise its publications held out. That because of its youth, its courage, its technology it would prove to be the vast uncompromised exception. I hoped that the ball which had been tossed across to Europe by [Louis] Sullivan and Frank Lloyd Wright had been hurled back by the European pioneers of the new movement with sufficient vim to leave no doubt as to its real character. That on arrival I should find it a baseball being pitched gloriously into the future to the plaudits of the multitude. Frank Lloyd Wright's genius continues vigorously but he plays alone. Otherwise I found a trembling notchball team playing to empty benches.

Americans are apparently a very romantic people about art generally and architecture in particular. Public reaction to contemporary design, which is not directly identifiable with unadorned engineering or streamlined industrial products, is as obstructionist here as it is elsewhere.

I learned this after I had seen a map published in one of the numbers of *Twice a Year*.[7] This map of outstanding examples of modern architecture in America is composed of dots, each representing an individual building. It shows a cluster of dots around New England, thinned out a good way south along the Atlantic Coast, another cluster in the northern Middle West, almost a complete blank all the way to the Rockies, in spite of the develop-

From an article, "Architecture and a New World," published in *Arts and Architecture*, May 1941.

ment of towns like Houston, and then once more two formidable
clusters centered on the Bay Area and Los Angeles. The number
of the western dots represents a surprisingly large percentage of
the total. This numerical weight recalled the astonishing prepon-
derance of work from California, illustrated in the American architectural press. . . .

. . . Whether it is because the relative remoteness of the West
has continued its feeling of self-reliance or because the prevailing
view in America is that the future development of a sane architecture must be a regional one, I kept on meeting with the
claim, both in and out of California, that this was precisely what
California was doing. Obviously, any positive regional or local
characteristics in a contemporary architecture could spring from
two sources: either from an eclecticism which draws on local
historical precedents, or through a clear view of contemporary
needs and possibilities which are translated into a real indigenous
"from the ground up" architecture.

Under the first head come the Spanish Missions, the Califor-
nian ranches of the early 19th century, among which is to be
found the noblest building in California of any period—the Val-
lejo farm near Sonoma, imports from New England, and finally
the Victorian, which in San Francisco produces a curiously satisfactory blend of merchant pomp and ship's-carpenter simplicity.
This last and finest tradition survives only in house backs. The
fronts have long been mangled, beyond reprieve, by the romanticism of the speculative builder. These noble backs of a real building tradition and the few isolated buildings of the same school
scattered up and down the Coast, recalling the best Georgian,
appear to have inspired fewer designers than the more romantic
and showy Mission style. The still later Beaux Arts and the Commercial Classic appear confined, for inspiration purposes, to
"monumental" buildings on campus and in civic centers. . . .

. . . In connection with later developments, it is interesting to
speculate about the extent to which the ranch influenced Frank
Lloyd Wright, before he in his turn let loose the flood of imitators
which persists to this day.

Tragically, the work of a true native genius, Bernard Maybeck,
which is contemporary with Wright's early work, mostly to be
found in the Bay region, seems little known and has produced no

followers. Yet his inventiveness, sense of material and space, make him certainly one of the outstanding architects in America.

Under the second head of influences of regional characteristics, which most obviously could direct the emergence of a native architecture, and apart from the ubiquitous building material, timber, are the climate, which makes outdoor living possible all the year round, the integral part played by the automobile in the development of California, and the progressive educational system which has stimulated research in school building and developed a number of interesting types. In this field Neutra's work has provided undoubtedly the basis and the best examples.

But, the effect of these positive influences on the emergence of contemporary architecture in California cannot be gauged without reference to the negative ones.

Development everywhere has been slowed up by opposition. Here, perhaps to a greater extent than anywhere, contemporary architecture has had to fight, on the one hand, the imported classicism of the Beaux Arts system, entrenched in the majority of schools, practitioners who have deliberately minimized the importance of the new movement, and the somewhat self-conscious preoccupation of their opponents with the production of a native style.

One of the unfortunate results of the latter has been an antagonism among progressives to the work of such men as [Richard] Neutra, as in the East they are hostile to [Walter] Gropius. Their inability to recognize the philosophy behind Neutra's facade reveals an inability to understand the basis of a healthy architectural growth out of needs and means, a principle of ever-increasing universality, which makes such labels as "International Style" a travesty of the truth.

The confusion about the main issues with which architecture is concerned has produced an astonishing lack of interest in design problems and a lack of perseverance necessary to overcome the obstacles of both reactionary opinion and obsolete practices. Research and experiment in industrial technique and material possibilities of our age are negligible. The line of least resistance is followed.

A majority of architects are creating new shapes and little else. They are forcing the wine of traditional materials and construction into the new bottles of their buildings, and are reversing the process, so to speak, in their cities. The same inertia, when applied to problems of planning, has been responsible for the continued sprawl of Los Angeles and the congested chaos of San Francisco, which are being carried to the surrounding hills, released for spoilation by the new automobile roads. The formidable array of dots on the map therefore resolves itself into exhibitions of individual ingenuity because the larger numbers of dots represents private homes. . . .

. . . The combination of climate and the automobile has produced a definitely original contribution to building types of the "drive-in" markets and cafes, and the super-gasoline station. So far, unfortunately, no good designer has had the opportunity of carrying these building types to their logical conclusion of making them into good architecture.

After these observations and reflections, one is forced unwillingly to the conclusion that in spite of the large number of modern buildings, and in spite of their individual interest, California has not so far made a very important contribution to the idea of modern architecture either in its general or regional sense.

The gloom engendered by this thought is not mitigated by the further reflection that the larger proportion of the total is made up of relatively costly private homes.

I do not mean to suggest that the individual house as such is an irrelevant subject for experiment, nor do I wish to belittle the exceptional talents responsible for modern California architecture, but rather to suggest, quite objectively, that really the total effect is disappointing precisely because the talents of such high quality might have been used to better public purpose.

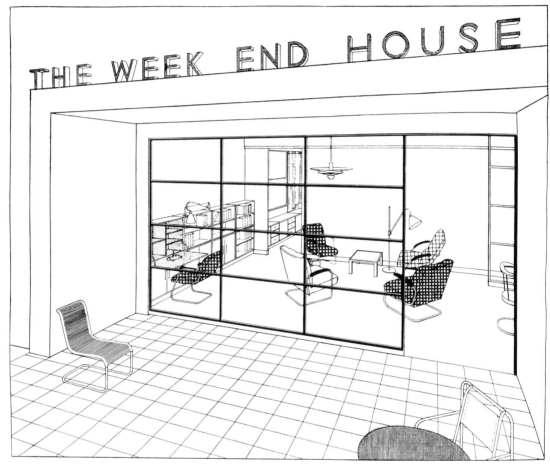

Model "Week End
House" at the exhibition
of "British Industrial Art
in Relation to the
Home," Dorland Hall,
London, 1933.
Furnishings, also
designed by
Chermayeff, were from
the catalogues of Pel,
Ltd., Plan, Ltd., Best
and Lloyd, Ltd., and
others.

As an architect and designer dedicated to the proposition that the nature of man's physical environment is one of the most important influences on man's thought and action, capable of destroying or creating health and happiness, I am most anxious to use this opportunity of presenting this argument and to make it clear at the outset that this is our objective as I understand it.

Certainly I am not participating in this meeting or any other activity of the Council of Arts, Sciences, and Professions[8] except to further the cause of peace and the continued development of planning and construction techniques in such a manner as to promote increasingly greater health and happiness for all mankind.

I am not here to propagate communism which, through the unscientific, repressive, exclusive dogma which characterizes it today, is the very antithesis in these respects of the philosophy and methods which I believe in as democrat, technician and artist.

It is, nevertheless, obvious that a situation in which we can function scientifically, technically and artistically at the highest level is one which demands freedom from fear and utmost liberty in thought and action. That is a situation of honorable peace. It is equally obvious to me that this cannot be obtained without understanding between the United States and the Soviet Union, the two greatest powers of the contemporary world.

This contemporary world of scientific and technical control of man's environment is developing at an unprecedented rate; a far higher rate of development and expansion of tools at man's command than is the development of man's ability to employ these tools to good constructive purpose.

Here in the United States, where man has achieved the world's

From an untitled address given to the Planning and Building Panel at the Cultural and Scientific Conference for World Peace sponsored by the National Council of the Arts, Sciences, and Professions, New York City, March 26, 1949.

highest standard of living, it has been calculated that we lack at least ten million dwellings of decent standard.

To this formidable number may be added many more millions of dwellings required to meet the minimum standards in many countries devastated by war.

In South America, Africa and Asia, untold millions more will have to be provided for people who have, until now, been completely denied this basic privilege of decent shelter.

All told, the dwellings alone which men urgently require today are to be counted in probably hundreds of millions. . . .

. . . If man were to apply his artistry, scientific and technical knowledge to the production of housing at the same level he is now applying these to the production of tools of destruction, and transportation such as the automobile and the airplane, one of the world's greatest problems will have been solved. . . .

. . . Such a program will undoubtedly result in the greatest single industry the world has ever seen.

The primary task in such a program would be the establishment of universally acceptable standards, of a social as well as technical nature, and will require the services of the best minds in every field everywhere in a vast program of research, development and production. It will require a large part of the human material and economic resources now being invested in the development of implements of war.

The nature and scope of this essential task implies the free exchange of knowledge and experience in a world-wide system of collaboration. . . .

At this moment man has means to control his environment undreamed of by our ancestors. We are already scientifically and technically capable of carrying the most advantageous climatic and other conditions with us where we will, employing means of transportation which make it possible for us to deploy our increasing numbers over the face of a still abundant earth.

Man's technical advantage over nature cannot, however, be used to its utmost if we do not remove the fears, hates and ignorance that tie us down in congestion, misery and poverty to places and things the value of which we may well question.

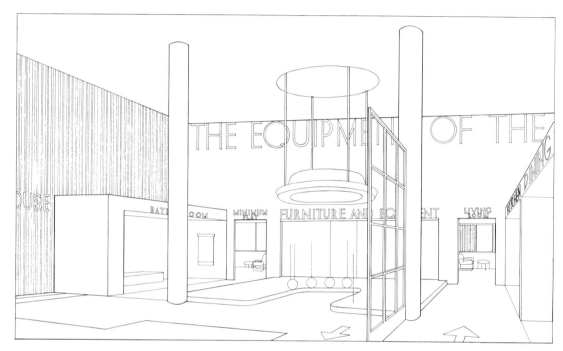

Exhibition of "British Industrial Art in Relation to the Home," ground floor entry, Dorland Hall, London, 1933 (in collaboration with Wells Coates).

Our cities are increasing in number and size. The problem of maintaining the good life, that is of human values as well as property or real values in cities, is also increasing. These problems are dramatically illustrated in the great metropolitan centers like New York, Chicago, Los Angeles. However these centers have special features of attraction which too frequently blind us to the ills with which they will be overcome, like all cities large or small, unless we do something about it.

Let's look at the suburbs. Why do we rush to the suburbs? They provide really only a pseudo-country life which involves great waste of time and human wear and tear, because work, entertainment, and commerce remain largely within the cities. Therefore we constantly commute, we increase the number of short car trips, and our roads and our parking facilities are becoming infinitely crowded. These great big shopping centers, the present-day decentralization of commerce, following suburban development, are really only a cure for traffic problems not a prevention. But we still prefer to do the kind of shopping we can do there than to face the kind of endless parking problems which we find in the middle of town.

Now I think the problem of urban housing for people who live in or close to towns has only been tackled at the apartment level. And apartments do not solve all urban dwelling problems, that is for families with children. Neither do I think an apartment necessarily to be in the grain of Americans, at least not all of them. In the production of separate houses emphasis is really on the pseudo-country house for what I might call the rural-suburban areas. It is free-standing, but on inadequate land, with eye-catching gadgets and novelties and placed with no relation to its neighbor. The untouched and unsolved problems of housing lie in the urban-suburban area where land is much more scarce and

From untitled notes prepared for an NBC "Home" telecast, April 10, 1956.

most costly, but even so it is wasted; where the amenity of privacy—that precious thing—is not provided. Communal facilities can and should be supplied, and it is the architect's problem to find ways of doing so.

It is, I think, important to provide both privacy outside our homes and for community purposes outside our homes. Let's look very, very quickly at the kind of subdivisions which we now find in the rural-suburban area. Is this kind of house a castle? Well, it may be so described, but it is surrounded by an extremely dangerous moat in which cars are parked all over the place. The moat is filled with dangerous intersections in which our children can be killed. Our yards are not really usable. All the gardens are private; there is no space even for a communal children's play-lot. When we look at a typical urban-suburban subdivision, we see every ill which is in suburbia, simply made worse. This is what we fled from. All the spaces are smaller. The houses are tighter. They are pseudo pseudo-country houses, with little tiny setbacks between them, all of which is waste space but paid for with the same dollar.

Now let's look at the project which you saw in *Life*.[9] By taking the same typical urban block and cutting out a few houses, space is provided for off-street parking and a little community park in the middle with room for a playground. This is a little better, but the other ills are still there. All the houses cannot face the right way. Some face north; some are south-facing. So the major problem of orientation has not yet been solved.

Now, however, look at a typical new subdivision. We can imagine one where all the streets are one-way streets, where all the parking is off-street parking, where all the houses are put close together and where the approach to the houses and to the community park in the middle is by very pleasant little footpaths, down which we can stroll in safety, and where our children can play and walk alone to the tot-lot which could be at the end of each block. Let's take this block here on the left and look at it a little bit more closely. It might have at the top two-floor row houses which would be the most economic kind of unit. Here are some with interior yards which might be described as sort of outdoor rooms, but completely private because everything is walled in. Behind your fence your world is your own. So we have here a double privacy, a privacy from the invasion of the street. Here we have even a sort of vestibule in front and in this, we know, the children and everyone else can mix quietly before they get into the traffic pattern. This is a safe and decent pattern. . . .

. . . In another kind of row-house with walled gardens front and back this idea of privacy is even more developed. On the left are the rooms which might be the owners'—the parents'. They have their own study; they could have the baby in this room while the child is still small. Then the kids move across the house. The other side of the living room and the dining space, which is the community space, is the children's own. Here they could have their own bedroom, their own little play yard when they are very small kids which is right under the eye of mother working in the kitchen. Therefore we have a buffer on two scales: inside the house, between the different tastes and activities of the children and the adults, for all our different tastes in entertainment, radio and television; and outside this little tiny neighborhood the buffer between the footpath world, which is safe for us and pleasant for us, among trees and shrubs, and the road pattern and the parking lot for the cars. This is what I mean by having our privacy and enjoying the good life.

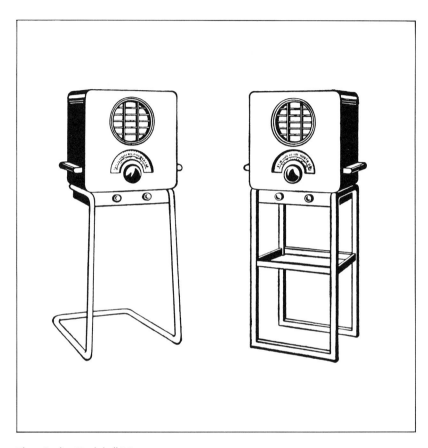

Ekco Radio Model #64,
designed for E. K. Cole,
Ltd., London, 1933.

. . . Humanity is on the verge of a total re-grouping. I'm not a sociologist and therefore I'll not attempt to describe the tremendous migratory patterns which are quite obvious to anyone who looks around him. Still, in general, I see that everything is in flux, that not only do we not have our own stable beliefs, but such beliefs as we do have have become transportable, and they're no longer immutable, but subject to verification, skepticism, and obsolescence. If we think of mobility in more specifically physical terms rather than in social terms, we could really say that what we are entering now is a period of deployment. Everything that we can now do, technically speaking . . . tends to move around, not to have a special locus; but to be universal, to have no roots, to be adaptable. We think of flexibility as a virtue rather more than solidity. So what I'm seeing at the moment, merely as an observer and not as an architect, is a new age of deployment which could almost be described as the age of the industrial nomad. . . .

. . . The question, of course, is how does one think about it. By upbringing and age now, I belong to the dying urbanity. I still like this as a way of life, and I really like my country as I find it. . . .

. . . These illusions, this psuedo-country, this pseudo-country house, this pseudo-townhouse, this pseudo-contact, all these things have somehow got to be modified and arrested. This is part of what I would call the architectural as well as the sociological problem.

If this is so we could ask ourselves, of course, the question of what our particular role here is. We have a doubly difficult one. Being in the position of pioneers, and having gone through all the agonies of the railroad age, and now being at present in the agonies of automania, we have to conserve and protect what we

---

From a lecture, "Design and Transition: Architecture and Planning Purpose Examined in the Light of Accelerating Events," given for the Great Issues Course, Dartmouth College, April 22, 1957.

had against these inroads, as well as build the new. But I'm pretty sure because of our historical advantage, people from all over the world and principally, of course, from what are ironically called under-developed countries, will come to us in order to learn certain technical devices with which to improve their purely physical condition. I don't think that those people will be particularly interested in going through the same agonies as ourselves.

For instance, the hucksters' dream here of the American automobile age as conceived by General Motors, is not going to stay here very long; I think it is already over. The two-tone Tyrannosori are practically obsolete already. And we can see the little beasts, you know, in the highways and byways, these little bubbles and scooters and so on, all waiting to take over. I think they will. Now I'm quite sure that the great areas which are going to be industrialized and which will want automation for very good reasons, will not go through the follies of being run over by their own traffic. I don't think they'll do that. So we have to be able to project at this moment possible conditions which eliminate our own mistakes and which may enable the next stage of industrialization and deployment in the world at large to take a reasonable pattern without interferences with the good life. This probably means, certainly from the point of view of traffic generally, a much more balanced notion of what traffic is about.

For instance, it is fairly clear that if we were drastic enough here to defy the hucksters (and you must remember that this exaggerated love of the super-automobile has been only recently cultivated by most intensive propaganda—it's only three years old), Americans could once again take their automobiles or leave them. Now they're mad about them. So, they could be "unmaddened" just as readily by some kind of shock treatment. I don't know what the medical term for this is. But in any case I'm absolutely sure that we have to have a balanced transportation system. If we did, we would be able to stop appropriate transportation at certain points.

So I can imagine—I won't call it a town because I don't know its shape yet. Let's imagine a new constellation of things which might gather, say, around a light industry, maybe around an institutional office block of some kind, like insurances. Or, it may be around an educational institution such as you have here in

Hanover; it may be any one of the specialized activities that we can conceive of, including staple-markets. I see no reason at all why "Stop-and-Shops," the great staple-markets, should be in towns at all, where they drag this infinite traffic with them; they should be out somewhere, very openly placed. But this could be a core of a certain kind around which would develop this constellation, as I call it, of its special character, which is special and characteristic of the function of this core. And they would all vary, and history would repeat itself, but the form would not.

A metropolis, on the other hand, would have to be preserved, either because it is an historical monument or because it is so dense and compact in its mass that it cannot tolerate the incursion of every whimsical trip by a gigantic bus. . . . Every time the little woman buys the forgotten box of corn flakes with two hundred and fifty "horses" at her disposal, this makes absolute shambles of any transportation and any taxation system. Who pays for the traction, who pays for the road, for the parking space here, for the parking space there? This is becoming a burden which society may not deal with. But we could very readily in a metropolitan area conceive of new kinds of things like transportation exchanges, could we not, where an entirely new kind of architectural entity, where rapid-transit or long-distance automobile haul would stop, where a new kind of automobile stacking would occur, where you transfer to some kind of public transit within the metropolis, not excluding taxis for those who can afford them, but certainly differentiating public domain of transportation from private domain of transportation. And at this point we very readily begin to see a new kind of pattern out of which a new kind of architecture could grow. If we separate these things in the terms that I've just described, we might get the notion of a true separation of the public domain and the private domain in a logical way, so that the one doesn't get in the way of the other. Just as I do not wish my child to be run over by a truck, neither do I want constant, shall I say, communality. I think that complementarity is all.

To enjoy communality, you must have the option of real privacy. To enjoy real privacy, you must have the option of a genuine and constructive communality. So at every level, whether it be city-country, whether it be public transportation or private transportation, whether it be road utility, services, de-liveries, and my private domain, I want each to be true to itself. I don't know whether any of you saw somewhat exaggerated pub-licity which has been going around lately to something we've been working on at school, at Harvard. It's a very simple notion, a kind of re-grouping of houses, with the houses themselves being so planned that you have the option of insulating the child from the adult, the adult from the child—I think that this is really coming to us adults after quite a long time, I think we deserve it. Also, we make zones where you can mix at will and by choice. And by the same token, we have a pedestrian world in which this car and this truck shall not penetrate, so that children may play there in peace and without carbon monoxide poisoning. And generally we try to recognize what we have, what we are likely to have for a long time, and to arrange our environment as a pattern. . . . I'm not talking now about its specific shape, . . . but as a pattern which would be at least logically defensible. . . .

. . . I'm not particularly in favor of introducing romantic Mediterranean piazzas in Chicago. I doubt whether they'd be used.

I think that there is already a great equivalence to a pedestrian world in new terms in every skyscraper which goes up in down-town New York. It is not an accident, for instance, that the, shall we say, institutional buildings around Park Avenue, these great post-war skyscrapers, are huddling together very, very tightly. Why? Because arriving by automobile from suburbia—of course, you must remember that the best paid men in this culture are those who flog themselves fastest into a grave—these men arrive by commuting; they go into this air-conditioned nightmare world of theirs, and they stay there all day long, communing with each other, without ever putting on a raincoat, fur coat, or anything else. They live in a world which is the mechanical equivalent of, shall we say, a mild-climate piazza. They commune in this way.

The downtown garment district is again another village of the same kind. The huckster mile on Madison is exactly the same thing. You can practically go from *Look* to Pip to Squeak to *Life* to *Time*, or whatever it is, without ever getting out of doors. So this is again another kind of pedestrian world. We are in one way or another creating really genuine functional environments. But they're not being very well done.

There's no question that some of the skyscrapers are master-pieces. When a Mies van der Rohe designs a building, tremen-dous sensibility in the proportioning, the materials, everything else goes into it. Indeed for all of them, technical resources are such that you can't go far wrong because really the rental space and elevator ratio is practically prescribed. Technically there are no mistakes to be made. But these are new worlds. They are the great pieces of architecture of our time because they are the new tools with which a genuinely modern architecture is being built. As we go out from these luxury centers, the further out we go, the more questionable the whole thing becomes. The peripheries of our cities, as you know, are blighted. They are slums. They are debilitated. The housing is beneath any standard that should be acceptable. Further out, the curve of rot takes an inverse bend; when you really get into the pseudo-flight area of suburbia, it produces extremely comfortable to expensive houses. Some-where out there, an equivalence in terms of technical equipment, ingenuity, expensive materials of the skyscraper exists but in a romantic image. It is nothing to spend 100,000 dollars, 150,000 dollars to 200,000 dollars for a house in Westchester, or Fairchild County, or Winnetka, or wherever. And yet you find that this house only is about six feet away from the party-line, which stands a few feet away from another pseudo-country house. Being pseudo-country houses, they open in all directions, and normally of course, you find that your bathroom opens onto the other man's bedroom, and so on. The actual distances are not enough to cope with assault on privacy and modesty. We simply ignore the neigh-boring house. We pretend that it does not exist.

And so, they, complete a row—about a million dollars worth of idiocy on one side. Then on the other side will be exactly the same houses, oriented the same way, for idiots with the same amount of money to spend. It is their privilege, but I don't think that this is the kind of thing that professionally speaking, ar-chitects should tolerate.

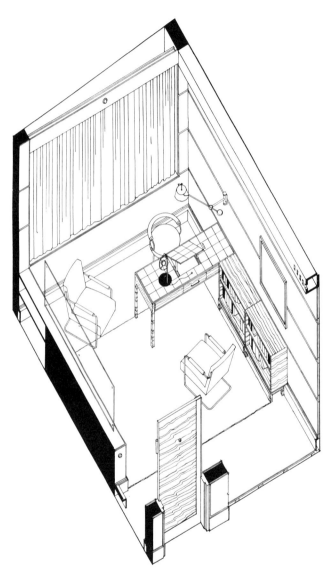

BBC Broadcasting
House, London, 1933.
Studio 3B.

. . . Recently I heard two men discuss my subject from their viewpoint. This is always a very happy occasion. First of all, John Whiting, an anthropologist, addressing himself to the Joint Center of Urban Studies at an informal luncheon, reported on his studies in progress on tribal, social space—that is to say, on structure and form as an anthropologist saw it—all the way from swaddling clothes through beds to the largest element he was prepared to tackle at the time, some sort of a compound for a group or family unit. What he discussed were tangible boundaries, that is to say, boundaries to places and experience.[10] The same evening Marshall McLuhan, the psychologist and specialist in communication systems, spoke of the "global village" of the technologically highly developed society. He spoke about instantaneous communication which meant the dissolution of tangible, tribal space. He described it in his own words as "central experience without margins."[11] Ernst Gombrich, apropos of the same thing in another context, said, "where everything is possible and nothing is unexpected communication must break down."[12]

An Englishman, a biologist, J. Z. Young, whose particular interest is the evolution of cerebration in the measure of evolutionary progress, speaks about randomness and rules: randomness being individual creations and rules being collective creations. I will quote directly from his Reith lectures given some years ago. He says,

Each individual uses the store of randomness with which he was born to build, during his life, rules which are useful and can be passed on.

Similarly, we can detect in the process of evolution the increasing randomness of all living things. The higher animals, in a sense, are more different from their surroundings than are the lower. We might therefore take as our general picture of the un-

From a lecture, "The Shape of Privacy," given at the Graduate School of Design, Harvard University, May 9, 1961.

iverse a system of continuity in which there are two elements—randomness and organization—disorder and order, if you like, alternating with each other in such a fashion as to maintain continuity.[13]

My question, and the question of many others, is whether our collective rules are in themselves becoming, by some quirk of circumstances, random.

All these observations by learned men, outside our field, suggest that the spectrum of space, ranging all the way from personal immediacy to collective abstractions, is actually our problem and our field. McLuhan deliberately cautions against continuing the development of central abstractions without marginal realities—that is to say, generalized notions at the expense of first-hand, abstractions without experience. He describes in fact the danger of making all experience totally vicarious.

This is a very general background of the particular I wish to discuss. Architects, and I include the planners, of man's habitat must ask what are the pressures which are now being exerted upon us to which design must respond. We must recognize and understand the crucial pressures of our own times.

As a somewhat vicarious planner and architect of our physical environment—all educators in our field run this risk if they really apply themselves to the task of education—it appears to me that the natural or man-made environment can be seen in terms of the spectrum of experience which anthropologists, sociologists, and psychologists, and biologists speak about. This spectrum of experience is of many different scales, but at each it must, if it be truly organic, be organized in a hierarchical order. Although the word "hierarchical" is in danger of becoming a cliché those of you who are familiar with it must bear with me because it has much significance in terms of my context.

This kind of hierarchical organization at every scale appears to me to be an analogous combination of ingredients. They appear to be a combination of social purpose and functional and technical, as well as formal, articulation and integrity. My immediate concern in this whole spectrum of experience, which is becoming infinitely vast, is with the small end. . . .

What is the background of my concern? Roughly, there are

three major issues; first, the population explosion; second, the growth of the man-made environment, which I think may be described as organization; third, the shrinking of the natural environment, which raised problems of conservation and redistribution of the random and varied. Nature is already, if I may so put it, becoming most unnatural—cake-eating bears in State Parks are testimony to this. Tomorrow, we may have total weather control and the family of man will have no escape at all from his handiworks.

If we think of our habitat in this way, it may be that even the so-called natural will have to be very carefully rationed in the future following a hierarchical principle. In other words, we will have to have nature rationed out to mankind in varying packages from the great wilderness on the one end to, maybe, the little shadbush outside your private window at the other. In any case, what we are concerned with is the issue of human ecology; that we are ourselves remaking the human habitat. We must recognize those issues that are a threat to our humaneness.

It happens that I am an optimist, as optimistic as one may be in these days, and I can imagine total design in which there is a deliberate reconstruction of our environment in relation to the *real* pressures of our time, the pressure on industrializing man, which may or may not be a prelude to human engineering or self-transformation. I prefer the mystic term to the quasi-scientific one.

In any case, in terms of what we may do about the transformation of this environment, which is beginning somehow to betray us, it seems quite reasonable to start with housing, which contains, culturally at least, all the opportunities at the first level in the social hierarchy in which the individual and the group share their lives. A community structure at this scale can in itself become a model and it may indeed be the kind of environment which we produce for a family which may influence beneficially the organizations at the larger scale.

. . . Everything that I am going to say tonight will have absolutely nothing whatsoever to do with esthetic considerations, nothing whatsoever to do with problems of style, nothing to do with problems of construction, but only to do with pressures which may be reflected in plans, which are not two dimensional

but are, in fact, three dimensional concepts of functional space.
. . . I am going to limit my discussion to considerations of the urban
house—that is, to the context of total urbanization with which we
may be faced.

There are, I think, two rather important pressures which have
to be reckoned with in relation to this issue. They are both the
media of communication, if slightly different in character. The
first, which I call Enemy No. 1, is excessive mobility and particularly auto mobility—the car comfort that I consider cold comfort.
Secondly, there is Enemy No. 2 which is noise. As we continue to
urbanize we have these several rather bad effects. We dissolve
what I would call the social, historic space, which is what Whiting spoke about, with the aid of the free-running, autonomous,
private car in public places. This car cuts the countryside to
pieces, and it dissolves the city. It has a strange and terrifying
effect of producing urban litter wherever it goes, and the boundaries between the country and the city, between that which is
natural and that which is synthetic, becomes dissolved in the
process. Furthermore, this extraordinary implement of convenience and mobility has produced the illusion of togetherness
which is expressed in idea of the ideal suburb. I think that any
continuation of the process or use of implements of this kind, of
free running, private mobility in public places, will tend to increase the process of erosion at both ends. . . .

. . . The second issue, however, is less conspicuous. Noise is
not yet recognized as a menace, yet there is the rising cacophony
of sounds. You can test it for yourselves, if you can uncork yourselves from your other neuroses, in terms of the jet overhead, the
gurgling plumbing and the perpetual communication systems
which have now become part and parcel of this civilization—
voices, voices everywhere and wonderful non sequiturs claiming
our attention all the time. From the jet overhead, the little transis-
tor in our hot and uneasy palm, these sounds are really with us
whether we like it or not, and we had better recognize it and the
immediate increases with which we are threatened. . . . Noise
moved into our houses just as surely and as dominantly as "the
man who came to dinner"; TV has settled down forever. . . .

. . . Today, I think, we are cultivating the gigantic, the conspicuous, the instantaneous, the loud, the vicarious. It is the

realm of vast community, which only produces feelings of awe as against the small, the subtle, the slow, the quiet, the immediate, the realm of privacy, if you like, the realm of delight. We lack somehow equilibrium in our ecology and our experience, which provides all experiences as a matter of course to satisfy randomness and rule principle of opposites as necessities. Variety is *not* the spice of life. It is the *essence* of it. We obviously require both community and privacy, and we require the option to enjoy either.

What is the practical planning application of such a principle or such a concern? The obvious things are being, if somewhat half-heartedly, dealt with. The separation of cars from pedestrians is now recommended as a commonplace by planners. At least we are giving pedestrian objectives a little recognition, and the hierarchical planning of traffic, dividing the fast from the slow, is beginning to have effect. However, we lack recognition of traffic complexity in terms of the public, the semi-public, the semi-private, and the private. We do not yet recognize that each may have its own appropriate transportation system. What is still less obvious is that even within the small community of the family there are exactly the same problems of communication and diversity of interest, the same cleavages, as there are in the larger world. We can say that the question of spaces and places, the differentiation of interest, and therefore appropriate functional definition exists in what we have lately considered to be single units.

This is simply not true any more even for a small, civilized, industrialized family shelter with all kinds of communication systems and increasing diversity of interest.

A family requires facilities for community, adult privacy, and child privacy. Every home in the affluent society, in the sense of being an environment, must recognize that there is cleavage and diversity, which is hierarchically a reflection of the larger environment.

In order to illustrate the argument in planning terms, I am going to consider it on two levels. First is the cluster, that is to say, the arrangement of dwellings as a group, having similar characteristics and having the same objectives of trying to prevent interference of the larger environment of vehicles and noise with the group and the interference of traffic and noise generated within the group with individual family units. Again, I want to emphasize that I am not speaking about these things either esthetically or stylistically or structurally, but I am speaking about them purely as matters of organization. . . .

Prevention of interference is really the question that is uppermost in my mind because the barriers between community and privacy may, in terms either of communication or traffic become all kinds of modulated and differentiated transition points between realms possessing integrity, or they may, in fact, be nothing of the kind, and that we may be unclear or dishonest about our objectives in life.

The principle of which I am speaking may be simply illustrated. It is the notion of barrier, translated into the notion of a sequence from the minimal passage, transition point into an organized transition area, and finally into the lock in which a new activity occurs.

Not only is the point of transition the essential joint between functional realms possessing integrity, but there is a second consideration; namely, that when two realms are joined and there is a transition point between them, it is very proper and reasonable to examine the nature of this to see whether it may not assume the function of a realm in its own right. To give a very simple example; if you take out the storage and dressing functions from the so-called bedroom, you might get a new transition realm which is an entity in itself and rids the bedroom of all kinds of encumbrances it presently contains in spite of its name. The new realm becomes, in addition, a buffer zone visually, accoustically, and climatically. . . .

For example, I need hardly remind any dweller in a contemporary society so loudly equipped as America, that the neighbour has become the enemy, particularly if he doesn't listen to the same program. We have a gentleman who sings. I have nothing against singing, I only object that I must hear him when I am listening to something else.

If all this is true, then the various problems, as previously stated, resolve themselves into the house problem in a very simple way. It becomes a question of social, visual and accoustic insulation. Each realm within the domestic domain, with its hierarchical order, ranging all the way from community to privacy, and containing the essential ingredients of communion between family, as such, family and nature, the individual and nature, and naturally communion with oneself the vital missing ingredient, the treasure going down the drain. Nobody can be alone any more.

I have mentioned to you two enemies of what I would call the rational plan—the car and the noise. I must now introduce you to my enemy No. 3, which is the "open plan." As I am not discussing here the abstract, beautiful space, I must look at the open plan as an instrument in relation to existing pressures upon its users: a dwelling very fully equipped, the desire for an open plan, and the equipment which is likely to go into it. The pressure coming from telephone, radio, hi-fi, TV, dish-washers, blenders, etc., is immense and is pushing privacy through ever intruding electronics and communication systems, firmly out of any kind of family environment. The analysis which follows estimates what happens when a family has these means of communication and the appetite to use them is housed in an abstract pavilion.

Mies's first house, which was very carefully zoned and had all the private sleeping quarters on a separate floor, with servant quarters which are very carfully isolated from the generalized living space, was somewhat formal. The plan which he produced only about three years later is the idealized pavilion, the Barcelona exhibition pavilion disguised as a dwelling. This plan, which is really exraordinary in its Miesean esthetic elegance, is curious in so far as only the disciples rationalize it as a housing plan. Mies does not. For him it is simply an ideal pavilion. If we look upon the space and we calculate the per foot cost, we know that this family would have two television sets, four radios, one hi-fi system, and it would be utterly incredible as a residence. However, Mies is not fooled by this. It is only his disciples who are.

Mies, in designing the earlier rational, practical family house with two entrances is absolutely clear. He recognizes the division of the adult world and its privacy, and the children's world using the service of the kitchen area as a vestibule between, and there is absolutely nothing wrong with the plan at all. It is clear and usable. This plan his disciples do not display.

From another older prophet, Frank Lloyd Wright, comes the 1938 *Life* house, projected by the magazine as a prototype for public consumption.[14] Here you see so many names to one single space—recreation, dining, etc.—which could not be inhabited today by a family. This is a single occupancy pavilion and has exactly the qualities of the Miesian pavilion which Philip Johnson enjoys in his house. It has absolutely nothing to do with family houses and anyone who designs family houses in this nature is either a fool, or worse than that, a cynic!. . .

. . . The philosophy, which I am offering for your examination, searches for equilibrium. By equilibrium I mean a spectrum of variety of experience. At each point, experience shall have its functional and its formal integrity—a definition of order wherever you may meet it, at whatever scale, whatever dimension, whatever place. I don't think that I can say anything kinder about the suburban sprawl or urban renewal than that they are both what I would call, pseudo-spaces or pseudo-places, providing pseudo-experience. Somehow, the suburb, particularly, is a dreadful mutative monster which was born of country out of the city. This monster is devouring both its parents. The instant communication, together with McLuhan, has transformed our human communications systems to such an extent that the medium has now become the message—a ghastly pseudo-message which is neither specific and particular, nor general or abstract.

In the search for the new equilibrium we seem to have two alternatives. Logically, one would be to preserve the existing equilibrium in our ecology between ourselves and our environment, and the other would be to introduce an equilibrium of our own making. We don't seem to be ripe enough to do the latter.

The vicarious, that is to say the second-hand, experience appears to be triumphant at the moment. The immediate, the direct experience from which all true judgments come, seems to be all but gone. Not only has it all but gone, but it is already suspect before its death. I have heard men of good will, in all seriousness, questioning the proposition that being alone is a good thing. I have heard it questioned that the lonely man has a way of life. They could be wrong. So could I.

I think that neither the natural environment nor our proper nature are being cultivated any more. We are in an age of rather special and somewhat irrelevant memories or exaggerated hopes. Esthetics, problems of style and structure of the man-made, are but a piece, as far as I can see, of a great organic hierarchy of form. These things, nature or the man-made, are not alternates. What we actually need, as I understand it from my learned colleagues in other fields, is the option of both constantly available.

You will have gathered from this that my concern is with man's condition and not man's comfort. We face problems of ever-rising densities, ever-rising densities not only of people but of traffic and of noise, generated by modern people. Urbanism on the humane side implies urbanity. I think we must learn once more to live at very close quarters, and what's more, we have to learn to live in ever-shrinking quarters, for space is running out with our rising numbers. It follows from this, in simple logic, that we must develop techniques to enable us to exercise the options which our humanity demands, and which our ingenuity provides or promotes, if you will, without damaging each other. We must learn to do this before we destroy ourselves. I have a feeling that the hour is late.

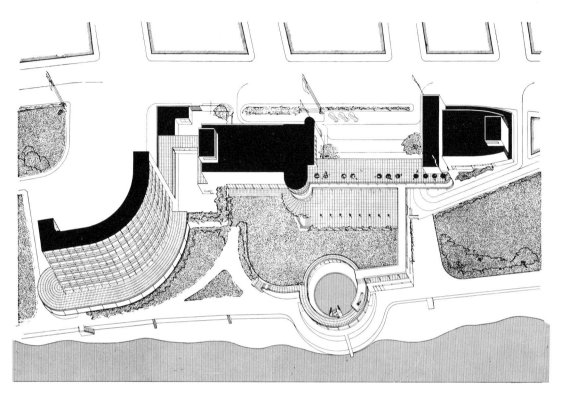

Entertainment Hall,
Bexhill, Sussex, master
scheme, 1934 (in
partnership with Erich
Mendelsohn).

Human ecology is a problem of the affluent society. For the first time, man is in the unique but uneasy position of being largely responsible for his own environment. But at the same time he is threatened by the very achievements which make this possible, the ever-accelerating scientific and technical progress of the last half century, which at one time promised an endless, benevolent plenty and comfort undreamed of in any ancient empire. . . .

. . . Looking back to slower moving times and processes we can recognize the forces which produced the cities of history: the need for transport exchanges, strongholds, production centres, markets, places of worship—each gave its city a special character and tangible form. The plan and structure of such settlements reflected the needs of the community for which they were the foci—intensively used and densely inhabited places for security and community. And the topography in which they were set, whether untouched, gently tilled, or fiercely hostile, was the natural complement to the man-made town.

But industrial man upset the balance between the recognizably natural and the designed urban. He eroded, with his products, the face of the old civilized world, and threatens to do the same to the emerging civilizations of Africa, Asia and South America. His cars, shuttling between the illusory pleasures of the diluted countryside and the equally illusory comforts of saturated cities, have muddied the outlines of both.

Soon this very freedom of movement, typified by the private citizen going where he will in his own car, may make both freedom of movement and cars impossible in densely populated places. We shall have to develop better forms of public transport, teach people to walk reasonable distances, and encourage the growth of a desire to stay put.

Meanwhile the inhabitant of this "affluent" environment,

From an article, "Private Affluence and Public Squalor," published in *Punch*, June 17, 1964.

driver and button-pusher and knob-twister, is ever more en-
grossed with minding his machines. Expensive equipment leaves
him little time to enjoy anything else. Car and TV dominate him
at home, and photographic apparatus abroad. Images and sound
succeed each other in an endless *non sequitur*. His observations
are superficial and his pleasures vicarious.

What effect will this chaos have on human minds, nerves and
tissues? It may be that the rate of transformation by man of his
habitat has hopelessly outrun his capacity to adapt. Bustle and
variety, the old attributes of cities, have been replaced by dangerous traffic and deafening noise, visible order by shapelessness,
special character by monotonous vulgarity. All are difficult to
identify, and therefore to adapt to. When everything is possible,
nothing is possible.

Modern man's preoccupation with his private comforts and
pleasures has left the public realm neglected. It receives little
attention until a major crisis forces private interest to take notice
of the public condition. The astounding difficulties any city planner or architect encounters in trying to provide the most elementary order and efficiency to meet new conditions are enough to
deter all but the most courageous and devoted. (Arrogance and
salesmanship help too, of course.)

As to such attributes as scale, character and aesthetic, which
distinguished the great civic spaces and monuments of the past,
these are simply no longer the architect's province. The careful
programming and loving care given to the production of the private realm are replaced by indifference and expediency in the
public realm. The honorable exceptions to this general, depressing rule, are not enough as yet to get public attention, recognition
and respect in a time when more has been built in one century
than mankind had built in all history. And the purposes for which
even these places were designed become obsolete under the re-
lentless pressure of rapidly changing technology.

Trying to adapt old cities to new needs, increasing numbers
and pace of people and their attendant things has proved at best a
temporary panacea. The pumping in and out of unlimited quantities into the existing cities has proved to be beyond the capacity
of circumscribed, preferred spaces. Even entirely "new towns,"
whether capital cities or satellites, do not seem to be appropriate

to need: they are old towns at heart; "closed systems" designed around central public, and civic centers. This pattern can no longer serve in a world, in which not only the city, but every segment of it is essentially a place of access in a global system of communications, and so must in itself become an "open system" susceptible to extension and modification.

Conceived in such terms, the larger world-wide urban organization may be likened to a great hierarchical system composed, in the manner of higher living organisms, of hierarchical functional systems such as nerves, blood vessels, digestive organs and muscles.

Public spaces form an analogous hierarchy in the urban complex. Man will have to design and provide a family of places of varied dimensions, scale, character and form appropriate to the special purpose of each. Clearly defined places we must have; the public places in cities are the breeding ground of "urbanity," culture, the arts and a sense of greater community, and it is here that they develop, become refined, and may flourish.

Shortly we may run out of "natural" spaces where man's spirit is refreshed. It seems unwise to confine construction on the grand scale to which we have already become accustomed without an equivalent program of "conservation." We shall have to provide a hierarchical parcelling of the remnants of nature, all the way from the great wilderness without to the small flowering shrub within the innermost city court. Patrick Geddes's and Lewis Mumford's admonition on this score over many years can bear repetition in the face of the bulldozer, DDT, and uncontrolled meandering of predatory man.

Even if we were to put into practice hierarchical planning and design of public space we would be hard put to preserve their individual integrity. For without continuous vigilance the process of interference of the man-made with the natural may continue. The equilibrium, the essential option, would once more be in jeopardy.

My random thoughts on the public condition became somewhat more clear when I completed a typically brief odyssey from the eastern seaboard of the United States, through the midlands and west country of England, London, Paris, through Provence and Sardinia to Rome, Athens, and the islands of the Aegean.

In the land and city-scape, in whatever public space the tourist moves, chaos prevails. Private retreats of serenity and silence only provide satisfying shelter from a forbidding jungle. A sudden influx of the new money, machines, crowds and strange noises creates as many problems as are resolved. These are apparently inevitable harbingers of a "higher standard" of life. The old squalor of individual poverty is replaced by the new squalor of chaos. Ancient monuments and quiet streets become defaced with illuminated slogans of the hucksters, aimless crowds of strangers and mechanized vehicles violate by their number, speed and noise places designed if not for tranquility, at least for a leisurely tempo.

Perversely, the ubiquitous car, designed for great speeds, hiccups its way through crowded cobbled streets, and comes to an inappropriate immobility, inefficient and costly, parked obscenely in some very unlikely place. The Paris and Rome of narrow streets still hold some promise of future regeneration if they are restored to pedestrian use exclusively.

London provides some poignant examples of incompatibility: traffic and pedestrians in Piccadilly Circus which may not be resolved by ingenious juggling within its confines, and the incompatibility of the actual immediacy of ceremony at St. Paul's for the few and the illusory immediacy of TV for the many.

On Sardinia the ugly whimsy of luxury hotels and villas, the roads for cars and docks for yachts with all the attendant crevice fillers are eroding the lovely land and sea-scapes faster than the sea ever did and threaten to erode the traditional Sardinian's dignity by pressing him too fast into unaccustomed servicing tasks and wealth from land sales.

Even without a car, Delos's sacred ruins have been desecrated by new museum and cafe buildings of incredible, and in the context, unpardonable ugliness. On a larger scale, modern Athens makes an unexpectedly sordid frame for the Acropolis.

Tourism has become a way of life for mobile and communicative modern man. If he is not the prey or the predator in this bedlam of public squalor, he cultivates in self-defense the faculty of subsisting on the half-heard or the half-seen and may be observed moving in vast crowds distinguished by indifference, lack of initiative, boredom or complacency.

Affluent society's privileged and sensitive few, in search of decent privacy, pleasure and solitude, seek this ever further afield. In the process, and for, of course, the best reasons, the erosion of a habitat fit for some future humanism continues.

Perhaps this drift toward universal "public squalor" in our environment may be halted by re-establishing a sense of "public responsibility" to match our prevalent pre-occupation with "private prerogative." If we can do this we may start on the uncomfortable return journey from the ridiculous to the sublime.

Entertainment Hall,
Bexhill, Sussex, 1935.
Auditorium preliminary
study.

. . . I have a feeling that the urban revolution is really a very significant change in human affairs. I think it was Mr. Roderick Seidenberg, another ex-architect, who said that from now on post-historic man will be as different from us as pre-industrial man was from pre-historic man.[15] This I really believe. There is a certain evolutionary tempo which, for convenience sake, I will think of as three different clocks. One is the biological clock which is moving so slowly that it is virtually at a standstill. There is the sociological clock which has been moving relatively fast in the development of human groups, mores, and cultures. To this has been added modern technology, a rather fancy name for tools.

This technological clock has been accelerating at a tremendous rate. It would be impossible to extrapolate it in a linear way. Think of it as a tremendous uprising spiral of social change. Consequently a problem, with which everyone seems to be concerned, is how to synchronize the disparity of the two clocks. In other words, reasonable control of technology is not achieved at the same rate as it is produced. There seems absolutely no possibility of synchronization, so the only things we can do is bring them a little bit closer together. Possibly in some distant world which I cannot possibly imagine, I shall be proved wrong.

In any case it seems to me the relevance to this of Environmental Design is that it must include very long-term predictions; prediction in that we may now make models and test their validity because we now have tools with which to implement theory in a new way. We don't have to turn theory blindly into action to test it. We can program, and we can test without the sometimes disastrous consequences of cause and effect procedures. In fact, we can do an awful lot without doing damage. Architects still con-

From a lecture, "Environmental Design and Adaptation to Change," given at the Urban Exploration conference, Florida State University, October 28, 1966; published in *Urban Exploration* (Florida State University, 1966).

tinue, of course, at the drop of a hat, to get things off the tops of their heads and ruin towns for generations. This is one of the main reasons why I no longer am one of them. I really believe, therefore, that prediction is a part of prevention of the predictable bad, and the inducement of the predictable good. I am not claiming in any way to be omniscient about what is good or bad. That is your problem.

I think we are going to have to say there are two things at work in this evolutionary process. One is the tremendous quantity of growth which, however, does not happen to be the same as the quality of change. We cannot merely extrapolate number and just adapt ourselves through our technology to the problems of number. We have to recognize the quality of significant changes of the most profound order. That means that we have to have new measures. For instance, we no longer think of location in terms of distance. We think of it in terms of time-distance, certainly if there is any kind of vehicle involved. Even for a pedestrian we think about the frequency of the trip, so you have a measure of time-distance-frequency. By the same token, you can think of quantities in terms of density, or number of people accommodated in or using a facility. At the same time you can put a parallel to that and say "density-intensity." How intensely is a place or a facility used? So the measure, then, becomes one of dynamic order-interaction, the continuous pumping between related phenomena. This change in process and organization has profound influence on values.

If all this is even vaguely true, words like city planning and regional planning begin to lose their meaning for me and must be superseded by something more significant. Because every time someone says city, up flood the image of the familiar city. Region—what region? Technical region? Ethnical region? Geographical region? There are so many different kinds of regions that I prefer to use a more neutral word like field or territory to describe what is really happening. What is the action field or range? Perhaps what we talk about as architecture now, or city planning, or landscape architecture, or design or this or the other current phrase, suggests a somewhat arbitrary division of labor. It has lost meaning. When architecture stops, where does landscape architecture begin? Where does architecture stop; where does urban design begin? It is almost impossible to define our task in these terms. Actually where it begins is in the minds engaged in the task; some better men can stretch themselves wider; and lesser men cannot. The latter concentrate on specialization. It seems to me that environmental design is a more accurate description of the design problem of our time.

It can be seen, also, in another way and I am coming to this as my most important assumption. Environmental Design is really an ecological problem. Almost imperceptibly, the man-made environment is becoming as important as the natural environment through which man has been accustomed to move. Urbanism is a system of man-made environments, a habitat, man-made as opposed to natural, which almost demands that we think of it as a special fourth ecology. It has been added to the ecology of land, air and water.

We are, in fact, not only creating our own environment in the terms of comfort, or cultural necessity, but we are interfering in a brutal way, as you all know, with the natural. It is a two-fold ecological problem of structuring one side and conserving the other side, not separately but simultaneously and always in direct interaction. Urbanism is really a new stage in the development and deployment of man. Instead of following the natural isotherms where we found him in great congregations, we are coming to the point when we can take our climate with the necessary controls with us where we will. Because of this capacity, astonishing quantities of men no doubt will just snap out of the natural ecology and take their own ecology with them in order to survive. This ecology, this urbanism, this redeployment exists on many, many scales, all the way from the global, from the point of view of instantaneous information, right down to the essential face-to-face contacts within family groups to the larger communities, tribes, clans, occupational groups, ethnic groups, nations, regional associations and so on.

All these have their particular boundaries which are largely social, but are describable also on various territorial scales. It is quite obvious, just take the very typical example of New York. There is a lot of talk about the governorship of New York and the elective power structure problem. The mayor of New York has to go, hat in hand, to a man who actually commands far less power in the real sense of the word than the mayor. New York is not a city, but a colossal, metropolitan region. Its technological boundaries are so enormously changed that it draws its energy and water supply all the way from the Canadian border. It energizes intercourse of a cultural kind for the whole United States. It is a technological imperative, not a moral one, but a political one, namely that we shall have redeployment of power structure under the pressure of technological realities in a very short time. The redistribution of legislatures is the first symptom of this, but it by no means represents the whole process of readjustment to which I suspect we are irrevocably committed. . . .

Today in America, there is no such thing as a city. There are only components in a metropolitan system of randomly distributed urbanism. Technology is, of course, concentrated largely on historic cities and we are trying to accommodate these to constant changes by various devices. Sprawl is the first symptom, along with suburbia. I consider these totally anti-urban as well as anti-conservationist and irrational.

But, we are now coming to an even greater problem. Our technocrats, pre-occupied with the logic and technology of mobility, are suggesting that, in fact, greater diffusion is now possible. In terms of frequency of travel and time-distance, of course, we can go faster. What would be the result? We would then have a continuing process of building up the illusion of greater freedom for those who are privileged enough to afford this colossal mobility. It is really much more expensive than people think. I have often wanted to get an economist to work out an equation for the real cost of mobility in general and cars in particular. I don't think anybody has computed this, but I am sure it would be colossal.

The other consequences of growing mobility is that historic congregations suffer in direct proportion, so that the places that we think of as historic cities are becoming degraded. Paradoxically that which used to be the privilege of princes, to be within cities, has now become the privilege, and the necessity, alas, of the new poor. The princes have sought refuge in pseudo-hunting lodges, the roads to which, of course, are all supplied from the public purse. I think the problem is really how to look at the metropolitan interaction of many of these components and to find an organizational theory, or a system or a model, which would somehow counteract this divisive quality of random motion and prevent the degradation of urban concourse, and the destruction (by tourism et al.) of ("vanishing") paradises.

You will, I think, understand from these remarks that I have a commitment. I am not in the least objective. I really have a commitment to community and urbanity which is the product of concourse and intercourse between many different minds. It seems to me that urbanism is probably the most significant and influential tool ever created by man for the improvement of his mind. That is what I am told by the wiser natural scientists and social scientists. We did not effectively change our brain structure for hundreds of thousands of years. We have always had something like fifteen billion transistors in our heads, but we have been using relatively few. We are going to use more and more and more as we interact people-to-people and people-to-tools. This interaction is what makes for the greatest expansion of the mind. Therefore, it seems to me that urbanism is a tool for the acceleration of the evolution of man. It is not something to be lightly dismissed because we can put anything anywhere, which is exactly the same as saying nothing can be everywhere. We shall move endlessly nowhere, spending more time in the process, in motion, for its own sake and not getting that kind of leisurely intercourse and interaction that is really the catalytic power that is life and human intercourse at its richest.

I am asking for a reexamination of priorities; random motion, although it seems to be infinitely convenient and comfortable, is divisive. It is divisive in a sense that if we had too many clusters it would follow that these clusters would tend to get smaller. It happens that high technology requires the prop of density in terms of numbers of users and in terms of turnover of use. Without this density we couldn't possibly have any of our service trades. We wouldn't have elevator boys or university presidents unless we had pretty high density-intensity use places. So what I am afraid of is, if we fragment our clustering beyond some critical point, we will almost certainly ensure a lower level existence. Only staples, absolute stereotypes and standardized facilities could subsist in small clusters because there would not be enough variety of appetite to demand the options and the number of choices. The other side of the same dismal coin is if we have staples everywhere, except where there is already built-in variety and specialty and excitement (namely the historic cities, where real options lie), we will have progressively more pressure on these concentrations which have not been designed to receive it. I don't believe, of course, that this divisive action has to be continued. I see no reason for it at all. . . .

. . . So it would seem to me that one has to think of urban organization, perhaps in an oversimplified way at first. Appropriate flow systems of motion and interaction. Appropriate container places for people, and I really mean people, uncorked people; people that are walking on their legs, or sitting on their backsides, whose eyes you can see instead of their headlights. More and more restoration of man in his natural state in relation to all kinds of human intercourse regardless of whether it is on a family level, neighborhood level or a city level, or a regional level or whatever the territory or orbit may be. This does suggest that we should abandon, as soon as possible, random flow systems. The car is perfectly alright where there is no concentration which will support a public transportation system. It should really be treated as an emergency vehicle where population is very, very thin, and therefore, where congestion is not an issue. It could be treated like a yacht. It should be something wealthy people can put in harbor until ready to go on a cruise and when the pleasure cruise is over, shove it back in the harbor.

Public transit as far as I can see, is a catalytic force. It is an instrument of cohesion because every stop on a transit system is potentially an exchange where man is restored to his concourse personality; where the passenger becomes pedestrian. Every exchange is potentially a concourse by definition; and it does give priority to the pedestrian.

I am against the kind of planning which zones for special purposes; dormitories only, for instance, or workplaces only. It means that these places become dead daily. They are wasteful in terms of their occupancy, but they will literally go dead in an urban sense. A technologically wasteful place in a densely populated area if designed for peak numbers for a very few hours during the day becomes dangerous at other times when it is deserted yet may have to be passed through. Every urban success that I know has been one of mixed uses where the town, like

Bologna say, or any of those little Tuscany towns, is alive twenty-four hours. The great capitals should be alive twenty-four hours. They are all intensely and constantly used and require mixed zoning.

High density use produced high land values. The public owns a tremendous area, in any urban situation, of rights-of-way of public roads and air rights. This capital of the most precious, preferred, most expensive land area should now be used in an intelligent manner. Big buildings for public purposes, health, education, whatever, should now with determination be placed not on speculative land acquired from some speculative developer at low prices, but should be placed in public air rights over roads already publicly owned, thereby having the advantage of "bridges" serving many communities sliced apart in that first burst of "automania."

If one has mobility and instantaneous communication, among the highest peaks of technology from the standpoint of physical planning, then I can imagine tranquility opposing that at the other end of the spectrum. I propose tranquility that is induced by designed places for leisurely concourse; I mean real tranquility. I don't mean something polluted, shall we say, by acoustic interference.

Consensus is not in any sense a good thing to have, not even in relation to political action. In order to get anything done at all, consensus is simply a temporary convenience for action which cannot maximize anything for everyone at once. It is not a theoretically valid goal except on the highest level of abstractions of general "good" which changes very fast. Obviously we are riddled with so many contradictions that we lose sight of the fact that most of the contradictions are not necessary. They can become simply the opposite ends of a hierarchy or spectrum of complementarity.

Let me give you just a few examples that will enable one to maximize either end of the spectrum which flows between rules and randomness. Too many rules are obviously inhibiting. Too much freedom is also obviously dangerous for public purposes. Rules, randomness; restriction, freedom; these are opposite poles of a hierarchy containing intermediary positions just like community and privacy which was previously mentioned. By exactly the same token you can say that in great concourses you have anonymity. On the other hand, in your small neighborhood group you have identity. Both are indispensable, but you cannot settle for median satisfaction because it would deny both requirements. Exactly the same things would be true in terms of time-distance-frequency. At one end you have accessibility. Things must be immediately accessible. At the other end, the value would be space. You go there more infrequently, but you get more space. So with staple-specialties, all the apparent contradictions are really complementaries. I am searching for a theory or system or principles, which are the major parameters of urban complexity. These would be adjusted in time. The action realities are the variables of cultures, of geography, of technology, economy, and of scale difference. They are measured in terms of place and time. But these are variables, and you can retreat from the theoretical optimum to the possibility of a given situation. A good game to play after dinner is to see how many urban complementary social and technical hierarchies you can put down in three minutes. You will be astonished how revealing this is. What would happen if we could resolve contradictions into complementarities?

Just in closing: no less a person than Max Born, a great physicist, came out unequivocally with very, very serious reservations about the usefulness of our spending billions on the space race and lunar landing.[16] In other words, what he was saying politely is we are all lunatics. Well, I commend you to the notion that we don't need a space agency for up there, what we need is a space agency for below—immediately.

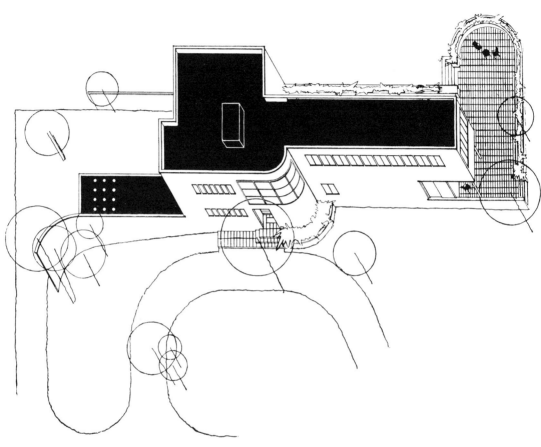

Nimmo House, St.
Giles, Buckinghamshire,
1935 (in partnership
with Erich Mendelsohn).

. . . I am going to talk, if I may, in most general terms about what I mean by shape of community, and about exactly what is intended by an introduction which really summarizes the whole book. Namely, there are some obvious available structuring devices in our existing technological culture of which by far the most obvious is precisely what has just been stated: the systems of mobility and communication. But as the talk is of transportation, it is quite obvious that we are going to discuss not the implications of communication systems, which don't have territorial limitations, but only specifically about those systems of communication which do have territorial implications: access to and from facilities and people.

A few days ago (it is very interesting that everything becomes topical so suddenly in America) a presidential candidate (Senator George McGovern) declared that his priorities included reconstruction of the transportation system, the rebuilding of our cities, renewing our rural economy and reversing dangerous pollution. Pollution, of course, is fashionable and is being discussed all the time and I am not going to get into that. It is very good news to hear a presidential candidate link urban development and housing with transportation.

It is particularly cheering because we have also heard in the last few days of the program to restructure government departments. Transportation will be put into the new Department of Economics, and problems of urban redevelopment and housing are going to be somewhere else, something which I think is called human resources. This is the kind of deliberate act of separating linked and integrated (logically speaking) systems which could help us resolve our problems instead of leaving them unrelated, contradictory and aggravating problems.

From a lecture, "Shape of Community," given at the Boston Architectural Center, January 27, 1971; published in *Transportation* (Boston Architectural Center, 1971).

All this, of course, is due to a very, very simple problem which plagues our society: the question of wasting time-space resources, tearing of nerves, sponsoring of lies. They are all results of a disease which I call "automania." The western world under the leadership of the United States, which is particularly hardware prone, is almost dying of this right now. . . .

. . . What the ubiquitous automobile does, among other things, is to tear society apart just like invisible cancer does. We have now any number of stereotyped ghettoes (to suit every purse) springing up in and around our cities. All these isolationists' islands in a sea of tarmac are very much like the very visible oil slick around other shores which is spilling over, growing in its dimension and reach. Our own spillage may be destroying humanity on the shores of our cities. You will gather I am not a suburbanite.

The human consequences of this technological extension have not been really truly examined. It certainly has not been understood, and the measure of all such things has not yet been taken. We have tended to extrapolate everything, as if, merely making more of something and better in any way touches the fundamental problem raised in the first place of why the something should continue to be made. In any case we have to admit that transportation, if we really face it quite honestly as a technique, actually provides an extremely small and infinitely variable part in the whole picture at any given time. . . .

. . . We have lost sight of the profound difference between communications systems which bring much second-hand information to many without virtually any territorial restraints whatsoever, and movement systems which provide access to real events of first-hand experience. They involve, of course, response immediately or slowly to the environment with which you have had this confrontation.

What I am talking about, of course, is not extra-territorial, working in fields. It is something which is very earthy indeed if we applied means of measurement which we have to, say, population growth, technological costs, and the accompanying automotive numbers per capita growth in one equation. We might very well conclude that eight hundred square feet of all available space, whether it be on the actual earth or in the corrugated extension of our structures, is a totally disproportionate burden which already urbanizing society cannot afford. It might be noted that all the current talk about cleaning up the car and its fuel will in fact only aggravate every single disease from which we are not suffering immediately. More cars will come into exactly the same places in greater number. It is not the pollution by the car which is painful but the destruction of our habitat. Nothing is more appropriate at this time than a discussion of such problems which are connected with this vital factor of mobility in modern technological society in a school which is actually dedicated to the improvement of professional standards. This is not a trade school; you are not taught here nuts and bolts, I trust. You come here to refresh yourselves in a relation to purposes rather than techniques. I will give you a few examples, in order to demonstrate my own priorities and commitment, and remind you of a very dismal record. Nearly four years ago HUD held a conference on urban transportation under the aegis and the help of our old colleague Charles Haar.[17] Some of you were there. Because our institutions are very poorly designed to respond to any crisis other than war, very little or no positive action has in fact resulted.

Last December the House and Senate negotiators—I love the word—"killed" a miserably inadequate three-quarters-of-a-million appropriation which could have helped cities at that time to meet current transit deficits. A much larger amount of money, of bad money, has already been sunk in the redundant SST and probably a much larger amount of good money still may be voted for it. The highway lobby, only two weeks ago, declared publicly that it needed for the next fifteen years 350 billion dollars—that is a little less than the whole of the national debt—in order to feed their juggernaut.[18] There wasn't a murmur from anybody.

Much closer to home, and I say this with all due apologies to my son, involved the proposal for the American bicentennial based on prototype mobility systems which could become both an exhibition and demonstration and an investment.[19] This is extremely unlikely to clear the assorted lobby and institutional hurdles. It is much too realistic in a true sense of that word. Generally I take a dim view of defoliation of green and pleasant lands. Continuous economic growth leads to more torment for the consumers, more capital for the consumer's paradise. We are not alone. The United Kingdom had a conference which characteristically in the English manner was called "The Countryside in 1970."[20] This was held to round out seven years of painstaking and meticulous research work. Not one of the discourses touched more than superficially upon the impact of mobility on that very confined island. Similar painful circumstances, you can add your own catalog of horror.

I would like also to report to you something rather good. Some years ago, Professor Robert Ayre of Yale (he has since left), in applied sciences, ran a seminar in his school of which he was the chairman. He had graduate students in engineering and selected college undergraduates in a seminar in which both were thrown together. All students were asked, each one in turn, to present a report on a typical engineering feat of large scale, not in terms of its technology, but in terms of its social impact. This went on for a whole year. It may interest you, although you may not be surprised, to learn that in this exercise the undergraduates came off very, very much better than the graduate students in applied sciences: the latter were already far too conditioned to operate in any sensible way.

We have all sorts of options opening up, and the observations, which I am now going to make quickly, are of compressed and parodied quotes from this book which is still buzzing in my head. It is called not only the *Shape of the Community,* its main title, but has a subtitle called "Realization of Human Potential." I think both are self-explanatory and I hope relevant to the purposes of this lecture series. The title and subtitle describe my commitment and my environmental priorities. . . .

. . . I hope that you will bear with me for at least one evening if I speculate about purpose. There is a sort of law which seems to operate in the phenomena of life of all kinds, not excluding mankind, in which maximization of individual choice of environments, events, or interactions is achieved by extending the spectrum of alternatives between tolerable limits of complementary opposites, as, for instance, between community and privacy.

If you live totally exposed in community, history will tell you that the community pays a terrible price. If you live entirely in the isolation of the utmost privacy as a hermit, history will also tell you that you pay a tremendous price for that isolation. There is no consensus center point which is ideal. That would be a dead center indeed.

What is operating, of course, is the constant process of interaction between compatible complementary opposites. Sometimes you find equilibrium between the two. You can never find equilibrium in an artificially-created situation which has a dead center. So, I hope that we may derive our environments and our structures of environments and their designs and their operation from rational choice rather than blind choice. This requires that we have some conceptual structural devices in the first place before we let loose the immense reserves of our technological skills and potentials and resources.

In very, very general terms, exploration of any kind by man is guided by human commitment to human ends, and these are quite visible and understandable ends or goals of one sort or another. The mutation of the human brain in the evolutionary process, remote in time, made it possible for us to imagine that even Cro-Magnon man 34,000 years ago was able to give attention to measuring the seasons. The most primitive man became the first animal to participate very directly and purposefully in the evolutionary process; but our participation so far has had very mixed results. The reason for that is, I think, quite clear. We have always had commitments, but we didn't always have the correct priorities in relation to our commitments. Now we see those two things as being essential pieces of this equation.

What we are really doing in broad terms when we talk about "urbanizing" man is a new stage of evolution. I like to think of this man-made environment as a third ecology, the human ecology, which is urban because that is where man is evolving. Urbanization, therefore, in the broad spectrum of this kind, appears to be a very significant step in the evolution of *Homo sapiens*, the social animal, the animal that has to interact with his own as well as with the man-made environments.

This process is apparently quite similar to every other process, which goes on in any form of evolution; it produces natural laws of slow evolution and sudden and yet inexplicable mutations which make our evolution not a smooth curve but a jumpy progress of surprising leaps into the unknown. We are at this moment in the biggest leap of all, the movement from pre-industrial society into post-industrial society.

We know in the United States the word urban has really lost any particular meaning as opposed to, say, rural. There is no such thing. It is simply that we have an infinitely greater exchange between people who are working in "A" field or who are working in "B" field. Both are totally interdependent and, as a matter of fact, totally interchangeable in the long run.

This process of urbanization is creating conditions which are quite, quite different from the classic notion of an urbanized society. This is a society of cities. Every single human settlement regardless of its size, intensity, density, frequency of use, whatever measures you like to apply to them, is in fact part of a global urban system in the process of developing as inevitably as the evolution of man himself. An ever greater interaction between these settlements increases their interdependence. This universal interdependence is extremely important not only in relation to the movement systems but in relation to foreign affairs, for example. No matter on what scale, whenever we have a communication system, all human beings regardless of their cultural condition, their educational condition, or economic condition, begin to operate slowly with the same structuring devices and the same capacities to choose their destinies and methods of operation.

I think of all settlements as an enormous hierarchy of places where people are, not necessarily as residents but simply as users, accessible to space or information of whatever kind for whatever purpose.

If we were to start talking about design of these sort of pieces of our urban environment in this immense hierarchy of settlements and interdependence, communication systems and access systems; namely, transportation, such systems would become prime structuring devices.

I would like to emphasize my priorities and the reason for my mistrust of any continuing adherence to a single "ideal" ubiquitous form of movement. (The car is the nearest thing to this we can now think of.) Everybody has the illusion of total freedom of access to everything provided there is a roadway. Shortly, as a matter of fact, we could have, the abandonment of roads and move around on air cushion, wheel-less vehicles of a design which could cross rough terrain. This however would not improve our conditions; it would make it worse, much, much worse.

What is really happening is that because we have random movement so highly developed technically, we are getting what I call territorial anarchy. All these bits and pieces of inhabited places scattered and diffused, served by the automobile, can only make the provision of extremely standard facilities just as standard as the automotive instruments of mobility themselves. We are getting in fact a stereotyping of our society and we are getting an illusion of choice, whereas, the reality is that we are moving more and more, wasting more and more time in this movement, moving from nowhere to nowhere because we only move to the already preconceived target which is exactly in the same set of targets as the one you have just left. Every shopping center is the same; every parking lot is the same; every point of arrival and departure now is fundamentally stereotyped. . . .

. . . We imagine we are getting more individual choice but in fact we are getting less freedom because the mass culture and the mass production systems scattered randomly over low-density concentrations of human beings can only support the stereotyped. It requires a very high concentration, full of ambivalence, uncertainty, mixed intensity, density, frequency of use, to induce the real variety which actually produces choices.

You can get choices, as a matter of fact, along Third Avenue, but I defy you to get a choice in the supermarket, because you have seen it all before and will again in every other supermarket.

What I am talking about is the lack of opportunity to meet other than preconceived purposes produces stereotyped people. People move from target to target, but they know what they expect before they get there and that is exactly what they get. There is no surprise, no adventure. There is none of the evolutionary pressure which difference, variety, mix makes. Therefore, it would seem to me that we could use the structuring device of public transportation mobility to reverse the divisive power of randomly moving automotive vehicles in private hands, heavily subsidized, of course, out of the public purse.

My journey to New Haven, in spite of the dollar twenty-five

which I subscribed to the toll booths of the pike to New York, actually is subsidized to a tune of between $4 and $5 per car trip out of the public purse to this day. Now, this is an unbearable burden for the people who don't own cars and who have to travel on the New Haven railroad which doesn't move reliably. There is a kind of inequity operating here which is taken for granted simply because we are automanic in our view of transportation. . . .

. . . Technological cost is rising so fast because its complexity requires, as a matter of fact, an immensely heavy turnover of use. Highest technology must have a 24-hour turnover and it must serve the optimum number of people. The measure of its efficiency in terms of not only what it can do but also how we can pay for it to do it, is intensity, density, frequency of use, and mix of use. I would say that the only way that we can possibly benefit from using technological costs is by having transit systems which will shift our stereotyped, special-use ghettoes—the residential sector, business sector, industrial sector, etc.—which none of us can police and certainly not even our $16,000-a-year policemen, because they have to be self-policing.

We have to have mixed zoning so that everything is occupied 24 hours a day to a greater or lesser extent. Can you imagine what happens around the empty garages, around St. Louis stadium in downtown when there is no game on? You can't walk around there. You would have your throat cut. And this is some of the most precious land that St. Louis has.

I am against peak load targets which result from this kind of indiscriminate use of transportation systems in the wrong place for the wrong reason. You cannot have peak loads in something which really requires a very regular pulse of frequency use throughout the 24 hours. I must keep on emphasizing this. We have already got the technology that is necessary and we have the existing rights of way which have been established by our roadway systems. They are not entirely evil. Our highway systems are marvelous, but we must take them over and make them work better than for the very low-carrying capacity that they actually have. Particularly they must be improved when the carrying capacity of these very efficient flows begins to falter and finally collapse, for example, as you get into high-density targets to which all these flows are directed: our highly-concentrated cities. We could reverse this process.

I am going to make a suggestion which is positive in relation to transit. If you have a considered hierarchy of transit systems at various speeds, but all achieving an identical, balanced time distance factor; if you wanted to be within five minutes' reach of whatever, then you would be using accelerated motion which is technically achievable. You would still be getting wherever you have to within so many minutes which is really the measure of accessibility. If you only had to wait three minutes or thirty time/distance/speed/frequency "units," then these must be counted in as a differential in this measure.

We all know the famous buses, one every ten minutes. But so many buses are now frustrated in New York, even with the one-way avenue flows. They have to proceed in groups because no bus can stop any longer except behind another bus. So, what you do is get fleets of buses at intervals between half an hour and an hour serving the New Yorkers standing shivering in the streets.

Transportation simply doesn't work in this kind of simplistic way. You have to have integrity of mass-transit based upon what this has to do. It has to meet time-distance-access specifications and particularly for the disadvantaged in our time as a first step.

The kind of transportation that I am now describing does not necessarily do away altogether with the conventional car. It is quite obvious that the further away you get from the high density, the car becomes more and more valuable, because no mass transit system can be maintained in low density over large areas. You get an inverse pattern of complementarity; places where the car really pays off and where the car really does not pay at all and other systems do. There are, also, many intermediary positions.

I can visualize a hierarchy of exchanges in which every stop in the system is in fact an exchange between passengers arriving and departing at that point for very good reasons and by several different means. . . .

We can bridge a highway which cuts a community asunder with all kinds of catalytic bridges of public services. These could be a school, a hospital and a health center. If everybody is within certain walking distance of quick sub-systems which meet there, most of the time for whatever reason, the cleverest fellows in private enterprise would nucleate around this publicly-primed new exchange. Exchange points in a transportation system are not just a way of moving passengers around, they make people gather together and enjoy first-hand experience at leisure. Separated from your machines for that brief moment of time, you see somebody as a man with long hair or short hair of a girl with nice legs or not nice legs; where boy can watch girl. Somewhere you can relax. That is why Europeans go thousands of miles in order to sit in piazzas everywhere.

We, on the other hand, treat our streets, the only public places for pedestrians, as traffic arteries themselves. You only have to walk down a sidewalk anywhere to realize that cars receive better treatment than men. Even in lovely Boston and Cambridge. What you see are fearful, frenetic passers-by who really loathe everybody they have to brush against in case they fall in the garbage. These are not meeting places, they are just traffic arteries in which people are dehumanized and become vehicles.

I don't believe it is economical any more to pursue the path of least possible investment in some undeveloped piece of land with the sure knowledge that the public purse will somehow beat a road to the doorsteps at colossal expense to all the people who are not going to use it.

We could invest in exactly the opposite way. We could invest in the most essential substructure with an absolute certainty that the intensity and density and frequency of its use will write it off as fast as we now write off development costs. This seems to be indisputable, and I think there is some evidence of this in other cities outside this country.

There are theories maybe and there are systems which already exist but which have not yet been systematically used. What we have to do in talking about transportation is not to discuss the hardware (whether it is a monorail or whatever) but simply what it has to do in terms of new purposes and measures. I think we would come up with entirely new answers. What I am really suggesting is that our fragmented society finds it so difficult to live in community now, because of stereotyping and ghettoization and polarization instead of public places which are meeting places. Places in which the privilege of being there and doing whatever it is you are doing there may not be disputed, challenged on the grounds of interference with traffic, where you cannot be a nuisance, where you cannot be told to move on.

In other words, we need kinds of contemporary agoras where all kinds of things may happen. There might survive some historic prime special centers in which, because of the number of people that want to be there, there will be generated all kinds of surprises and adventures. Surprising first-hand experience and the extension of choice would occur through meeting the unexpected. We would not have the limitation of choice by only going to that which is already known.

Many years ago, I think it was in 1956, a school was very carefully designed as a bridging device, so that two sides of a split community could in fact meet in a freshly designed, extended facility. Bridges could be a university or a regional hospital. Points of transfer can be designed to be of infinite richness as learning places. I am against the idealized beautifully-landscaped walk from school to residential sector which eliminates any possibility of a child meeting the adult world until it is too late for him to learn what it is all about.

I want places in which the old and the young and the middle-aged and the workers and the idle all mix together in the most natural way as a daily necessity where we become rehumanized again. If we have a perfect system—that is to say, technically a perfect system, and socially secure—then the easy walking distance, which is still the cheapest to ten minutes' reach that we can use, can be expanded slowly even for the child, the perambulatory child, because his territory will be increased faster, more safely, and will include much richer experiences than today. If you are poor, until you can get a car and a driving license, your experiences are really street corners. If you are the "privileged" suburbanite kid, you are carted around in the back of a station wagon endlessly and miss everything between the targets, whatever they may be.

This is a horrible, horrible way of growing up. I would like learning places, and they can only be produced by weaning our children away from the notion that the passport to adulthood is a driving license. The passport to adulthood, as a matter of fact, is understanding what the adult responsibilities are and how to behave in an adult way.

I am trying to put transportation, transit systems into such a relationship with meeting places that pedestrians become imperceptibly passengers and can again be seen as persons and not as machine minders behind the headlights. That way we may get new agoras.

I had better stop now. I have a very short peroration, you will be relieved to hear. It is quite evident I hope to you that I am talking of very different sorts of transportation systems than the ones which are currently operating, not because we can't operate them, but because we won't. A hierarchy of appropriate systems for many conditions must be much more than just merely expedient or sporting. Moving about must not be anxiety creating. Everybody now is concerned with departures and arrivals because they involve us with the disposal of monsters to which, we have been tied by some kind of invisible umbilical cord; such as a Mobil credit card.

I am advocating a system of mobility which can help enlarge access of choice for poor or rich alike. This is terribly important for a democratic system of movement. One of the most humanizing instruments I have known is, as a matter of fact (not in the rush hour of an inadequate system in New York) a subway in the morning going—I used to take it—to Brooklyn. I got to know an awful lot of New Yorkers that I never could have seen before. Good mobility in a complementary sense is simply the other end to satisfying tranquility.

We cannot enjoy constant mobility and anxiety created in its wake in the present form. We will have an ever-increasing leisure time which may be forced upon us if we do not plan for it and know what to make of it when it comes. I can imagine even now places where people become, as a matter of habit, peaceful citizens instead of competing consumers; places in which spontaneous events will be made possible and above all in which compassion and tolerance of strangeness may once more play a part; places of escape from forced unanimity and suspicion; places which are self-policing around the clock; inviting places and learning places.

If we cannot create simple things of this kind, we may be facing imminent deterioration as human beings far more terrible, perhaps, than sudden extinction through a nuclear blast.

We shall deteriorate slowly and we shall see our limbs and our organs waste. We can lose our humanity in places which are empty of meaning or surprises, but we must not do this.

Thank you.

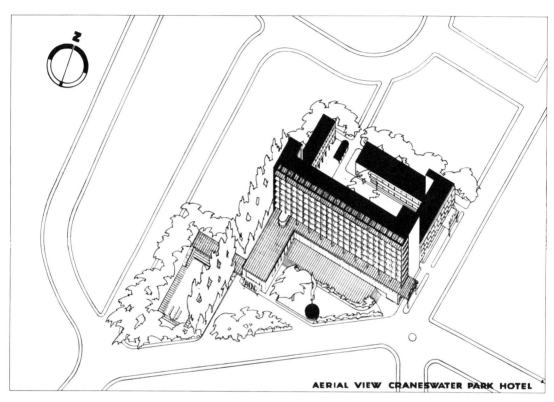

AERIAL VIEW CRANESWATER PARK HOTEL

Craneswater Park Hotel proposal, Southsea, Isle of Wight, 1935 (in partnership with Erich Mendelsohn).

SHAPE OF COMMUNITY: REALIZATION OF HUMAN POTENTIAL

A journey from New Haven, Connecticut, to Auburn, Alabama, is in itself a depressing lecture on planning failure. The journey starts with a two-hour drive along a six-lane turnpike which at most hours of the day or night, approaching New York City, is a bumper to bumper nightmare to match the Los Angeles horrors. Large cars compete with enormous trucks; the first are all too empty, the latter overloaded.

The traveler arrives with shattered nerves at one of the world's "great airports" in which the acoustic climate is hell. Noise wraps around anxiety or boredom. It is a non-place of insecurity sustained by interference.

In the air you enjoy relative comfort and, if you are not a compulsive reader of magazines, you can enjoy the vista below of a great metropolis. The view reveals nothing of the mayhem on the ground but which at night presents, to anyone interested, one of the greatest spectacles of man-made mountains twinkling with a million stars, a beautiful fantastic creation. Then you recall that this consumes, in behalf of some twelve million people, more electricity than the whole of Belgium.

The drive through Alabama is, by contrast, a journey from nowhere to nowhere until one reaches Auburn University, a campus ghetto with little visible connection with its surroundings. Students seem isolated here. The traveler begins to think about the prevailing, most uneven distribution and consumption of energy. It is depressing to move around in the highly developed technological world of the U.S.A. Contradictions and failures are apparent. Planning appears to be non-existent.

We appear to be trapped in a technological hell. The appetite for more technology seems uncontrollable. Perhaps we will not learn to curb materialism in time for survival. The United States

From a lecture, "Shape of Community: Realization of Human Potential," given to the Graduate Program in Urban and Regional Planning, Auburn University, January 18, 1972. Published in Samuel Snow, ed., *The Place of Planning* (Auburn University, November 1973).

consumes some forty percent of available physical resources. This small percentage of humanity already consumes more per capita (statistically) than the rest of mankind. But the American appetites for mechanization, an exponential increase in energy consumption, are spreading over the inhabited globe, and no end is in sight.

A recent visit to India's cities is a picturesque form of the same traffic mayhem in which cars compete with bicycles, carts, beasts of burden, and pedestrians along the same street. Of course, the same situation for cars and pedestrians, and whatever, exists in all developed countries.

In a very, very few cities is there any public, mass transportation to help us live in high densities. Buses, as in New York and London, competing with private cars for the same road space, are virtually useless. Yet there are very few plans for transit of equality, for poor and rich alike, in congested urban areas. These areas are now under increased pressure from suburban cars still moving regularly in to and out of the unique facilities of great cities.

The suburbias, dependent on the private, random-running car, which can be built anywhere where public roads may lead, suffer from another aspect of the same mechanized mayhem. People can live in ghettos of their choice. The commuters, shoppers and children can move in station wagons or some such "essential," from house to some familiar goals in dreary daily routine. For them, everything between remains unexplored. It might be said that they move from nowhere to nowhere: a poor environment, empty of everything except convenience.

Yet ubiquitous, essential movement has become a major portion of technological man's waking hours, and this has fourfolded in a single generation. The business of why to move, to where, for what purpose, and the manner of moving and its costs, are in fact more important than the technologies of mechanized movement.

If our current thinking leads to the improvement of cars— cleaner, safer, smaller, more economical; then, if we do not eventually provide viable alternatives, including walking, employing manpower only, our energy resources will be consumed faster and the death of cities will have become a tragic reality.

It must be noted at the same time that ubiquitous, predigested, edited, standardized man-communication messages will complete our mass-culturization. For there will be no adventure, discovery and creative interpretation left for the individual to enjoy.

The real invisible problems for planners have little to do with formal design. The priorities are in the realms of social betterment through politics reaching toward new systems of power.

Your problems as students demand new priorities, also, of reaching out toward new sources of knowledge, ethics, morals and ideals. These are not currently available in dogmatic departments devoted to narrow enquiry.

Nobody is indispensable, but some people invent and contribute more than others. So what we should really be doing in any university is searching for that free, creative talent which needs few textbooks but which will come out of an entire reorganization of our needs and system of enquiry. Those concerned with public good today are not looking for easy answers but for simple questions that have to be asked before any plans or programs may be formulated. And this applies to all students in all universities anywhere, and will be required in greater, fairer measure, if we are to slow our march toward oblivion. Otherwise, our artificially created appetites and mindless ambition will destroy our humanity all too fast.

Thirty-three British scientists quite recently made the following sober judgment: ". . . that to avoid a world environmental catastrophe, we must soon stop building roads, tax the use of power and raw materials, and eventually cut the population in half. . . ."[21] Another scientist, Loren Eiseley, has quoted an Eskimo: "We fear the cold and the things we do not understand. But most of all, we fear the doings of the heedless ones among ourselves."[22]

Now is the time to set up new, viable commitments. These are individual and political ends and decisions to be made toward the attainment of these commitments. You can try to see problems in the light of highest public purpose. You can then examine notions of organizing action and the means necessary. At the bottom of the list of things to be done in the planning process are the tools of implementation: the available technology. They are somewhere around the corner and waiting. They are already in somebody's head. All you have to do is call for them.

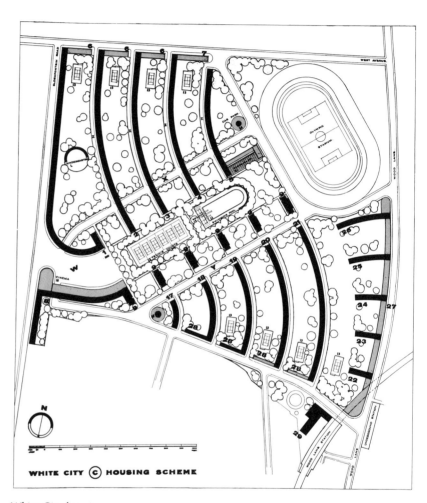

White City housing
proposal, London, 1935
(in partnership with Erich
Mendelsohn).

I am deeply moved by the honour bestowed on me in memory of an old friend and colleague.[23] I am also deeply moved on this occasion which celebrates your society's fiftieth anniversary. This coincides with my entering my eightieth year together with another old friend and your past president Milner Gray.

He reminded me recently that the founders of your society met in my London office. You will, I hope, overlook any inadequacies on my presentation on this occasion which recalls distant days almost forgotten by this old man, and who now speaks as an American living in the U.S.A. . . .

. . . Many friends and colleagues here today shared with me the hope and aspirations of the "twenties" and the "thirties." Today I will address myself to immediate and rather grimmer problems: the maintenance of continuity and acceptance of change which challenge our concerns and commitments.

The world war stopped designers from practise they were accustomed to but provided a much needed opportunity for reflection. During the war I became a teacher; after the war I was encouraged to continue as one. As a result I did more thinking about my profession and what services it was to provide. I came to think of design as an all-embracing activity which should ignore the somewhat arbitrary boundaries established by emerging specialists. In the "forties" I described this broader spectrum as "environmental design."

Since my retirement I had time to think at leisure. This last decade established the imperative need for viable theory, ahead of action. We were approaching a crisis; violence and abuse of nature and humanity have increased all over. Violence may be encountered on any doorstep anywhere. During my life revolutions and wars, great and small, have never ceased. They are now escalating. Yet scientific, economic and technological changes

---

From an address given on the occasion of the fiftieth anniversary of the Society of Industrial Artists and Designers, London, October 10, 1980.

are occurring on an ever-expanding front. In the western world, in which I have lived, I have witnessed growth and change, greater and faster than in any recorded period in human history. Time itself has accelerated. The industrialization process which began earlier moved more slowly toward the twentieth-century affluence.

Abundant resources were obtained, too often, by questionable means. However, the results were never questioned in the civilized world until quite recently. The almost miraculous advances in science and technology were accepted as compensation for tremendous casualties and the passing of great traditions. Newness at any price was grasped without comprehension of the growing complexities of the new processes and their consequences. The older cautious steps, moving from simple things to more complex ones, were superseded by immediate acceptance of the "instant" benefits of material improvements. . . .

. . . Growing expectations and appetites for more material comforts coincided, unfortunately, with the exponential growth in world population. As Joan Robinson, an economist, has observed:

. . . An increase in the expectation of life is a clear gain but an increase in the number of bodies (with all their mechanical extensions), in a given territory is by no means an unambiguous benefit. A higher density of settlement (above a threshold, that is soon passed, permitting adequate mastery over the environment) means a lower average availability per family, of natural resources, including cultivable land, and it becomes professionally more onerous to make good the deficit by investment as density increases. . . .[24]

It seems that we have to learn how to simultaneously preserve and recover more of nature while we learn how to live better in greater densities. It is only in the last decade that the civilized countries have been forced to recognize the limits of power and world resources which they have been misapplying and squandering without regard for the aspirations of the rest of mankind.

Heinz von Foerster, a biologist, underlined our dilemma as follows:

. . . the processes of change that were thus initiated are even in retrospect difficult to comprehend—history—as it was and is now written—is merely descriptive, and even at that highly defective, because of arbitrary selection of descriptors in the absence of guiding concepts of communication and control.

These conceptual difficulties, of course, arise because man's genetic pool is exposed no longer to a more or less stable ecological cultural system; a constant "milieu exterieur artificielle" but to an environment which itself evolves as a consequence of man's ability to project and objectivate thoughts and descriptions. It is not merely change one has to contemplate, it is the change of change that complicates the issue of a development devoid of almost all continuities; resembling a cascade of discontinuities, of "quantum jumps" in kind . . . .

Von Foerster asks:

In the face of socio-cultural eruptions, what does planning mean? How does it help? What can still be designed that is not obsolete by the time it is produced? How can one foresee a future? . . . in a dynamic system, however, "Scenarios of the future" are meaningless for they are envisaged as being the same as today's with only quantitative variations of otherwise unaltered qualities. . . .[25]

Today some of us recognize that more cars, irrespective of whether they are smaller, safer, cleaner and more economical, will produce more and wider highways, larger suburbs and traffic mayhem. Above all they will increase deaths on the roads. They are hardly a prescription for an urbanizing world. Wilfred Owen, writing in the *Bulletin of Atomic Scientists* of last November, asks:

Can the burgeoning cities of the world avoid massive congestion, disorder and social ills . . . . By the end of this century the world will be more urban than rural . . . .

. . . Everywhere the attempt is being made to accommodate growth and change by simply adding on to what is already there. . . . In earlier times cities were able to cope with imbalance caused by growth because neither growth rates nor changes in

technology were great enough to damage the system. Today the changes affecting urban areas are massive and precipitous. Improvisation is not enough, and a process of consciously designing the environment and managing growth has become essential. . . . The effort must be aimed at substituting urban design and redesign for the accidental city. . . .[26]

What I am discussing is urban ecology in the expanding man-made world. Urbanization appears to be a significant step in the evolution of *Homo sapiens*, the social animal. This process in its nature is not dissimilar to the evolution of the universe and other forms of life in it as we know them. On a general level the human community in man-made environments seems to follow some of the laws of natural evolution and mutation—interdependence, conflicts and adjustment—an interaction without end between living things and their environments. Man has added another dimension to ecology.

The new technologies of communications and movements are so pervasive that they now play the role of a cultural catalyst for every environment and induce an ever greater interaction between settlements and increase their interdependence. Industrialized (developed) societies have already become components in a global "urban" system; others are following at different speeds.

This universal interdependence appears to operate in much the same way irrespective of the spatial, cultural or other dimensions of settlements; the traffic and communications of historic capitals operate in a similar way to all metropolitan centers, old and new, and their various extensions. Together they constitute a global hierarchy of settlements in constant interaction linked by movement and information sub-systems, which are the two most conspicuous components of a technological super system now emerging.

In spite of this technological reality (a new condition in the evolution of man and his habitat), most societies continue to be directed by institutions rooted in simpler, self-sustaining economies of an agrarian era or in ideologies of the early industrial period. Both, at the time, were manageable and satisfactory in various degrees. In the past the effects of the products of the land or of factories were comprehensible to all concerned. Most of the

time reality coincided with the illusion of a stable society and
economic success. If something went wrong, it could usually be
corrected by appeasing the gods or their delegates on earth, by
throwing them out, by annexing neighboring resources or by mi-
grating to greener pastures.

These relatively simple remedial steps have become ineffective
rather suddenly. In the foreseeable future neither intervention,
whether divine or military, nor increased production alone holds
much promise. Migration is already no more than search for employment. (Thereafter, in a more distant and unimaginable,
equitable future of genuine universal abundance, movement on
earth may be limited for the majority of men to the search for
rewarding leisure.)

The present "urban revolution" has produced unprecedented
crises because in the highly developed societies of our time most
men live in urban environments. Existing, crowded cities are
hardest hit, but the effects of change extend everywhere. Social
and technical conflicts are only magnified in urban situations.
Poverty, injustice, alienation, illness, pollution and congestion
are failures which reached the existing cities first, but these and
other technological and sociological plagues and absurdities
threaten man's entire habitat. . . .

. . . The city dwellers in developed societies have suddenly
become reluctant to leave their destinies in the hands of obsolete
institutions controlled by invisible experts or all too visible politicians, who until recently were believed to be the dispensers of
technological cornucopia. The habitat of the most "affluent
societies" where the citizens live, work and should find their
pleasure has been deteriorating and becoming ugly and obsolescent at a frightening rate. Technology is racing ahead of social
need.

Lady Dora Russell finds today's world (at the age of 85) less
hopeful than in the 1920s. As quoted recently in the *Times*, she
says: "I don't believe it would be possible to educate children
now as I once believed they could be educated. Who cares about
the human race anymore? . . . Either we turn our planet into a
machine, or we return to some form of civilization. It is a savage,
difficult choice."[27]

Now even the most privileged or our citizens have suddenly been jolted out of their complacency. Everyone is looking for a tolerable accommodation to critical change: the depletion of natural non-renewable energy resources and the need to reduce consumption on a scale never before envisaged. Some symptoms of general concern are already visible: the options of "hard" (technologically sophisticated) production systems based on depletable resource, and "soft" (labor intensive) based on non-depletable resources of sun, wind, and vegetation systems. The Schumacher philosophy "small is beautiful" is being examined with appropriate seriousness. There is a growing mistrust of collective profiteering; bureaucracies, big government, big industry and big business are generally suspect.

Rich people are still enamoured collectors of anything antique or old looking, perhaps a symptom of sorrow for the vanished craftsmen as much as random acquisitiveness or of hope of safe investment in inflated ancient or modern art. The fashion of fifty years ago (love of new shapes), however, still continues for the new not-so-rich. The "luxury" garbage, advertised in full technicolor in the pages of our magazines, is evidence of cultural decline.

It appears that man is confused by too many options; historicism has supplanted history, simplicism (superficial answers) simplicity, aestheticism (affectation of sensitivity) aesthetics, mysticism about art (the mysterious and unique prerogative of genius) the path of natural intuition. The "creative," intuitive approach to a problem is made to appear superior to the processes of intelligence. Artists, while they claim superiority, seldom have to accept responsibility for their actions. The facile now passes for the gifted. In all this I detect a return to formalism and eclecticism which was the fashion at the turn of the century. As Sir James Richards has observed: "Our new eclectics are reviving almost anything."[28]

I have become conscious of the trivialization of my profession. It has become clear that the difference between intuition and knowledge can no longer be so easily drawn. In any field whatsoever, the protagonist has to draw on many other sources to complete his own work. In the planning and design professions, of course, this broader frame of reference is essential. A simple sketch no longer suffices to project an image of something actually very complex which has many aspects. Any design process must employ a variety of skills and methods with both intuition and intelligence in the search for a model.

Indeed, the process of designing complex things has become a technology in its own right. But we still have technophobes in our midst. Yet all model building must start with questions of general need, definition of precise purpose—the organization of parameters—and finally the utilization of available means for action. This principle still holds good in spite of the claims of self-appointed pseudo-masters.

In the beginning of this century, artists, painters, sculptors, architects, graphic designers, industrial designers, engineers, planners, natural scientists, philosophers, joined forces with writers and emerging film makers to project appropriate, significant forms to meet situations without precedent. Optimism was predominant; opportunities of reconstruction after the devastation of the first world war appeared immeasurable. In the wake of redeployment of intellectuals from many countries, "the modern age" was ushered in. It is still with us.

In the period between the two world wars designed products were part functional and part fashionable. The early definitions of "form follows function" were simplistic, largely mechanical in content, and materialist in cultural purpose. We now recognize that functionalism is a complex composite which affects every aspect of our being. This was described by John K. Galbraith succinctly, as the techno-structure. (He included culture.)[29]

Whatever was produced in the last few decades indicated a progressive movement away from making "things" to the understanding of "systems." This new knowledge made it possible to discard simplistic analogies between living organisms and man-made things which were merely matters of organization at a much simpler level.

We are beginning to abandon the notion of creating "complete" things. We are recognizing that we are participants in a process of evolution: "change and growth." We not only are getting more but in the process are becoming different. In other words, change in quality is the inevitable other aspect of quantitative increases.

Over the years my own preoccupation changed from things one

imagined could be personally mastered, such as a painting or a sculpture, to structures of use, such as industrial design or architecture in which you could perhaps master the client first. But then one found, of course, that in addition it was necessary to master the economy and compromise with the existing culture in which one was supposed to be making an independent, creative judgment. Today planning and designing cities is even more difficult.

After some lucky practice I found this activity unsatisfactory and moved to more theoretical involvements; trying to understand more of the larger environment and its physical and social complexities generally and the urban problems in particular. . . .

Whenever anybody now accepts the role of the designer he or she must accept the burden of great responsibility. The myth of creative uniqueness and superiority must be forgotten. The jolly independent artist is out. So is the jolly hermit. So should be the gay playboys of the Western world and their extravagant shenanigans. Much of this escapist extravaganza is, of course, a symptom of boredom among rich exhibitionists. Boredom, alas, is but a short step toward cynicism, disgust and destruction of old and new values. It is a black comedy of contempt; gallow's humor. . . .

. . . I suspect that many "uncreative" people, are so described because they have never been given the opportunity to exercise their latent talents. In a university, one can not only build intellectual and intuitive bridges through methods and mechanics of learning but actually raise both to new levels of excellence.

Scientists continue their research; scholars have been continuously searching. In my own field, which I have come to think of as environmental design (irrespective of scale), I am convinced that the essential ingredient of research, now missing, must be immediately supplied. Our educational and professional spectrum must be extended beyond the conventional three to five years of "professional training" for the "business" of "architecture" or "planning" or whatever! Designers and planners must know more. We require post graduate, ongoing work in research as a career. I can imagine that such studies could be structured to include both individual and group work and would involve students and faculty from other disciplines at the very beginning. No school of "architecture and planning" can afford to work alone. We must be prepared to design and build new cities and we are faced with drastic reconstruction and reorganization of existing ones. We need new protagonists.

May I suggest a few priorities for this giant enterprise: existing world cities are already linked by aviation and by rail and road transportation. Mass transportation systems must determine the location of new cities and industries. All cities old and new must be structured or restructured within by appropriate economic mass transit and public vehicles-systems. Private automobiles must be kept out of high density city cores. Movement systems and supporting flow systems of services and utilities should determine the location of the various container systems: the inhabited places, and their supportive facilities.

It is my belief that everything observed in nature or in the man-made environments is a vital aspect of the learning process. It follows that everything of excellence that man creates, conserves or saves from destruction is an invaluable learning opportunity, thing or place. Such places which are to be designed for the new technological environment must include those designed deliberately to promote social mix and awareness in concourse. There are few mixing places in our present culture. I speak as an American. As we move enclosed in our automobiles from familiar target to a selected target we leave everything between unexplored.

We need exchanges between public transportation systems which become public places where pedestrians old and young, poor or rich, will find themselves as a matter of natural, daily necessity to observe and mix with each other at leisure and in security, while sharing the amenities provided. We must learn to welcome strangers once more.

Without profound changes in our attitudes toward urbanism as a way of life, which now appears to be our inevitable next stage in man's evolution, we shall not be capable of designing rich containers for life. If we succeed, these may never be perfect, but the desperate conditions bordering on disaster and despair may surely be vastly improved. We will need an enormous number of humane places, and we will need them fast. The four ecological clocks—biological, sociological, methodological, and technological—have for all too long shown a progressive synchronization failure. This has reached a critical stage. Man faces the options of survival or catastrophe. Time is running out.

I began this somewhat rambling discourse with a reminder of continuous alarms and excursions, wars and revolutions, which have been constant accompaniments of my life. The mosaic of my prejudices and preoccupations which I have laid before you is not intended to alarm you but to challenge new generations to face harsh new realities and hopefully to overcome them.

The events of the last decade tended, in my retirement looking outward, to change me from a tentative optimist to a distressed near-pessimist. But, of course, I could be wrong; the events of the next decades may well be drastically changed toward a better human condition. I shall not see it. In the meanwhile, I hope you will perhaps share some of my concern and commitment or at least find them useful while developing your own priorities and responsibilities.

You will remember the poetic warning of Auden's: ". . . seek-ers after happiness it is later than you think." Another poet Anatol Kuznetzov has provided a more eloquent closing than I can:

It is not my intention to be original, and what I am saying is common knowledge. But I should like to mention vigilance once again. I want especially to remind all the young, the healthy and active, for whom this book is meant, of their responsibility for the fate of man. Comrades and friends! Brothers and Sisters! Ladies and Gentlemen! Please pause in your pursuits and recreations for a moment. Not all is well with the world . . . comrades and friends, brothers and sisters, ladies and gentlemen! CIVILIZA-TION IS IN DANGER![30]

For Chermayeff, the title "architect" evoked, above all, inescapable social commitments which took precedence over aesthetics. His ideology imbued the new movement in architecture with a clear social mandate, leaving the issue of a new style as a secondary concern. The "art" of architecture, as he loved to paraphrase his mentor, Eric Gill, would always "look after itself." The threat of the corruption of the social purposes of modernism remained a constant concern from the earliest days. A blend of socialist politics and commercial expediency encouraged modernism in Britain. Chermayeff, who was introduced to adulthood via the Russian Revolution, placed his architectural priorities clearly on the side of politics. To Chermayeff, British complacency was inexcusable in the midst of the crises of modern life. He saw the activities of the architect in the larger context of world events—a world which was shrinking in terms of communication while expanding in terms of social and technological complexity. The moderates of the architectural profession briefly embraced him; he became the youngest Fellow in the Royal Institute of British Architects. But his professional euphoria was shortlived. His demise was most deeply rooted in the framework of twentieth-century capitalism. As Chermayeff was to point out so many times, capitalism embraced a view of professional priorities for architects which countered his own.

By the end of the thirties, disillusionment came with the final European economic collapse and the certainty that the largest-scale product of modern technology would be the holocaust of war rather than social betterment. A decade later, Chermayeff's hopes for reformation of the profession of architecture in the United States were devastated similarly by the subtler, but ultimately more pervasive, commercialism of the fifties. Petty business pursuits replaced the driving intellectual forces of the thirties, and the social basis for modernism collapsed in the face of the crass superficiality of modern practice. Chermayeff abandoned practice, except as a small-scale pleasurable activity, and devoted his time instead to academic research outside of the marketplace. But academia was not exactly immune to the business of architecture. As Chermayeff would point out, both remain inextricably tied to each other, permeated by many of the same commitments and subject to the same corruption of purpose.

The threat of corruption of the social purposes of modernisn appears as early as 1930 in the manifesto written in conjunction with the proposed exhibition of the Twentieth Century Group (Brief Statement of the 20th Century Group). The "group," consisting of Chermayeff, Wells Coates, Raymond McGrath, and Mansfield Forbes, was one of the many publicist coalitions organized in the cause of modernism in Britain. The authors compare the lack of initiative in England to the impressive foreign efforts involving recent exhibitions —for example, the Paris Exhibition of 1925, the Stockholm Exhibition of 1930, or the Berlin Exhibition of 1931. Their proposed exhibit was intended to contribute toward an understanding of the "true meaning of modernism" by both manufacturers and consumers. They express concern that if designers pursue their arguments only at the level of "fashion," the larger purposes of the movement ultimately will be lost. And indeed, one of the strongest arguments for modernist "functionalism" had to be social amelioration for a public long conditioned by traditional design.

In 1932 another important early theme surfaces—that the goals of the modern movement could not be separated from professional reform (A Tonic for Architecture). Chermayeff parted company with many other modernist colleagues on this issue. His extemporaneous remarks, which follow a talk by Joseph Emberton, put some distance between what they each believe should be the required degree of reform. The imagined or real "critic-journalist" who became the object of Chermayeff's impetuous comments identified the general importance of critical writing to reform efforts; and in fact the majority of the young British moderns not only designed but also wrote extensively about design.

In 1935, Chermayeff delivered his most expansive critique of the profession of architecture up to that date (The Architect and the World Today). Correlating professional reform with public service, he draws the line between progressive and conservative political causes within the limits of architectural practice. Chermayeff disparages the relationship of the architect to sources of economic and political power; and he recognizes that the transformations of recent history simply replaced old royal patronage with corporate patronage. The new patrons still lack social responsibility and are even less desirable than the old royalty because they lack their "picturesqueness and imaginativeness." The architect, reduced to "lounge lizard" and conditioned by consciousness of "the buttered side of his bread," excludes important considerations. These economic dependencies are an obstacle to needed reforms, which must expand professional concerns beyond "the application of materials and art to building" to more conscious social purpose. In general, Chermayeff presents a view of architecture as a rigorous intellectual pursuit, in which practical and theoretical knowledge extend beyong building technique or aesthetics.

By 1939, on the eve of Britain's entry into World War II, Chermayeff's priorities for the profession of architecture remain unfulfilled (Architects and Modern Society). He advises the architect-survivors of the holocaust to start again—above all "as intelligent and political beings, to lead the fight for an active and fruitful existence." In effect, he identifies the end of the modern period, as it came to be defined in the thirties, by pointing to the futility of a discourse limited to "classic facades for commercial exuberance, or the bare bones of functionalism for an A.R.P. shelter." He argues for a fresh start, using what was learned to reformulate an intelligent coalition of technical, aesthetic, economic, and social forces, to produce an architecture which might go beyond modernism. This mandate became his own personal credo in the following decades.

Chermayeff carried the issue of professional reform to the United States. It is the central theme of his first major talk after immigration, given at Harvard and Yale in 1940 (Crisis in Architecture). He again argues that the shortcomings of the previous decade must be studied rather than ignored and that corrective action should be pursued at the level of a broad professional consensus. He traces much of the professional demise to the "inherent contradictions" within the architectural profession as well as to the "economic structure of our society." He accuses the profession of preoccupation with superficial stylistic debates and of escape from practical reality through artistic pretention while more and more building is done by others. He advocates use of the war years, when building activity would slacken, to develop a new theoretical basis—to pursue new

aims, self-education, and public education and to prepare for re-
sumption of activity after the war. Chermayeff first uses the words
"environmental design" here in relation to a discussion about
broadening the scope of architects' design activity, so that it may
"embrace all problems of shelter and its equipment and their relationships." And Chermayeff clearly envisions a new generation of
modern architecture in America, which could question the results of
the pioneer efforts in Europe.

In 1941, some dilemmas of large-scale planning are explored
(False Gods). He voices concern that large projects run the risk of
further separating professionals and their "narrow set of dogmas"
from the "desires of the people for whom they plan." A nervousness
surfaces about the megalomanic tendencies of planning ideals which
were growing out of the unprecedented scale of private and public
planning initiatives. He is concerned especially about the social implications of oversimplified and overscaled projects. He affirms the
need for such projects, however, and takes notice of the political
naiveté of professionals who anticipated a national building program without federal intervention, which would leave the issues of
human need to bankers and realtors. But he is optimistic about future
prospects, especially with the precedents of the great "architectural
frontiers" like the Central Valley and Grand Coulee projects.

By the end of the decade of the forties, however, as the postwar
pattern of architectural practice developed, Chermayeff's optimism
had already faded. In a talk at Harvard, in 1949, he counters the
growing professional interest in monumentality with a plea for interest in "anonymous" building (Anonymity and Autonomy). He sees the
previous three decades of "research and development" being translated into an "architectural neurosis" rather than a "new architecture," and he identifies the emerging strategy toward cities as one of
its most blatant symptoms. This strategy of deurbanization based on
"fear" was expressed in the systematic removal of the ideal of urban
proximity from the United States culture-at-large and from the architectural language in particular. He strongly implicates the hypoc-
risy of architects, who "are anxious to justify our profession socially,
and to rationalize our position as artists," thus "deliberately evading
many things. . . ." In 1950, he challenges those who claimed that
the profession was held in the force of circumstance and could not
control its own commitments (The Profession of Architecture). He

argues that the professional establishment set its own rather conservative priorities and warded off alternatives. This talk is one of his most direct attacks on the politics of the profession of architecture, and it was made at a critical point when the forces of conservatism triumphed after the previous decades of sublimation, which were caused by the social crises of deprivation and war. His talk also reflects the foment within the old progressive alliances—for example, his displeasure with the position of Joseph Hudnut.

Debate on the relationship between artists and architects was fashionable in the fifties. In 1955, at one of numerous forums on the subject, Chermayeff paraphrases the question posed earlier by Giedeon at several CIAM meetings: "At what point does the functional requirement begin; . . . is it sufficient for the artist to exist in a vacuum of his specialization?" (Framework for the Arts). He feels, however, that the question is not very useful, or at least not answerable, because the marketplace prohibits the axiomatic ideal of integration of the arts. The artists' position in relation to his patron is reduced to "embroidery." Chermayeff also argues that the culture is against integration. A "common denominator" cannot be found in a society in which "diversity, diversification, variety, uncertainty, rather than discipline, dogma, belief, faith, common experience are the rule." In 1957 he further explores the issue and points to the "fallacy" of thinking of architecture as pure art (Design and Transition). He criticizes the "cycle of romantic involvement," which uses the architect as artist as a professional rallying cry. Once again, he states that the basis for "art" should be social need and that if artists are involved, "art" will be produced. He relates the question to a larger issue of professional identify and states that the architect is neither artist nor businessman and ultimately not professional because of the ambivalence about social responsibility.

In 1959, he discusses another fashionable subject of the decade—the relationship of art and science (Shape of Quality). Chermayeff disparages the myths of incompatibility of art and science and the lack of interest in technology of the architectural aesthetes who sought to justify a profession on its aesthetic contributions alone. He argues that "scientific discovery" and the "explosion of technology" should inform the concerns of "pure art"; and that these new developments should influence method away from the necessity to "lean upon the past or upon genius" and away from "our kind of personal, private view—to see an infinitely widened spectrum." He compares the "Freudian fifties" to the 1890s and to the Victorian response to technological and cultural changes of the nineteenth century; and he registers his disagreements with the new Victorians—Paul Rudolph, Edward Stone, and Philip Johnson, with their "monuments of porphyry and pressed glass." Theirs was the architecture of the "courtesan," as described in 1962 (Designers Dilemma). It was "expensive, exhibitionist indulgence for rich patrons" by architects who "have absolutely nothing to do with the humdrum realities of day-to-day family life." In this Easter weekend talk, the level of popular discourse in architecture was compared to a rivalry between "Easter bonnets." Chermayeff saw more hope for change in the university than in the marketplace, and he suggested professional support of alternatives to traditional practice, which would be related to advanced academic research, creating a clear choice between marketplace and other architectural activity.

In 1964, Chermayeff points to the lack of a substantial critical architectural journal in the United States as further evidence of the dominance of commercial values (Architectural Condition). The magazines have "little to do with architectural criticism, history or theory" and more to do with "business purposes" of cataloguing architectural products and architects' public relations. He also criticizes the dominance of commercial values from the point-of-view of diminished interest within the professional lobbies, such as the American Institute of Architects, toward encouraging public service as an alternative to private practice. He offers the opposite example of the Royal Institute of British Architects with its long-standing advocacy for public practice. He correctly senses, however, a growing interest among "anonymous, unknown, usually young architects" in practicing at a "public level and close to decision-makers" in "urban renewal offices and city planning offices, staffed no longer by sociologists and economists and demographers, exclusively of the slum clearance era." In fact, as the social activism of the 1960s unfolded, this mode of practice did enjoy a brief period of support from young progressives.

The last three essays are reminiscent. In 1972, Chermayeff discusses his earliest period in the United States, during World War II, when the outlook for initiative and innovation within the profession seemed brighter (Shape of Community Revisited). In this address, given at Yale, he dismisses the campus, which boasted a prodigious number of new buildings designed by "stars" of the profession, as being a "cemetery of buried architectural hopes, disconnected monuments . . . ." They belong to the category of "publishable exemplars . . . really so many shiny needles just stuck into an enormous haystack of unfinished business." Yale's monument-building, blessed with the complicity of the architectural profession, might serve as evidence of the "inexorable law that all institutions and 'truths' must finally lag behind emerging realities"—a proposition which he defines in 1974 (Institutions, Priorities, Revolutions). He points to the condition that "high technology and much good art are all too often serving contemptible purpose." He again examines that critical postwar political transformation which left him an apostate most fundamentally, with a political position which had no professional constituency.

Finally, in 1979, Chermayeff reminisces about the thirties—the period which molded his own professional commitments (Thinking about the Thirties). It was a "revolution intellectually absorbing and emotionally moving: a political and cultural ferment among scientists, writers and artists." Its survival was brief, and what followed was pallid by comparison. As for Chermayeff and the profession of architecture, the example of his own involvements rather than his words puts in evidence his most devastating critique. "Bentley" in Sussex is an extraordinary architectural moment. But possibly a more extraordinary and ultimately more useful lesson is how the concerns that its architect voiced in the decades afterward contributed to the public discourse of the period.

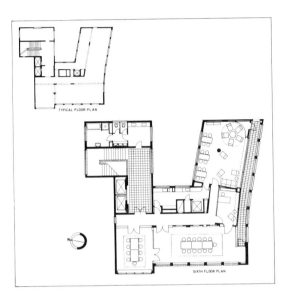

TYPICAL FLOOR PLAN

SIXTH FLOOR PLAN

JAMESTOWN ROAD

OVAL ROAD

Office building for W.
and A. Gilbey, Ltd.,
London, 1937.

1. That in England, with few exceptions, manufacturers have had no contact with designers.

2. That modern design has been abused by ignorant fashion-mongers and has been commercialised in the worst sense of the word.

3. That the true meaning of Modernism is not apparent, in the midst of all this medley to either maker or buyer.

4. That manufacturers have depended largely in making contact with the public through trade buyers, instead of associating themselves directly with serious designers.

5. That such exhibitions that have taken place have been commercially handled and have demonstrated the need for reform in the method of procedure.

6. That after the foreign precedent of exhibitions in France, Sweden and Germany, the time is now ripe for a similar exhibition of rational modern art in England.

7. That if such an exhibition comes into being it must not be lost among others which have been so mishandled and further compromise modern work in this country.

8. That such an exhibition should be controlled in its arrangement and selection by designers, who would guarantee the omission of spuriousness and misconceptions.

9. That it is our job to establish in the minds of the public and the manufacturer that modern art is not a fashion, but an expression of contemporary life.

10. The 20th Century Group[1] was formed by designers to bring about a concrete demonstration of these beliefs in the midst of

From an undated typescript probably written by Chermayeff with Wells Coates, Raymond McGrath, and Mansfield Forbes, 1930.

widespread bickerings and discussions which have been completely unproductive up to date in this country.

11. That in such an exhibition all our aims could only be defined in rational terms of public requirements and not of their whims.

12. That our aim is to demonstrate in an exhibition modern ideals without undue stress of individualism and without self-consciousness.

13. That the Group's particular job is concerned with housing for living, learning, playing, and their appropriate planning and equipment.

14. That the primary aim would be to demonstrate the economic values of new materials, mass-produced articles, the application of science and their new value in terms of producing things for people of all standing and incomes.

15. That a building or a thing can be cheap and yet possess a quality of appropriateness and beauty.

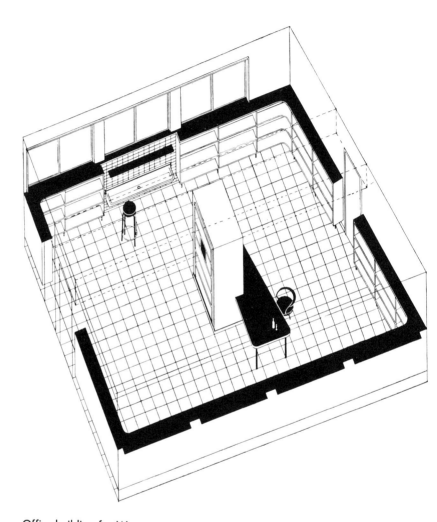

Office building for W.
and A. Gilbey, Ltd.,
London, 1937. Tasting
room.

I have much enjoyed both my dinner, Mr. Emberton's address and other speeches and am at peace with all the world. What I am sceptical of, however, is whether the world outside this charming assembly is quite so much at peace with the gathering or if others share my feelings that we should be at peace with the world.

Mr. Emberton has given you an invaluable prescription for a tonic to be administered to architecture and kindred design.

A tonic presupposes a state of convalescence or mild ailment. I should like to suggest an earlier step to achieve this comparatively desirable condition. The first prescription should be for a strong antidote against poison in the English architectural body.

I can best illustrate my meaning by telling you of some remarks I heard from an eminent art critic. I believe them to be relevant.

This critic-journalist and author, after a very pleasant dinner, protested his complete contempt for the cinema as neither at the moment possessing nor ever able to possess artistic or intellectual qualities of value. He condemned, with the full weight of his omniscience, the whole thing as unworthy of attention. He condescendingly told of his one experience of this depravity, an evening with Mr. Chaplin of the film, not of the flesh, which irrevocably confirmed his opinion of the unworthiness of Mr. Chaplin in particular and the cinema in general.

It appeared to me that the gentleman was posing. He may pose, for all I know, in his writings and art opinions, but that does not prevent his sayings, his writings from being taken seriously.

His pride in his unawareness of arts outside his pet subject left, as far as I can judge, an imcomplete art critic, intellectually at least, a half man—or briefly, a half wit.

Similarly obstacles bar the way to rational thinking, art appreciation, architecture and design.

Remarks made in a discussion following a talk by Joseph Emberton entitled "A Tonic for Architecture" given at the Design and Industries Association, London, January 26, 1932.

Similar incomplete gentlemen among industrialists, politicians, councillors, who pride themselves only on their special experiences, who dogmatize about this life-long preference, that consistent condemnation, belief in bricks and lathes, mistrust of concrete and plywood. Their one-mindedness, no matter if it has passed the period of relevance, still lays claim to control and guidance of public affairs.

These unaware gentlemen, Aldermanic protoplasm, "Adam's only" architects, complacent, conservative half-men, or half-wits, are undoing daily the constructive work others may do.

In the past it may have been argued that these half minds were a counter-irritant and soothing influence to the extremism, but I do not believe that such an argument could be reasonably advanced today.

To continue the medical analogy, when Novocain or similar local anaesthetic is administered to paralyze nerves, the dose is well under control and the effect transitory, and it is given to make possible painlessly the drastic measure to follow.

English architecture and design appear like some poor victim to whom anaesthetic has been administered, regardless of cost, in numberless injections until the whole body is swollen and deadened to reaction and syncope is not far off.

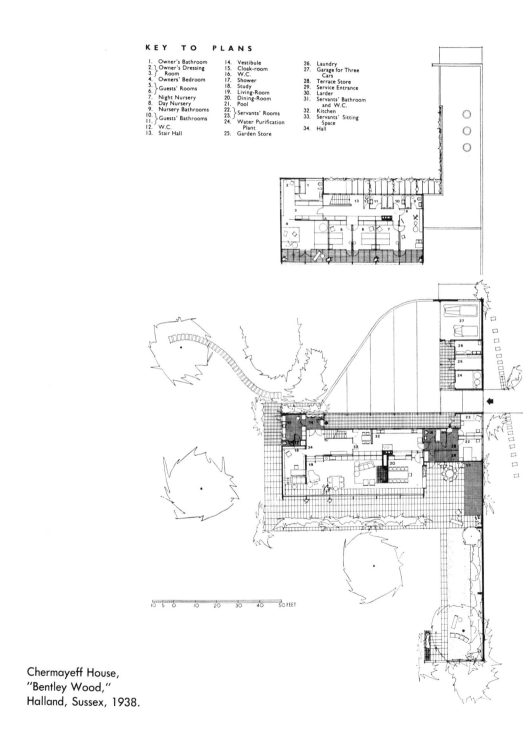

KEY TO PLANS

1.	Owner's Bathroom	14.	Vestibule	26.	Laundry
2.	Owner's Dressing	15.	Cloak-room	27.	Garage for Three
3.	Room	16.	W.C.		Cars
4.	Owners' Bedroom	17.	Shower	28.	Terrace Store
5.	Guests' Rooms	18.	Study	29.	Service Entrance
6.		19.	Living-Room	30.	Larder
7.	Night Nursery	20.	Dining-Room	31.	Servants' Bathroom
8.	Day Nursery	21.	Pool		and W.C.
9.	Nursery Bathrooms	22.	Servants' Rooms	32.	Kitchen
10.	Guests' Bathrooms	23.		33.	Servants' Sitting
11.		24.	Water Purification		Space
12.	W.C.		Plant	34.	Hall
13.	Stair Hall	25.	Garden Store		

Chermayeff House,
"Bentley Wood,"
Halland, Sussex, 1938.

THE ARCHITECT AND THE WORLD TODAY

The promise of democracy has not been fulfilled for the creative artist or technician. It is evident that the architect's traditional role as the artist protégé of a rich patron is persisting in spite of every indication that this is no longer possible. Individual patrons, the kings, the princes and the priests, have disappeared as effective supporters of the arts and remain only in relatively few isolated instances as more and more tired curators of collections which are being virtually assimilated by the state museums. Their nineteenth and twentieth century successors are individual industrialists, merchants and financiers, who are becoming less and less satisfactory patrons except as bidders at charity balls for useless trifles. The patrons of the architect for work of any scale are local governments and large firms, trusts and syndicates. The only possible alternative patron to these that the architect can look to is the state—so far the architects have not had that opportunity of serving the community through so disinterested a patron. In consequence, the architect is being driven to reliance on individualist clients. He has become a sycophant. In most cases he remains a sort of architectural lounge lizard; more rarely, if he is adroit in other directions than architecture proper, he may achieve, at the age of sixty, or so, the stature of a lounge lion. But all the time he will have remained acutely conscious of the buttered side of his bread, to the exclusion of his social and technical responsibility, which he is essentially qualified to assume as a direct consequence of his special training and experience when he is young, healthy and at his best.

The architect is being exploited by a system and is having his activities and contribution controlled, together with those of millions of others, by private interest individualist patrons, who today, for the most part, lack the picturesqueness and imagina-

From a lecture, "The Architect and the World Today," given to the students' section of the Architects and Technicians Organization, London, March 18, 1935; first published in *The Architect's Journal*, March 21, 1935.

tiveness of their earlier prototype. In fact, the architect today is not able to do what he could and should be allowed to do. He is not economically independent.

New planning and new design of structure is not merely a variation in aesthetic principles, a consequence of new discoveries in structural materials. It is infinitely more. It is the expression of an earnest desire of intelligent and highly trained people to change living conditions in proportion to the immense strides made in general education, medicine and applied technique. The problems in building, which require the architect's fullest attention and concentrated effort, are problems of economic planning in housing and industry. The problem of building is to build for reasons and with means which will not saddle the obsoleteness of bygone ages on millions of our contemporaries or those who will come after. In architecture it is quite clear that research is not far advanced, while the means of applying the fruits of any research objectively do not exist.

But the application of technique to building is only one side of the problem that faces us in the raising of our standard of life. To quote from Sir Stafford Cripps:

We must have some economic system which enables us not only to produce, but also to distribute, the products we are capable of making. Indeed, one of the great difficulties that we are experiencing today is that there has been a revolutionary advance in the technique, without any change in the underlying economic structure of industry, which controls distribution and production.[2]

Technical invention has far outstripped social invention in its advance, and it is now necessary to invent some new economic methods which will prevent our suffering from the too rapid technical advance and enable us to obtain the full benefits of the work of our scientists and inventors. A great many processes, which can be used by the architect for the benefit of the many, are finding an outlet only in work of a luxurious character for the economically privileged and are hailed as a sign of returning prosperity. Sir Stafford Cripps continues:

It is a mistake to assume that luxury production increases the national wealth. If ten thousand workers are occupied on the production of luxury goods while there is still an unsatisfied need for ordinary commodities, the labour of these workers is being wasted. Just as in times of war the whole productive effort of the community is concentrated on war materials, and all luxury production is stopped because it is wasteful, so in the great war that must be waged on poverty and disease, all productive effort should be spent on overcoming these evils before it is wasted on the wholly unnecessary luxuries.[3]

Public attention is side-tracked from the importance of problems such as housing of the masses to demonstrations of individual ingenuities of an exclusive kind. . . .

. . . The practice of architecture should embrace far more than the application of materials and art to building. It should include the application of technique to thinking. Architects can no longer concern themselves with construction in a separated professional compartment. They must participate in the reconstruction of society.

If this purpose were fully realised and became commonplace among architects, it would become eventually in their hands a tremendous educational force which would change the attitude toward building, the architect's function and legislation concerned with building.

Few of us are concerned with building in any form who are not aware of immediately the specialized building forms peculiar to our day, and who are not aware of equally the advantages which modern building technique has to offer. Equally, there are very few among us who do not constantly meet with a stream of examples of misapplication and misunderstanding. We see the most complex examples of modern structure arising here and there, not for reasons of progressive service to the community, but as the results of speculation and profit making—uncontrolled, unplanned and, unfortunately, for the most part rather ugly. These buildings, with few exceptions, are the consequence of technical development, aggravated, mishandled and overdriven by capitalist growth with its particular requirements of maximum profits from minimum outlay.

More dangerous than these are the commercial circles which are exploiting people's stupidity, sentiment and snobbery. The examples of this exploitation are bespattering the countryside and disturbing our streets with hideous parodies of old styles or with exercises in wasteful ingenuities.

All these people are a nuisance to progress. But the real danger lies in the practices of the large concerns, the monopolies and the price-rings. It does not require long experience in architecture to discover that many materials invaluable to the building industry are prohibitive in cost for no good reason such as scarcity or imperfected production, or that most manufactured standard articles are controlled by price-rings, and would become economically possible for the architect to use for the benefit of the whole community if these monopolies were broken.

In fact, the architect is very often faced with the amazing paradox of, on the one hand, not being able to use certain materials or processes toward the making of his building or, on the other hand, being forced to use others against the dictates of his reason and conscience. Architects are being asked, as it were, to build "as cheaply as possible, at whatever cost." And yet we know that there is no technical obstacle to the reduction of cost or to the full freedom of use, in a most rational and effective way, of all these things which are required for building today, that would enable the architect to offer the benefits of these things and his knowledge to the community.

We have the machine-worked materials and the machine-made goods. In fact, mass production, the inevitable purpose for which the first power-driven machine, the modern tool, was invented, today can be utilized for the production of essential elements for the millions who at the moment lack them. Bricks alone are not enough. Mass production and pre-fabrication of all essential structural parts of simplest dwellings could contribute some form of standardized architecture such as has been attempted already in U.S.S.R. and America.

Through collective technical effort, the materials required for the making of essential buildings could be controlled to facilitate the production in this country of all those things which the mass of humanity lacks but which it is their right to know about and to demand and all of which the technical resources can give them. But we know that the mention of the word standardization or rationalization represents to one part of the community an attack on individual expression—actually the loss of possibilities of private profit. To another, it stands for the exploitation of the working classes, because up till now these have never received the benefits of technical advance and only have seen it exploited for the benefit of the few. It is for architects to prevent the continued misuse of technical development and, particularly, at all costs to prevent the continued misapprehension of rationalization and its real possibilities.

We as professional men are facing a crisis which demands collective and objective action. The contribution being made by most professional bodies in this direction is negligible. They are individualists fundamentally. This critical period does not appear to be the time for individualism. We are faced with economic problems in reconstruction affecting the lives of millions.

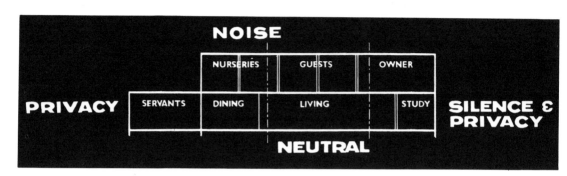

Chermayeff House,
"Bentley Wood,"
Halland, Sussex, 1938.
Section organization
study.

You have invited me to give you my views on the architect's place and purpose in modern society.

A few months ago such views might have been debatable; they appear to me less so now. Then we might have discussed the extension and strengthening of the line drawn from [Walter] Gropius to [Lewis] Mumford without arriving at an immediate plan for action.

Such a discussion on *technical* grounds could have led to the acceptance of our age as one of technology, rapidly expanding and self-transforming, having no "style," this being impossible in its dynamic condition.

On *aesthetic* grounds we could have greeted the appearance of isolated solutions of contemporary problems, beautiful and exciting enough to win our spiritual allegiance and to give us a promise of a new aesthetic to emerge in the future but rooted in the technical transformation of our particular times.

On *economic* grounds we would have accepted this period as one of transition, with the old type of patron rapidly receding into history and growth of new, more impersonal, and vast combinations of government and industry to replace him; we could have compared the architectural possibilities of large-scale building under imperialism and social planning like the T.V.A.

On *social* grounds we would have come to the conclusion that large communities everywhere required the urgent services of trained technicians to fulfill their most elementary needs, in accordance with our knowledge and resources so far available to an archaically privileged few.

We might have concluded that we had to shift our grounds from individual self-indulgence in "art" to technology and social service in the first place in the hope that we may have built a better world for quite ordinary people to live in.

From an article, "The Architect's Place and Purpose in Modern Society," published in the *Northern Architectural Students' Association Journal*, February 1939.

Latest political developments can make us more objective. They require a futher readjustment of our attitude which in any case would have provided material for a life-term programme.

We may now observe that little has been gained in our lifetime through technical ability or newly developed social conscience, for lack of opportunity to apply them intelligently, except possibly for the erection of air-raid shelters fit for heroes to survive in.

The survivors among the architects must start again, but not confused by an academic education on the one side and a world of practical problems on the other, but as intelligent political beings in the forefront of the fight for an active and fruitful existence.

Faced with the present situation to voice a "design preference" for either classic facades for commercial exuberance or the bare bones of functionalism for an A.R.P.[4] shelter, one may justly come to the conclusion that both alternatives are equally futile for the purpose of determining an architectural attitude. The latter alternative has at least the point of being an immediate necessary objective.

What can the position of an architect worth his salt be in a society which hails elementary progressive steps as utopian, and where reaction is so firmly entrenched that it has become an accepted commonplace, instead of being recognized for what it is? I suggest that we must first equip ourselves technically and politically for a fight which will ensure that some day architects may practice an appropriate architecture in a new society which they themselves have helped to create.

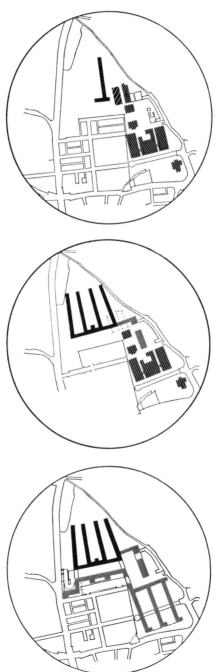

Imperial Chemical
Industries laboratory
complex, Blakely,
Manchester, 1938. Site
phasing study.

I hope I may be forgiven in presenting a case to you which appears to be based on foreign experience and which you may decide has no relevance to your own, the American, situation. I believe, however, from what I have learned in the course of my brief contacts here, that those problems which face you are in many cases very similar to those with which we were faced in England in the few years preceding this war.

The war itself is not only a violent interruption, a sort of curtain rung down on progressive work in architecture and in cultural life generally, but has acted, at the same time, as a magnifying glass under which both the achievements and, what is more important, the shortcomings of the architectural field were quite clearly revealed.

The general state of confusion and conflict, of which the war is a symptom, exists to a greater or lesser extent everywhere, and it seems that architects must make their particular cultural and practical contribution to dissipate or at least modify this prevailing chaos.

The war has stopped temporarily, possibly for a much longer period than we dare admit, the development of architecture in Europe. . . .

. . . I believe that here as well as in Europe, in spite of certain isolated examples of gain, both our profession and our art are in a very serious situation, and it seems necessary to review our position, restate our objectives and aspirations, and consolidate whatever positions have been won, against all attacks of reaction, which continue and may continue for many critical years.

I would ask you to recall, as I speak, that my first hand experience is a European one generally, and an English one in particular, on which my criticism and report is based.

It took us some years to realize that the principal handicap the

From a lecture, "The Crisis in Architecture," given at Harvard University, April 18, 1940.

architectural profession suffered from was caused by inherent contradictions, or incompatible conditions, within their own ranks. Architectural education for the larger part had remained maladjusted to the social and technical changes. It continued to grind out an increasing number of architects on an obsolete pattern, throwing these onto a market or, if you prefer, into a society which was quite incapable of assimilating them, which had not, in fact, provided sufficient employment for the larger number of their predecessors, except in intermittent periods of economic booms.

The attitude of society towards architects was perhaps best expressed in figures: never has the percentage of the annual total cost of building carried out under architectural supervision in England exceeded twenty percent. The average figures over a period of ten years has been approximately ten percent. This percentage has dwindled to almost nil since the crisis of September 1938.[5]

In England there were, in spite of this, about 13,000 registered architects in 1939. This number was reached after a steady increase since the turn of the century, when architecture became a respectable alternative profession to the army and the church for the younger sons of gentlemen. . . .

. . . Architects, apparently, had no contribution to make in a war effort, although paradoxically a modern war is admitted to be largely a technical problem calling for the cooperation of scientists and technicians. They also had made little or no impact on those who were responsible for the peace programmes, either of state, provincial, municipal or industrial undertakings. The immeasurably larger proportion of research, planning and design which we have long since recognized as our province—such as city planning, housing, building construction, research in material, production and assembly, direction of taste, all our most vital and important problems—was initiated and controlled by politicians, engineers, surveyors, and commerce.

This state of things appears likely to continue after the war if a sufficient number survive from that large number of students, who are today certainly better equipped than they were ever before to assume responsibilities of initiative and leadership in a society which requires most urgently reform and an enormous increase in supply of shelters and their equipment.

Where lies the responsibility for this deplorable situation in architecture? I believe it to be shared equally by the profession itself and by the economic structure of our society.

A recognition of our position in time is necessary; this is a transition period from the chaos of the first impact of the machine to a clearer appreciation of its present and future possibilities. We are still in this revolutionary period.

One of the most significant results of this change is the disappearance of the individual type of patron, to whom architects looked for employment even very recently, and his replacement by a new type. The patronage is of groups, rather than individuals. Communal or group demands, whether they represent industry, commerce, local authorities or the state, present new problems and impose new tasks on the profession.

These new demands as yet have been neither fully stated nor recognized. The new patron does not yet know his own problem. At this moment in the history of architecture I do not think that these patrons, still in their adolescence, appreciate the difference, only recently apparent to very few among the architects themselves, between the conventional pre-industrial figure of the architect and the new architect, who emerged at the beginning of this century and who is growing up in the more progressive schools today in increasing numbers.

The outside world is unaware of the broader implications, sociological and technical, of planning and design, which is an integral part of a contemporary living architecture. It still looks upon the architect either as a gentleman, doing a gentleman's job and living a gentleman's life of polite conformity to an unchanged culture, or as an eccentric artist, whose decisions on matters of art, which "have no contact with practical problems," need never be questioned because their significance is purely formal and superficial.

Within the profession, to an equally great extent, the same confusion exists as to the scope and responsibility of contemporary architecture. Within the profession itself there continues a conflict between two schools of thought.

Among the enemies to the sane and healthy growth of architecture, are those who are simply unacquainted or out of touch, by accident or by deliberate intention, with contemporary developments. Among the deliberate escapists are those who are afraid of or, as often as not, simply incapable of grasping the new problems. They prefer archeology and scholarship, which they transmute into a second-hand, ready-to-wear culture of a known style, to the more difficult task of research, experiment, definition of new aims and a new integration.

Our task would be made easier if such escapism was confined purely to a withdrawal from the scene of action. Unfortunately some of the escapists become active opponents to the new movement. The still formidable strength of the obsolete, academic attitude leads to those forms of fantastic contemporary building which fulfill neither a rational nor an emotional need. We must disassociate ourselves from this group to avoid their eventual fate and to escape being buried alive in the graves of their own digging . . . .

. . . We are still spending, pretentiously, I believe, vast sums on building for eternity. Yet reason suggests, that in a transitional experimental age, where the technological obsolescence period is very short, the life of buildings might well be curtailed to an economic minimum to avoid both waste of our present resources and the saddling on future generations of useless and cumbersome possessions. . . .

. . . To add to the confusion of the architectural scene, we continue ridiculous squabbles on design preferences, continue to erect pretentious, illogical extravagances which are supposed to represent the ultimate goal of a successful practitioner, while inefficient, substandard building continues to increase. Architects are fiddling while Rome burns and then complain that their prestige is vanishing.

And it must be remembered that as long as this false picture of architectural aims and qualifications persists, so long will a haphazard employment of architects continue. The private practitioner will fight for the occasional plums of monument building and will be forced to pay low wages to his assistants and to monopolize any kudos, real or assumed, to survive the periods of inactivity.

All these things, either pretentious or stupid, unscientific and inartistic, are symptoms of a general confusion on fundamental issues, a state of chaos, in which, as yet, there are an insufficient number of exceptions to which to point, and in which no sane architecture can at the moment function fully. . . .

. . . I believe that the new architect cannot in the first place win recognition from the general public as an artist. He must, I think, take up his first stand as an individual fully cognizant of the sociological and technical needs in an enormously broadened field of design generally.

Until such time as the profession itself has clearly defined and come to a general agreement on principles among themselves, the world will only accept the immediate, practical, elementary benefits of the new architecture, which they can easily understand.

We cannot achieve a basic condition in which a complete, sane and healthy architecture can exist and flourish and its new concepts of scale, space enclosure and relationship and aesthetic principles be understood until we have won public confidence.

Until the actual shortage and inadequacy of existing standards in housing and city planning are recognized and solved to a greater extent than they are now, we will not achieve the recognition of the new aesthetic or the "moral imperatives," as Lewis Mumford calls them, implicit in the practical advantages of the new techniques.

I do not mean to suggest that we should at this stage confine ourselves to purely practical issues, but rather that the prevailing habit of theorising on esthetic, a dead scholastic end in itself, should be supplanted in education particularly by a programme of actual work, of real experience grounded in immediate practical necessity, out of which will grow a spontaneous, organic expression of a new scale concept and new forms. In fact, out of this a new and richer esthetic will emerge.

We can dismiss as incomplete for our purpose the architecture of the engineers, who merely provide a technical solution. We can also dismiss that spurious employment of new elements which is the architecture of fashionmongers, a contribution just as valueless to today's building problems and as misleading as the gratuitous fancy dress borrowed from any other period . . . .

. . . The first task is to define our aim, and to have it accepted by the majority of the profession. . . . Should reaction prove too strong, for whatever unforeseen reason, it may be wiser to diassociate ourselves entirely from the opposition and drop the use of the label "Architecture" as long as it is discredited. . . .

. . . The range of design must be broadened to embrace all problems of shelter and its equipment and their realtionships, which is environmental design, and which is more often than not curiously separated at this moment from the conventional limits of architecture. Within this widened sphere of design activity many architects and designers will find satisfying opportunities for creative work. I do not see them performing these tasks as blinkered specialists, but rather as more aware, better informed and equipped creative individuals.

The second important task might be described, perhaps, as a process of self-education arising out of the first. It is a program of research in collaboration with scientists and technicians in other fields.

There are, of course, a number of such isolated pieces of research started already. But the rate of progressive growth and amount of valuable contribution would be greatly accelerated and increased if a larger number of minds trained in this method of thinking were made available.

Lastly, and, perhaps, this is one of our most urgent tasks, is not within the field of architectural education and the profession itself, but outside them. . . . Happily, the necessity of making the new architecture known coincides with the unfortunate situation of the architects today. We have much unoccupied time on our hands in which to take stock, talk and write because at the moment at least there is too little building for us to carry out.

In England we succeeded in forming spearhead groups of allegiance and collaboration with international organizations, such as C.I.A.M. (International Congress of Modern Architecture) of which M.A.R.S. (Modern Architectural Research Society) was the English group, as well as such groups as the A.T.O. (Architects and Technicians Organization) now the A.A.S.T.A. (Architectural Assistants, Students and Technicians Association) to which private practitioners, salaried assistants and students belonged.

The free interchange of ideas on all subjects affecting architecture, which these groups made possible in the end, created the stimulus which, in a very short space of time, completely revolutionized architectural education in England, at any rate, as for instance at the A.A. (Architectural Association).

As soon as the demands of the students became coherent, with the backing of a few progressive architects in practice and one or two educators of exceptional quality such as Professor Reilly at Liverpool and Professor Leslie Martin at Hull, the break with the past was made.

Last summer saw the first meeting of the Northern Architectural Students' Congress, with representatives of spearhead groups in all the important university and other architectural schools. In 1939, appeared a student sponsored and produced architectural journal, *Focus*, which established itself immediately as a new critical and constructive force.[6]

It is the student body itself which realized that the old education was less conducive to employment than merely a good family or business connection, a thick skin, the ability to hold large quantities of liquor, or a repertoire of good stories, and certainly less useful than a professional integrity flexible enough to allow one to take a hand in what was quaintly known as "honest building". . . .

. . . May I sum up in conclusion: I believe that the task of contemporary architecture is threefold.

That its programme of activity will be based: firstly, on *research* into contemporary contributions of science and technique, in collaboration with the workers in the fields; secondly, a return to first principles in design—a *restatement* of the architectural task, and a re-definition of the scope of our profession—a revision of educational method. Thirdly, the *information* and demonstration to the outside world of architectural aims and possibilities which will create a condition for an architecture.

That which has been achieved by the pioneers in the old world and the new world alike must be consolidated and taken to their next stage of development here in America because the old world, temporarily at least, is hobbled. That is the only possibility and is, like many other issues, the responsibility of America. You are more than equipped to assume that responsibility, if you have the will to do so. . . .

. . . Here will be continued the process of what Gropius calls the "crystalising out" of an architecture really worthy of that name, representative of our recent discoveries and future aspirations—recognisable as organically part of our contemporary scene.

That it will be comparable in essential quality of design if not in outward form to the best of the past, we have already a sufficient number of examples to make us feel completely confident.

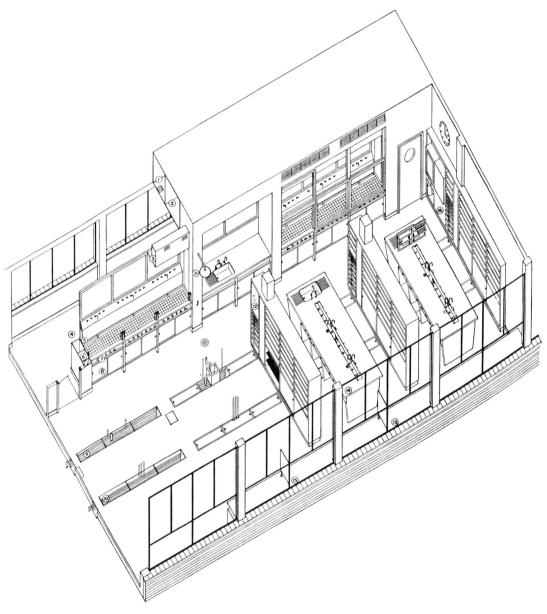

Imperial Chemical
Industries laboratory
building, Blakely,
Manchester, 1938.
Typical laboratory.

"Planners," "architects," "housers," "sociologists" et al. grasp at straws drifting about in a capricious wind. The scramble goes on whether the straw happens to be the establishment of a housing or planning authority, the construction of a housing project or some isolated specialized building, an overpass or a light standard.

To deduce some fundamental professional shortcomings from these antics does not imply the underrating of such excellent individual works as have been completed, in spite of the haphazard method of going about them.

The fact that the author of any such work may have stepped out of the ranks of planners, architects, designers or what have you merely suggests that the present arbitrary subdivision and classification of professionals has no real meaning. Then what about the actual purposes for which these professionals are being so assiduously trained?

Are the objectives quite clear in the minds of these various groups? Are we deluding ourselves not only with regard to the validity of procedure but also about the effectiveness of the completed work?

What is the impact of so many professionally treasured things on society as a whole? Are not professionals developing a narrow set of dogmas which are rarely understood and certainly almost never shared by the very people whom they believe to be benefitting? . . .

. . . Are reformers, full of goodwill, technicians, complete with excellent remedies, going about their job in the wrong way? The fault is not merely material; "souls as well as slums, *minds as well as money*" are involved.

An anthropologist chimes in with his own query into our chorus of inquiry: What is this era of unprecedented planning basing its plans upon?"

From an unpublished manuscript prepared for *Task* magazine, 1941.

We have a representative set of answers supplied on both sides of the Atlantic: in England the *Architectural Review*[7] in its masterly reconstruction number and here in the planning issue of the *Architectural Forum*.[8] Both appear to share a defect while being excellent on the material side.

The defect, I suggest by agreement with [Tom] Harrisson, the anthropologist, is: "They suffer from the detached view of the superior technician who wants a tidy and esthetically pleasing scheme, and has seldom asked basic questions about the desires of the people for whom they plan."[9]

The *Review* I feel inadvertently bogs down over a phrase. It says: "Planners are divided into 'Social Planners' and 'Technical Planners'" and goes on to define the "Social Planner" as "one who might be called a *territorial* planner, for his raw material is *simply the land.*"

We cannot agree with the authoritative *Review* and must here side with the layman Harrisson who points out that the social planners' material is: "*the man, the woman, the child, and the relationship between these and the whole community.*"

Architects will be poor technical planners if they have not at least a close relationship to social planners by this definition.

The *Forum* has a planning prescription which, covering some seven pages, leaves little room for doubting the intention that it wants a building program on a national scale but without Federal action. In effect, it proposes control of building operations by industrial monopolies to serve a nation of individuals. Quite positively the *Forum* wants to eat its cake and have it . . . .

Are we to continue to project into the public mind narrow professional interests about land, building materials, the building trade politics, methods of finance, shapes, sizes and sequences? Or are we going to devote at least part of our time to find out what makes people happy?

Is not this fundamental research, this "Architectural Mass Observation," of what sort of communities people what to live in, of what sort of houses people want, of the degrees of satisfaction, both private and communal, which they get from the different sorts of planned communities which have already been built, again of what makes people happy, an important task which can be performed only by such as *architects* and *psychologists* and certainly not by such as *realtors* and investment *bankers?*

To clear the prevailing confusion it appears as important to find out about the whole community as it is to set our own "planning," "architectural," "designing" house in order.

The sooner this desirable preliminary task is performed, the sooner will the professional body in the U.S. be able to get on with their exciting job.

To get a correct evaluation of any data which may be collected will involve breaking down artificial, obsolete barriers between the various professions concerned with environmental problems as much as the breaking down of equally artificial and obsolete barriers between professional and the community at large.

When we emerge from our water-tight compartments from which, like so many blinkered babes, we have gazed through tiny quartz windows at the outside world, a magnificent horizon will be realized. Some tangible reasons for the broadening of our field of vision suggest themselves.

Projects like the Grand Coulee, the Central Valley and the St. Lawrence offer unique opportunities for a long term program of research and action. Within the framework of specific large scale programs such as these, which have to create from the ground up every element of a new environment from industrial shelters and items of their equipment to whole communities and industrial and transport systems, planners, architects and designers can find opportunities for complete and convincing demonstrations of principles which have to date remained largely in the realm of theory.

It is not to underestimate the intrinsic value of isolated great works to say that however complete and satisfying these may be in themselves, their value is diminished because, nearly always, these examples are isolated among unrelated surroundings. Therefore their true significance is blurred or entirely obscured. But such planning and building, as part of the federal projects, may be done for people who by the very implications of the situation may be more tolerant of the unfamiliar and more apt to give experiment a fair trial.

The Grand Coulee and the Central Valley are architectural

frontiers. To equip ourselves for their conquest we require preparation. Such preparation involves not only reorientation of the professions, but their identification with the mass of people *with* whom, as well as for whom, they must work.

Planning and architecture are no longer a technical and esthetic problem alone. As Lancelot Hogben has said, an architect is a scientific humanist, but a humanist above all, or else he renounces his claim to leadership.[10]

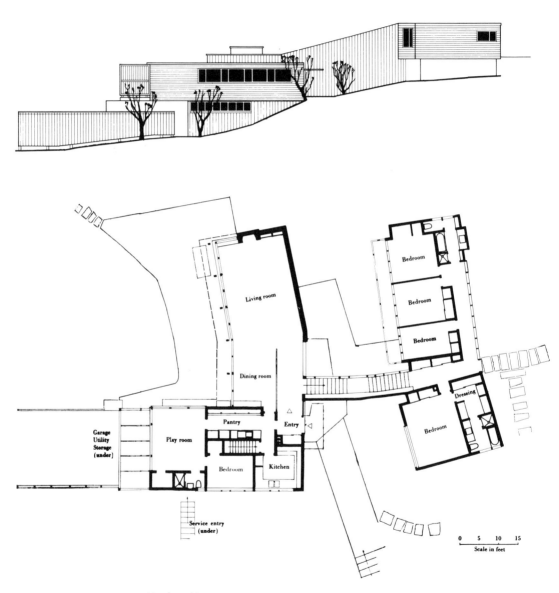

Living room

Bedroom

Bedroom

Bedroom

Dining room

Dressing

Garage
Utility
Storage
(under)

Play room

Pantry

Entry

Bedroom

Bedroom

Kitchen

Service entry
(under)

0 5 10 15
Scale in feet

Mayhew House,
Piedmont (Oakland),
California, 1942 (in
collaboration with
Clarence Mayhew).

ANONYMITY AND AUTONOMY

. . . Architects do all sorts of things in a haze of an amazing complacency. Meanwhile a new architecture is being made by others. Architects fortunately do not have the monopoly in building design. I think it is high time that they really become identified with the nature of the whole field of building and construction activity.

Let me first explain what I mean by anonymity. This can be illustrated perhaps by telling you of the impact Cambridge has made on me today after two years absence. I was absolutely delighted coming from Chicago, which has things about it which I will not underestimate, to find myself in the older, civilized surroundings of New England in which you are privileged to go about your daily chores. The effect of the homogeneity of the New England architecture in the small towns and villages is always a joy to see. I also wanted to see what was happening in terms of the contemporary additions to this civilized environment after two years. So I went to see new dormitories in Cambridge and individual houses just outside: the big building, toward one end of the architectural scale, and the small dwellings at the other. I was struck forcibly by the curious paradox illustrated by these. The big building was leaning over backwards to be small, to deny the fact that it was a big building. It appeared to be curiously romantic to me in this desire to be something other than it really was. And at the opposite end of the scale, the small houses were all shrunken palaces, trying so hard to be individual, larger and more important than they really were. Apparently we want every single building which goes up to be expressive, one way or another, to demonstrate a principle or to exhibit the designer's skill, instead of being what might be described as a good tool for a given purpose, conceived and constructed by workmen confident of their powers. We are so obviously *not* confident today . . . .

From a lecture, "Architecture: Anonymity and Autonomy," given at Harvard University, April 11, 1949.

. . . Surely, having gone through twenty-five to thirty years of research and development, we have a number of things which we can accept as being socially good and technically useful and esthetically satisfying. Yet we seem to be lacking courage to translate these into a new architecture. Even the masters are suffering from the architectural neurosis of our time.

Architects have one of the greatest problems of our time to solve. This problem has grown beyond all manageable proportions even in this country which has the highest standard of living in the world. Something like sixty-seven percent of the population (and it is still rising) has come into the cities in order to get the advantages of proximity. And what are we doing? We are not introducing on the perimeters of our cities the new kind of urbanity which recognizes the situation but actually introducing into them the new kind of cow path and the new kind of romantic earthiness which simply does not belong there, which does not ring true within the context of the urban pattern. We are creating situations which are indefensible and then finding ingenious arguments with which to rationalize our peculiar behavior.

I do not see why we should be afraid of urbanity. I do not see why we cannot conceive the provision of shelter as the first task. Where are the definitions of purpose, for instance, as against the demonstration of ingenuity and inventiveness? Every single building is shrieking at you to be noticed. Some of them lean over backward in exaggerated humility and want you to admire them for their omissions. Others are leaning in the opposite and calling upon you to recognize them for their extraordinary ingenuity. Is it not possible to have house and entire street and neighborhood in the contemporary idiom? It is this unanswered approach to an urgent problem which requires an architecture of anonymity. It requires a deliberate act on our part as architects.

Actually society *is* producing anonymous building, but not at the architectural level. The builder's building is becoming anonymous, except to the scholar who can say that it derives from this or that architectural prototype. Indeed, we are too often content to console ourselves for our inadequacy in action by being knowing scholars. We are missing the whole meaning of the devastated wood because we know all about a particular tree. I am offended by this attitude, and I think that it has become a canker within the architectural school system as well as in the profession. Therefore, I will make a serious plea for the idea of anonymity and the emphasis by architects today on things which must first be inconspicuously useful commonplaces and not on things which are aggressively exhibitionist.

There is a confusion now because of the strength that the modern architectural movement developed some twenty-five to thirty years ago. This movement became powerful, in the first place, because it set out to fill an obvious rational need. It has since become an irrational fashion. Today quite simple and unpretentious people are "expressing" themselves through architecture. In previous times, it was the privilege of relatively few patrons. But with wealth more evenly distributed and each individual conscious of his value in a democratic society, anyone who can possibly afford it would like to express his individuality through architecture. He does it unfortunately eight feet away from another totally different individual expression.

I believe that anybody who at this moment instead of providing the simple thing called "shelter" makes this a monument to the client is actually betraying the profession because he is doing so at the expense of urban society as a whole. Every architect's house nowadays turns out to be a very individual solution. As a result a new homogeneousness of architecture, which would be a genuine expression of our time, is being sacrificed to individual display; an architecture of anarchy for a world tending inevitably to integration through action.

. . . In architecture we have an extraordinary situation in which we are becoming blind again to all these things which were so extraordinarily clear to us about ten, fifteen or twenty years ago. Something has gone and I think we have to recapture it . . . .

. . . I do not see why if we think of shelter as a technical problem, which it so largely is, we could not devise shelters which have a comparable integrity. When we had done that, we shall have the material with which to make our kind of new modern architecture. I do not know what that new architecture is going to look like, but I am pretty sure that it is not going to be at all like the architecture which we now call modern, which fundamentally is old architecture made with new materials and shapes, or vice versa, and which is repeating the appalling errors of the nineteenth century.

. . . We are building fundamentally very conventional houses with excellent new components, whenever we can get hold of them, but we haven't done much to promote higher standards of living. Practically the only unconventional thing about them is their appearance. We dote on the open plan without questioning its social repercussions, which might be questioned by any parents with small children. We are spreading the cult of the large window and are frequently compelled by external circumstances to cover it up again for privacy and against glare. We are developing a set of escape clauses for ourselves in magnificent rationalizations. We say: "How beautiful this juxtaposition of stone and redwood is, below desirable tensile strength and much above a desirable hydroscopic content, but so charming." We make a virtue of primitive materials and esthetics exclusively and let economy, efficiency, etc., go hang. This is called modern architecture.

I do not see, however, why we have to go on doing this if we realize that this primitive enclosure, which we are being so romantic about, is enclosing tools of the highest level of technical efficiency. In terms of time the technical differential between a refrigerator, radio and a number of other essential features and the so-called modern structure which contains them is probably about five hundred years. The differential between the most modern house and its automobile controlled urban environment is probably as great. We look at these discrepancies, but do not see them. . . .

. . . I am a little frightened at the vagueness of people talking about architecture as a social art. I believe I know what it means. I am perfectly sure we can talk about it with considerable intelligence. It is extremely difficult, however, to find examples of the principle in action. We are not practicing what we preach in a fundamental and comprehensive way. We are anxious to justify our profession socially and to rationalize our position as artists. In the process we are deliberately evading many things which can be scientifically examined and which may be technically mastered.

As a result we are not producing the tools with which a genuinely modern architecture may be made. I believe we have reached the point at which this first step must be consciously taken by ourselves and nobody else: the architectural or designing profession. If we do not do it, it is quite obvious that this essential activity is going to be taken over by the people who are in the business of producing, in one form or another, the kind of tool that people want. They will do this at a far lower economic level than we are currently capable of doing and at an unnecessarily high cultural cost to society.

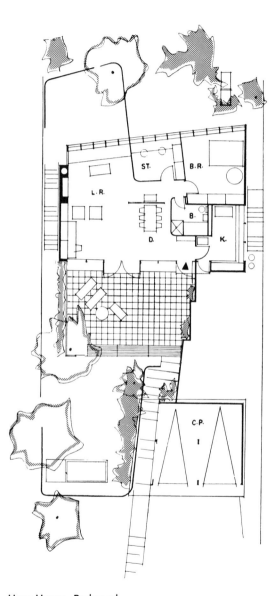

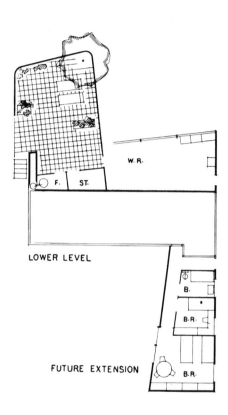

LOWER LEVEL

FUTURE EXTENSION

2

Horn House, Redwood,
Marin County,
California, 1942.
Study plan.

I'm grateful for this turnout because as a rule, you know, a prophet is without honor in his own country and certainly I've been put into the position in the last few years of addressing more audiences outside my own private bailiwick.

I've called my talk a report because I felt that I had to share with my own students and colleagues some of the things which have been very seriously on my mind for a considerable number of years and which, apart from moments of elation and optimism which come into everybody's life at all times, have on the whole been rather sad years. I don't mean to depress you; I think that the future is your own. I'm talking about the immediate period ahead which will be my somewhat tired future.

. . . There is a profound split within our special world. Too many people think about things now in contrasting absolutes of black and white—in totalities. This is becoming a very bad habit. A very dramatic example of this presented itself to me when I was invited some six or eight weeks ago to participate in a forum at the Architectural League in New York which was conducted under the general heading of "Must Architecture Be Sterile?"[11] When I received this invitation, I was forcibly struck by the suggestion that at any time people could believe in all seriousness (and the people who arranged these talks were certainly intelligent and well educated people) that an abstract symbol—a word—can be "sterile."

Quite obviously, architecture, which is an abstract word symbol for activity of men, cannot in itself be sterile. It is, of course, extremely likely that some of the participants in the activity can, indeed, be sterile and more. When I received this particular invitation, I searched around for data to help me clarify my own mind.

It occurred to me that the simplest and best thing to do would

From a lecture, "The Profession of Architecture," given at the Chicago Institute of Design, November 2, 1950.

be to look at the evidence provided by the practitioners themselves: Architects, of course, with a capital "A," the profession.
It was very easy to do that because I receive the *A.I.A. Journal*
regularly. I'm a member of that honorable—if slightly senile—
society, and I could, therefore, read the writing on the wall as
they themselves wrote it with a slightly sweaty finger and on a
fairly dusty wall. This is exactly what I did.

What I propose to talk about today is based on immediate
evidence that this profession—like almost any other set of people
today—is split from top to bottom, that it suffers from schizo-
phrenia of panic and sterility on the one side and hopefulness and
creativeness on the other. It is also extremely important for us to
observe that the official face of the profession is, as a matter of
fact, a face of fear. It is, for instance, becoming very clear to me
that those people who have now appointed themselves as the
defenders—certainly they are self-appointed defenders—of the
thing which we are talking about—architecture—are those people who are either frightened or greedy or stupid or just plain
illiterate. The people who are actually making architecture, of
course, are not in the least concerned about the future of architecture; they are just getting on with the making of it. . . .

. . . It is pretty evident, that one of the main troubles with the
so called profession is that it is not a profession any more except
for very few. It is, as a matter of fact, nothing more than a
business and, by a turn of fortune's screw, a great number of
people who are now architects might have been suspender manufacturers. They are so patently in business that we have to disen-
tangle somehow this confusion and ask ourselves, "What is it
really that we are talking about when we discuss the profession of
architecture?"

In this same series in which I participated at the Architectural
League under this schematically and semantically incorrect title,
"Must Architecture Be Sterile?", another session was given by a
very venerable dean—in the past a very important dean—from
one of the few great architectural schools in the country.[12] This
dean addressed the professional body in New York on this subject. I did not hear or read the full text of his speech; I did receive
reports on it by a number of my own kind of colleagues who were

incensed and by others—not my own kind—who obviously loved it! So I think I had a fair report of the speech.

It amounted to something like this: we've overdone this functionalism business, boys, so go easy on functionalism. On the other hand, we are missing this rather undefinable quality which might be called inspiration. (This reminds one of a similar skirmish fought between Eliot and Lawrence Bynyon about poetry some thirty years ago). The dean prescribed a return to the spirit of the Renaissance. This advice is about as relevant and as wise as that which somebody might give, say, to Mr. [Norbert] Wiener at M.I.T. or any of the physicists at the University of Chicago to the effect, "Go easy on modern physics, boys, and return to the spirit of alchemy." Such advice would not be terribly useful, of course, to a man who is interested in nuclear physics or theoretical physics. It just wouldn't work! This is the typical kind of nonsense which belongs to the department of fine speaking and writing for which this particular dean is so distinguished. But this piece of nonsense was enunciated in all seriousness to a body of professionals of whom a small number were properly nauseated, but most of whom were absolutely delighted because this provided a neat cloak for their own uncertainty.

Here is another example from which I am going to quote. I picked up the *A.I.A. Journal* from Washington and also the *Bulletin* of the Chicago Chapter where I found a very interesting article: a preview of [Ralph] Walker's, president of the American Institute of Architects, forthcoming book. It is going to be called, believe it or not, and it's written by an architect, *Collectivism Versus Individualism*.

Part of the revelation provided by Mr. Walker is that he "hates three things: faceless people, faceless architecture and those who believe a faceless, international formula-architecture is inevitable." He attacks "the myth of the house as a machine." He identifies "the forces of collectivism, not only with Communism, but with every governmental and business bureaucracy." He wants to "encourage unusual individuals who, in turn, will create an even better way of life, always striving for the development of responsibility and leadership which alone is capable of keeping any culture and civilization alive," and so on, and so on, and so on.[13]

This is the president of a professional society speaking in 1950. It is very interesting. Here we have a very typical situation in which words of absolute meaning are used loosely; where meanings are distorted; where fine shades are made into blacks and whites; where obscurantism, evasiveness, equivocacy—which have long been, of course, the stock in trade of the demagogue and the ward politician—suddenly become the tools of a professional man, the man who has actually been elected by his profession as its representative.

I find this most peculiar and also most distressing. The only fact, I suppose, to mitigate against this very distressing business is that it is election year.

Let us look at it a little more closely and ask, "What is Mr. Ralph Walker really doing?"

He is doing, of course, exactly what Mr. Stuart Chase's—you remember *The Tyranny of Words*—influential and powerful senator did just before the reelection of Roosevelt. This senator told Mr. Chase that he felt the next election was going to be won on the issue of "Americanism," and when Mr. Chase, who at that moment was interested in semantics, asked him in all innocence what he meant by "Americanism," the influential and powerful senator replied, "I don't know, but I think it's a damned good word with which to win an election!"

We can recognize exactly the same situation when the president of the American Institute of Architects, by talking about collectivism versus individualism in terms of black and white, sneers at every true issue and really has done absolutely nothing else but jump on the band wagon of popular politics, thereby establishing, at least to me, that he is very much interested in the business of architecture and not so much in its responsibilities.

Is it really possible for an intelligent man, which Mr. Walker unquestionably is, to confuse the issues so utterly? To despise collectivism in this kind of totalitarian way when he himself is the elected representative of a professional collective; when he himself has to deal with the product of collective industrialization? Among his best clients are, after all, the Bell Telephone Company, an extremely collective phenomenon. Does he really feel confused on these issues? Was the fact that he designed the

M.I.T. library because an individual gave this job to him as an individual because they liked the look of each others' hairdos or something? Or was he not in fact dealing with a great collective? And did his firm not get the job because it was an organization or collective equipped to furnish the required services? Does he not realize, for instance, that none of his buildings—his most ambitious and most rewarding buildings—could have been built except as the result of a tremendous labor force, the trades union labor force, which is a collective peculiar and special to our time? Or is he against these organizations? Does he not realize that every time he employs refrigeration or air-conditioning or this or that technology that he is using the total resources of a great collective science and technological development? Of course he does; he knows all these things.

I'm sure he knows them just as well as I do and yet he is writing a book on collectivism versus individualism. I think this is a non-professional act. I find very little comfort in it.

I go on looking for further evidence in the *A.I.A. Journal.* In that little issue there is a series of little letters—and they really are very little letters; annoying little letters—written with all that whimsical humor which professionals always use when they are seriously upset. There is a Mr. Loomis of Baltimore, Maryland, who spends some three or four hundred words in establishing with false humility his inadequacy and inefficiency and then attacks [Lewis] Mumford with some fifty words. He attacks Mr. Mumford on very simple grounds: that he [Mr. Loomis] smells (and I am using this word advisedly; it's purport of his letter) behind the professions of Mr. Mumford as a city planner, welfare-statism. And then he goes on to say (these are his exact words), "Mr. Mumford doesn't seem to quite understand the people of the 'provinces' still love to go to the big city just to gape at the monstrosities, to get a thrill from the change, and to get back home where they can tell about the wonders, but more particularly, about the horrid undesirable ways and bestial surroundings of the city slicker."[14]

So, in this whimsical way, he is, as a matter of fact, in all seriousness recommending that we maintain slums, congestion, squalor and so on so that the provincial or the country man may enjoy the thrill of seeing people miserable in a different way from his own so that he can go back to his little sub-rural community and lull himself into a false security.

In order to feed these wretched little microbes, we have to keep gigantic organisms in a nice state of constant decay. Wonderful thought!

There are two letters of this kind and, of course, the significant part is not the fact that these letters were written, because there are always a hundred fools or knaves for every Mumford, but the fact that The American Institute of Architects publishes those letters not only without comment but with a kind of between-the-lines glee. Apparently they don't like Mr. Mumford either.

Now I come to the last indictment which is based on another item in this same issue. Mr. William Scheik, who is a director of the Building Research Advisory Board, set up in Washington as some of you may know, whose purpose it is to advise how best to invest funds which have been voted by the House of Representatives for research into the problems of housing, building construction and other problems within the field which might be generally described as architecture, explains in this issue of the *A.I.A. Journal* what BRAB (Building Research Advisory Board) is and why.

This is what he has to say in the opening paragraphs: "The only handicap with architects on the subject is the fact that it deals with research and architects collectively don't seem to be research-minded."[15] This statement of simple fact of immense significance is addressed to the architectural profession with the utmost diffidence so that Mr. Scheik may get the maximum cooperation from this professional body. He has to say in all honesty that the architectural profession as a whole seems to be conspicuously unsympathetic to the one thing which is preoccupying men of responsibility and intelligence everywhere else. It's a tremendous indictment.

Can we not say that within this one little *A.I.A. Journal* there is evidence produced by the architectural profession itself of its obsolescence?

I don't hear protest or lament from, let us say, Mr. Owings or Mr. Skidmore or Mr. Merrill. This firm has a wonderful exhibition in the Museum of Modern Art in which again you see that the

American collective genius, technical resource, power for organization have absorbed an enormous amount of Corbusier, Mies and Gropius and are in fact producing exactly that kind of anonymous (or as Mr. Walker would have it, "faceless") architecture which Mr. Walker so definitely deplores and which apparently the Museum of Modern Art thinks deserves the accolade of having a special show: the first non-individual show that the Museum has ever put on.[16]

This show is an admission that this "faceless" thing, this "collective" thing, this functional act which is so deplorable, according to Mr. Walker, the frightened dean et al., is setting decent basic standards and is good and right and peculiarly "American"—if it is not all of architecture.

At this moment all these other people cry, "No, no! Let us not do that; let us go back to the spirit of the Renaissance and let us keep functionalism out of it." They don't tell us exactly what is the pinch of Renaissance or functionalism which is permissible and which makes a stew of architecture perfect.

All these little people are saying much and doing little while the others are doing much and say little.

I think we can conclude from all this that we are in search of basic principles again upon which we may build a program of action. We have been doing this for a very long time one way or another; we shall continue doing that. We shall never find entirely satisfactory solutions, but on the whole I think we are going in the right direction. This we are doing with a full consciousness, I believe, that modern architects are not being exceptional and are not trying to escape from the responsibility or even from the general climate of our time, but on the contrary are identifying themselves with it—and I think very properly—because this kind of identification is—with the prevailing temper of our time—unconscious, unmannered and profoundly serious.

Nobody really knows what we are going to achieve finally because we are in a stage of transition, but there is a direction.

What could that direction be described as? I think it was described most accurately for me in my most impressionable years—some twenty-five years ago—by Lancelot Hogben. You probably all know him as a biologist and philosopher. He said, when asked to define his position, that he was a scientific humanist.[17] I think this is the closest definition which I know of the kind of position which the architect of today may adopt.

And by architect I mean somebody who in fact performs all those things which are now roughly lumped under the heading of architecture for the lack of a better and more convenient term. I have often pleaded and would plead again that, as a matter of fact, we drop this particular term because behind it are sheltered somewhat irresponsible, insensitive, illiterate and frightened people and others of rather dubious persuasion, professionally speaking.

I would rather not identify architecture with them at all. Perhaps we need another word to define our activity and until we restore the word architecture to its original meaning and dignity. Perhaps we are scientific humanists concerned with a new kind of tool making and for a new set of purposes and conditions. Certainly by so doing we would share in the position of integrity, humility, intelligence and achievement which distinguish the scientists and humanists of our time.

I think that the most humble and, at the same time, the most effective people of today are those people who know that which may be discussed and that which must be done. And those people who are least convincing are those people who enjoy vagueness or emotionalism, who wish to escape from realities or reason. These discuss the undiscussable and they leave that which may be done undone.

I believe we should not identify ourselves with these latter.

I believe we should proceed scientifically; I believe we should now be scientifically disciplined even if we possess artistic sensibility and imagination.

We should, as a consequence of that, pursue a technical path with the greatest caution and integrity, keeping in mind that really there are no technical problems. The problems which face us are not technical ones but are problems of purpose and principle. And then I believe we must really go back to that which humanism stands for. It is the study of man: human ecology.

It seems to me that we've forgotten the man for whom we are making architecture. We've forgotten all those beautiful and simple things which were so beautifully and simply stated for us by people like H. G. Wells—for instance, *The Fate of Homo*

Sapiens.[18] It's a great and simple book which restates in very elementary and non-technical, non-scientific language many things which have been rather obscured by complications of over-specialization since. It seems to mark, as a matter of fact, the passing of a brief age of clarity and the entering of the new age of babbling and confusion which people quoted are providing for us. Bernard Shaw and H. G. Wells belonged to that bygone era. They kept on repeating—and I think we, in our own special attitudes about our work, can properly follow their precept; "Let us look at facts; let us look at man himself and, if we have new tools and ideas with which to improve his condition, then let us use every tool and every idea at our disposal for that." And we have so many possibilities now. Why don't we examine them and use them?

What is it I am declaring I am going to do when I say I am going to be architect? We need not mind whether the rose is called by any other name and you say in the somewhat obscure language of the Institute of Design, "I'm going to be a shelter designer." It's a euphemism; we can call it anything you like—it really doesn't matter. Anyhow, what is it that I am going to do? What is my objective? And I think my first objective must be, if I am going to preserve my integrity, to say there are so many things going wrong and there are so many things, in spite of it, which are coming out right that I must really ask myself honest questions. I would put man as I may observe him today in the first place and what is he and what does he need, I ask. Buildings are for man; they are not an abstract idea.

This is not individualism versus collectivism; it is not the battle between fascism and communism; it is not the battle of this ism against that—not these magnificent abstractions which have become scapegoats for every fool and rogue. These are simply conflicts between people's differences which you can identify. We can cater to ascertainable common needs in spite of the individual variants: pleasure in nature, children, color, in health, security, in collective as well as individual achievements, in crowds and privacy. We can look at these needs and we can really begin to examine our problem, but we have to do it on the basis of ascertainable needs. We can't be satisfied to take refuge in either aesthetic aspects alone or say we will examine the problem of our profession from the point of view of environment control or from the point of view of technology of structure. How can we be satisfied to do this when others are actually fighting our architectural cause on political grounds?

We also have to fight on that ground; we must. Professional responsibility is indivisible. You can't have peace in our backyard and be satisfied to have our war in Korea. Wars and peace—all these things are completely indivisible. Integrity is indivisible. Technical competency is indivisible. We can't be competent about economics and be utterly incompetent about art. This is impossible. We can't allow sensibility and ethics to become atrophied while materialism is being more and more perfected for doubtful purposes.

I think we have to take a view of an architectural totality in which we must play a part with unshakable integrity. Now our profession always has, of course, professed aims and ambitions. The only reason why I have taken it upon myself to make this brief report is because I feel that there is a dangerous enemy to be fought in spite of my prevailing optimism. In spite of all these quite magnificant things which are happening, there are pretty dreadful things happening and we have to keep our eyes open. We have to act according to the wisdom which comes of consciousness. This I think is tremendously important to us. And at this point I would conclude. I am absolutely sure that we are on the right path. I'm completely sure that we are the significant and virile minority; I am also equally sure that we could take a hell of a licking before we come through. I believe we really have to gird ourselves for a hard fight. I had in mind to warn you that it is not going to be easy and to tell you that it is going to be glorious in the end.

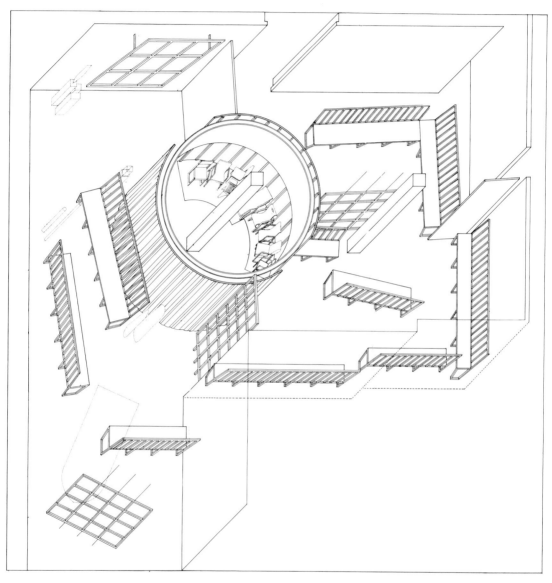

"Design for Use"
exhibition, Museum of
Modern Art, New York,
1944.

As an architect primarily and as a sort of second hand painter, I am concerned with this problem from the point of view of providing a framework for the arts. The CIAM—International Congress of Modern Architecture—has batted this thing around for many years. Three congresses, that is six years, ago, at the instigation of Giedion, the problem of esthetic was put very squarely to the architect of this international gathering.[19] The problem, as he put it, and I think it was a correctly stated one, was: at what point does the functional requirement cease and at which point does the artistic interpretation of the requirement begin; is it sufficient for the architect to be alone; is it sufficient for the artist to exist in a vacuum of his specialization?

I do not feel that the general way of propounding this question, which is mainly how do painters, architects and sculptors collaborate, to be the true statement of the problem. I believe much more sincerely that it is a question of how do the arts of architecture, painting and sculpture act coherently and concisely together. It is fairly evident that in more closed cultures, in the pre-industrial era, there was a certain kind of cultural cohesion when, in fact, every architect knew exactly what the other man would do, whether he be a sculptor or a painter, and could change roles with him. He could be ambivalent. In the great days, the painter was also a sculptor, if he had the talent and the craft, or he could become the architect. There are many examples, of which the obvious ones, of course, are da Vinci and Michelangelo. But generally, the liberal artist was able to function in closed cultures which had their own disciplines and rules. They could not only function because they had their own cultural drives behind them, but they could also function because their patron was part of the culture. The problem of our time, in the industrial society as I see it, is that we do not know who anybody is—there is such a diver-

---

From remarks made at the symposium "The Visual Arts: Their Relationships," Graduate School of Design, Harvard University, February 8, 1955.

sity of tongues speaking about everything, removed in time and space. There is no specific culture. We are simply made aware that every culture and every product of every culture is accessible to us should we take the trouble. This means that diversity, diversification, variety, uncertainty rather than discipline, dogma, belief, faith, common experience are the rule. So, although I believe philosophically that the architect, the sculptor and the painter should in fact act together in the common creative act, in visual, plastic, space and order-forming, I see little of it.

How can, in an industrial society which tends towards diversification, where everything regardless of time or space is available to us, people come together? How shall they find a common denominator, a reasonable base for action, which would enable a painter to elect himself as the natural collaborator of a sculptor, or an architect and so on? It would seem to me that this is a very grave problem of our time. The only thing that I can see is not therefore the collaboration as a problem but a cultivation of the integration of the arts as such. If this were true, then the spectrum of time becomes rather large. At that point, I may not with all good intentions in the world pick a collaborator. This would be a brash thing to do unless he had already preelected himself through intimate intercourse over many years, through common beliefs, through the sort of exchange which rarely occurs now in our very diversified and mobile society. Where could you safely say: I know this man; I know that he knows what I know and that we like the same things? This would be a base for collaboration. But when I am faced with the possiblity, as I am a painter—I put myself weakly in this position—of being picked with a pin by an architect, who is picked by fortune's pin to put up a doubtful blockbuster on Madison Avenue, and asked to embroider the doubtful, palatial entry with a very doubtful piece of sculptural or painting enrichment, I would really not know where to begin.

As a result, I find that this kind of fashionable desire to do the right thing more often than not leads to rather negative results. This does not, however, in my mind, preclude the necessity for trying to nurture a ground, or a base, or a philosophic comprehension or understanding among all the visual artists. So, therefore, I would say that wherever we may create a place where somebody may rest—by this I mean really a pedestrian area, where there is room and time for contemplation, for peace, for reflection—there shall we find the kind of architect who understands, and where a painter or a sculptor may contribute to the total environment. I do not see the possiblity of this kind of collaboration, myself, in the automobile-bound world and the rush of the elevator, which only gives a fleeting glimpse of something which is supposed to be good. I question it. In fact, I more than question it. I am very cynical about it.

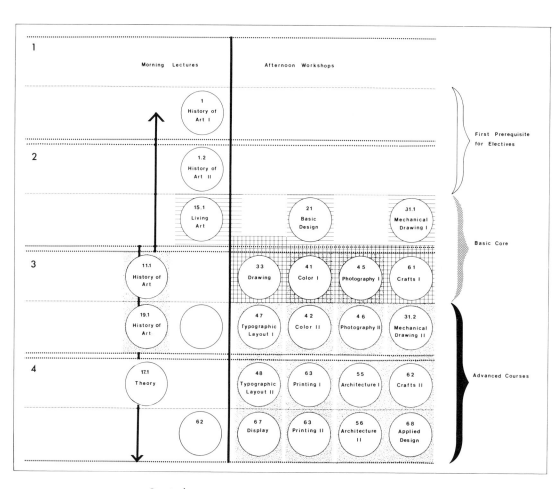

Curriculum structure,
Department of Design,
Brooklyn College, New
York, 1944.

. . . Somewhere we ourselves—by we I now mean the intelligent people conscious of architectural and planning and urban responsibilities—have to have ideas. It is the idea born in perhaps one single mind. A great man said that all revolutions are born within one mind. I think there's a great deal of truth in this. You see, we have to produce a sensible notion, which will then become generally acceptable and understood, that on this basis we can build an architecture. Because, for me at least, the notion that architecture is purely art is a fallacy. What we really need is a field of action within which people may humbly work in order to produce things corresponding to identified needs and designs. If there be artists participating in this program, we shall then have art. If there are no artists participating in this program, we will get some quite adequate but perhaps hideous tools.

We are doing exactly the opposite now because of the cycle of romantic involvement: everybody thinks that we can actually cultivate artists simply because we've got a guilty conscience. I think it is very nice of us to finally recognize that materialism has got somewhat out of hand. But to commit the opposite folly of saying that because we are hungry for culture, rather than mere civilization and comfort level, we can therefore turn out artists with the same facility that we can turn out chemists and engineers is a great mistake. I don't think that we can do anything of the kind. In fact, I cannot conceive of any chemist or engineer setting out to produce an artist-engineer or an artist-chemist, even though the great ones are exactly that. But they don't set out to produce them. They simply set out to solve problems.

I think, therefore, our critical moment now is to return to humility and recognition of, shall we say, programs, needs, requirements, in other words, the building of a base. It happens that we are very fortunate, certainly in this country (I say this in

From a lecture, "Design and Transition: Architecture and Planning Purpose Examined in the Light of Accelerating Events," given for the Great Issues Course, Dartmouth College, April 22, 1957.

all humility), because of the great pressures of disaster elsewhere. There is a tremendous reservoir of talent. But, I say this
again with all humility, this reservoir of talent has been very
largely wasted, because of our rather foolish preoccupations with
art with a capital A. This would be bad enough if we spoke only
of the artists. We, of course, know that the artist in this peculiar
last hundred years has been the man without status . . . the person who has no real position in society because of great diversification. We do not know what art is any more. Stop anybody
in the street and say, "What is an artist?" and he would probably say, "painter." But is it true? How many media can you think
of in which there are legitimate creative artists? Hundreds—
literature, photography, films, graphics, theater—anything you
like to mention, there are artists performing in it. Therefore, we
might reasonably say that the cycle now has gone all the way
around. We have sort of exhausted ourselves by chasing our own
tail and missed art by trying to create it synthetically. . . .

. . . If we are doctors, we do not cut out somebody's appendix,
just merely because somebody turns up and says, "Doctor, I'd
like to have my appendix out" . . . . We examine him, find out if
it's good for him, and if an appendectomy is not in order, we just
don't do it. Architects, apparently are of a different kidney, although they call themselves professional. They're quite prepared
to remove somebody's appendix if only the client wants it. I don't
think that this is a professional attitude.

So now I'm going to come right around and ask, who is it who's
talking to you—this abstract man called the architect? Is he the
businessman? If he's a businessman, he's not a very good businessman. Because certainly the profits are negligible. . . . Architects are on the starvation level. Doctors are earning 18,000
dollars average; I think the architect's average is 7,000 dollars
according to the latest figures. So a businessman, he's not.

Is he an artist? I doubt it very much, because what is he going
to be artistic with? He's really often nothing but an arranger of
catalogue items and the line of least resistance in respect to his
client's wife. And this doesn't even exclude corporations, because there's always the chairman of the board's wife, who has a
decorator or actually was a decorator herself. So he hasn't very

much to be an artist with. He's not a professional, because he doesn't accept social responsibility. The question is who is this hypothetical architect? Who is this mythical animal? . . .

I think that we could redefine him by saying that he is very uneasy about his position, as are the scientists, as are the responsible industrialists, who suddenly are beginning to recognize that nothing much really exists in these comfortable little parcels and vacuums which one finds when one first puts up one's shingle. There are tremendously complex interrelationships operating in an industrial economy and a culture in transition. It is only by taking note of these complexities and very deliberately thereafter saying, "All right, I cannot be a master of all this, but I can, within this framework of reference, select one or two tasks, which I rather like to do, or which I am competent to do, and attack them very, very humbly." I can try to solve a problem by writing an intelligent program because when I write an intelligent program you practically have a solution coming out at me. This kind of attitude is a reasonable one in all fields and therefore should not be unreasonable for people who now call themselves architects in a beautifully vague way. If we did adopt reasonable programs, we would find our artists, we would find them very readily, and we wouldn't have to go out looking for them. . . .

. . . "Anybody can produce art"; it's as easy as that. And by the same token, anybody with a slight facility for drawing, everybody with a good memory for the last pages of the *Architectural Record* and the *Architectural Forum* is a self-appointed genius in architecture. He arrives in school ready to conquer the world and to tell his professors, in particular, what to do. The most arrogant and therefore curiously out-of-kilter man still to this day is the pseudo-artist. He has all the overtones of frustration, all of them. He still doesn't belong.

Therefore, in conclusion, an architect, who is only another kind of an artist in the classic sense is really an animal which doesn't exist. What I want and I recommend very strongly to you, not only as potential architects but as potential consumers of architecture, is to let art look after itself. As Eric Gill said, "Beauty will look after herself."[20] But you must insist on getting logical action, tackled with complete humility and utter relevance to the problem in hand. I believe that if we go on with these notions long enough, and make our programs wide enough, we shall get an architecture worth talking about. In some distant future when somebody comes to talk on this subject again in this room, he will have something very positive to say.

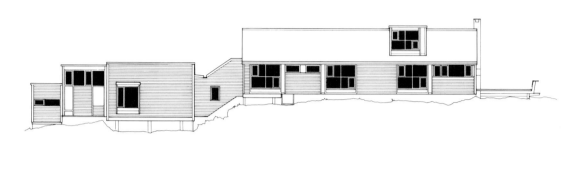

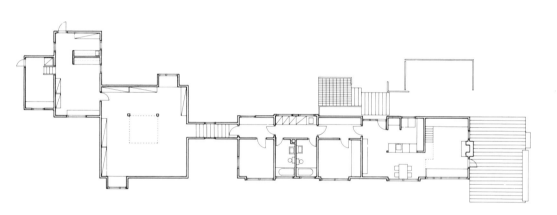

Chermayeff House,
Truro, Massachusetts,
1945–1972.

. . . I want to describe the attitude of scientists to our age as opposed to the characteristic architectural attitudes of the younger men, who should certainly have learned to know better, who are looking to the past prematurely. That used to be the prerogative of the middle aged, if not for the elderly! By the same token some of our elders, who should certainly know better, have been sketching a futuristic future. All too prematurely they have been drumming up issues instead of looking at forces which are in fact at work.

Professor H. J. Muller, a geneticist and Nobel prize winner speaking of the slow emergence of scientific thought, says the following:

In place of a rational system of knowledge, men erected pretentious edifices of misinformation. Within these walls they imprisoned themselves, tied up by bonds of emotion, and of hopeful compulsion. Inside, a puppet show went on, in which the leading roles were played by spirits, and the main mode of operating was magic. Even the areas of knowledge in which real progress had been achieved—astronomy, mathematics, medicine—were perverted to the pseudo-sciences, such as astrology, numerology and exorcism.[21]

You can make your own architectural analogies. . . .

. . . Industrialization on a world-wide scale removes this distinction and we shall have to take totally different attitudes in the sense that we shall choose that which is appropriate when everything will have become available. In the whole picture, the shape of quality is not the shape of a particular but rather the essence of any thing which we may think of as excellent. This is true of all art—fine art, visual art, architecture, the making of artifacts, urban design. As far as I am concerned the only thing which

---

From a lecture, "The Shape of Quality," given at the Graduate School of Design, Harvard University, April 16, 1959.

actually counts, and has counted for many years, is a visible sense of order—something which can be seen, understood, felt. This order can be either physical or philosophic, but its presence must be evoked. I am going to quote Professor Whyte from his book *Accent on Form*, which I commend to you. In the preface, the introduction to his own writing, he quotes A. M. Dalcq: "Form poses a problem which appeals to the utmost resources of our intelligence, and it affords the means which charm our sensibility and even entice us to the verge of frenzey. Form is never trivial or indifferent; it is the magic of the world."[22]

Mr. Whyte himself says the following:

Physics seeks to penetrate the music of the atomic spheres, biology the harmony of the organism, and neuropyschology the melody of thought, and though they do not yet know it these three sciences may be seeking to discover the same universal principle of elegance. This principle must be simple, and must define the character of change in complex systems. There seems to be little choice. It must surely express a natural tendency towards simplicity *pervading all realms.*[23]

I find this a wonderful statement. It is scientifically, I am sure, correct, but it is also poetic. In other words, we now have poetic scientists. The question is: can we match this by producing logical architects? At the moment there is no evidence that we can. . . .

. . .We have to switch from the pressure to produce to discover a process for production appropriate to our time and to the needs of our time and appropriate to the extremely differentiated functions which any professional man or any artist may indeed perform in our time. The greatest agents, however, for prescribing methods of production in slower moving times, in a pre-industrial age, were history and tradition. Included, of course, was the cycle of action and reaction, the swing of the pendulum within any series or epoch. But in any case it was a relatively slow process in which any functionary could very easily refer to that which was familiar, to needs which were known, to tools which were well tried, and even reproduce forms which were well understood and assimilated. There was a cultural continuity sustained by a great elite.

Today something quite else occurs. Traditions have been rudely interrupted by tremendous events. Most slow moving developments have been upset by scientific discovery and an explosion of technology. In such an age, we may not lean upon the past or genius. We must substitute something for the slow process, the empiric method. We have to admit that this substitute will have to be a quick decisions process. This is what [Christopher] Alexander has described very accurately as the programming of a decision-making process.

In general terms this probably requires the definition of principles, the analysis of needs in a more precise way than we are now doing, by asking right questions, and developing methods of arriving at solutions. Above all, we have to get ourselves in the mood of asking questions based upon a logical system of thought rather than upon emotion and all too quick a response to the pressures which I have previously described . . . .

. . . In housing alone, if we face up to the real need of the world, we will have to produce something between eighty to a hundred million units in the next decade. This can certainly not be done without industrialization, and without in fact typifying housing in relation to its purely functional elements. If what I am suggesting is even remotely true we will have to switch our minds rather rapidly from our kind of personal, private view and force architects to see an infinitely widened spectrum.

If industrialization does begin to operate as a tool which architects may intelligently use at one end and, at the other, which the monument builders will continue to use to produce monuments in a diversity of techniques, this astonishingly widened range will reveal images, symbols, monuments, housing, urban renewal, and, above all, remembering Dr. [Martin] Wagner, a reduction in the cost of housing as a primary objective of architects. What has the priority? I suggest that those people who wish to come in at the pure art end are privileged to do so without condemning the others or sneering at those who elect to come in at the other end. In fact I believe that architecture is indivisible. It is like art; it does not have to be of any single handwriting or type to be excellent. All purposeful action is completely honorable. . . .

. . . We need all sorts of prototypers in the new society now in the making. The despised "planning factories" are performing a tremendously valid task in such a society as ours. Skidmore, Owings and Merrill, although their work may not be uniformly excellent—the mere immensity of turnover would preclude this, and the pressure under which they have to produce would mitigate against this possibility—are nevertheless doing a tremendous job by staying within certain limits of kind but not quantity. They have been able to improve the quality of the things in which they have been interested—structural systems and detailing well beyond the small office capacity.

These people are performing astonishing digestive functions, and in the process they have produced some of the most excellent prototypes certainly not invented by them but certainly polished to a very high point by their organization. Their consistency does not compare with some of the other planning factories where you will get a little classic number if that's what you desire, modern number if that's what you want, on Thursday next. I think this sort of technical architecture has to be respected because it is useful to all of us.

Mr. [Paul] Rudolf used as a title for his talk "The Rise and Fall of the Curtain Wall" for no better reason than that it was a very good title.[24] He really doesn't believe a word of it. It is quite unlikely that he should because it is quite patent that the technical perfection of the curtain wall is such that it can produce an art form. The trouble is that it decayed because it was misused for the most part. Curtain walls will continue, I am sure, where they are in fact needed. I suspect that in our kind of industrialized society, in which characteristically gigantic structures are put up, where capital and operational costs are important and the speed of erection is paramount that this will persist. I am sure that these things will persist wherever industrilized production off site will be the appropriate means of erecting a building.

Nothing which has happened in the crustacean world has yet convinced me that there is a better substitute for an infinite array of alloys, synthetics or glass with its infinite versatility. These are still the most useful envelope-making materials which we have at our disposal. I would add a footnote; the virtues of hygiene and smoothness are not to be sneezed at when there are too many pigeons about!

What is suggested by all these remarks is that the very stretching of our possibilities and potentials requires very careful
stretching of our minds and new kinds of thinking about the real
problems in hand. We really have astonishing new possibilities in
front of us. Just as the last revolution was built on the shoulders
of the Paxtons, the Eiffels, the Cottoncins, the Fressinets, so we
have today an opportunity to build something on the shoulders of
Owen Williams, Ove Arups, the Nervis, the Candelas, the Frei
Ottos, the great form-making masters of our time. It would seem
to me that the art of architecture must be to put these new resources to work and to noble purpose.

    . . . This, of course, echoes what I said more clumsily in rela-
tion to the task of form-makers (speaking of architecture), an
even more poignant cry from Dr. [A. R. J.] Grosch, who says
unequivocally that there is no point in zooming off into outer
space. We can spend our money better in caring for our under-
fed and over-crowded millions.[25] For my money, Here! Here! I
would really prefer to come up with a method of reducing costs in
housing in the next ten years than to build a monument of porphyry and pressed glass if I understood Mr. [Edward] Stone; Mr.
[Philip] Johnson, et al. I think we have to stop searching for forms
just for a minute and search for solutions. . . .

    . . . What sort of conclusion can one make? There is very little
doubt that the masterworks will survive. We have contemporary
masters whose actions are so conspicuously excellent, the quality
of whose faith is so unequivocally good that their work will survive. More than that, we have a whole school derived from those
masters, and among the followers are people of sufficient excellence that their micro-masterwork in the master's mood will survive. I am also quite sure that there will be emerging prototypes
of an entirely new kind if we seek new solutions rather than new
forms. I am pretty certain that we are at the end of an era and the
beginning of a new. I am quite sure that the extravaganza of what
I like to think of as "the Freudian fifties" will join in oblivion the
bustle and the garbage of "the naughty nineties" and the
artificiality of the art decoratif of "the gay twenties" and that
something else will come up. However, my precept is one of
caution and this is probably reasonable.

    I am interested in things that take time to develop. I believe that we have to re-affirm principles, purposes, and methods. In other words, I suggest that what we have to do now is to go back to a new "commodity," a new "firmness" and I am quite confident that, as a result, we shall find a new "delight" in good time.

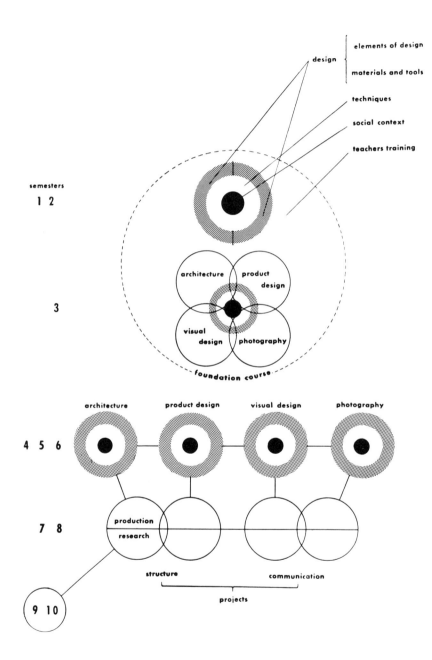

design {
  elements of design
  materials and tools
}

techniques

social context

teachers training

semesters
1 2

3

architecture   product design

visual design   photography

foundation course

architecture   product design   visual design   photography

4 5 6

7 8

production
research

structure   communication

projects

9 10

Curriculum structure,
Institute of Design,
Chicago, 1949.

I should say immediately that I feel myself highly privileged to have been asked to participate in your exercises, but I was somewhat confused as to what would be suitable comment about my private concern as an artist and architect to an audience composed of a community of these functionaries. I started looking around for some departure point and I found it very conveniently in Mr. Edward Logue, an erstwhile New Havenite. He was a director of the urban redevelopment, and his report was discussed by that admirable critic, Mr. Walter McQuade, who himself has taught here, at a symposium in the Museum of Modern Art held only recently. This report was in *The Nation*, and I would very much like to quote Mr. Logue, as quoted by Mr. McQuade. He categorized the architectural profession, which he thought rather silly, as follows:

(1) those who buy jobs under the table from crooked politicians; (2) those who eat in businessmen's clubs every day, coax jobs from businessmen, themselves become business men and deliver business buildings, not architecture; (3) those hungry young architects of talent—the only respectable category to him—whose competitive situation forces them to deliver buildings on low budgets but whose own ambitions make them want to build great or even good architecture, and who eventually turn into; (4) the "great architects," who blandly ignore budgets, and also have the devastating habit of entirely despising one another's work.[26]

Now I don't know what New Haven did to Mr. Logue to evoke this. It may, of course, have been Boston later. In any case, I agree with Mr. Logue, if perhaps for different reasons, and I propose at least to start by giving to you my explanation of his last categorical statement that all architects despise each other's work. People capable even of having critical judgments can be

From a lecture, "The Designer's Dilemma," given to the annual spring convocation, Yale Arts Association, April 14, 1962 very easily explained. I think that the artist and architect in our society are treated very largely like courtesans—expensive, exhibitionist indulgence for rich patrons—who have absolutely nothing to do with the humdrum realities of day to day family life. Behaving accordingly, our spoiled artists resent each other's for the most part eclectic work, either of art or architecture, just in the same way as any woman might who encounters a rival at a cocktail party in the same Dior Easter bonnet. . . .

. . . It is ironic that in an age in which man is indeed transforming his environment at a pace unprecedented and in quantities unprecedented, the group of professionals who, by definition, are among the prime shapers of man's habitat are deprived of prime responsibility, namely, to make decisions. The trained shaper of environment is in a subservient position, and this is true in spite of all declarations and slogans of the professional organizations or the very arrogant assertions of a few favored individuals. The fact still remains that less than ten percent of total annual value of building in the United States is architect designed. Even if architects are involved, the writing is on the wall in the negative sense that their name is rarely mentioned. Certainly it is mentioned far less frequently than that of bankers, the real estate men, the politicians and the lawyers or even decorators. It is fairly evident that the designer is a functionary operating on many scales in a society which is now developing; that designers, dubbed architects in the traditional sense, have all but vanished as prime builders because many others are designing, deciding and building. Not only is the activity therefore changing, but it is enlarging and stretching in its spectrum, and I suspect that for those reasons alone, we need an entirely new deployment, a rather different set of functionaries for the vast task ahead. . . .

. . . The designer's dilemma will not, however, be resolved by the profession as a whole or even by the schools. It will have to be resolved eventually by being assisted in new attitudes. They are developing, I think, primarily in the schools with the help of a handful, a tiny handful, of practitioners, very rare practitioners.

I would like just to enumerate some of the things which I believe to be of primary importance for the resolution of the dilemma I am discussing. Probably the most generalized one and the most important one is the recognition that there are new

forces at work. I don't discount the force of new structural technology which is enriching our vocabulary of form. This is a very
important aspect of it, but not primary. At the same time I suspect that the current over-exuberance in form-making, which is
the result of the pent-up hunger of many war years and which
puts hyperbolic paraboloids on dog kennels, is not a primary
force. More importantly, we are shifting, for reasons already indicated before, our focus from individual buildings to their relationships to their immediate environment and to each other. We are
shaping again the outside spaces with the same diligence as interior spaces, and this endeavor, of course, distinguished the greatest monuments of history.

We begin, in fact, to think and design urbanistically, in clusters, in complexes and organizations, and having made something
beautiful here, we look very askance at the ugliness across the
street. We have learned from the natural scientist a great deal in
the intervening few years since the war. We are conscious, for
instance, of the various elements and aspects of the physical
environment. We have begun to understand them much more
clearly, and we are developing techniques of controlling this environment. We have begun to understand them much more clearly,
and we are developing techniques of controlling this environment, or making it work to our advantage instead of trying to
buck it. We can of course, and must ever more move as our
population and mobility increase, take our habitable climate with
us wherever we go, to desert, mountain top, jungle, where you
will. We have already shown our capacity to do so by taking it
dramatically and very expensively into outer space.

In the full knowledge that our environment shapes us just as
much as we shape it, we have begun to realize that it is the
underlying organization of components which is the true basis to
form. This could be described as organic in the sense of the great
masterpieces: that form is only the expression of such organization, and that the importance of our action becomes quite clear
when we think that there may be some interrelationship between
the total chaos and incoherence of the physical world and the
growing neuroses of its inhabitants. Perhaps chaos in the eye may
actually accelerate confusion in the mind.

We are beginning to understand now that programs very often

make plans and shapes much more convincingly than hunches or whimsical or willful invention. In our society, which is technically complex, and which in dimension is shrinking because of our growing communications, possibly the need for specialized monuments is becoming relatively rare as compared to the need of universal prototypes. These are things that may be useful anywhere in a world which will be very rapidly industrialized precisely because of communication which permits us to share more and more common knowledge and common interest. We are learning from other disciplines techniques of prototype programming which, like technology itself, is not exclusive or particular or local, but quite universal, generalized and anonymous.

Therefore, within this widened spectrum of mere necessities we have to provide, we shall also need a variety of designers capable themselves of applying their talents and intelligences to an infinitely greater variety of problems. They are needed to solve such problems as I have just described of the universal prototype at the one end while we shall still require others who will have the sense and the sensibility to cultivate the indigenous and the special. Both these and all the possibilities between will have scope and scale ranging from the intimate and small to the communal and gigantic.

Not only is the spectrum of design much wider, but so is the action of designers potentially much deeper. It is also of course infinitely more complex. As in the Renaissance, we find it now, perhaps even more so, very difficult to draw clear lines of distinction between the sciences and the arts, including the science and art of regional and city planning or urban design or building design, which is uniquely and erroneously called architecture today. Why not include product and equipment design? This situation of unclear boundaries of responsibility and action is very much the same as is the problem of distinction between the fine and the applied arts, when these comprise the overlapping activities of painting, graphic design, photography and film sculpture and exhibition design. For the talented tyro, all these final acts provide but alternate paths, and any one or more of these may be followed by the dedicated artist in his maturity. Therefore to summarize, we can really say that we are not living in a black and white world which we find so convenient—this world of easy category and of polarity—but in an infinitely complex hierarchy of possibilities. Within this hierarchy, the opportunity exists to pursue the personal objective and reap the fruits of privacy, and at the other end there will be the more demanding but no less rewarding tasks of social responsibility and commitments to the larger community.

Both the private and the public are the artist's province. In an age of very rapid industrialization within this great hierarchy of potential, greater architectural responsibility, as far as I am concerned, lies at the community end of the spectrum, for we cannot stop the good man withdrawing into himself. The trouble is how to prevent the bad men from spreading themselves wide? We have to get designers or architects who so equip themselves for the new immensely complex task as a group of functionaries in industrial society, who will, in fact, earn the right to claim a share in the process of decision making. At the moment they have no such claim. Perhaps as a result of actually staking out this claim, we may eventually breed another Pericles rather than dozens of Diors.

However excellent schools and professionals may be, it will all be too late if we as a society don't recognize that this dilemma is common to designers and to consumers or patrons alike. The dilemma is fundamentally one of quantity, the affluence that so many people are talking about, the speed of events, the exploding population, exploding urbanization, and astonishing acceleration in energy consumption. We have to recognize this problem without delay, and we have to back this recognition appropriately with laws, adminstrative action, and, of course, dollars. This task must be performed at all levels.

The established designers or architectural education I think needs today the stimulants of post-graduate study to enable our most gifted and dedicated architects to stay out of the marketplace if they so wish. I do not suggest that some of the best architects should not in fact go into the marketplace where their particular talents will find their expression, but I think we must provide the other option, and we do not provide this option today. For we must have a continuous and essential research in environmental design comparable to some of the programs in other disciplines, notably natural and social sciences, for we too are here concerned not with cures but with prevention.

I believe that the arts and sciences of design—because it is becoming a science as well as an art—require assistance, more and more, in professorships, expanded facilities, and, above all, in fellowships for the best minds. Our current compressed professional curricula do not yet have adequate preparatory education. They tend to reduce each class group to the lowest common denominator and to spread very thin the essential information for each group and for each individual. Therefore, I think reform perhaps is needed most in education so that we may within the process of education provide opportunities for the best minds among their peers. We need a budget for constructive action, in which I place the making of our physical environment very high up, to protect us against ourselves; we need rather more in fact than we are currently allocating to the armed forces to protect us against others. We do need a ministry of urban affairs today to cultivate an urbanity in an urban society just as much as we needed a ministry of agriculture for an agrarian society, possibly more because of the compression of time and the expansion of population and economic growth. For if we cannot shape our environment intelligently, and if we cannot equally intelligently conserve such pieces of that environment as are good for man, we shall have dehumanized ourselves by dehumanizing our environment, and the condition of man will not have improved.

We are witnessing at the present moment the dissolution of habitable or great places and, if we continue on this path, the dissolution of appropriate place. The loss, therefore, of the proper occasion for which the place has been designed will have been completed. We shall need no Pericles because the possibility of an acropolis will no longer be ours. We shall subsist miserably on an annual production of Easter bonnets, but the reasons for the Easter parade will have vanished forever.

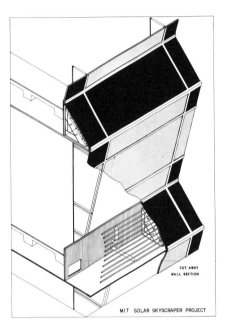

CUT AWAY
WALL SECTION

MIT SOLAR SKYSCRAPER PROJECT

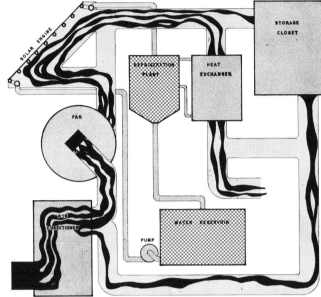

Solar skyscraper
project, Massachusetts
Institute of Technology,
School of Architecture,
1952: Design studio
project with MIT
students.

. . . There is a very great need to study what has been absent from discussion so far: the larger problems of urbanizing men in great numbers and great complexity. The word urbanism, or any substitute for this general notion, has been totally omitted from discussion so far. I believe this larger expression of architecture in our time deserves priority over single building quality.

For similar reasons I resigned from the AIA some years ago and have not since had any reason to change my mind. I have remained in the RIBA, partly out of sentiment of course, partly because they made me a Fellow, but mainly because they are extremely serious-minded about the responsibility of architects who, by definition, are *professionals first and foremost.*

A professional, as far as I can make out, is somebody who acts *pro bono publico,* in other words, who has social responsibility and is *not* a businessman. I have a quote here which I am going to read. Mr. William Allen, whom some of you may have met because he was a visitor all over the place here, is now the Principal of the Architectural Association in London. He had this to say after his visit on the occasion of a discussion at the Royal Institute as to whether they should up their fees: the Royal Institute felt that they needed all the money they could get their hands on to consolidate the position of what is a weakened profession.

This is what he says about us.

I was in America about six months and talked to educators and architects across the United States and Canada. I became increasingly aware of the tremendous difference between the professions here and in America. We are all accustomed to look at the glossies and admire the work of Kahn and others, but when you drop below that level and talk to architects doing ordinary jobs, you find them

From a lecture, "Random Thoughts on the Architectural Condition," given at the AIA-ACSA Teacher Seminar, Cranbrook, June 9, 1964; published in Marcus Whiffen, ed., *The History, Theory, and Criticism of Architecture: Papers from the 1964 AIA-ACSA Teacher Seminar* (Cambridge: MIT Press, 1965).

up against extraordinary difficulties: terrible fee cutting, fee com-
petition, chiseling of all kinds . . . .

In other words, we are not a profession any longer (those of you who are architects). Most of you are historians and that is still an honorable profession—but be careful.

He continues:

. . . cities that are terrible investments to the future, for the most part rather horrid places. They do not like public architects over there, they think they are in competition with private practice. The real difference begins to show up when you look at some statistics. Here in England we have fairly good knowledge that we have something like sixty percent or more of the building indus- try's total volume of building. The highest figure that anyone could guess at in the States was thirty percent and the lowest ten percent and the general notion is that it was going down and not up as it is here. This is a very serious state of affairs for American architects, if it is true.[27]

All this is, as a matter of fact, undeniably true, and more and more of the building dollar is spent without any help from ar- chitects whatsoever. It is therefore perhaps reasonable at this moment to speculate why this is so.

Bruno Zevi has already told you, and I entirely agree with him, that no matter what you do, how wisely you behave in the class- room, it makes not the slightest difference to the field. The field gets more and more inefficient and vulgar, further away from the public purpose. For the world in general terms, this means that private appetites for those comforts which are now in the hands of a minority in the western world, of which we happen to be the chief benefactors, are still unassuaged. If we are going to provide increased and widely distributed comfort, hygiene, health and leisure, we had better be very, very careful ourselves because people all over are going to look to us for example. We must not continue on a path of self-destruction. Architects, in particular must begin to design components of an environment which would be worthy of the aspirations of the rising masses of any country. Uncommon men must learn to serve common man.

I would like, if I may, to go on freewheeling. I have a manu- script, not written for this occasion, in which I marked a few relevant paragraphs which I will read. I agree with Mr. Zevi unequivocally that although modern architecture has produced some most excellent formal statements and really great inventions, we still have not got one single piece of architecture of total excellence such as the earlier examples in simpler cultures. Of course, new diversity and complexity has something to do with our failure.

We have not built anything, for example, which is so admirably designed for contemplation and communion as the great temples, churches and cathedrals of history. The reason for our own failures lies in the program behind the act, the consideration of true purpose, the "why" of building, which has been overlaid by obsolete cliches in a backward-looking culture, so frightened of the future that it finds comfort in imitating the past. We are faithless cowards of the worst kind. . . .

. . . There is another problem, in this country particularly, as Mr. Allen observed: the ubiquitous private practitioner. In architecture there are few public servants; nobody talks much about public service; it is only very recently that the notion, because of the pressures of the time, is emerging at all. Public-oriented planners and designers are now getting into urban renewal offices, and city planning offices, staffed no longer by sociologists and economists and demographers exclusively of the slum clearance era, are projectors of reconstruction and a total architecture. These anonymous, unknown, usually young architects are operating at a public level and close to decision makers. This is important not only because they are doing an important task but because they are involved in expenditures which would make even SOM jealous. One city, like Chicago, could spend in one year everything that SOM was responsible for in decades, and they are not doing badly as pioneers. A new activity is emerging apart from the private practitioner and on a new scale. This is a very significant change.

Under all these pressures, the private practitioner runs the risk of losing his integrity: all that star-making, which makes *Time* magazine covers, is part and parcel of the prevailing hucksterism of our system.[28] Architects are now not only subject to being exploited by the professional hucksters but they themselves are to become hucksters.

I have a feeling that what has really been happening is that architects have completely missed a position among decision makers. They are worse than hucksters; architects really are hustlers, they are the second oldest profession today, they stand on street corners waiting to be picked up and they think it is a good thing to be picked up by people with a lot of money.

I am sick indeed of expensive scenery. Mr. Zevi, walking around with me yesterday, observed that the scenery close by, the great portico which splits the world of the fountain source from the world of the water tower is just waiting to be taken down. It looks exactly like a theatrical set, you just turn off the lights, you knock down the flats and you take it to the next fairground. It is just scenery, and if you look at it very carefully, it becomes worse and worse and more and more emptily decorative and finally slides down into the slough of purposelessness. . . .

. . . Apparently we cannot have several serious architectural magazines with criticism in America; we simply confuse things. Why would an advertiser of a simple commodity for sale or a simple business architect who is looking for how-to-do-it buy such a magazine? Architectural magazines which are admirable catalogues, second only to Sweets' catalogue, have little to do with architectural criticism, history or theory. So, by definition, a profession which cannot sustain a magazine except for business purposes doesn't deserve a good magazine. . . .

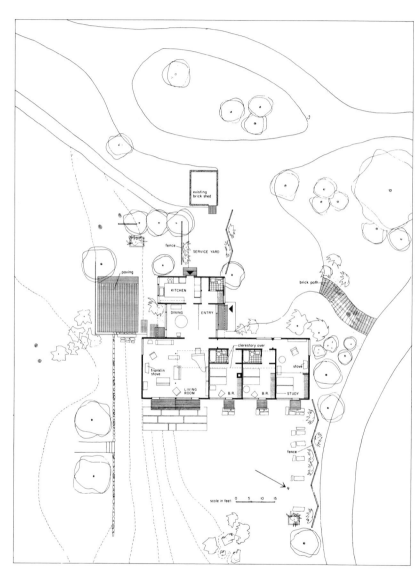

Payson House, Portland,
Maine, 1952.

. . . Forty-one years ago I was elected as fellow of the Royal Institute of British Architects without any formal professional education of any kind, simply because I had plunged in and done a few things which seemed to have the approval of the establishment of that time. Thirty years ago, maybe a year or so less, I passed, here in this country, the senior exam of the National Architectural Registration Board and I got ninety-five percent, which I think was the highest at that time. I am not boasting about it; I am merely stating it as a simple fact. Twenty years ago I resigned from the A.I.A. because it was a totally useless institution for reasons that will become clear presently to you. Generally speaking, I never had any particular taste for the hustling for clients. We are the second oldest profession you know. I never cared much for arguing with bureaucrats, mostly rather stupid, or watching greedy contractors with an eagle eye lest they cheat a client who deserved it.

If I may, I will turn to the period which I have in mind. It was an expression of the kind of professional community to which I belonged during those years. It runs really from war to war. Three rather eventful decades. The Second World War was really a morally acceptable response to an attack from a totally immoral threat and it caused, of course, the complementary response from people who were not directly engaged in the war as such, of stimulation, hope, some kind of elation about the possibility of the future. I arrived here just as America was joining the war because I had no part to play in the other end, and they wished me to get the hell out so as to save a few gas masks; because I could do something over here; and I had an engagement. So in this country I had a very short spell indeed of practice, on the West Coast actually, in which I was rather flattered in

From a lecture, "The Shape of Community Revisited," given at the College, Arts and Architecture, Yale University, April 26, 1972.

being invited to design an architect's house for him.[29] He wasn't a bad architect; he was simply afraid of his wife. . . .

It was a very interesting time for the profession as such. There being no commissions, a lot of intelligent architects, some immigrant architects, like myself for instance, got together with a lot of forward-looking American architects, among whom were Oscar Stonorov and his then partner, Lou Kahn. George Howe, who later, as you remember, became the chairman here at Yale, invited Lou Kahn to come here and design the Art Gallery next door, his first and distinguished sizeable piece of work. We formed a society to think about the problems which would arise after the war, the American Society of Planners and Architects. I want to draw your attention to the fact that planning was put first and architecture last. This was, of course, in a way, a hangover from the pre-war activities of the International Congress of the Modern Architecture, C.I.A.M., and the notions of Corbusier, who invented the word urbanism, in case some of you don't remember that. We sat around and thought and planned for the future. I'd like to just mention in passing that the pattern in which Stonorov and Kahn were then engaged was social planning, tenant protection, and they worked very closely with Walter Reuther who came down from Detroit to Philadelphia in order to develop the unionized labor consciousness of their responsibility in relation to environments, a most unusual situation which has long since been forgotten.

George Howe was the first president of this A.S.P.A., which of course dissolved with the war, and in his opening speech, I think at the Waldorf, where it was almost obligatory to have opening speeches, he made a wonderful peroration in which he invited the architects and planners present to make "master plans for master politicians" who might consider these after the war was over. It is a beautiful phrase and a very useful statement.[30] It is quite true, of course, that master plans are no longer really possible. We don't have master plans which are a finished product. We have simply programs for on-going, open-ended change in a rational and reasonable work.

I saw to my dismay that my old friend Peter Blake who was also an apprentice in my office with [Erich] Mendelson nearly fifty years ago, who is now the editor of the *Architectural Forum*, is

preparing a kind of valedictory number on my old friend Lou
Kahn. Lou Kahn, in the preview in the *Forum*, which most of you
must have seen, was described as the architect's architect.[31] Of
course, it was true in a sense, except that I really think that as
time has passed he is much better than that because the run-of-
the-mill architects are not much good. We have the preview of
the architect's architect in Frank Lloyd Wright and Corbusier,
certainly. The trouble with Frank Lloyd Wright's architect's architect was the awful vision of Broadacre City, an ever sprawling
sub-rural sprawl, worse than the sub-urban sprawl. Corbusier
invented "urbanism." He was supposed to be the architect's architect but he was much more than that. And then they finished
up with choosing Kahn for this, somewhat unflattering title under
the circumstances prevailing.

I think Blake quoted Lou as saying that the ultimate work of art
is the city. I don't believe a word of it. An ultimate work of art of
any kind is an accomplished fact, a complete and discreet entity,
that is what a work of art is, whether it is a Venice or a painting or
a sculpture. I don't believe for a minute that Lou, if he snaps out
of his mystic moods, will believe that a city will ever exist in this
discreet and finished way at any number of hands, far less one
man's hands. I think what we are actually entering is a global
system of urbanism, which is an infinite pattern of interdependence and interaction, which will only be started by wise men but
never, never, never be finished by anybody but a dangerous fool.
So, I think Mr. Blake is wrong and I don't believe that Lou really
thinks all he occasionally says.

I remember in 1954, ten years after the war roughly, that Philip
Johnson, Edgar Kaufmann and I, immediately after the completion of the Frank Lloyd Wright Bear Run, went there with George
Howe as guests of Edgar's. We were taken by George on a tour of
Philadelphia in order to see his and Lescaze's recently completed
Philadelphia Insurance Skyscraper. It was the first genuinely
modern skyscraper, rather fashionably, modishly formal but still
fundamentally a good departure. I remember very well going
round slowly with Philip and George, and George said, "Look at
this neo-classic post-office, I built that. Look at this city hall and
the pseudo-romanesque, I did that," and so we went on and on
until we arrived at this skyscraper and then I turned to George

and I said, "George, it is obvious that you have sold out for a pot of message." He had a very handsome, very handsome practice indeed of no significance whatsoever and he had the decency and integrity to recognize it. He thought this remark was rather funny. Ten years after that, after he had been chairman here and after Lou Kahn had built the art gallery, the architects had all gone back to business as usual and it was only a few men like Howe who could look ironically and contemptuously at the scene of this decline, which has since been galloping of course as you all know.

It is fairly obvious to me that any profession, in the last decade, which is dependent upon fees as its reward based upon estimated costs in an inflationary period is simply bound to perish like dinosaurs from the face of the earth. No designer outside this astonishingly archaic and obsolescent profession would dream of entering into a career so precarious unless he is stupid. Of course, the stars who command commissions discovered this long ago. [Gordon] Bunshaft of S.O.M. I think invented an appropriate system. Most of their business is of course with the deductible dollar, so when he builds Chase-Manhattan he takes it at cost plus for his time and all other expenses which include fantastically complex and costly components, an infinity of drawings, computer services, or whatever. In fact, the people for whom it costs nothing, are very persnickety about the architecture they get and they don't think anything about scrapping 50,000 dollars worth of plans and starting again, nothing! It doesn't cost them a penny. It costs you and me, if we work on estimated cost fees, a pretty penny. So, we could say that the profession, economically and technologically in an inflationary age, is, together with all bureaucracies, about a couple of generations behind the realities of our time.

It does this, unfortunately, not on the same moral basis as the thinking of the first stage of these three decades I have described, the Second World War, but because we are now in the last decade of the most obscene, shameful and demoralizing, meaningless war of immense cost, which, if reinvested, could have done all the things that the profession has failed singularly to do at all. So, demoralization and deterioration are both physical and social, and this does not, in any way, exclude the profession which is now distinguished by being, in fact, the servant of the rich. It has done absolutely zero for the poor. The rich are getting richer and more mobile; the poor are getting poorer and they have no place in which to stay. Economically, socially, environmentally and architecturally we are bankrupt.

Just look around you here. . . . It's like a cemetary of buried architectural hopes, disconnected monuments, just like little tiny tombstones to suit every purse, capped, of course, by the most expensive mausoleum ever built in the middle of the most expensive granite desert where there should have been a busy concourse next to commons, and next to a library.[32] A more inane thing I have seldom seen done by an intelligent community anywhere. And architects were all party to this disgraceful thing. I have come to the conclusion, in spite of my regard for an awful lot of excellent performers, that the profession has become obsolescent, if not senile, irrelevent for the purposes of new realities and new needs. And publishable exemplars that you read about in all the magazines and which our pseudo-critics and historians spend so much time in exalting and discussing, are really so many shiny needles just stuck into an enormous haystack of unfinished business, untouched and fomenting inside ready for spontaneous combustion at some unpredictable moment. And the needles will not hold it together.

The expensive, tax-deductible facilities and monuments have absolutely nothing that I can see conceivably as the architecture of our time or as an expression of a moral professional obligation which attends any social art. My own predilection, of course, as you can see is really asking questions. I am not terribly interested in designing facile solutions. . . .

. . . The new A & A Building designed by [Paul] Rudolph had great dignity and it held out some kind of stimulus. Now, this same reminds me of nothing so much as those Normandy churches in the First World War after the German Cavalry decided to bivouac overnight and burn the pews for warmth, and stable their horses in the transepts.[33] The only difference is that there were horse droppings there and now apparently here are dog droppings. But it is an obscene desecration of something that could be used for better purpose. It may be unusable as a working space; it certainly would be usable, as I recommended to the president only recently, as an extension of the Art Gallery in order to accomodate the growing collection of growing sculpture, a very nice kind of environment I might add. The spaces would match the majestic aspirations of our welders. . . .

. . . What is planning in the sense of the priority put upon it for many years, many decades? It is now no longer planning for some accomplished fact, it is really programming a process. It's building complexity through models, employing means of simulation equally technologically complex as the problem itself. It means that we can now avoid the infinite social mayhem created by thoughtless and mindless experiments which had to be proved through use.

This is the most expensive kind of period of technological misuse I have known of in these three decades. People put up anything that comes into their minds at the drop of a telephone receiver, and then wait to see if it works or produces a revolution. We don't have to do that any more; therefore, we can accelerate our redemption in order to match the accelerating doom which other people promise us if we don't follow this path. We have not yet, however, become used to the notion of using sophistication, technologically speaking, with humility of enquiry, morally speaking, as complementary opposites in order to work toward open systems. We want to see something finished, rounded off, and refined by us. This, of course, is in itself ridiculous.

Our programs should actually become programs by prevention, not so much cure. They should prevent the probable and perhaps imminent extinction of humaneness as we now think of it. Shadrach Woods, you know him by name I'm sure, described the people who now are the telephone receiver order taking prima donnas as "Sunday urbanists." They see everything as scenery. The profession, and particularly the architectural schools, which are professional schools dedicated to the design of environments, are particularly vulnerable to this today because they are surrounded by the yapping packs of frustrated, ignorant and greedy which can be roughly described as technophiles or technophobes.

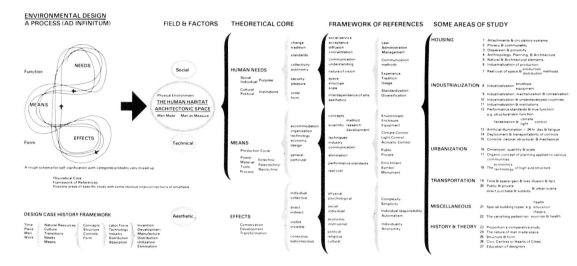

ENVIRONMENTAL DESIGN
A PROCESS (AD INFINITUM)

Function:

NEEDS

MEANS

Form

EFFECTS

A rough schema for self clarification with categories probably very mixed up.

Theoretical Core
Framework of References
Possible areas of specific study with some obvious interconnections of emphasis

DESIGN CASE HISTORY FRAMEWORK

Time	Natural Resources	Concepts	Labor Force	Invention
Place	Culture	Structure	Technology	Development
Men	Transitions	Controls	Industry	Manufacture
Work	Needs	Form	Distribution	Distribution
	Means		Absorption	Utilization
				Elimination

FIELD & FACTORS

Social

Physical Environment
THE HUMAN HABITAT
ARCHITECTONIC SPACE
Man Made   Man as Measure

Technical

Aesthetic

THEORETICAL CORE

HUMAN NEEDS

Social
Individual   Purpose

Cultural
Political   Institutions

change
tradition

standards

collectivity
autonomy

security
pleasure

order
form

MEANS

Production Cycle

Power
Material   Eotechnic
Tools   Paleotechnic
Process   Neotechnic

accommodation
organization
technology
economy
design

general
particular

EFFECTS

Conservation
Development
Transformation

individual
collective

direct
indirect

visible
invisible

conscious
subconscious

FRAMEWORK OF REFERENCES

social service
acceptance
diffusion
concentration

communication
understanding

nature of vision

space
structure
scale
interdependence of arts
aesthetics

Law
Administration
Management

Communication
methods

Experience
Tradition
Usage

Standardization
Diversification

concepts   method
scientific research
development
techniques
industry
communication

elimination

performance standards

real cost

Environment
Enclosure
Equipment

Climate Control
Light Control
Acoustic Control

Public
Private

Enrichment
Symbol
Monument

physical
psychological

social
individual

economic
institutional

political
religious
cultural

Complexity
Simplicity

Individual responsibility
Automatism

Individuality
Anonymity

SOME AREAS OF STUDY

HOUSING

1. Attachments & circulatory systems
2. Privacy & communality
3. Dispersion & proximity
4. Anthropology, Planning, & Architecture
5. Natural & Architectural elements
6. Industrialization of production
7. Real cost of space & production, distribution methods.

INDUSTRIALIZATION 8. Industrialization envelope, equipment
9. Industrialization, mechanization & conservation
10. Industrialization & underdeveloped countries
11. Industrialization & institutions
12. Performance standards & true function e.g. structural skin function, fenestration & climate, light control
13. Artificial illumination – 24 hr day & fatigue
14. Deployment & transportability of controls
15. Controls natural, structural, & mechanical

URBANIZATION 16. Dimension, quantity & scale
17. Organic concept of planning applied to various communities
18. The economics, technology of high size structure

TRANSPORTATION 19. Time & space (gain & loss) illusion & fact
20. Public & private, direct purchase & subsidy & urban scene

MISCELLANEOUS 21. Special building types, e.g. education, health, theatre
22. The vanishing pedestrian: exercise & health

HISTORY & THEORY 23. Proportion a comparative study
24. The nature of man made space
25. Structure & form
26. Civic Centres or Hearts of Cities
27. Education of designers

Curriculum study,
Harvard University
Graduate School of
Design, 1953.

I have the privilege to address you tonight on the evening of May Day and on the eve of an International Conference on "The Professions and the Built Environment."

I am happy to see the word "Environment" used again in the context of the Graduate School of Design. I first applied the term "Environmental Design" to a course of study at the Institute of Design in Chicago in the forties. Soon after Dean William Wurster adopted the same broad definition to his new school in Berkeley (with, I am sure, the blessings of his wife Catherine Bauer). "The College of Environmental Design" then came into being. In the fifties I used the same description for the integrated first year for architects, landscape architects and planners under my direction here at Harvard.

On May Day it seems appropriate, by way of preface, to remind you of earlier revolutionary steps (or evolutionary mutations) in the thorny path of architects and planners, urban designers, landscape architects, et al., soubriquets now somewhat confusing to my mind when arbitrary boundaries of separation between specialists have become smudged in practice. . . .

. . . In the aftermath of the First World War and its devastation in the western world, there followed the frequently completely spontaneous, independent development among pioneers: practical idealists working toward a systematic, programmatic approach to design. Revolutionary changes appeared in architectural thought and action in many countries simultaneously. To quote Gabriel de Mortillet: "Like-working of minds under similar conditions;"[34] or, in the words of Colin Renfrew, ". . . the advance-part in the universal process determined by the very nature of man."[35] Strangers at first, these men established national associations for research. Finally an international organization

From the Gropius Lecture entitled "Institutions, Priorities, and Revolutions," given at the Graduate School of Design, Harvard University, May 1, 1974.

emerged. All these are milestones in the evolution of environmental design and an expression of new aspirations familiar to
you.

For a small group, still living, who had the privilege of working
with the pioneering heroes, sharing in debate, in design and the
writing of the manifestos, those days seem far away. Even here,
when Gropius came to Harvard in the thirties, at the invitation of
Joseph Hudnut, this influential event now seems remote.

The classic base of the Beaux Arts, together with the master
workshop, was challenged, if in a somewhat different manner, by
Le Corbusier and by Walter Gropius. "Facts" were no longer
immutable and were linked to theories. Better theories changed
the facts. Gropius came to Harvard from a unique school of his
making, in which gifted collaborators, faculty and student alike
were encouraged to research and innovate.

Perhaps more vivid in some memories were the meetings during the Second World War, here at Harvard and in New York,
when enforced unemployment gave some of us the necessary
leisure to speculate and plan for the post-war opportunities to
build a better world in our fashion. Equally vivid still are the
international meetings which followed and became an influential
force: the "International Congress of Modern Architecture"
(C.I.A.M.). There were many days of hope then, here and
abroad.

The collective hopes were not realized. Discrepancies between
philosophically based collective intentions and the individual
concern with the immediate present quickly grew into unbridge-
able gulfs. Today I have to confess to a deep dislike for disre-
spect, only matched by my mistrust of uncritical adulation,
shown to heroes of yesterday. I have learned, rather late in life,
that a profession is a process of involvement with principles that
have a longer life than personalities.

I have been lucky enough to learn that the past, the present
and the future (recognizing our new powers of projection) are only
different aspects of a comprehensible, continuous activity with
which an individual may identify himself, plug-in, so to speak,
into the "eternal present," of which Siegfried Giedeon wrote. We
have yet to create a mutual tradition to match earlier, more pro-
tracted periods. The thoughts of vanquished and departed heroes

are still very much alive in a very real way, in spite of the growing turnover in near-heroes or less. You may recall in this connection the early ironic warning of Percy Wyndham-Lewis: "Bury your dead, they are alive!"

Still, many not so famous men continue to be concerned with new purpose and unprecedented problems and continue to ask penetrating questions about the future of urbanizing humanity, in which conservation, perhaps even more than construction, must play a role. Professional responsibilities will surely have to be redefined in the face of new realities.

One of these appears to me probable: progressively larger segments of humanity will continue to live in cities in ever higher densities. A corollary to this seems to be that urbanism has emerged as a vital instrument in human evolution. Yet, at the very moment of this realization, urban man runs the risk of becoming an endangered species without any assistance from mad bombers. We continue to urbanize in the wrong way.

Paradoxically, our high technology has created the sprawling shapelessness of suburbia. Suburbia has polarized the random groups of which it is composed at the very moment when our extended human interdependencies are seen to be inescapable. The "shrinking world" of the League and later the United Nations has been forgotten, or worse, has degenerated into a platitude complacently repeated by isolationist protagonists of many feathers: politicians, professionals and marketeers.

Suddenly, however, the stale cliché has become a disturbing reality. Our world *has* shrunk. The design profession, in the meantime, has become a very private practice, busily serving private satisfactions and vested interests, leaving the tougher problems in the public realm to new protagonists emerging from the expanding ranks of scientists and engineers. The tough new problems are, alas, further bedeviled by a cultural decline into vulgarity, superficiality and anarchy. This new reality will not go away without much work and agony and changes in priorities.

Institutions and practices established earlier have reached a period in which many can be seen to be obsolete. They are no longer susceptible to old remedies, gradual change, violent revolution from within, or war from without. It is unfortunately true that not even the most disciplined professions (among whom I do not number the architects) are immune to the inexorable law that all institutions and "truths" must finally lag behind emerging realities.

Perhaps professional conferences past and present (including tomorrow's) may bring timely reform. Perhaps the all-pervasive powers of conglomerate business will be persuaded by professional eloquence. But as no one seems to be in control of the timetable and of priorities involved, it appears likely that we, at the end of the line, may lose both our technical advantage and our moral strength.

You will, I hope, forgive my temporary pessimism. Priorities of new purpose and new timetables and measures for improving man's condition in the public, collective realm are currently given insufficient attention. Our communicative world is dominated by persuasive arguments for the acquisition of a questionable assortment of goodies. Essentials are too often overlooked. The momentum of inexhaustible, disconnected propaganda, mendacious answers at the drop of a telephone receiver for the affluent and informed, at the push of a button on TV for the deprived and misinformed, have almost replaced thoughtful questions about real needs. Quick, profitable projects for the few have replaced responsibility toward the many. Real estate has become the last frontier.

High technology and much good art are all too often serving contemptible purpose. New and seemingly benevolent media of persuasion are surely more deceptive than those of old tyrannies. The nouveau-riche patronage is largely illiterate and materialist in its demands. The remembered tyrants of the past were, on the contrary, very knowledgeable about the same ends and means for providing pleasures and satisfactions, as were the artists, architects, musicians, poets and other providers at their service. In our time both the patron and all too often the pro cannot even read anything strange or prefer not to, a new form of illiteracy.

In the past courts of peers could apply themselves to most problems at leisure denied to contemporary bureaucracies working fast against imminent change: change, which usually means critical issues without precedent, face to face with innocent or uninformed personnel. To date complexity, for the most part, has been tackled sporadically in disconnected portions. But pieces, no matter how excellently shaped intrinsically, can leave the greater whole untouched.

Today we can, if only partially, assess the successes and failures of the professions as against the remarkable gains in resources and opportunities of our unfolding technological planning era. The hopes formulated remain unfulfilled even in America, only indirectly touched by wars and revolutions. American designers' advantage and promise and attainments are still not the true measure of their potential. Let us by all means praise the few great and the many not so famous men, but at the same time let us ask searching questions about the future of collective effort.

Looking back on the eroding post-war prosperity we can now see that the brief moments of reflection we were granted during the war soon gave way to opportunism. Design and construction were competed for savagely. Rationalizations were easier than rational research. Intriguing forms won over substance and quality. Excellence competed with exhibitionism. Efficiency competed with imagination. Pent-up frustrations in creative people temporarily won over the good intentions. Technical journals celebrated the exceptional while the profession as a whole did what the client wanted, and industry mass-produced miserable housing stuffed with mechanical and electronic gadgets. People and their possessions and extensions have become profligate consumers.

Professionals have become fundamentally submissive to market pressures and indeed are businessmen themselves first, abdicating social responsibility. Professors, often practitioners in disguise, trained assistants, rather than educating new functionaries and encouraging free inquiry. Academies who chose heroes to lead their architectural schools ran the risk of having their students become pale images of the master or apprentices to the status quo elements in the profession. In either case free inquiry by young talent and intelligence was delayed.

It seems to me in retrospect that more was gained by teacher and student alike from research in the sciences without than from the somewhat stereotyped improvisations in the design curricula. Nevertheless, between the world wars the profession did become acquainted with the elegant new geometries which emerged from the hands of mavericks of various callings. Giant spans, trusses, shells, domes, membranes and moldings became accepted new organic structures and forms. By contrast, the eclectic niceties, arbitrary sculptured buildings accompanied by a vast literature of rationalization, became a bore. Yet, in spite of the onrush of new means and ends, the profession seems to be to this day remarkably resistant to change. It is still not research-minded.

Sometime during the war years George Howe, then elected president of the American Society of Planners and Architects (A.S.P.A.), just formed, exorted the members in a speech: ". . . make Master Plans for Master Politicians!"[36] I know he intended to say "Master Statesman." There being none interested even mildly in our deep concern with environmental subject matter, the Association died soon after. Creative men went their separate ways; for the others, business as usual prevailed.

Splendid photographs continue to ennoble less splendid buildings, and extravagant praise and circumspect criticism continue to promote the stylish along with the merely picturesque. To this day the profession seems to be dazzled by potentials of public relations and continues to deliberately design photogenic palaces for humble purposes. . . .

. . . I recall a most memorable and relaxed Bicentennial conference in the forties at Princeton, devoted to a purpose not dissimilar from tomorrow's.[37] Foreigners and Americans met in celebration of survival and in friendly debate. Frank Lloyd Wright spoke to Robert Moses, fresh from parkway triumphs. The cows of the open spaces confronted the cars of suburbia. Alvar Aalto received a gold medal. Mies van der Rohe observed all these goings on with Buddha-like detachment.

Soon, after the genius of Taliesin stood "Broadacre City" on end in "Mile High"; pigeon cots replaced cowstalls. [Robert] Moses continued on his parkway spree. Neither the master of the prairie nor the master of the parkways gave much thought to the consequences of peak traffic which would be aimed at peak reception targets. This knotty question was left to some unnamed authority or divine providence for another day. About the same time Alvar Aalto commented on a rather boring presentation to a M.I.T. jury: "It's all very nice—but where is the tiger?", thus anticipating Exxon by a generation. . . .

. . . Meaningful and comprehensive attempts to rehabilitate

and possibly restructure the urban fabric are still waiting for the essential massive funding by government and new laws at every level to fit the new realities. Any rational environmental action must of course wait for a fundamental change in national will and for the reordering of aspirations.

A noted European critic-professor sang the praises of the car capital of the world, where cars are worn like boots for the most trivial errands, and where no one walks except in sandals on "strips."[38] Los Angeles, on closer inspection, turns out to be the highest density suburban super-cluster with maximized travel time, in the sun, for the affluent. The poor public remains unrecognized. You will recall the closing line in Brecht's "Threepenny Opera": "Die im dunkeln sieht man nicht" (Those in darkness can't be seen).

The "built environment" which faces us still remains threatening: anonymous skyscrapers surrounded by canyons of darkness, dehumanizing slabs standing deep in parking lots; suburbs are thinly disguised as "new towns" (sometimes elegantly custom-tailored). None can convincingly hide the deadly components in the neglected public realm around them. Without community places, without public transportation, without pleasure places requiring no entrance fees, the impoverished public spaces in growing cities reveal our failure.

It seems that for a while yet, many unpublicized but noteworthy intellectual events must compensate for ubiquitous physical failures. Perhaps some conferences will be remembered after many monuments will have been pulled down to make way for more profitable buildings to be occupied by the submissive and the uninformed. The streets will probably stay littered.

At the same time, and in spite of these familiar failures, great things *have* come to pass if only in small quantities. Prototypes of elegance, in project form or realized in association with enlightened patrons and consultants, have evolved and have raised our hopes again. A formidable arsenal of new tools for designers has been added to the old and well-tried. These await proper reorganization and application by responsible decision makers.

Let us face it. While law, medicine and engineering are conspicuously prosperous, architecture is struggling to save what is left of its living and of its professionalism. Fees based on shaky estimates of cost have little meaning for the rank and file, caught in an inflationary spiral. Even the great personal successes among architects may be threatened if their fees for private institutional monuments, on a cost plus basis, paid with now deductible tax dollars, become suddenly few and far between.

John Dyckman, a planner, observed in 1963 that the survival of his profession was also threatened as the rank and file cooled their heels in the corridors of insecure bureaucracies. Perhaps this is better than cooling heels at street corners waiting for unknown clients with muddy purposes? It is hard to decide. What new collaboratives from many disciplines will be in the position to deal with great problems of the public realm, with the help of what powers? "To make Master Plans for even Master Statesmen" is no longer tenable in a changing world. Planning professions must move up into the hierarchy of public power together with form-givers. Perhaps we need a new and comprehensive Department for Environmental Defense.

Evidently environmental design will embrace many not yet defined functions. New organizations will have to face problems of research and programming not yet clearly visible. They will further have to find new yardsticks and measures for complexity, so far not invented. This emergence of a different personnel may be slow and painful and require a caesarian. But symptoms of imminent birth are visible. . . .

. . . A repository of enormous but unused intellectual resources is at our disposal, which dwarf the already visible achievements of technology. It has been there for a considerable time and our knowledge is growing exponentially. The trouble is that the gap between knowledge of the few and ignorance of the many is growing at the same rate. Another greater trouble, as James Edmonds, a physicist, has pointed out, is: ". . . that it is the widespread application of science which has produced the growing crisis. Lack of wisdom, not of knowledge, will be our undoing."[39]

We have enough talented form-givers to join their peers among other talented functionaries, one hopes with humility, renouncing past false claims to leadership for the future. It is out of redeployment of our existing human resources that a new and viable environmental design profession may evolve. My optimistic guess is that the larger part of their activity will be devoted to research. Universities will have to assume this reponsibility in our field.

The Bulletin of the Atomic Scientists, "Science and Public Affairs," is currently asking some searching questions which apply directly to our common purpose: how will the environmental designers communicate to the government their ideas of which resources ought to be funneled into certain types of research? How can we set priorities in any field after an era of plenty? We have the pressure to allocate our resources today, and will have for some time! Caught up in a runaway growth, we are asked suddenly to consider the quality of life.[40]

. . . Professionals can no longer leave decisions on what to build at the mercy of investors nor the location of buildings to developers. You cannot leave the decisions of how to move from place to place to the mercy of the automobile industry, oil interests or highway lobbies. In short, you can no longer abdicate your professional responsibilities toward public purpose under pressure of vested interests.

Having at least partially and unconsciously abdicated, we have lost our sensibility. We have lost contact with nature, while building our man-made environment too fast. In the process we lost our sense of wonder and compassion for other living things. We have invaded the natural with our endless machinery. We have learned to think of all things as "hardware," which can be produced, appropriately enough (in modern jargon), by "soft-ware." We have lost our dignity and have lost sight of our true selves in our acquisitive drive for possessions. We seem to live behind screened picture windows, blinding headlights and impersonal license plates. . . .

. . . The main body of professionals engaged in diverse day-to-day tasks still remains, by training or temperament, unsuited for systematic research or creative prototyping. The survival of many professions is in jeopardy because to a large extent the purposes for which they were originally established and the means which they have learned to employ have become suddenly and simultaneously obsolete. The next stages of comprehensive design, requiring many and probably most unexpected kinds of protagonists, will no doubt be slow and painful for all well-established professions. Perhaps least damage will be done to both humanity itself and other living things if man finds a new urban symbiosis.

This is a time of troubled transition from one epoch to another in the midst of crises born of disillusionment and expressed in cynicism and opportunism, in protest and violence against existing order. We all share much of the prevailing disillusionment with the present, but some have a vision of environments in the future which will provide greater freedoms instead of the mendacious rationalization and unfulfilled promises of the mass-cultures manufactured by corporation powers. John Kenneth Galbraith, the most quoted Harvard professor, in his last book *Economics and Public Purpose*, says: "The need for remedial action to align the use of power with the public interest can no longer be escaped. And such remedial action ceases to be exceptional but becomes, instead, an intrinsic need."[41]

The young generation of today *is* the caretaker of the future. It will *perhaps* build in good time institutions corresponding to new realities, able to adjust to the new ecology and to the new aspirations of humanity everywhere.

I want to quote Gunnar Myrdal, the great Swedish economist, from *Against the Stream*. He learned, in spite of dissatisfaction with things in present day America, to love this country. So have I. He writes:

At this particular juncture the generation preparing to take over responsibility for this country certainly needs to be ahead of its time. If the nation is not to go downhill into reaction and disaster, the many serious mistakes in policies, committed by the older generation, must not be perpetuated . . . This is how I feel when, as now, I am speaking to a youthful audience.[42]

And finally I want to read my favorite quotation from a generous friend and mentor whom you are memorializing in these lectures from a letter to students written in January 1964:

For whatever profession, your inner devotion to the tasks you have set yourself must be so deep that you can never be deflected from your aim. However often the thread may be torn out of your hands, you must develop patience to wind it up again and again. Act as if

you were going to live forever and cast your plans way ahead. By
this I mean that you must feel responsible without time limita-
tions, and the consideration whether you may or may not be
around to see the results should never enter your thoughts. If your
contribution has been vital, there will always be somebody to pick
up where you left off, and that will be your claim to immortality.[43]

During my lifetime, entirely and precisely of this century, I
have witnessed a series of events in my chosen field announcing
profound change: I have seen eclectic architecture respectfully
buried. I have observed, with some pleasure, that the mythical
beast "International Style" did not rise from the ashes of World
War II. I have seen with deep chagrin the anarchic, fashionable
western shapes confront the dull paraphernalia of western commerce in cities, and even in remote islands, all over the world.
Embassies, universities, hospitals, housing, offices, and factories—western buildings are placed without rhyme or reason
and become interlopers in cultures, places, economies, and cli-
mates unable to accommodate them.

I hope that our "shape-makers" will, like old soldiers or the
cheshire cat, fade away along with their "creations." I hope to
see these replaced by "problem-solvers." I hope to see an "International Space Agency" established for here below. I continue to
believe that artistic independence is not a myth. I am therefore
confident that the beauty of nature and art will join the elegance
of science in a new amalgam. And I feel that once this is
achieved, this new excellence will be recognized.

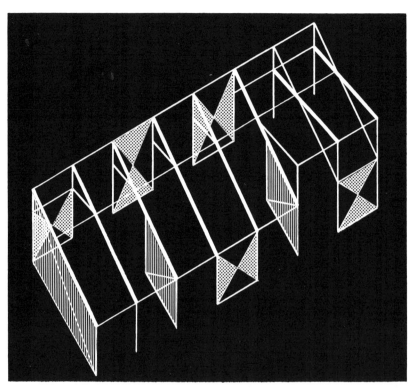

Wilkinson House, Truro,
Massachusetts, 1954.
Structural study.

It's difficult to look back to the thirties across fifty years and three thousand miles with any accuracy. I hope that the inaccuracies and omissions will be forgiven by old friends and colleagues who are still alive. This was the most rewarding decade of a long life. I had found my avocation and my dear wife in the late twenties and had become an Englishman. The painful aftermath of the Russian Revolution had receded, and the future appeared bright. I found myself in the middle of another revolution intellectually absorbing and emotionally moving: a political and cultural ferment among scientists, writers and artists. All professionals, whom I had the privilege to meet, were involved somehow in reconstruction, reform, and literally rebuilding another continent where I visited frequently my surviving relatives who had settled in Germany and France. Removed from the constraints of war, ideas and activities spilled across national boundaries, and the pressing needs of reconstruction, of rebuilding the physical destruction, made the new ideas into new forms. These new expressions of purpose made an enormous impact on my generation. Exciting novel prototypes, settlement buildings, industrial products appeared in profusion. New technologies fired the imagination of professionals in planning, architecture and design. New professional associations suddenly became international in intent and character.

England, where I felt most at home, joined in this movement later than the Continent. The young designers in England inevitably emulated an older generation already active in Germany, France and in the U.S.A. Some of the designers of my generation visited Europe and saw the works of the European pioneers. An English chapter of C.I.A.M. (International Congress of Modern Architecture), MARS (Modern Architecture Research Society),

From a manuscript, "Thinking About the Thirties" prepared for *The Architectural Review*; published as "An Explosive Revolution," *The Architectural Review*, November 1979.

was formed in the beginning of the thirties and was followed soon by other professional associations dedicated to the purpose of redefining professional responsibility, technical competence and social purpose. Purposes without precedent were to be met by means without reference to history. Form was assumed to follow function.

Le Corbusier, [Walter] Gropius, [Marcel] Breuer, [Erich] Mendelsohn, Naum Gabo and Berthold Lubetkin, came to England. Architectural exhibitions in Scandinavia, Germany, France and Holland were visited by designers of every nationality and a common cause came to be recognized internationally. The similarities in expression, it seems to me in retrospect, were the direct result of a shared knowledge in the techniques available and their application to clearly recognized needs and purposes. Variants in available resources and climatic and social conditions did not override the basic affinities. But, the perverse suggestion that there was a conscious effort to establish an "International Style" in the twenties and thirties now seems nonsense.

Conventional, eclectic "style," established by "eclectic" architects, was challenged by designers interested in problem analysis, technical research, and enquiry into social and environmental factors. Men of talent, in the words of Eric Gill, "assumed beauty to be able to look after herself."[44] Programmes and models emerged as new tools for designers. Architects presented projects to prospective clients and found the latter receptive. In short, an explosive revolution: the redeployment and regrouping of a profession for exciting new ventures. A surprising number of protagonists of the modern movement in architecture achieved success without any formal, that is, (conventional), training in design. Gropius's Bauhaus was dedicated to the development of a new kind of school which would fit new conditions and use a non-historical perspective. Subsequent events proved this to be effective and influential throughout the world.

These personal assessments of the architectural environment should perhaps be supplemented by an equally personal account of how I came to be engaged in it. It was almost accidental.

On very slender credentials, by pure luck, I was commissioned by Lord Waring of Waring & Gillow to design a "Modern Furnishings Exhibition" and direct a Department of "Modern Art" at his establishment on Oxford Street. My designs, developed with a talented group of younger men on my staff, were produced by the Waring and Gillow Factory. This was staffed by a remarkable group of elderly cabinet makers of great knowledge and skill. They, to my surprise, welcomed the change from a tradition reaching back to the eighteenth century, and they became enthusiastic collaborators. I never learned so much so fast: how things were put together out of what. In addition the Wilton Carpet Factory produced our rug designs. I was able to purchase the etceteras of furnishings from many sources on the Continent as well as in England.

The Exhibition, completed within one year with Paul Follot doing his own section in it, was an instant success, and I became an instant designer. Wells Coates came to England from Japan via engineering in Canada and combined technical precision with elegant form. Lubetkin came soon after and established the group office "Tecton" with other brilliant, socially oriented designers. Both became my great friends and unconscious mentors. None of us, it seemed, sought commissions. They simply came. We applied ourselves to any problem which was offered irrespective of scale. We must have had most reasonable clients, for they never interfered, but encouraged and supported us.

Early in the thirties, Wells Coates, Raymond McGrath and I were commissioned to design the offices and studios of the BBC's new building on Portland Place. Mary Adams, director of Educational Television of BBC organized a series on architecture. Both were well received by a growing public concern for the modern movement.

Throughout the late twenties and the thirties it was my good fortune to have made friends with the talented men of science: Desmond Bernal, Hyman Levy, Alfred Bacharach, Julian Huxley; with the artists: Henry Moore, Ben Nicholson, John Skeaping, Barbara Hepworth, John Piper, Eric Gill; with the engineers: Owen Williams, Ove Arup, to name a few. As a result, my architectural "proselytizing" became well rounded. Helped by a certain facility with words, I was invited to advise many groups as were Lubetkin and Coates. Professor Charles Reilley in Liverpool, Leslie Martin in Hull, Frank Yerbury, director of the Architectural Association in London, invited us to lecture and address symposia held in their schools. I was invited to address the RIBA and to my surprise was elected a Fellow soon after. Among points stressed then I recall protesting the categorization of designers as city planners, architects, landscape architects, industrial designers, or whatever. We found this too confining and in fact tackled any problem offered on its merit. The wide spectrum stretched from hardware, to fixtures, to furnishing interiors, to housing, to architecture and landscaping, to city planning. Our public relations were extended through exhibitions and successes in open competitions. Many components designed for special projects became manufactured products and gained wide distribution. The 1934 Dorland Hall Exhibition, "British Industrial Art in Relation to the Home," was particularly successful.

My brief partnership with Erich Mendelsohn after he fled from Nazism was invaluable. I learned architectural organization and design of some complexity including both schematic presentation and meticulous detailing. Our winning the Bexhill Pavilion competition provided me with essential experience in work supervision. This whole project proved a great success and commanded great attention.

Throughout the "thirties" our work was well received in the architectural press. Everything we designed was extensively covered. The *Architectural Review* and the *Architects' Journal* in particular remained loyal friends and supporters. My debt to de Cronin Hastings, James Richards, Morton Shand, John Betjeman, is inestimable.

Our relatively small offices were largely influential through our method of work. Possibly they helped to accelerate the demise of "successful" practitioners who designed large buildings on a very small scale and left their completion, with minimal architect-supervision, to the surveyors and contractors. The interiors were left to clients and their hired hands. Our method of designing was based on team work: principal, assistants, engineers, consultants and quantity surveyor participated from the conception of a project to its completion down to the last component detail. I am heavily in debt to my engineer Felix Samuely and surveyor Cyril Sweett, whose loyalty and patience never wavered. Many of my collaborators in the early Waring and Gillow work, Eastland Fortey, John Early, who followed me into architectural practice with

Whitfield Lewis, and Berkin Howard I remember most fondly. Their support, patience, continuous enthusiasm and hard work has never been forgotten. Their talents and skills surpassed anything I did. Everything we designed was conceived in three dimensions as a structure-space through which we could move comfortably in our minds until it could be presented rationally in graphics and models. Every detail was painstakingly developed. Some were actually invented. Nothing was too trivial to receive full attention.

I still have recurring pleasure in remembering the work of my friends and colleagues: Lubetkin's and Tecton's Zoo pavilions, Finsbury Housing, some modest elegant country houses; Connell, Ward, and Lucas's houses of fine technical invention; Wells Coates's BBC sound effects studio, Cresta Shops, Prince's Gate Flats, Brighton Flats, and Sun House projects.

I enjoyed my own Cambridge Theater Auditorium, which offered a focus on the stage by lighting; Gilbey's Offices, which defeated air born and structure conducted noise; I.C.I. Blakely Laboratories, which provided multi-floor organization, flexibility, and climate control.

Leaving our house "Bentley" in Sussex was painful. It fitted and grew into the landscape. Its occupants could all enjoy amenity and privacy. I still think it was beautiful.

Chermayeff's direct involvement with academic life did not begin until 1942 except for the unsuccessful attempt to organize the European Mediterranean Academy in the thirties. In the early days, however, he participated in an informal educational program which contributed significantly to the development of modernism in Britain. The use of media—the printed word, radio, and, later, television—was critical because the populist aspect of modernist ideas required wide public understanding and support which could be cultivated only through the mass audience. Innumerable exhibitions also contributed to the cause, since they served to unite designers and manufacturers with the mass buyer, and they were events which received enormous publicity. The numerous new professional alliances and organizations also served purposes of self-education among others. Many of Chermayeff's earliest writings originated as talks and discussions centered around such organizations.

Early talks and discussions, such as the one given at the London decorating firm of Heal and Sons in 1931 (A New Spirit and Idealism), set forth the tenets of the modern movement within Chermayeff's rudimentary outlook. Created by "problem solving" rather than "from some preconceived idea of what the finished work should appear to be," modernism was said to transcend style as a spontaneous expression of a "new spirit." This would counter the snobbism of the elite, who could still "demand luxuries, expressed in the old tradition of handicraft." The work of modernist architects and designers would offer the common person an alternative to copying the rich. The modernists would translate the new materials and technology to achieve "new standards of beauty in itself, without meaningless borrowing of embellishments from other times, and without striving after preciousness and exclusiveness which can stimulate snobbism."

Changing political and economic realities played an important formative role in the development of Chermayeff's outlook. He argues that the "economic necessities of our time" could not be recognized adequately through "simplification of some classic form"; and that Britain could not fulfill "its economic function in the world of today by virtue of its achievement in the past." He comments on a "retrospective stupor" in relation to the "modern world movement," which the Parliamentary proposals to adjust tariffs or the gold standard would not address. Britain's "retrospective stupor" did seem to have in fact curtailed the introduction of modernism and probably contributed to both the force of its introduction and the strength of the opposition. The introduction of modernism occurred first in the marketplace. Academia remained largely unaffected until the end of the thirties, when new economic and political crises decimated the previous flurry of commercial practice and the modernists began to shift their interests toward the schools of architecture.

Participating in the change in emphasis, Chermayeff visited a number of schools by the end of the decade, sometimes in the company of professional colleagues such as Wells Coates or political sympathizers such as J. Desmond Bernal. Chermayeff spoke at Liverpool, Hull, the LCC School, and the Architectural Association, among others. The schools were seen as an important key to breaking modernist impasses. In 1939 at the Architectural Association, Chermayeff points out that architectural education can be as critical to defining professional purpose as professional purpose can be to defining architectural education (Training for What?). He discusses the lack of initiative and innovation within the schools and the general lack of "standards." The earliest arguments surface for the integration of the study of architecture with other related disciplines such as town planning, building technology, and visual arts. His argument vaguely follows that of the Bauhaus model but enlarges the scope of concern. He shows a developing interest in pedagogy as well as purpose, and he takes notice of some of the contradictions between architectural "training" and professional "function" in a society in which most building is erected for profit, with the percentage of architect-designed building remaining almost negligible. Ultimately, he sees that changes in both the schools and professional practice are inextricably tied to political change.

Chermayeff's earlier ideas on education were elaborated immediately after his immigration to the United States. During his stay in California in 1941, he developed several proposals for new architectural curricula at Stanford University and at the University of California at Berkeley (Contemporary Planning, Architecture, Design and Design Education). He mentions the pioneer modernist curricula in the eastern schools such as the Armour Institute, Columbia University, and Harvard University and the greater possibilities for continuing reforms in the United States than in Europe, which was already engulfed in war. Enthusiastic about the potential for innovation in the western United States, because there were few established schools of architecture and unprecedented design and planning initiatives such as the great hydroelectric projects, he felt that perhaps the West could escape the resistance to educational reform which he found elsewhere. He associated the resistance with "an obsolete philosophy of materialism inherited from the nineteenth century, which segregated architecture and the arts from the so-called 'realities' of everyday life" abetted by "entrenched academicism and boom-time practitioners." And he points to a theoretical lineage from Geddes, Sullivan, Wright, Le Corbusier, and Gropius as precursors to the new wave.

For Chermayeff, the potential of the West never materialized, and it was at Brooklyn College in 1942 and later at the Institute of Design in Chicago that his first academic opportunities were realized. In his inaugural address upon his appointment as president of the Institute of Design (Education for Modern Design), given in 1947 at the juncture of the Brooklyn and Chicago experiences, he assesses some of the philosophical and institutional limitations of many modernist precepts. He notes the lack of resolution between forces of tradition and revolution within American culture in relation to everything from social patterns to product design and states that the activity of design should be informed consciously by the increasingly complex larger world without retrenchment into "fine art." And he voices a warning about the danger of substituting technique for imagination or purpose.

By 1950, the Chermayeff curriculum had been well established in Chicago (Architecture at the Chicago Institute of Design). In summarizing the intentions, he gives ample recognition to the Bauhaus origins of the Institute programs, but his goal was to build on them rather than to preserve them. The "American cultural climate" is credited with having influenced many of the changes, yet this climate is already moving in a hostile direction. Chermayeff takes notice of the growing "new romanticism" which was to contribute to the fate of the early modern movement in the United States with its "propagandists" who "continue to stress the formal aspects of design while making fashionable and over-simplified statements about function at the most primitive, pre-industrial level."

The Chermayeff ideal attempted to grasp the problems of function as well as form, and he sought to establish within the Chicago curriculum the attitude that "architectural activity carries with it social responsibility." Architecture and environmental design became the primary focus of the curriculum, built upon the "Foundation Course" of more abstract visual and social principles, with the latter much more highly developed than under Moholy-Nagy. The advanced architectural design courses distinguished between the "functional, the typical, anonymous and economic" building and the "ceremonial, ritualistic, individual, specialized or unique"—thereby insuring that both categories were fully addressed. Other revealing distinctions were made, for example, between research and "pseudo-research"—alluding to the perceived demise of the evolution of modernist education. The student was "not to study the master, but the principles and factors the master himself had to study," in contrast to Beaux Arts pedagogy.

The innovation at Chicago was terminated by Chermayeff's removal to MIT and Harvard, and it was not until 1954 that he again had occasion to implement a broad new curriculum when he restructured the Harvard first-year program and departed from the long-standing Gropius sequence. An important component of the new program was the Environmental Design Seminar, which was integrated with the design studio, and like the studio was required not only of architecture students but students in planning and landscape architecture. The 1954 transcript from the seminar, then in its infancy, is an interesting interlude which records discussion concerning pedagogy (Environmental Design Seminar). Chermayeff begins, however, with a sharp, eloquent statement about Philip Johnson's performance on the previous evening, when Johnson delivered his widely-publicized talk, "The Seven Crutches of Modern Architecture." Though Chermayeff quickly dismissed Johnson as a "palace architect," there were points of agreement between them. Still, their shared concerns on the shortcomings of the contemporary state of the modern movement had, by then, taken fundamentally different political directions. After discussion of Johnson's talk, the seminar shifted to the new program. Chermayeff addresses a number of

issues, including the inefficiency of the traditional design studio for-
mat and the great untapped potential for collective student "research" which could produce results far more significant than the
simple sum of the individual design projects.

During the following several years, the gap widened between
Chermayeff's position on architectural pedagogy and the directions
taken by academic programs in architecture across the United
States, which continued the gradual reconstitution from Beaux Arts
to modern. His attempts at Harvard to create an advanced gradu-
ate-level curriculum met with disappointing resistance, encouraged
by xenophobic "professionalism"; and at Brooklyn, where he had
begun his academic career in 1942, he found retrenchment upon his
return in 1957 (Modes and Manners in Art). He warned that his
pioneering "design" program, the first in the country to replace "fine
arts" within a liberal arts college, suffered the danger of joining the
new "Beaux Arts"—a premature academicism. He found that his
fundamental "design" inquiry was replaced by skillful but superficial
pattern-making, limited by a false sense of professionalism. It was
undoubtedly apparent that in the schools of architecture, perhaps
even more than in the profession, reform had been usurped by a new
aestheticism; and in general, by the mid-fifties, whatever role the
modern movement had played as a catalyst for institutional change
had lost its momentum.

Chermayeff's own pursuit of an advanced curriculum and research
in architecture at Harvard in many ways isolated him further from
mainstream educational priorities. Those priorities were in evidence
at the 1964 Association of Collegiate Schools of Architecture
Teacher Seminar at Cranbrook shortly after his move to Yale (Architectural Condition). On this eve of the riots in Watts—that great
signal of the beginnings of the recent American malaise—
Chermayeff's social priorities in relation to the theme of "history,
theory, and criticism" stood apart from the others. The problem of
history underlay much of the seminar—a reaction to alleged post-
Bauhaus dilution of the importance of history in architectural curricula. While Chermayeff agreed on the need for restoration of
history, he saw it in terms of "new appropriate ways of presenting
history as process" rather than static study of periods and styles,
cleansed of all but aesthetic considerations.

Chermayeff was most forceful in his growing concern about the relationship between academic programs and the professional marketplace, which he felt tended to dominate educational values and priorities. This situation was heightened undoubtedly by the values engendered by the enormous prosperity of the sixties. He points out that the practitioners who control architectural curricula also use the schools as a source for cheap labor—at the same time tending to see their own academic salaries as a "subsidy" while "waiting to get sufficient earning power to practice." He recognized that this closed circle could only compromise the development of a serious academic discipline.

In 1967, Chermayeff argues that schools should be "by definition scholarly, exploratory, adventurous, philosophical . . ." instead of "exactly the opposite" (Design as Catalyst). Rather than being an end product in itself, limited to the realm of a marketable skill, design education was seen as a "catalyst" for other inquiry within the university. It could bring together many disciplines which share a common concern about the environment, especially at the graduate level. It was a conception which he had already applied to his Masters class at Yale. Essential to this conception was an "elimination of the myth of artistic separateness" and elimination of the artificial distinctions between the design disciplines which had evolved in the previous three decades—industrial design, architecture, landscape architecture, city planning, et al., all of which dealt in the contradictions of "self-appointed generalists" organized into "splinter groups of specialty." Beneath his argument was the conception that "creative action" should no longer be "confined to the traditional frames of the 'Fine Arts' " but recognized as the essential ingredient for "any individual at work."

In his 1973 acceptance speech for the Royal Canadian Institute of Architects gold medal in education he further alludes to the importance of "research" as an academic activity in architecture ("Obviously Something New Is Abroad"). He acknowledges, however, that "it is as yet not a term which can be properly applied to this activity in architecture." He expresses his continuing interest in "problems without precedent" and admits to remaining "an amateur of sorts during a period of growth of specialization." He pleads for a reaffirmation of the public responsibilities of those who enjoy professional privilege and their "camp followers in academe." But with inimitable style, he admits that they, "together with the excesses of fashion, have their uses, of course, as irritants." Finally, in 1978 he places an ultimate hope for resolution of the moral dilemmas of the profession in the university rather than the marketplace (Values and Ethics). He warns that "in the final analysis, we are running out of time . . . we must put some limits to gradualism; some actions cannot brook delay."

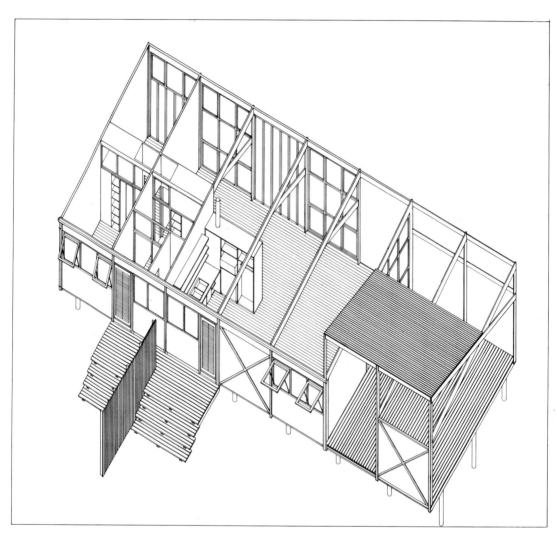

Wilkinson House, Truro,
Massachusetts, 1954.

Out of the twentieth century—our times and their own particular conditions—there is growing a new spirit and idealism. The only works and their creators who can be classified within the term "modern" are those who have contributed to the expression of this spirit and those ideals which are peculiarly of our time.

This establishes that the work in any period tradition, excellent though such work may be, is not relevant or significant to modernism.

That such a new spirit exists can be observed in all the changes which are taking place around us, whether in the realms of science, economics or politics. Constant experiments in new methods establish beyond a doubt, even to the most sceptical die-hard, that new minds are being brought to bear on old and new problems alike with ever-increasing understanding and success.

These minds have been produced in this age all over the globe by the concerted influence and pressure of new conditions. They have created, in different countries with no direct social intercourse, at identical, or nearly identical, times, theories and practices in structure and arts which have a common denominator. Spontaneous desires for expression have resulted in works measurable by a common standard.

These modern creations came into being in spite of obstructions and without being self-conscious contributions to this or that "ism," such and such a style. They do not come under any category other than that of "modern" in its true sense: expressing the contemporary spirit and achievement. All things in their time may have been modern.

All thinking people obviously realize that the twentieth century is but another stage in evolution. We do not claim a moral superiority, however more advantageously we may be equipped today for creative effort. On the contrary, we must live up to our

From a lecture, "A New Spirit and Idealism," given at Heal and Sons, London, October 26, 1931; first published in *The Architects' Journal*, November 4, 1937.

predecessors' tradition of creating. The craftsmen of other days realized that this was the tradition of art.

Mr. Aldous Huxley wrote a short time ago that tradition is the next best substitute for talent.[1] Modesty would verge on stupidity if we believed ourselves to be unable to progress. This age cannot be satisfied to copy where conditions demand new things without precedent.

Measured by time, we are not far removed from our predecessors. However we are not merely just distinguishable from the men of the nineteenth century; we are divided by the barrier of the Great War, and the changes it has brought about.

The post-war period can be described as the beginning of the age of applied science. Its various aspects have been developed and made appreciable and measurable by every member of the public. This development and application of science to all things to be encountered in the walks of everyday life is developing the consciousness of man and stimulating a more varied and wider demand on industrial processes to minister to his needs.

Exchange of ideas through easier international communication has established in everyone's mind, on his own particular scale, the need for and immediate solution of problems of work and leisure; the fulfilment of a desire for comfort and hygiene. The continuous combination of these factors has stimulated achievement towards aesthetic expression in terms of economic and accessible productions. This developed consciousness of man, and its increasing curiosity as to means of achievement, has stimulated invention. Increasingly subtle, we are getting a greater profusion of new materials. These, in their turn, demand new forms for expressing them.

Conversely, the new type of creative mind stimulates, by its demands, the discovery of new processes and fresh technique. To make these accessible, man is being superseded in his average inaccuracy by machines in rationalized production in industry. These machines, which are accurate and fast, are mass-producing components of structure and all commodities which are rapidly raising the general standard of living.

These new implements of creation are emanating from different brains and are being controlled by different hands from those

which in other times dealt with superstition, extreme individualism and vanities. Rich patrons of course still demand luxuries,
expressed in the old tradition of handicraft.

If I may reiterate, therefore, the forces within this age have
produced new talent and new channels for its expression. We
cannot deny the existence of a movement all round us which is
daily finding greater scope and is gathering force with its growth.

Seen in architecture, in the interior equipment of public institutions and private dwellings, in advertising, painting, sculpture, literature and in every convenience that civilization is
bringing nearer to all, these forces are finally being accepted as
something which, perhaps only in its infancy in this country, can
nevertheless, not be overlooked, or worse still, pigeonholed
under some ridiculous label.

Those who would see the significance of modern work must see
it as an expression of sanity, consciousness, and mental and
physical hygiene and in terms of usefulness primarily. Through
architects and designers these have achieved new standards of
beauty, without the meaningless borrowing of embellishments
from other times, and without striving after preciousness and
exclusiveness, which can only stimulate snobbism.

New forms resulting from the solution of new problems are
arrived at through the process of solving and not from some preconceived idea of what the finished work should appear to be.

The designer of today, no matter what his speciality, must fulfil
the requirements of all the wider demands made on him. However, while having to be a conscious, cultured man and technical
exponent, he has a third and most important function: that of
selector. This quality of selection is the undefinable quality of
taste of the artist. There are usually several equally efficient
solutions of a problem. A selection has to be made. Therefore,
the designer is an aesthetic arbiter. The principal factor arising
out of all these forces which give the impulse to modern creation
is a general sense of organic unity of our times.

The following bring down to a few simple terms or definitions,
the expression of these beliefs in all modern design: (a) fitness for
purpose, i.e., materials for a purpose and not for effect; (b) form
and colour are of a thing and not on it; (c) decoration as such is
redundant; directness of expression is essential to fuller under-

standing; (d) simplicity is essential in a scientific age of complexities, if we are to retain our sanity.

The new art of simplicity, as I see it, will in fact produce such things and make them accessible to the average man's home: there it will relieve the variety, which is itself becoming monotonous of ingenious machinery, travel, advertising and pleasure, and their accompanying noise. We cannot escape from it even in our private lives.

To turn to interior equipment particularly, we have arrived at a point where all these considerations converge in one plain indication, which is that the furniture for today and tomorrow must be strong, cheap and mass-produced, of good, simple and machine-indicated design. To serve the special and peculiar needs of our time a new style is evolving, a new furnishing "period" is opening before our very eyes. Small, simple, hygienic pieces are needed, and few of them. Today, there is no room for furniture that does not fulfil some real function in a way that needs least attention and work.

Parallel with these changes has been a growing respect for the machine on the part of designers and on the part of the public. They like machinery. Perhaps subconsciously they appreciate the beauty of it. Machines are a part of their everyday life.

The old designers of furniture, fabrics and fittings were antagonistic to machinery or shy of it. It was supposed to be at war with craftsmanship. The result of their attitude was that machinery did without designers, and its ghastly products ran amok over the face of the land. This encouraged the designers to stage the various period revivals and the arts and crafts movement. All this is coming to an end. Modern designers are embracing machinery as a heaven-sent opportunity to develop and multiply good design.

On the continent, furniture of simple beauty and complete efficiency is mass-produced in standard forms by machinery. It enjoys enormous sales, and these in turn have effected further economies, so that the German, Czech and Scandinavian artisan can furnish completely, and in the best taste, very cheaply indeed. The modern aesthetic is therefore understood and established abroad. The position in England is one of transition.

In England, to a greater extent than anywhere else, the middle classes copy the rich. When the rich collected antiques, a demand sprang up among their followers for the sham antique. Now that every magazine and newspaper bears evidence that people of wealth have been converted to the modern aesthetic, the proletariat are turning as well.

Perhaps there is less sheer emulation this time and a clearer view of the practical issues involved. There remains, however, the same risk that in answer to their demand they will be fobbed off with wrong-headed imitations.

We have obviously not yet achieved the final form and are only on the road to a simple direct art. We are now passing through experiments between the designers, trades, draftsmen, available machinery.

The crazes for a change which pickled and petrified oak, and limed it, forcing on old things the indignity of some grisly ritual of exhumation and vandalism, and then, latterly, the illiterate manufacturer's fashion which has merely dressed old forms in new clothes, borrowing decorative motifs from all sources regardless of artistic or functional merit, have produced a procession of Elgin marbles dressed in top hats and petticoats, all marked down as bargains.

I should like to go farther and even say that to my mind, modern creation cannot be achieved any better through elimination than by additions. We are creating nothing by simplification of some classic form, adapting it to the economic necessities of our time. Those who believe that this can lead anywhere are making a vicious circle of evolution.

England seems to be in particular danger of not fulfilling its economic function in the work of today, by virtue of its achievement in the past. It should be justly proud, but not to the lengths of falling into a retrospective stupor. Unless we participate in the modern world movement and create appropriately, imposition of tariffs or going off the gold standard will not avail.

"Modernism" has been exploited since the war like a milliner's fashion. That such significant arts as design should be allowed to deteriorate and lose its significance through lack of understanding is unthinkable. Even if some ingenious charlatan in Paris persuades women back into bustles, let us, at all costs, not go back to Egyptian railway stations and Gothic petrol pumps.

Fabric designed for L.
Anton Maix, New York,
1955.

The title which was given to me for this talk is "Training for What?" One might equally say "What Training?"—it comes to the same thing. It is a question of which came first, the hen or the egg, and I propose to take the last first. I imagine that the Architectural Association School goes back to about the same beginnings as most schools, and these educational establishments, these seminaries for the training of the sons of gentlemen, had, I imagine, one definite guiding principle: their primary aim was to produce wage-earners. That meant, roughly speaking, conforming to usage, continuing a known tradition of craftsmanship and type and design, in fact, a drawing-board technique which explains the rag-tag ends of classicism which still stick. It meant concentrating on the production of design which was safe and which would sell well.

This good behavior, this politeness, this safety, this acceptance of the *status quo* resulted in the production over many years in all architectural schools of the average. The aim was to produce a good average standard all round, and conformity to the accepted principles of design rather than encourage individual brilliance or any freedom for individual curiosity or inventiveness. In spite of that, it can be observed that all these various establishments which were, so I believe, striving to achieve this end, were quite prepared to cash in on any student who was tough enough or independent enough to survive and to make a spectacular success in after-life; in fact, the spectacular and exceptional success was probably the most effective and at the same time the most misleading advertisement for the system of the school.

As I see it, the machinery, and therefore all the elements in that machinery—the various cogs of the controlling body, the staff, and so on—by preference tended to be average and steady and

From a lecture, "The Architectural Student: Training for What?", given at the Architectural Association, London, May 23, 1939; published in *Focus 4*, Summer 1939.

safe, which as far as I can see roughly means middle-aged. Education was not experimental, and in this preservation of safety and this taking of the easiest line, the line of least resistance, the production of the readily assimilated product, the educational system as such became crystallised a very long time ago. All that crystallisation really means a lack of fluidity, an inflexibility. The enormous social changes outside, however, have demanded change. They demand and, in fact, presuppose an enormous flexibility on the part of any student, and this flexibility, this suppleness, is, as far as I can see, both physiologically and intellectually the attribute of youth. It is this essential gap between the middle-aged structure and the youthful student today, who is aware of the impact of the educational and architectural, and those aims and aspirations which the young student has.

This question of awareness and intelligence must, I think, mean to any students who have an intelligent contribution to make, whether it be scientific, technical or artistic, that it is quite impossible, to learn while the school or system of education in which it is operating is, so to speak, a watertight compartment removed from realities of the outside world, while it is still carrying on with something which no longer has validity.

That is particularly marked, of course, today, when we are right in the middle of a transition stage. The student, aware of this transition, aware of the impact of the outside world, whether it be cultural, physiological, technical, scientific or anything else, is becoming daily more and more aware of the limits which this empirical, traditional, educational system possesses. To recapitulate by analysis: there are first of all the economic limits. The students spend five or six years in the school and then go out into the world, and something or other is supposed to be guaranteed. Secondly, we have academicism, caution, gradualism, the fag end of the devotion to styles. The machinery, in fact, is completely inflexible, whereas the material is becoming more and more supple. How are the two things to be reconciled?

I can only make a guess at it. I know very little about education and the structure of a school and the difficulties of making the machinery operative, but there are some obvious suggestions to be made. The first one, which may not appear to be immediately relevant, is this. As far as I know, anyone today can go to an architectural school, sign on the dotted line, pay his fees, and say, "I want to be an architect." It seems to me that in this state of emergency in which not only the world but architecture as part of that organic whole is in a state of crisis, it is absolutely essential to make sure in the first place that those who enter this very exacting profession have, at any rate, some small talent for it. In the second place, it seems expedient to make sure that the numbers are limited at a moment when society is unwilling or unable to assimilate them all. I would, therefore, suggest that it is extremely important that any architectural school should have, as part of its machinery of entry, a questionnaire: a test paper which would be prepared not by architects but by psychologists and scientists in order to see whether the potential architect, who is probably choosing the profession of architecture just as casually as a few years ago he might have chosen the army or the church, is in fact fitted to go through a long period of education with the necessary devotion to an exacting subject, apart from any personal talent which can only be developed and not inculcated in the process.

Secondly, it seems to me that this word "architecture" should be dropped. It is high time that it was dropped. We need some other general term such as "design," which would cover town planning, construction building in the architectural sense, if you like, as apart from engineering industrial design, the study of materials, and so on. Again, and here I may be suggesting something which already exists, there seems to me a very great need for the introduction of new subjects into the curriculum of any design school. The things which immediately occur to me are geography, geology, sociology, and sciences which are concerned with the movements of peoples and the development of rational groups. Then there would be landscape gardening as one of the architectural elements with which one builds, the study of all forms and form generally, texture, and colour, the study of contemporary development seen in historical perspective, sculpture, painting, typography and layout, photography and nature itself.

You may be in the fortunate position of having that kind of education, but it seems to me that a Henry Moore or a Ben Nicholson could give infinitely more to the potential architect in terms of their insight and knowledge and activity than perhaps an architect could give. I should also like to see practical construction as part of the curriculum of any school and an examination of the properties of materials. I would not limit construction to known forms of construction in building, but would also include abstract constructivism, constructions without purpose, a sense of form and enclosure in space. All this has been more clearly stated by [Walter] Gropius, and it seems to me to have had, and still to have, validity as the basis for an architectural training. We have had Gropius here and we know his teaching. We have lately heard Frank Lloyd Wright and we know roughly his philosophy. There must be something valid for us here to be drawn from both those sources—perhaps adjusted and tempered, but in any case used. That is roughly, as I see it, the problem of what planning should be, and I am sorry if it is vague and nebulous and generalised.

Now let us come to the egg or the hen, or whatever it is this title of "Training for What?" It seems to me that only a stable society could give an answer to that particular question. If this were an accomplished fact, the question would not arise. This is not only a problem of training but a question of function. Generally, architects who have anything to contribute at all are constantly asserting and protesting rather than building and designing. On the other hand, there are their less qualified colleagues who dine out while some of you, if you are fortunate enough, will be able to design for them in their absence, and as Frank Lloyd Wright would say, "And how!" We might easily deduce from this that there was something very wrong with architecture and the function of architects generally and their position in society. This question of training is part of the whole cogent problem, namely, that of what you are going to do as architects. We know the percentage of building which has not been designed for use as a principal factor is large. The amount of building which is designed primarily for a specific use is relatively small. Most buildings are erected for profit, whether the return is taken in terms of dividend on earth or in terms of dividend in heaven by producing monuments or memorials. A memorial form is a little too extravagant and unreal, as far as I am concerned at any rate, to be regarded as a living architecture.

Assuming for the moment that this motive of profit is to be accepted and that capitalism should continue as a system, at least we know that it does not work at the moment. It cannot assimilate you potential architects when you leave your school into the pattern of its own making, no matter what your qualifications may be. Even the privileged children of the wealthy, those connected with the ruling classes, the very well conducted and polite, the sycophantic, will probably find that the only architecture that this system has to offer is the architecture of barracks and shelters, at any rate so far as the immediate future is concerned. I look keenly forward to the first shelter with a slightly Georgian flavour!

You may be able in that way to eke out a living propping up basements—quite a number of you are doing it now—for some years; but that, if it is a job at all, is a job for engineers. Meanwhile, engineers, commercial people and politicians will be doing your job for you as they are doing it today all over the face of England—and that face is too small to stand this treatment for very much longer! You will probably have an opportunity of adding to the range of memorials. This question of appeasement of conscience is no longer a private matter between a man and his confessor; it is another opportunity for advertisement, and you will, no doubt, be invited, should you wish to accept the invitation, to design very expensive but obsolete hospitals, schools and housing in terms of glory to some alderman or other. You will also through them provide for posterity a mausoleum for the system which is asking you at the moment to pay fees for the privilege of being able to function. That will go on until you tear these mausoleums down yourselves. There seems every probability, of course, that in the interim there will be a war which will save you some of that trouble, but unless you do something about it—and it seems to me your immediate task—the gap will soon be filled and you will be providing further memorials after the next war, memorials to that "backbone of the nation," "the people who pulled you through in the end."

Some of you may be like myself and not want to have anything to do with all that, but the opportunities, unless you make them yourselves, are going to be extremely few and far between. These opportunities require making unceasingly. The condition of society in which society as a whole has a sense of responsibility in design has to be brought into being by students who believe in those principles in which you believe. It has to be done by students not as ephemeral artists, not as pseudo-architects, but as far as I can see, as political and social-minded technicians, so that you may bring about a society which will accept design in terms of its own position in time and with full reference to its technical knowledge and resources.

All this has already been far better stated by people like Walter Gropius and Frank Lloyd Wright, and I do not wish to enlarge in my own way upon it; but it is only with persistence that this condition in which you can function as architects may be brought about. No matter what training you receive at the moment, unless you bring about that condition you will have wasted your time, and it seems to be obvious that such a conception of design and its proper position in society cannot be developed in the water-tight compartment of a school which retreats from realities and practises the art of archaeology or any other equally remote thing. Equally, it cannot be confined to specialists; it must be shared with the outside world. Perhaps if this putting of your own house in order—which is your immediate problem—goes on it will have very valuable repercussions outside, and will be invaluable for giving a further impetus to a movement which, although at the moment it seems to be imperceptible, is actually like a terrific landslide gradually on its way.

In conclusion, I should like to say that "Training for What?" seems to me to require only one answer: to create a condition, some day, as soon as possible, with all the means in our power, in which we can practice that thing which at the moment we are only talking about rather loosely as architecture, and which, as far as I can see, is at the moment not worthy of that name.

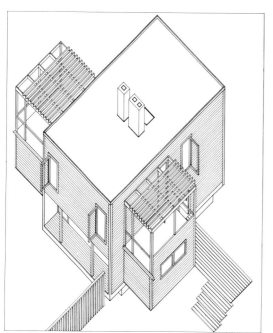 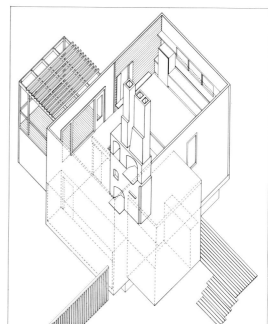

O'Connor House, Truro,
Massachusetts, 1956.

As a result of the various conflicts in Europe and in the Western Hemisphere, there exists a serious conflict of mind within the profession of practicing designers everywhere, concerned with our contemporary environment, whether they be planners, housing specialists, architects, or designers of building equipment, and a great confusion as to the purposes and potentialities of these in the mind of the community as a whole.

The conflict in the professional minds is due to lack of adjustment of the majority, to rapid social, scientific, technical and artistic change, and the inability to grasp that the term "architecture" in its obsolete academic sense is completely inadequate to cover the broader and more complex pattern of modern society. It is due, further, to the inability of the majority to grasp the concept of organic unity of all design problems and their relationship to other sciences, humanities and the arts.

The confusion in the mind of the community as a whole is due to the prevalence of an obsolete philosophy of materialism inherited from the nineteenth century which segregated architecture and the arts from the so-called "realities" of everyday life. This segregation has been, for the most part, deliberately preserved by entrenched academicism and boom-time practitioners. It has further been intensified by blind specialization with its lack of exchange of ideas and close cooperation between specialists as well as between those and the general public.

At this time the United States appear to offer the only possible situation in which a serious effort can still be made on a sufficient scale to avert the complete disintegration of a valid concept of these problems. It is the only place where the gains made by the pioneers of the new movement from Patrick Geddes, [Louis]

From a manuscript, "A Summary of Report on Contemporary Planning, Architecture, Design, and Design Education" (1942), written as part of recommendations prepared for the University of California at Berkeley and Stanford University.

Sullivan, Frank Lloyd Wright, Le Corbusier, and [Walter] Gropius, to many other workers in this field today can be consolidated.

Here the idea of a planned architecture may be invested with a richer and fuller meaning and where it is possible to prepare a body of professionals able to see their task in the proper perspective and equipped to deal with the vast problems which lie ahead.

This is possible only because the U.S. may remain outside the main stream of war, but also because there exists here a very large number of people of vision and integrity among administrators, professionals, students, and others.

Valid contemporary philosophy of design is being developed in centers such as: Harvard and the M.I.T. in Boston, Columbia University and Pratt Institute in New York, and the Armour Institute in Chicago.[2] These few centers are, however, not sufficient for the main purpose.

In the West there exists nothing comparable to the above. Yet it is precisely in the West that the situation demands the establishment of an enlightened and active design center from which both ideas and personnel will emanate to deal with the design problems presented by the Grand Coulee and Central Valley Projects.

It is within the framework of a specific program which has to create from the ground up a whole new environment, which embraces all aspects of design from individual units and their equipment to whole communities, that a complete and convincing demonstration of new principles can be made.

The prevailing chaos appears to be in danger of persisting, because, with few exceptions, the scattered and apparently unrelated examples of good planning and design illustrate only separate facets of the problem. Due to lack of understanding or deliberate resistance, the new architecture is either compromised or confined to theory. At best, however complete individual solutions may be in themselves, their real meaning and quality is obscured by the physical confusion and ugliness of their surroundings.

The Coulee and Central Valley Reclamation Projects, on the other hand, offer a unique opportunity for an uncompromised demonstration, if this task is well prepared for. The need for the establishment of an educational center, capable of producing a personnel and material for this work, is urgent if the usual inadequacy and waste, born of haste and expediency, are to be avoided.

Such a body as is envisaged here could start its function through the establishment of a nucleus of a single director attached to an existing college or university.

This nucleus would grow quite organically as the work developed from preliminary survey through analysis of special problems to a program of synthesis and design. It would be the aim to correlate all the factors involved, social, technical, artistic, and economic. The work on these problems would produce a wealth of material upon which an educational system for planning, architecture, and design, could quite naturally be built.

The program of work would embrace not only the training of fully qualified technicians, but would include such work as is necessary to obtain the sympathetic cooperation of industry, labor, and the general public, as well as to provide material for the education of children in all grades—elementary and high schools—where little or no information or interest is given now on precisely these problems.

It is in this latter educational range, perhaps to a greater extent than even in a reactionary university, that the archaic forms of design in all its branches is complacently accepted, and architecture in particular has ceased to be regarded as a living art. The majority of human material which reaches the most enlightened educators is either uninformed or conditioned by an obsolete attitude towards design, both at home and in the schools. Unless, therefore, an attempt is made to prepare a body of public opinion aware of the issues involved, the task of putting into operation an intelligent planning and design program will remain extremely difficult.

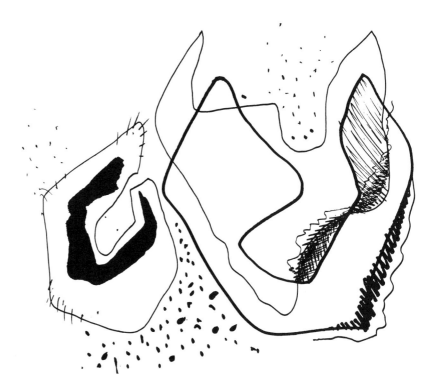

"Living Fragments,"
drawing, 1956.
Reproduced by
lithograph (17" × 22"),
1974.

The impact of the industrial revolution on the nineteenth century, with the tremendous acceleration of scientific and technological development, and the expansion of economic frontiers, was of almost explosive character and force. So rapid was the material development that its social implication and future technical and scientific possibilities were only grasped by a very few and by them only vaguely.

In our special field of visual arts, where through the intrusion of many intangibles the issues are not so clear cut, full realization of potentials came even more slowly than in science and technology, and adjustments were made far more timidly. Matters affecting tastes, habits and associations born of experience at a pre-industrial era die hard, because, as in all other experiences less precisely measurable than technical and scientific fact, we find it more comfortable to preserve an illusion of security than to adjust ourselves to the needs of a harsher reality. Much of the chaos and uncertainty of the nineteenth century has spilled over into our own century.

Some of the symptoms of the disease may be easily identified:

(1) Our prevailing inability to see clearly the true nature of industrial means of production and apply these to traditional things—houses, furnishings—with the same freedom with which we have done it to non-traditional things—automobile, airplane, telephone, and refrigerator.

(2) Inability to see clearly the profound changes in social structure, in family and in the individual, which are the result of the industrial development and the consequent changes in the desires and vision of contemporary man exposed to these new experiences.

(3) Timidity in developing systems of thought and tools with

From the inaugural address, "Education for Modern Design," Chicago Institute of Design, February 4, 1947; published in the *College Art Journal*, Spring 1947.

which to shape our environment more nearly to coincide with contemporary civilized man's genuine needs.

Too many of us are content to put things which we perceive through our visual senses into water tight compartments; on the one hand those which we have become accustomed to regard as "art" compensate for those which we regard as material tools. The latter we are apt to consider different from the former in terms of pleasure content. We have gotten into the habit of accepting ugliness as an inevitable attribute of many such things. Our towns and houses bear constant witness to this complacency and inertia. All too often we apply art as embroidery or disguise to the seamy side of our environment—a weak palliative at best, which leaves untouched the essential inadequacy beneath.

The need to develop a clear cut philosophy upon which to base a program for action with which to counteract these inadequacies, was recognized and the first steps were taken as far back as the turn of the century. Since then the work of development has continued and today we can safely say has reached a point of acceptance through its undeniable record of solid achievement. This guarantees its further growth and enrichment in civilized society.

Some of the premises upon which this philosophy rests may be perhaps sketched in this necessarily brief talk:

(1) That contemporary society with industrial means of production has to employ entirely new tools, instruments, for living consonant with our needs, spiritual, intellectual and material. The *needs* of an industrial society are in many respects without precedent and certainly the means at our disposal with which to meet the needs have been extended and enriched immeasurably.

(2) To produce the type of creative personality which we require, to use the means at our disposal and to understand clearly the purpose which the product has to serve, we need in turn a process of education which will develop a broad imaginativeness as well as a specialized skill which will be operative within a society using modern industrial means of production. A process of education, in short, which will make the designer state the problem in terms of "what for?" as well as "how?"

(3) To accept, in fact, as part of the designer's responsibility,

the formulation of a clear statement of the problem in the first place. The transition which we are making from backward looking pre-industrial thought and action to forward looking thought and action essential to our survival and happiness requires a restatement of each problem, without sentimentality, complacency or timidity perhaps to a greater extent than ever before in man's history.

(4) To emphasize, particularly in the U.S.A., which has without question reached technologically the highest point in industrial production, the responsibility of the designer whose design will be mass produced by thousands, tens or hundreds of thousands whether it be a piece of furniture or an advertising layout as compared to the very limited production of an eighteenth century chair maker.

(5) To break down the obsolete barriers between the so-called "fine and applied" arts and to present to the student the integrated and organic whole which is "visual experience," in its fullest and healthiest sense.

(6) Acquaintance with basic elements, which go to the making of all forms, color, texture, light, volume, size, and so on, their relationship to each other and to the total environment, is equally essential for the purposes of a painter, sculptor, industrial designer, typographer, or architect. All students of the Institute in the first place are introduced to and experiment with these basic elements and from them proceed to the discovery and mastery of techniques which are the tools and media with which to articulate these elements, to integrate them and through which these elements achieve their significance in the content of a completed work.

The media for visual expression in our time are not only the traditional media of drawing, painting, construction using traditional tools and materials but they also include light, still and moving photographs, new graphic techniques and an ever increasing range of new processes and scientifically produced materials with physical properties widely differing from natural materials and offering new possibilities of form making.

Students at the Institute have the opportunity not only to develop knowledge and control of such tried and proven traditional materials and methods but to implement this basic knowledge with research and invention into entirely new materials and techniques.

In short, we believe that the Institute's work is to produce creative designers who combine imaginativeness with technical skill and educators able to transfer these in their turn to others within the framework of a highly developed industrial society.

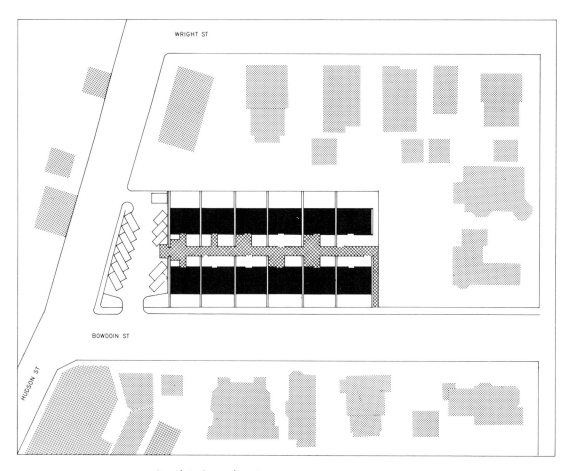

Bowdoin Street housing
proposal, Cambridge,
Massachusetts, 1956.

ARCHITECTURE AT THE CHICAGO INSTITUTE OF DESIGN

The educational philosophy of the Institute of Design continues in the tradition of the principles originally established by Walter Gropius and his collaborators in the Bauhaus. These are too well-known to require restatement here. [Laszlo] Moholy-Nagy's imaginative and inventive development of the basic training problem together with his Chicago collaborators, Grygor Kepes and Robert Wolff in particular, has been clearly stated in Moholy's *New Vision, Vision in Motion* and Kepes's *Language of Vision*.

In the last few years those principles have been strengthened and the teaching method made more effective by closer recognition of the highly disciplined methods of Joseph Albers in Black Mountain College. Further, both had to be adapted to the requirements of a larger school which the Institute of Design has become since Moholy's premature death. At the same time they were adapted to a more professional objective than intended by the Black Mountain College liberal curriculum and the original New Bauhaus of Moholy-Nagy. These later developments owe much of their success to the work of Hugo Weber and Richard Koppe, in particular, in the first stages of reorganization and to Buckminster Fuller during the past year.

For various reasons, mostly products of circumstances or war rather than intention, architecture at the school under Moholy-Nagy never became the major design field in spite of excellent work done by such gifted architects as George F. Keck, Ralph Rapson and Robert Tague. They participated at various times in the school work, but did not achieve a complete curriculum for professional training. The last two years have been largely devoted to the development of a basic course as groundwork for advanced courses in the field of architecture.

The new curriculum and the architectural philosophy underly-

From an article, "Architecture at the Chicago Institute of Design," published in *L'Architecture d'Aujourd'hui*, February 1950.

ing it, obviously has been influenced profoundly by the American cultural climate of uninhibited curiosity and willingness to try out the new as well as the predominant technical excellence and abundance.

Unfortunately and paradoxically, the transition period from the nineteenth century historical eclecticism has had a chapter added in America, in which the discoveries, experiments and fundamental principles of the pioneers in search of a new architectural order have become the clichés of new romanticism. With few exceptions the propagandists for the modern movement continue to stress the formal aspects of design while making fashionable and over-simplified statements about function at the most primitive, pre-industrial and pre-scientific level.

The defenders of the "modern movement" in the U.S.A. appear particularly susceptible to the inroads that science and technology are making into a traditionally "artistic" field. But the predominant character of architecture is picturesque and pseudo-humanist and so-called modern architecture continues to apply pre-scientific principles to planning and employ pre-industrial construction techniques.

The qualitative disparity between the "modern house" enclosure and its mechanical equipment, such as the refrigerator and the radio, is conspicuous enough, but the disparity between the most completely equipped modern house and the automobile and the airplane is glaring. In more specialized circumstances, such as a hospital, the disparity between overall standards applied to building enclosure when measured against medical and scientific processes within becomes accentuated to the point of the incredible.

This and similar evidence suggests that in our present stage architectural activity has been perverted and degraded. At such an historic period, the revaluation of educational responsibility in the field of architecture becomes crucial and the fundamental revisions in the total structure of professional training essential.

The Institute is making an attempt to achieve this. We are setting up as our immediate objects:

1. *The restatement of principles:* The uninhibited measuring of every phase of existing practice against the yardstick of scientific

knowledge, technical efficiency and plastic sensibility of the highest order of which we are capable.

2. The establishment in the student's mind that *architectural activity* carries with it social responsibility and the ethics of comprehensively grasped new order beyond the lesser requirements of technical and business efficiency.

In the U.S. at this time, there is an indication that the training of architects is following the prevailing pattern of more and more education for more and more students. The result is too often more and more of less and less. The conventional curriculum is inadequate in time and content for the task and it is becoming apparent that the economy cannot employ the vast number of "degree" and "license" holders supposedly adequately trained for their exacting work in a contemporary industrial society.

The Institute has therefore established as one of its goals the training of an elite of designers of *"effective controls of man's physical environment,"* capable of "thinking and designing comprehensively, an emerging synthesis of artist, inventor, mechanic, objective economist and evolutionary strategist" in the words of Buckminster Fuller.

Perhaps the uniqueness of the Institute of Design's curriculum lies in the extent and thoroughness of its foundation course and the completeness of its technical workshop equipment. In this course, which is required of all students irrespective of their specialization later and which lasts three semesters, very little is design in the conventional, technical sense.

The contents of these three semesters may be summarized as:

1. *Experiment:* free manipulation of media, materials and tools without looking to finished results, in the course of which the students develop a visual vocabulary, recognition of order underlying all structure and an imaginative approach to design.

2. *Control:* mastery of materials and technique. A wider range of visual perception and order is developed through a progressively sharpened and extended technical discipline.

3. *Application:* comprehensive thinking, understanding of design purpose, and the development of scientific method of problem analysis as applied to tools capable of extending man's control of environment. Architectural, product and communica-

tion design are studied simultaneously. In the process the student sees the interrelationship between the various fields and becomes increasingly space and purpose conscious.

Throughout, the process is more important than the end result. Work is judged in relation to individual and group effort without competitive grading at any stage.

Parallel to the workshop experiments the student attends lectures in science, sociology, economics and history to enable him to establish firmly the meaning of design in the total social context.

It is of interest to note that in spite of the length of time devoted to the foundation course, three semesters out of the total ten, the technical quality of professional performance at the more advanced stages is actually strengthened and compares more than favorably with the work of conventional schools, all doubts to the contrary.

In the third semester architectural design study falls under two heads for seminar discussion: first, analysis of man's biological and social functions and his reaction to physical environment; and second, composition with architectural elements both constructed and existing in nature. The latter continues the free manipulation of plastic elements and materials pursued in the first year and carries over the principles established into the realm of man—object—space relationships of architecture.

Following the foundation course, study begins immediately of structure (construction), climate control (heating and ventilation), illumination control (natural and artificial light), sound control (acoustics), hygiene (physical and mental well-being) in a natural sequence following previous analysis. These become basic factors in planning and design thereafter and yardsticks against which the functional aspects of design are measured.

The extreme technical-mechanical specialization developed in these subjects has meant the virtual writing of our own syllabi in the course of work in the school. It has received little or no help at the time of writing from specialist technicians. It is part of our program to produce a new professional, capable of presenting basic, functional factors underlying design, rather than the remedial or compromising post-facto services now rendered by engineer-technicians to the designer-artist.

Exercises in design begin with the simplest dwelling required to meet specific conditions in a variety of frameworks of reference for comparative purposes and progressively move on to the design of essential elements in a contemporary industrial community.

By restricting the scope of design experiment in this manner, the student can work in the familiar framework of his actual experience in connection with which he has acquired genuine value-judgments. The student avoids in the process the common pitfalls of pseudo-research into unfamiliar and often unnecessarily technically complicated situations. He does however establish in the process basic principles for all design problems and develops method and discipline in procedure.

The students' solutions to various problems grow out of ascertainable factors and their own sensibilities. The student does not study the master but the principles and factors the master himself had to study.

Throughout the advanced studies the school differentiates between two major categories of architectural design to meet our needs today. On the one hand there is the functional, the typical, anonymous and economic; on the other, what might be conveniently described as the ceremonial, the ritualistic, individual, specialized or unique structure.

The analytical study of "attached dwelling" completed this year and partially illustrated in this issue belong to the category of inquiry into anonymous or type shelter for families with children in an urban or suburban situation. The study, conducted under Gerhard Kallmann, endeavored to establish a system of standardized building elements, parallel to the development of flexibility or plan and space character.

Unfortunately, the studies completed under Buckminster Fuller which included the production of visual demonstrations of his "Energetic Geometry" and a new structural and interior space control developed from these principles are not at this time ready for publication.

Realizing that no one school can be all things to all men, the Institute of Design's architectural department has as its principal objective the education of designers capable of assisting the essential revolution in building construction and planning techniques.

Thus our specialized activity might be described under these heads: the provision of a firm framework to enable our students to continue specialized advanced work intelligently at institutions possessing special advantages of equipment or personnel; to train designers particularly equipped to participate in the development of contemporary, anonymous shelter and the industrial production of structural and other elements for these at the highest technical level; to develop and make available to others educational principles, methods and instruments which will extend man's advantage by any means at our disposal.

At the time of writing the high standard of performance by Institute of Design students at the Graduate School of Design at Harvard suggests that our basic work is on the right lines. This year the architectural department will have had its first fifth-year period, and it is our declared intention to extend this training into a program of advanced research into standards and into industrial mass-production of building elements in the form of a post-graduate school of research centre.

In this connection and following the participation of Buckminster Fuller in 1949 in the school's program. Konrad Wachsmann will join the staff in 1950 on a special project with advanced students.

Lest the foregoing description of advanced work in architecture be misconstrued as having a predominately technical bias it should be restated that throughout we are concerned with the development of well integrated functionaries in the field as a whole.

To extend opportunities for the display of painting and sculpture as essential furnishings of private and public architecture is, of course, an admirable goal. It is not, however, enough. We are here concerned with the more fundamental esthetic principles which enable the artist-architect to produce architectonic space-sculpture and painting (Max Bill, Fernand Leger) and the architect-artist the plasticly complete enclosure (Le Corbusier, Mies van der Rohe, Frank Lloyd Wright).

It is clearly part of our educational responsibility to create a

climate within which social purpose, technical means and pleasure content are organic parts or, in other words, an activity
which will embrace and correlate into a single field of activity the
work of artist-scientist-technician. On this principle, which is an
integral part of our program, we are collaborating with Frederick
Kiesler. He will come also to the school in 1950 for the continuation of studies in "correalism" which he has been pursuing for so
many years.

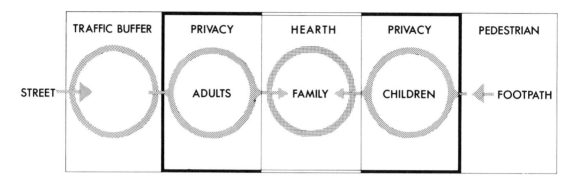

Bowdoin Street housing
proposal, Cambridge,
Massachusetts, 1956.
House organization
study.

Let's start our discussion. There are two possible subjects.

I know that you all rather enjoyed the theatre of Mr. Johnson.[3] I think he is very good theatre, and I think he did exactly the right thing in what one should do at a public lecture in a university, by making it exciting, interesting and gay instead of possibly being more accurate and extremely dull. If you want to discuss this lecture for a brief while without making too much of a postmortem out of it I will be very happy to do this.

To begin with we could list his seven or eight crutches (of architecture), which were a little bit specious because he omitted two of his own: history, economy, structure, function, comfort, controls, clients. Is that it? The ones that he omitted are that his architecture is palace architecture, which means that the use of expensive materials and so on make necessarily a great architecture, and the other is that there is only one kind of client. He is the man that you know . . . the friend client. These particularly are an over simplification, and, really, he did it quite deliberately.

Everyone can do only one thing when they lecture about philosophy, so to speak, and that is that they project their own beliefs. Projection of a belief is fundamentally a declaration of a special prejudice. When you become a great philosopher your prejudice simply embraces more things and has a more logical structure within its own chosen environment. So I do not see any reason for decrying the fact that he has prejudices, but when he talks for instance, about cheapness (economy) as having nothing to do with architecture he simply is speaking as a palace architect. When he talks about the client, he is obviously thinking of the man with blue eyes, with whom he drinks, who commissioned him to do something.

But this is not at all the architecture of the industrial era, and I would prefer not to call it the seven crutches of architecture. I

From a discussion in the course "Environmental Design Seminar," Graduate School of Design, Harvard University, December 17, 1954.

would rather call it the seven facets of architecture, because there is no single architecture in our time. As a matter of fact, in an industrial society, as we have discussed here frequently, there is an invisible client whom you never see at all, who has no special site, because you don't know the site. It cannot in any case be the dramatic, national site of an acropolis, nor the dramatic, special, private preserve of a Taliesin west. Most of our architecture simply has to be squeezed in between other architecture in urban centres and so on. This cannot be ignored, however much Johnson may feel disinterested about it.

So, it simply begs the question to say that the client is always right. The client is not always right and nobody in their senses would suggest that the man who is designing for an industrial society, where most clients are anonymous, would design prototypes and parts for production. You do not even know who is going to use them. You speak about the average man. So he stands completely condemned where we don't even think of the client, but we hope that our image of the client will finally make clients in accordance with that image. We are on Johnson's side there, but it is rubbish to talk about it that way.

As for the economy, it is no good denying the fact that we have got to produce an architecture of economy in our time, because we are distributing architecture to a larger number of consumers than ever before in history. And as the proportionate ration between poverty and riches is a completely quantitative one, there is no question at all that as we go on industrializing and humanizing and universalizing we shall have more and more cheap architecture, not less and less at all. So to beg this question and say it is not the architectural issue is ridiculous. It is also rather a pity, if I may suggest it, to go to the lengths and take this beautiful walk through the acropolis up to the Parthenon, and approach the Master in his Taliesin west temple. This was really extremely well done. I think there is a story in the description of an amazingly sensitive man, of a gifted, sensitive man. Very few people can draw such vivid images with such conviction, but I don't think architecture resides entirely there. I think we could go in to some very dark street and I think we could extract from that darkness somewhere any number of examples of the private, the invisible, and the unknown great architecture. Greatness does not reside in drama. Greatness can also be part of simplicity, intimacy, privacy and so on. And architecture is, I think, where you find it.

What about this question of structure? Johnson attacks Buckminster Fuller because he provides us with a kind of engineering in which it is difficult to place a door. Johnson uses door with a capital D, and therefore it has very special significance. I think that is his privilege. But if there were not the Fullers, not thinking about doors but thinking about structure, Mr. Johnson would have nothing to work with. It is really due to the fact that a great number of people spent really concentrated time developing rolled steel joists that he can now work with very elegant framework in the manner of Mies. But he could not have arrived at that. It really took an awful lot of private devotion to the subject matter of structure and principles of structure of that kind, and welding in the later stage, in order to make it possible for Mr. Johnson to make elegant joints instead of using a lot of cleats and bolts and so on. So again, we have to give due where due is due. To merely wipe off other people's interest is just as ridiculous as it is to do anything else of that kind of dogmatic exclusiveness.

I really do sympathize with him on another subject. The whole business of the photogenic presentation of trivia is almost destroying our sense of balance and judgment. Every dog kennel now is so magnificently rationalized and photographed that we can fill untold pages of magazines with thousands more pages of advertising, with negligible rubbish. The pretty picture is always taken for that fact and I think most of us are acquainted with architecture through photographs now. But this is not a substitute for architecture of course, and he is quite right in pointing this out. . . .

STUDENT: What do you think of this kind of comparative study of architecture, studying plans and projects of things which have never been built?

CHERMAYEFF: When we speak of the physical experience of architecture these are of things which are actually built. When something really exists the true test of its architectural validity is to go and see it, walk through it, touch it, smell it, turn your back on it, turn around and get the hell out of it, creep up on it again, and in other words experience it in the true sense because it already exists. It is not enough to evaluate it through the very limited mono-focal view of a camera, pre-selected for you from points of great advantage by someone who probably doesn't share your particular sensibilities. On the other hand, I think it is equally true to say that sometimes the thing which is unbuilt is of much greater significance than the thing which is built. There is no question at all that the prototypes, which were drawn but never built, are often very much more important than the accomplished fact.

Johnson is, I imagine, a very disciplined disciple and collaborator with his master, Mies van der Rohe, on the Seagram skyscraper in New York, which has just been given to them. And I will tell you in a moment the story of how they got it.

The thing that one hopes is that *le cercle est bouclé*, or that history has completed itself because the first projects for the *true* skyscraper were drawn long before they were built. . . . For a long time in history, the high rise building, say of Chicago and New York, had not found the idiom of the skyscraper because they were really nothing but the continuing sandwiching of a known kind of space and fenestration and so. Suddenly the Chicago school, as you know, through [Louis] Sullivan, principally, [Daniel] Burnham and [John] Root, and [William le Baron] Jenny, discovered that within this multiplication, vertical multiplication, lay new rhythms, new possibilities. But they were not so clearly understood, as a matter of fact, by the people who were involved in the buildings as by the people who were watching history. The men across the channel, the Gropiuses and the Le Corbusiers and the Mieses understood what was happening in Chicago, understood much more clearly what was happening there than the people who were engaged in getting the apartment block up, or the mocked-up building of a Pirie Scott. They saw the consequences more clearly because they were more didactic. If you remember Mies designed a wonderful skyscraper, the cantilever, with a sort of undulating front, roughly of three sort of amorphous cylinders arising around the core cylinder of elevators.[4] I am just hoping—I don't know of course—that this will have been built on Park Avenue, because then the whole history of the understanding of skyscrapers will have been completed. The master will have come home. Really the notion of the cantilever was never exploited here. We haven't got any skyscrapers of that kind and it is high time we had. The first thing that the others did was to put the columns inside the slabs so that the curtain wall could be a continuous curtain wall and so on. No, the projects are very often more important than the reality. . . .

[In reference to Johnson's own house], most people suspected that I made the remark about "fancy seeing a house in which you take the garbage out of the front door."[5] I say this, in reservation, because there is a general notion that such problems can always be ignored, and as we all do it, I don't think there is any particular reason for not saying that this is the measure, but it does seem somewhat illogical.

The idea of function and comfort is something you don't start with, but on the other hand you don't neglect it. Johnson, himself, doesn't neglect it. His glass box is extremely comfortable, very well heated and very well controlled. . . . We were talking of course in a private club of people who believed in modern architecture, that is to say, of architecture in accordance with a desire, appetites, and need of the time, so we know that eclectic architecture is not a very contributory kind of thing.

I am in disagreement with him because he left so many prejudices quite definitely unexplained, but I am in agreement with him on so many other things. . . . I think his particular attachment to the grandeur of [H. H.] Richardson does the great man somewhat of an injustice. Sever Hall is not one of his best buildings. It is one of his worst, and Johnson knows that just as well as I do. I don't think there is any particular glory between the intersection of the roof slope and the wall, but it is rather well proportioned as everything that he did was. I think another point arises out of the fact that he was very sensitive to what he was working with. All his stone buildings and his brick buildings are Romanesque in character. They are massive masonry with perforations, and the perforations are therefore obvious. That is what his architecture is about—mass perforated in depth. At that point one can see the perforations, positive and negative. This is a good test of whether it works or not and I think it does. Either as dark holes in daytime or as light holes in darkness—it is really like a positive/negative exchange. They work very well within his own idiom.

Now I want to change the subject. I just want to clarify for ourselves a procedural logic which would help you to gain your own personal ends in the project you are starting. I think it is extremely important to start to define any problem, regardless of its dimension, in some kind of clear way and to recognize at least those parts of the problem which are unequivocal. If you remember, in talking to groups of you over your models, which you were sanding (and I hope you are all through now as there is nothing more boring), how does one start organizing a complex inhabited by three groups of people? By groups, we mean groups of people divided into three different types of dwellings or residences. It seems to me perfectly clear that I would have to rationalize the position of each group as far as I was able. Whether I was right or wrong, I would still have to have a rationale. And if I had that rationale, I would have to have another one which would be so equally convincing that it would make me hesitate between the two, and I would be faced with a choice. Whatever method I adopt, whatever solution I adopt, I would need to say in the first place, "where should group A be" in the logic of the situation; "where should group B be" in the logic of the situation; and "where should group C be" in the logic of the situation? And this is simply a question of placement in an empty but quite large site—the relation of the environment to each group.

This would be, to me at least, a first step of an essential kind and all else would follow. This step seems to me to be unequivocally demanding of clarification. That's where I start. But a lot of you have immediately plunged into the architecture, presumably because of your hunger for self-expression and so on, by saying "what can I do with the block? Supposing I did this or this or this?" But these questions are jumping the gun with a vengeance because, again, variety, which this kind of displacement of your little individual cell produces, is the consequence of other events taking place, previous to that. You may not want variety. You may be more creative in solving more radically basic questions with a solution where more variety would be damaging rather than contributory. You would try and simplify and calm. In other words, I don't think you can come to decisions where taste or choice can operate until you know your whole story. I think the story cannot be written in this kind of haphazard way. You can't just suddenly start with an invention and then build around this invention a series of situations which would fit the invention. The purpose is to get an invention which would fit the situation.

So that I want you to bear with all your instructors during all those first exploratory stages and control your very natural anxiety to give this some kind of personal flavor, to arrive at a solution which you call "architecture." I think it would be very much better for you to set up the problem in a manner which would give you, because you are working in groups, the accomplishment of "research." I am saying this in absolute seriousness. The only advantage of being amidst research activities and resources such as libraries, information, and above all manpower, is that these are resources which you cannot have alone. Research tasks require this tremendous cooperative action. That is why research is done in universities or in great industries, and why the kind of thing that we are thinking about can only be accelerated in our processes of research and discovery, which will be valuable to each one of you if you do exploit your collective advantage. This is the whole base of working in groups. And as we are trying to extract from this collective advantage certain principles and methods, if we can stay with this impersonality as long as we possibly can, we shall know at the end of this semester. After that you will be on your own because you will know the picture and will be able to deal personally with the results of your common effort.

What can we then do in logic of this situation? Suppose that we went to an architect now and said we commission you to do this. Will you do a preliminary research on it? How much will it cost? He is going to work five weeks, with three people, and even assuming that they are no more skilled than you, still command 2 dollars an hour. This research, therefore, in terms of what you have to spend (and indeed you wouldn't be able to get 2 dollar labor), would in the end be a tremendously costly operation. So, let's squeeze everything we can out of our situation here.

I would say that among our fourteen groups you ought to get the possible variants so that we can all look at things which do not correspond to our personal taste but do correspond to the physical possibilities. I think on one side we should press, as far as the program permits, for the minimal amount of building and the maximum amount of open space, and at the other end we should press, within the limits again, of the logic of the situation, for a very dense coverage and great intimacy, and so on. Then we need all the intermediary stages. I want you to be conscious of this process because this is the only way that we are going to learn, all of us, three times as much. I believe that when we finally look at fourteen different versions they will be different for a good, simple, impersonal reason. You will come along and say, "I have put this here, in this form, with this distribution because . . . ," and we will listen. Somebody else will say, with the same powerful conviction, words about a totally different situation, and we will listen again. We will not only listen but we will look and at this stage perhaps the actual forms will begin to introduce into the problem all kinds of secondary considerations, which none of us saw, none of us anticipated and none of us could have invented. It really takes this process.

What we are really talking about the whole time in these seminars is what we can do to help ourselves so that when you get to the point when you are on your own—and it's going to be awfully fast, at the end of this year—you will have the equipment in which to tackle problems. How does the program get started; how does one turn any program into the organization of work which will use the collective advantage for each individual purpose? These are all very important things. To begin with, for instance, you don't know how to use your time. You have to know this. It is terribly important. I am not saying this because I am an impatient man. I am really saying this because a lot of other people just don't say it. Some professors don't say the unpalatable thing. It is ridiculous to have three days assigned for critiques, Tuesday, Wednesday and Thursday—where all three of your instructors are available to you, and presumably with you, because they are rather good and useful—to be doing homework, a private design assignment in this time. It is a very bad use of your time. It's not only bad use of your time but it is a bad use of the implement of instruction. Instructors are also people, and when the instructor feels there is nothing to grasp, when the activity for which he is there is not in fact developing, he is frustrated. He wastes a great deal of time getting into the vein of your thought, and you waste your time and his. You waste above all the commodity which we are trying to jointly cultivate which is interaction between.

You must learn this first year to really conserve and organize your time as well as your wits, as well as polish your technique. Then you will not waste either time or people as you go along. It makes me mad to see people in the advanced years waste weeks of time because they have never been taught method. Then they go on charrette, and everyone goes mad with fatigue. What happens is that students go into juries and practically all classes, at the lowest ebb, exhausted because they have been working all night to finish their drawing. And then they are expected to be interested in criticism, and above all they are supposed to be interested in criticism of somebody else's work. By this time, of course, they don't give a damn about anything. This, I think, is technically ridiculous and in a great university it shouldn't occur. We cannot work in the uncoordinated, unorganized way of high school children.

So to recapitulate, in this matter of self-discipline: first, remember that we are doing a collective job. Therefore we must distribute our energies and our experiments in such a way as to reward the whole group. This is not the time to show what you can do personally. You are going to show what you can do collectively. It will pay off because we will learn a great deal from each other in terms of method and principle. The second thing is that you must discipline yourselves so that you are not always exhausted at the wrong moment or doing something at the wrong moment so that you waste some of the facilities. These are the two things that I wanted to say about our present situation. In order, however, to console you in the next stretch, in the spring semester, all the talents that you inhibit now can come out into the open. You can have a wonderful orgy of self-indulgence. Each one will be working on a certain segment of this problem on his own and will be master of his own destiny.

Now, do you think that this group work is not rewarding because of factors which I may not perceive, or do you think it is working out alright? I think it would be bad to push a group against its group will. But we will have to get into this thing a little bit, and then we will see. There will be tendencies developing, and we can encourage those tendencies.

Mr. [Albert] Szabo yesterday was with a group that wanted to consolidate and chuck out the row house type.[6] Well, that was a sort of declaration which makes it possible to arrive at that position. Somebody else may come to the opposite conclusion and then we will sort it out from there. What about this group work, does it get on your nerves?

STUDENT: Isn't that a secondary consideration?

CHERMAYEFF: Well, we are not really expecting results. I say this with all diffidence because I know if people end up with something that they can really love they can't be absolutely frustrated. I think, on the other hand, that if the class admits openly at the end of this first year we will have done a great deal of very useful work, of which these will be examples in process, this alone will be very much more important than if somebody arrives at a beautiful solution. I just don't think we are looking towards solutions at this stage. What we are looking for is how do we work.

STUDENT: The only trouble seems to me is that we only have a week to complete this study.

CHERMAYEFF: There are several stages even in this first stage.

STUDENT: We are in the first stage now. As I understand it, in the first stage we were to go into the various solutions and then we were going to merge from there.

CHERMAYEFF: There are several stages even in this first stage. When do we actually finish? At the end of the semester, and that is a long way yet.

STUDENT: I am talking about the thirty-second scale model.

CHERMAYEFF: Well, I think there is only going to be a sketch idea, but it will be, at least, a "three dimensional sketch." The reason for making it three-dimensional is, as you are probably aware, that one doesn't really know how things are unless one is very highly trained in their graphic symbolism on paper. I think one really has to look at an idea as a physical fact. . . . I couldn't really see certain relationships, but when you started putting all your little blocks together yesterday I got, for the first time, an extremely pleasant surprise . . . . I didn't know whether it was going to be too crowded or not, but on the whole it seemed quite feasible. By the time that you have finished this first week's sketch you will know what is wrong with the possible variants. You will also know what is right with the principle. You may have a broad outline, but you will see the faults. Then you will continue to define within this framework, making the framework constantly more and more precise. When it is eventually finalized in terms of the general plan, it will include everything, including the pedestrian and vehicle circulatory systems and everything else. You will deal next semester with the problem of the individual cell.

STUDENT: It seemed to me that the real reason for the group was physical and moral, in order to come to some conclusion. When you get three people working on the same problem with the same background, at the same level, you find it a great waste of time. CHERMAYEFF: No, I don't think so. If we had fifty people, each struggling for the solution and going through this thing it means that the instructor's time would have to have been trebled. We just haven't got the time. So, number one, you cut the thing down to manageable dimensions of communion. What you are really trying to do is to find out things. It doesn't matter whether in a group there is someone who has contributed nothing at that particular stage. Somebody else may have been the master of that first sketch, but the other two have probably participated somewhere. Anyhow, we have arrived somewhere. At that point the people who have made no contribution might make the next very important contribution, and so it goes. This is a self-aiding kind of process, a snow ball process, and I think you do not waste time that way.

[SC then tells the story of how Mies and Johnson got the Seagram skyscraper job].

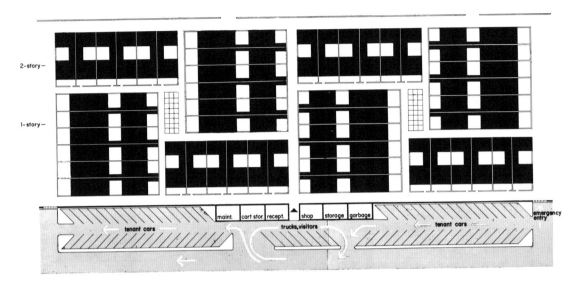

2-story —

1-story —

| maint. | cart stor. | recept. | shop | storage | garbage | emergency entry |

tenant cars

trucks, visitors

tenant cars

Harvard Urban Family
House Study, 1960.
Typical site plan.

One of the most dangerous things I know is to come back to old pastures because one becomes tremendously sentimental and objective values fall away. I am, in fact, deeply moved that the trees have grown so enormously, but as one moves through these familiar asphalt walks nothing else seems to have changed very much. Then I looked at the exhibition and I thought, well, I don't think things have changed very much here, either. I don't know that this is a good thing. I don't know that it's a bad thing. I am unable to speak of the intervening years except in a very general way. . . .

. . . So, if you don't mind, what I will do is to tell you what I think is the role of the kind of department which is so ably conducted by Professor Robert Wolff and his colleagues and what it has to do in relation to higher education as I see it in retrospect after fifteen years. I think it is fair to say that within those fifteen years the idea that the practice of the creative process, the ordering of things, the putting things together in various media, was considered, more or less, the necessary counterpart to intellectual exercises which we have taken rarely together as being education. This kind of complementarity which has developed on a philosophically defensible level has, however, produced all kinds of peculiar results in action. . . .

Art is being sold seductively, right and left, in the popular magazines and it has become a commodity today, which belongs to the marketplace. This suggests that we have come to the end of a cycle and that we had better take great care about the next. We might drive art straight into the ground before it has even begun to blossom. We are beginning to plough it in right now. That is why I am going to speak, in the first place, somewhat negatively. Then you can always point to your own situation as being the exception to the rule. It is always, of course, the other school which is doing the nonsense and you, yourself, are performing an admirable task, wherever you are.

From a lecture, "Modes and Manners in Art," given at the Department of Design, Brooklyn College, May 20, 1957.

If I am really to recommend any kind of curriculum in high education to deal with the arts, I would be most careful to stress the notion of the indivisibility of the arts. It is almost a reflection of the academy when in the world outside it we are so pleased with our knowledge about art, we are so pleased with the fact that the local museum possesses well-advertised objects of virtue in the field, that we are able to have museum art on Sunday, while we proceed, unseeing or blind, through the slums which are our visual weekday experience. . . .

We are also tending to substitute a few exercises in sensibility for being in fact sensitive. I do not know quite how to overcome this except, perhaps, by avoiding as far as possible any attempt at professionalism within the college art department. I think that any student who frames a painting exercise during his college career is probably committing a major sin against art as a whole. It would be lovely to think that humility prevailed and that all these nice exercises were put into portfolios only to be looked back upon with great private pleasure by those who go into some other activity or as documents in the process of development by professionals later on who will have battled with the difficult things within the field.

The reason I think we have to be cautious is because, in spite of everything, we still have only vague values in the realm of esthetics. If one looks around painting galleries today, and I am saying this with great respect towards the serious painters, I am speaking now about the general vulgarisation of something which I believe to be a very high level of activity, but if one looks at the enormous production and sales of vulgarisation, one sees the traps into which one may fall. Although it could be said that there is no task undertaken by man which does not have its proper discipline, it is also reasonable to say that if you start with painting, within the field of the visual arts, this field is the least disciplined of them all. The judgments are the most evasive, the technical requirements are the least demanding. Structural problems are almost non-existent as compared to, say, sculpture, where the constructional problem begins to emerge, however modestly—relatively modest compared to the technical and other demands of, say, architecture and planning.

The tendency today is to adhere, in the world of art, to that which is easiest and to proliferate this, not so much for artistic reasons but, as I suggest, for psychological reasons. As evidence of this trend, we have the fact that all too often introductions to painters' catalogues draw attention to the psyche of the painter rather than make any reasonable comment about the process or the product. This is a period of preoccupation with psychology. Too many teachers, in my view, particularly those who are emerging from the teachers' training centres springing up all over under the pressure of need in this vast and economically prosperous society of ours, rush into the classrooms not so much to start processes of humble work as to hunt down neuroses. They are self-appointed saviours of the lame and the perturbed and so on. The battle between the art teacher and the campus psychologist must be continuous and I imagine you must have suffered from that.

There are, in fact, so many traps surrounding this thing called art, into which we fall all too readily, that I am very anxious at least to, in so far as I am able in the short time at my disposal, give you reasons for my cautions as to the expanding programs which are going on everywhere since the very bold and, I think, remarkable and courageous experiment started here by President [Harry] Gideonse and in which I participated in a very small way (but it taught me a great deal). I have seen the rise of this thing. It is a form of education really now going through the whole body academic. We are very much in danger of becoming completely "beaux arts" in a new way. We are becoming academic prematurely.

I see the same exercises, the same tricks, performed all too fast because the time is not there—actually the process is slow as you well know. The temptation to skip the essentials is always there. In education, *the process is all*; the end product at this stage of education is absolutely nothing except a pedagogical yardstick to be kept private amongst teachers, perhaps of statistical interest, perhaps as a corrective to the method itself, but *never, never* of the smallest public interest as art. That is why I welcome the way you have set up your honors program—what you have asked the students to put up here is the result of their after-school work and not the in school exercises. This, I think, is really the clue. I would never encourage myself the school work to be treated as anything more than an exercise, but I would test people's capacity to absorb what has been learned and to have transformed this into something they do of their own.

There is no question that we have a tremendous body of people much better brought up artistically during the last fifteen years than ever before in the United States, from whom, presumably, the schools and the professional ranks will draw a large number of revealed talents which might otherwise have been lost. So the new education is partly a way of finding out whether in our body of intellectually, certainly, rather alert, young people there also resides a sufficient quantity of creative talent. Creative in promise, however, without adequate experience in the medium.

I would interpose my second caution whenever a college course tends to become specifically painting or sculpture. Art of any media which is normally associated with a mature personal work and a familiar tradition becomes dangerous, for me, at this stage of development. I much prefer, at the college level, to put away the word art because it is a heavily loaded word and the word craft which is its weaker, or its uglier, sister, but is also a heavily loaded word. I prefer to substitute the word Design, free of confusing associative meaning. Thus one could be free to experiment and to set in motion many things which were already well understood by John Dewey and were developed in a direct line of descent from him. Design seems to me a more appropriate description of the educational intention, and I am perfectly prepared to be corrected about this, because it might involve people in mere ordering as an end in itself—without an organic relationship with man's needs and aspirations. There is value, however, in the process of inquiry which tells us how pieces come together to make structures which are logically defensible, esthetically defensible, communication-wise defensible, symbolically recognizable and so on; a process which reveals that behind apparently disparate events and processes the same principles of careful, really humble, exact structuring exists. The doodle, which is one of the simplest and also the most useful of exercises in this general way, is becoming rather over-done. It is not an accident, I think, that the subjective approach and suggestive forms have now replaced the careful programmatic approach and the logically constructed forms. . . .

. . . Perhaps this exaggeration is the sign that we are closing a cycle, that we have to start again. I don't know where to start. I have no ready prescriptions. I am going to give you my own private summary. I painted for some seven or eight years, just like hundreds of other people painted who were not painters. To be a painter means to be a painter all the time. I was not a painter all the time, but I found a considerable pleasure of a therapeutic kind in painting in a manner which is sometimes described as abstract expressionism. Then I started to look again at painters like Lorenzetti and Piero de la Francesca, and I came to the conclusion that I could turn them upside down and find they were better and more significant abstract forms than I had myself painted. They had many, many things which I had never even attempted to reach. So I suddenly saw myself in rather a poor condition, and I stopped painting.

I have tried to pay increased attention to what I was fundamentally the whole time, which was an architect. Looking at architectural form and purpose, I have come to the conclusion that this is my base, not only now as an architect but also perhaps as a teacher and therefore perhaps equally as a student. Inevitably, every teacher is, of course, a student by the turn of events. I really believe that we have to admit that chaos is the prevailing cultural pattern and that this art, which we have looked to so peculiarly and so intensely, has in fact become a compensation for this fact rather than a thing *an sich*. I would really like very much to see more, in higher education, of turning towards the lessons of "ordering" from the point of view of the human habitat, the environmental factors, the buildings we inhabit, the streets, the spaces between, to feel that we are absolutely conscious of the fact that everything is relative. We cannot pretend that we can have, say, a domestic architecture of a romantic kind when we destroy it with a Detroit-made implement of a conspicuously (plastically speaking) different world. They are incompatible. Wherever I look I find incompatibility is actually the prevailing pattern, and that little cherries (of art) are no longer even decorating a fruit salad. They are sitting in garbage cans.

This doesn't solve the problem of garbage disposal. I think we have a tremendous task and I would say that it is in the city colleges, which are so close to insatiable productivity and also close to the horrors that are some of its by-products, that we should start. It is within this framework that we should continue with the correctives. We can't do it in private colleges among charming landscapes remote from ugly reality. They have too little in the way of stimuli to offer except, again, in the form of romantic compensation and escape.

I felt that here in Brooklyn—and I have never forgotten this—that the student body is utterly responsive and reacts fully both inside and outside school. Daily, the student body is pumping in and out of the campus. Here we should start again very, very carefully to reconstruct the relationships, or the notion of the relationship, between the human habitat as it is and as we hope to make it. Think of a more appropriate department or of a more appropriate framework of reference than one you have already established here to emphasize less fine art and more design. Perhaps slowly it could begin to do more planning, more architectural and industrial design, message-making forms, shapes, orders, as a path towards a general improvement in the standard of life. Within this, the artists' work will, in fact, be a natural extension to a higher level of an understood activity rather than a compensation with something remote and without status.

I am sorry if I have suggested in any way that I do not like what is being done. As a matter of fact, I have had no opportunity yet to look systematically at what you are doing here in the school. I am pretty sure that you are doing extremely good work. I am sure there are tremendous benefits to be had from it, but I would just plead for more emphasis upon the critical situation in which we find ourselves in terms of the total aspect of our physical environment. It is getting out of hand.

It is really getting out of hand. I don't think I have anything more useful to say at this moment, but I am looking forward to seeing the work which will, perhaps, clarify more things for me. Thank you very much for listening.

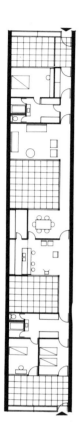

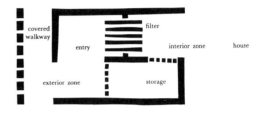

covered
walkway

filter

entry

interior zone   house

exterior zone   storage

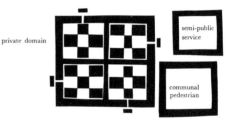

private domain

semi-public
service

communal
pedestrian

Plans and analytic
diagrams from
Community and Privacy,
1963.

The distinguished chairman has kindly left out that I am an apostate in this company. I don't like much what you do, I don't like very much *how* you do it and I don't believe what you are doing serves any good. Quite unconsciously, my good friend, Jean Paul [Carlhian] provided me with a text. His talk purported to be theory but actually was a catalogue of specious items. I am less interested in *how* things are done; I am more interested in *why* things are done. You can build without columns and make great architecture.

There are things which perturb me about this particular meeting. The thing which first shook me was your bibliographical list, a document which, I would say, is loaded. I think it has such singular omissions, conspicuously, the weak documentation of our present times and dilemmas. I cannot understand, for instance, how, Mr. [Peter] Collins notwithstanding, one can omit from required readings for your professed purposes: Mr. Greenough, who by the way first said, "Form follows function," and not Mr. Sullivan, who merely repeated it; Mr. Sullivan's own *Kindergarten Chats* I find more refreshing than anything you list; Mr. Wright who, in spite of his egocentricity, had great principles to announce. Where are the writings of some of our contemporary prophets such as Le Corbusier and Giedion, the documents of CIAM, and lastly those of Buckminster Fuller at the moment when the International Union of Architects has adopted his proposals for world wide inventory of resources with which designers will in fact have to work? Not the things they *imagine* they are going to have to work with but the *actual* things they are going to have to work with. The first two volumes can be obtained from Southern Illinois University and I recommend these to you and

From a lecture, "Random Thoughts on the Architectural Condition," given at the AIA-ACSA Teacher Seminar, Cranbrook, June 9, 1964; published in Marcus Whiffen, ed., *The History, Theory, and Criticism of Architecture: Papers from the 1964 AIA-ACSA Teacher Seminar* (Cambridge: MIT Press, 1965).

any which may follow from this source: a great deal of very useful data of which we are so happily, or shall we say, innocently unaware.

And lastly, of course, I am shocked deeply not to find my own book on the list, which I obviously also recommend strongly, and another discussing on a very high level the theory of form: *Notes on the Synthesis of Form*. It is a Ph.D. dissertation, just recently published by Harvard, by Christopher Alexander, who was my collaborator on the book *Community and Privacy*. Anyhow, it must now be quite clear to you that I am not of your company because I am obviously not well read except outside your field, and I commend to those of you who are young enough to catch up with your reading to do exactly that. . . .

. . . Perhaps Western cultures are on the down grade because they have little hope, and perhaps the African and Asian people will come up because they are filled with hope. Perhaps they will use art to better effect. I hope so. Somebody has to. It doesn't look as if we can. Maybe this is a depressing notion? Actually I am feeling extremely optimistic personally. I am having the best time of my life being a hermit.

Nevertheless I think the architectural profession, as it is, is obsolete. Much more importantly, architectural education is in danger of becoming obsolete. For that reason it is always heartening to hear that some great schools which are in very influential positions are about to change radically their methods and attitudes.

The professionals in the field, the practitioners, require continuity of attitude, interest and skill, and they really practice expediency. Their nature is practical and they are, in fact, conservative. Any deviation or invention in their profession is a very useful piece of public relations or propaganda, providing it doesn't radically depart from the general line. And yet these people who are conservatives are allowed to inspect and accredit the schools of architecture from which, of course, they draw their assistants and, more often than not, their so-called inspiration.

But schools are by definition scholarly, exploratory, intellectually adventurous, philosophical; that is, what I mean by theory and principles is that they are philosophically long-term minded. Their interest is to deepen and widen the field as a whole without exaggerated regard for the immediately familiar and practical. Their method is imaginative inquiry. This is true in relation to architecture in the larger sense of the word, in schools which have planning and other related departments and, of course, more particularly in universities with great extra-departmental facilities and resources. The search for widening and deepening is not only a moral but an intellectual obligation, and the student and the teacher and the researcher, in spite of themselves and because of the pressures from the marketplace, have become, in fact, opponents of the practitioners.

I am not a historian, as you can obviously see, but I would like to inject an amateur idea which occurred to me as history was being discussed. The practitioner and the academician, until only very recently, could be the same man because each had more or less a common concern. The further we go back in history the clearer it becomes that everybody was involved in the act of building, in its maintenance and its reconstruction, and everybody was absolutely and completely familiar with every purpose of every building put up in the culture in question.

This meant that you had continuity of a cultural and technical kind which permitted the refining of that which had been found acceptable. You could polish to achieve superb excellence. Later users gave a post facto accolade and the excellent and even the merely good became art and architecture. . . .

. . . Man is both extended, and, at the same time, he is deprived. He has become imprisoned in his own devices and frustrated by his own ambition. He is driven mad by his own noises. He is run over by his own mobility. He is inhibited by his own "education." Every time some bright, but not bright enough, administrator or professor thinks that it would be awfully good for architectural students to receive, within a miserable time package, another message from another god, it goes into the curriculum.

Our physicists are beginning to learn much more about how to educate, also the mathematicians. What happens in architecture? Schools expect the student in a very short slice of their experience labeled education to drink in many more impressions than in fact it is humanly possible to do. . . .

I am going to suggest two things which may not be properly

taught in the spectrum of time as short as the formal slices of education dedicated currently to architecture. You may not teach art because that is post facto evaluation of work accomplished, and you certainly cannot teach much technology because mostly it becomes obsolete before the chap gets out of school. So what is left to teach? Exactly what everybody had been hinting at and not coming out with: principles, a philosophically based process of tackling problems of organization. It is a set of intellectual and ethical rules of behaviour and guidance toward appropriate choice of tools as and when the specific and the particular becomes visible. The artistic act and technical knowledge are quite different from general principles; the two shall not be muddled in the mind. Lacking educational help, it has taken me forty years to separate art from technique and the philosophical principle from the particular case. So I assume maybe that the revision in education of future designers is in order. . . .

. . . May I remind you of an editorial by Mr. Peter Blake, who you know is an ex-editor of an ex-magazine on architectural education. . . . In an editorial about many schools which were about to search for new deans, Blake discussed various means of going about it. He mentioned, among other things, the star system resulting in part-time deanship instead of a whole time administrative job. I would like to read the last two paragraphs of Blake's editorial and parts of my comments.

The trouble is, unhappily, that education suffers (as a result of this) and suffers badly. For education has nothing to do with star-systems or competitions for endowments; education is a serious business. It requires teachers dedicated to (and skilled at) teaching, and programs designed to turn students into professionals capable of dealing with tomorrow's problems—which will differ very radically with those faced by artist-architects skilled at producing exquisite but isolated monuments.

It would be better for all concerned, for students—for students, for faculties, for the country as a whole—if heads of architectural schools were picked not for their glamour, but for their teaching ability and teaching enthusiasm; and if programs were written not in terms of one great man's "style," but in terms of the widest

*problems—social, technological, economic, as well as esthetic—
that are likely to confront the profession in decades to come.*[7]

I commented in part: that the good and almost invariably needy
student can now shop between several of the "very best" schools
for financial assistance. "The best fellowship- and scholarship-
endowed school wins the good students more often than not."[8]
This student really has to overcome something which is tacked on
almost accidentally to his education. So the needy have to shop
around for money, not for teaching. "Endowment is seldom if
ever directly obtained . . . in an architectural school, but by the
university obtaining this for very general educational purposes,"[9]
and I find in my experience, that the kitty is nearly always re-
served for the more fashionable sciences and architecture gets
short changed, for the very simple reason that it is really still
thought of as useless art. It actually isn't; it is a science as well as
an art.

Architectural schools are still relatively poor and science
schools relatively rich because the usefulness of the latter is immediately recognized, whereas architecture, even to very enlightened presidents, has a lower priority. The less enlightened, like
most patrons, are satisfied to build with the help of the merely
competent or decorators or status architects.

Under any conditions of course, schools need good faculty as
well as good students and current practice in faculty appointment
reflects the practices of the affluent society which is busy in the
marketplace. The architects who teach practice first and teach
second. (Historians are honorable men and are history teachers
on a full-time basis.) The voice of the marketplace has invaded
the university sanctum. Many schools have become victims of the
originally rational principle of practising preachers which has
now become abused. In too many schools teaching salary has
become subsidy for those waiting to get sufficient earning power
to practice.

"These observations are not intended as a wholesale condemnation. There are many teachers whose ideals and skills and
integrity are beyond any question and who are sometimes
teachers first and foremost in spite of being successful practitioners."[10] I have nothing against the master studio. I think one of the

great advantages of the Beaux Arts was that students simply lived with the great man, and worked with him for three or four years, and even if he taught you nothing, even if he only grunted at you, almost by osmosis something was transposed of his genius through common involvement. The student knew everything about the man; he didn't have to justify himself in every encounter, you only were with him because you knew what he stood for and what he did; he didn't have to explain himself. . . .

In addition to what I said in that letter, we don't need more architectural schools as much as we need a great subsidy to the sensitive and talented, to increase direct subsidy through fellowships, loans or whatever other aids together with absolutely free passportless exchanges and travel in a growing global society. We have to give people opportunity to remain students, to stay out of the marketplace and the privilege of being what they are, perhaps superior and sensitive hermits of our new world. We have to subsidize their advanced study and research in our field.

What we are doing at the present moment is reducing every student group to the lowest common denominator. This way we may not produce an appropriate education for architects of our time. Gropius became a great teacher because he had a purpose. He didn't have a special methodology or whatever; he had purpose, just simply that. He was a great teacher at the moment when teachers with fresh attitudes toward architectural responsibilities and potentials were needed. The Bauhaus was unquestionably very influential and the students of the Bauhaus and the later Harvard and Institute of Design period, and many students of those periods who were not directly Bauhaus, Harvard or I.D. students, benefitted enormously from this new turn in education.

So I don't agree that the Bauhaus failed to produce method. Actually it did have a method. The method was to encourage direct experience in form-making. It is perhaps true that deliberate omission of history courses was unfortunate. But Gropius could afford to omit them at that time. To be saddled with an obsolete historicity would have been damaging to his purposes. We still require new, appropriate ways of presenting history as continuous process.

Maybe now we are at a comparable period when much questioning already is being done by students more frequently than by members of the faculty, if current practices are really valid and if we have to re-evaluate the scope and nature of architecture in order to illuminate educational purpose. We cannot keep on tinkering with an architectural education in terms of courses when we don't see the end product that we are trying to get, and nobody is ready to define it. It is quite evident to me that the new broadened architecture (which is a loaded word) could with advantage be called by another name for the time being.

The entire spectrum of environmental design has been so widened, so immensely widened, that it is already out of the scope of any package deal in education. It is just too, too much. It cannot be squeezed into four years, and it cannot be squeezed into five years in which the last year in a "master" class, so-called, is nothing but another unnecessary exercise for impatient boys or a demonstration of premature genius or just a finishing school for the status seekers. This certainly is not education.

The first requirement is to use the best tools for making educated men. This includes, of course, education at every appropriate level of human development, which means that you have to reformulate education, which we now think of as elementary education or higher education or post-graduate education, into its proper doses in accordance with the individual human development and potential. It has already been demonstrated that you can teach higher mathematics and several languages very easily and simultaneously between the ages of eight and twelve. So then why wait until a child's capacity for learning certain things has been atrophied and then try and stuff him like a goose for rich liver.

The real education we are talking about, of structuring or order-making, of the comprehension of inter-relationship of things, must be pushed down as well as up. It implies an extension of the whole educational spectrum in two directions: down to the kindergarten through elementary school, through high school, and then up after the so-called professional training, which is really for one kind of practitioner only, into post-graduate research which may become a career in itself, as it is in many other fields.

This notion pre-supposes a reparcelling of learning-time.

Somewhere in the middle of this enlarged slice of learning and experience gathering and practice for certain people with demonstrable design ability, perhaps after two years of college, basic training, in making visible physical order or form, would start. Two years of this would be good for future painters, graphic designers, photographers, sculptors, architects, urban designers and industrial designers, et al. We could go right back to the Bauhaus; we haven't invented anything better since. At the end of that period you would have found out who really stands out in creative or intellectual capacity, or the technical, analytical, logical capacity sufficiently to go on further towards more serious tasks in a chosen field. The purely facile, the gifted and talented could peel off and could become whatever "beautiful" image-makers we need in society. Others would go into a technical two years in which exploration would be made of the ability to transform talent into systematic, purposeful action. They would receive an honorable degree as very useful functionaries in our society because we need a great many of them to translate imaginative thinking into actualities.

But the remaining students would be asked to start designing, that is to say, to organize new complexity into new visible order. There might be two or three years in this course, including a year or two years of apprenticeship to be chosen by the student. The apprenticeship would not be limited to going to the assemblage building construction industry, to mixing skilled and advanced administrative ability and simple technology, but it might include the option to put together administrative ability and very advanced technology in production industry itself.

Finally, without any time limit at all, any properly qualified person could come back to research and study in environmental design and control in order to make the fullest use of the human resources and facilities of a great university. We would then have a diversity of *real* architects, who would be able to fill out the architectural spectrum. Some of these would be *most* particularly engaged in *special* interests and at the same time others would become *the most needed specialists of all, the men without particular involvement* like the ideal President of the United States,

men capable of making great decisions after briefing by specialists, without being seduced by them.

All I have said of course has been said before and better.
Finally, if this is in order, I would suggest that this meeting before
it adjourns pass a resolution, addressing the bodies which en-
abled them to be here, to ask for an independent inquiry and
report to the profession at large as to the end-product, this "architect" we need in our time.

Chermayeff House, New
Haven, Connecticut,
1963.

. . . Obviously to assume that all goes well with University in our time and culture implies a serious neglect of "constant vigilance." We are today still lamenting the recent interference of politics with University and the shameful dismissal of President Clark Kerr. Perhaps it is appropriate on an occasion such as this to recall that a similar shameful incident occurred here in Illinois some fifteen years ago when another great President, George Stoddard also was dismissed summarily. Should we not doff our hats to absent friends? Before that, a quarter of a century ago, Lord [Bertrand] Russell, one of the great minds of our time, was deemed unfit to teach in the City College of New York.

In spite of such setbacks University is being transformed, liberalized, broadened and deepened in its quest for knowledge, just as it is undergoing profound changes in direction and purpose. . . .

. . . In these terms of our cultural dilemma it should be added that "the old idea of University as a Community of Conversants" has been pushed aside by the Baconian vision of knowledge as power. As in our history we separated the church from the state when the church dogma threatened the advance of democracy and liberalization of thought and institutions, so today it seems we must for similar reasons separate University from the power pressures of politics and the marketplace as well as guard it against exploitation by ambitious academics which, alas, abound in many areas including my field of design.

I will attempt to put design into the new framework of University and the urban environment of which it is a vital component. This is a new context less ambiguous and ambivalent than the prevailing ones, an artist's studio, a trade workshop, or a business office, or, worse still, the street corner, but in any case one where the professional is looking out for a prosperous client.

From a lecture given at the Founders' Day Ceremony, University of Illinois, Urbana, March 13, 1967; published in *Socio-Economic Planning Sciences* 1 (1967).

It is becoming evident even to the practitioners themselves that their procedures have become obsolete, organized as they are in splinter groups of speciality: industrial designer, architect, landscape architect, city planner, et al. Yet all become self appointed generalists always prepared to cross the boundaries of their own making at the drop of a telephone receiver and to operate at any scale with any medium in the environment shaping process. Such excursions into the unknown more often than not wind up in exercises distinguished by aestheticism, historicism, scientism according to individual taste, and mostly collectively, simplistic thinking.

Typical recent examples come from an A.I.A. speech offering the recipe of "aesthetically acceptable answers" or, as in the case of a large committee's report to Mayor Lindsay of New York, an introductory sermon suggesting that the "what" (the thing) is more important than the "how" (administrative, economic power) but leaving out entirely any discussion of "why,"[11] the prime mover in any process; namely, purposes more far reaching than immediate habit and appetite.

I think the architectural profession as it is is obsolete. But what bothers me much more is that architectural education is in the danger of becoming obsolete too. Professionals in the field require continuity in attitude, in interest, in skills and in the practice of expediency. Their nature really is conservative. Yet it is these people who are asked to inspect and to accredit schools of architecture from which they draw their assistants and more often than not their inspiration. But schools are by definition scholarly, exploratory, adventurous, philosophically long term minded. Their interest is exactly the opposite. It is to deepen and widen the field as a whole without exaggerated regard for the immediately practical. In a school devoted to architecture and planning, and more particularly in a university, this search for the widening and deepening is both a moral and an intellectual obligation. Therefore I think that the student, the teacher, the researcher, have in spite of themselves but because of the pressures of the marketplace, become opponents of practical men across a table which is supposed to be shared by both. . . .

. . . It is ironic that in an age in which man is indeed transforming his environment at a pace unprecedented and in quantities unprecedented, the group of professionals who by definition are among the prime shapers of man's habitat, are deprived of prime responsibility, namely to make decisions. The trained shaper of environment is in a subservient position, and this is true in spite of all declarations and slogans of the professional organizations or the very arrogant assertions of a few favored individuals. . . .

. . . The re-definition of the field as comprehensive design of environments eliminates the questionable distinctions between architecture and landscape architecture—industrial design— urban design—regional design, etc. These traditional divisions can no longer serve any useful purpose for they are essentially quantitative. A commitment to the study and design of the human habitat can produce qualitative variations and help build intellectual bridges between many disciplines. It is clearly the responsibility of universities to produce a new variety of professional excellence in a broader spectrum of environment studies and a greater understanding generally of the complexity of human ecology in a man-made environment. A comprehensive program should attract the diverse intellectual resources of the college and bring to design a greater diversity of talents. At this time it is almost uniquely identified with "art" which all too often attracts the merely facile. A declared broader purpose backed by appointments of widely recognized excellence to guide the postgraduate studies program would go a long way to correct our situation. Social, economic and technical issues have to be finally resolved in physical terms: visible, comprehensible order, "broadened architecture." But we cannot begin the process from the wrong end. . . .

. . . The design professions which could contribute to the resolution of critical problems and give visible and comprehensible order to the new complexity are handicapped through lack of the latest scientific and technological information on contemporary pressures being exerted upon both the man-made environment and man's historic and natural resources. They are, by tradition and training, collectively uninterested in research and unsuited to the new task. Architects are generally aesthetically formally oriented and are technologically "innocent" or backward. City planners are trained for administrative rather than creative functions and are sociologically and economically oriented. Professionals require a broader background and a more systematic approach to their problems.

A comprehensive, responsible and far-reaching program of research and education in environmental problems should now be developed in great universities because these are communities where the necessary diversity of skills and knowledge are available in a climate of enquiry, removed from political and market pressures. Germinal studies could be considered with advantage as a school of "environmental studies" and could concentrate on graduate and post-graduate research following the example of other disciplines. No single university department can any longer be "all things to all men" in either urban theory or design. The situation demands, as a matter-of-fact, complementary activities in many universities and institutions.

Current architectural education in "accredited schools" has adopted almost exclusively in their design curricula the method of "practical professionalism" within the framework of existing conditions and in the context of "real" situations of structure, site, etc. This provides "designer" personnel to professional offices without opportunity or inclination for necessary research into changing conditions. This method is not practical because it makes the obsolete an ingredient of the future. New formal invention remains without a foundation in new realities. We must search for a new method.

The bulk of knowledge and information in urban affairs lies outside the design professions and schools. We require first and foremost access to this. Secondly, because this is so and because we do not have the adequate knowledge, it means that we have to have within the school of architecture or urban design or whatever a superstructure such as has been developed in other departments, namely, advanced post-graduate, post professional work, so that this work, this intellectual ferment at the highest level of sophistication, can trickle down into the professional school. There is another effect which can now work in the opposite way; you can think of the whole as complementary pyramids. From the top, the advanced special studies sophistication, from the bottom, the great liberal spread of college. As our higher education gets better, so the intensity of spread of knowledge and interest increases. Thus, professional schools are, so to speak, shaped between the liberal bottom and the highly sophisticated specialized top. The importance of post-graduate studies at the most sophisticated level, intellectual and artistic maturity, is no more important than the liberal preparation for order making decisions and processes. Visual order is only one of many analogous orders.

It appears necessary therefore to remove all vestiges of "art" mystique from courses at the college level. Perhaps the best way to do this is to revive and develop courses across many departmental levels so as to put problems in form making to a greater variety of students employing media as varied as writing, music, logic, mathematics and physical constructions in a series of comparative studies. The greatest flexibility, invention and imagination seems to abound in the pre-specialized intellectual and emotional conditions to be found among our most gifted or talented undergraduates.

As suggested earlier, just as the future strength of design lies in its catalytic capacity at the graduate and post-graduate level, so may it also lie in a workshop of the performing arts, the most public art of all, which today should not be limited to stage performances. It may prove to be the most effective catalyst at the college level inviting collaboration between diverse gifts and talents. In any case, it has become obvious that the spectrum of creative action is no longer confined to the traditional frames of the "fine arts." It may be even asserted that the best work of artists in the affluent societies is performed within new frameworks of their own evolution and invention. Universities have lately made any number of bridgings and boundary-crossings between their departments and disciplines, and these have become a commonplace in the natural and social sciences. We must now recognize that the creative act of a gifted individual at work, doing things, has to be revealed through the educational process as a system of work. We have developed teaching methods based upon self-discovery and practice and the feedback process in learning. These should not be limited to intellectual means but should immediately include the "intuitive" processes. Indeed, are we not discovering that the line between the so-called intelligent and intuitive processes is not so easily drawn? If we can bring together individuals of special gift to demonstrate their way of work this may reveal that some tasks actually are simpler for those with special creative gifts and might help us to destroy the mystery about art. We may even see issues of great stature born of unexpected new liaisons; I imagine, out of wedlock.

Another priority in my mind is a catalytic college course bridging several departments concerned directly or indirectly with physical environments. Such a course in human ecology would recognize the man-made urban habitat as a growing inescapable reality and give the study of design of habitats equal status with the natural and social sciences and the humanities.

I am pleading for the elimination of the myth of the artistic separateness, for the abandonment of the star system which tries to manufacture excellence like any other commodity and over-loads these artificially created paragons with artificially created demands so false that these might corrupt even the genuinely superior person. I am pleading for a moratorium to enquiry into the nature of the creative process until a more propitious time when we are less self-conscious about art and more confident in our value judgments; when indeed our social purposes may have become clearer. The artist is the "truth-teller," as Robert Graves describes him, and a creative individual is someone who can push solutions to problems further than the less gifted.

Let us also have a moratorium on artificial culture. Can we not concentrate for a while on honest striving for improvement of man's condition? In the final analysis neither accidentally arrived at aesthetic pleasures, nor sophisticated technology, nor good in-tentions alone can produce even an adequate human habitat at any scale. Certainly a significant, if not a great, architecture must be the measure and expression of unequivocal purpose at all scales. I would not voice any concern for the current condition if I were a pessimist. I do so in the firm belief that we can identify our ailments and therefore devise and design remedies. This makes me think that an environment fit for humanity may yet spring from reasonably conceived programs, employing intelligently and honestly the highest technology. We have recently read of the expanded role of space planners (outer space of course, God help us, poor lunatics). I commend to you the notion of the expanding role of space planners here below by the creation of a single field of environmental studies. It will accommodate the genius of science, technology and art on an equal footing and with equal opportunities. For it we shall need new semantics, new methodology and above all a new spirit.

Without this revolution in attitude toward man's responsibility to ecology generally and without the acceptance of the design of environments as a segment of this, an equilibrium between construction and conservation "architecture" and "design" will have a hollow ring, and the inadequately prepared practitioners of this complex art and science will remain outside the process of decision making.

URBAN HIERARCHIES IN COMPLEMENTARITY

Physical Components in Interaction

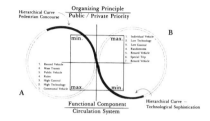

FUNCTIONAL HIERARCHIES IN COMPLEMENTARITY

Public and Private Interest

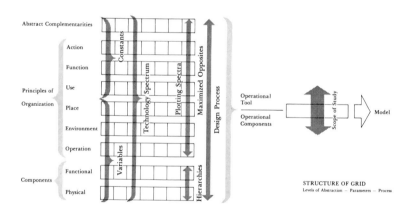

STRUCTURE OF GRID

Levels of Abstraction — Parameters — Process

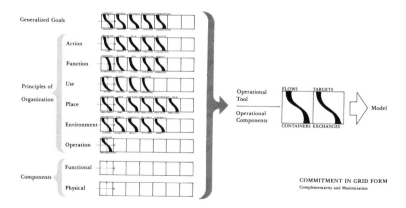

COMMITMENT IN GRID FORM

Complementarity and Maximization

Yale Model, Principle of
Complementarity, 1967.

Your institute has not honored me alone. Whatever good I may have done could never have been done at all without my many students from all over the world. For many years we have collaborated in speculation about purposes and priorities. Research is as yet not a term which can be properly applied to this activity in architecture. We worked together on a search for reasonable questions which might lead to viable answers. Anyway, we learned to mistrust easy answers to problems without precedent and with new excellent tools, or great preparation. We tried to apply ourselves honestly to issues and to "let beauty look after herself" in the words of an old friend and mentor, Eric Gill.[12] We learned what we knew full well; that mastery can only be acquired through long experience and was never taught even in the master's class. That real masters will not be denied and don't need any defenses or claims.

As a result of this experience I have remained an amateur of sorts during a period of growth of specialization, a most demanding pursuit, and avoided becoming a pseudo-expert. This occasion in a full life has a special significance for me: *obviously something new is abroad*. In this instance, it is the honoring of a minor prophet slightly to the left of rather private professionalism.

Something analogous has been happening in the world of sports, as you Canadians well know, a very public and prosperous business. It seems that more and more *coaches* get into the "Halls of Fame" along with *heroes* of the arena. This seems to be your special program. It is an honor to join your splendid company of medal holders. Somewhat south of here, happily, exactly the reverse is occurring in that most public of all realms, politics.

This coach, to whom you are being so generous, has had a lot of luck all along (including a revolution). I grew up a young man in

---

From the Gold Medal Acceptance Speech, Annual Convention of the Royal Architectural Institute of Canada, Montreal, June 1, 1973.

England in the company of an emerging, new elite of artists, writers, philosophers, scientists—contemporaries, colleagues, and friends—sharing in and stirring up a powerful new brew, as events proved later, broadening and deepening the scope of design and bridging old separations.

By the accident of war and revolution in my pre-professional years, I met with, and fell in love with, the creative processes all around me and their precision and integrity which had so many faces. I found them and ever since deep delight in beautiful logic and form: *in excellence*. Wanting (subconsciously, I suppose), to share all this, I became a teacher and have been one since World War II. The profession swings like a pendulum between war periods.

First, rational acceptance of new pressures and acceptance of new public responsibilities emerged. In the second, came relief and opportunity to express in action the artist's dreams and half formulated purposes—personal expression delayed or frustrated by great events.

In the second we witnessed retreats, led by the U.S.A., from public obligations toward private prosperity for some professionals. The public realm, where the critical priorities existed, was a dead thing—buried by bureaucrats. While the public cause was dead to the many, private practice became private indeed.

It seems that the pendulum of change is about to swing even more forcibly in the opposite direction. Professional concern with public affairs, a sensible and moral response to growing crises in an urbanizing and shrinking world is reviving once more. The familiar cry, "I don't want to get involved," has a hollow, ghostly sound.

The stereotyped practitioners and their camp followers in academe are, however, still a dangerous majority with predilection for quick answers of historicism, estheticism and scientism. Search for high purpose is still largely obscured by self-serving invention and private squabbles about the commonplace. These, together with the excesses of fashion, have their uses, of course, as irritants.

Anything disparaging I will say, or may have said, about professional activities, of course, does not apply to those present. The irresponsible "other fellows" are somewhere else. Professionally, I have been lucky to be able to work alongside an excellent minority of colleagues. All were concerned and pioneering. Much of their "strangeness" is now beginning to find general acceptance.

It seems to me, in retrospect, that leadership in these matters has been conspicuous in Britain and in Canada where public interest was never dead, where public works is an ever-present priority and where a continuity of civil service is built in. Canadian concern in public things spilled over, in the forties, as far as Chicago where I met Donald Buchanan again, who sent to the Institute of Design some splendid students.[13] Later, I had the pleasure of working with Canadian visitors to Harvard, fine "pros" dedicated to public affairs.

May I close on a personal note? Over thirty years ago when we landed in the new world I was launched on my teaching career from Montreal. Today I received the highest honor at the end of that career here again in Montreal. "Le cercle est bouclé."

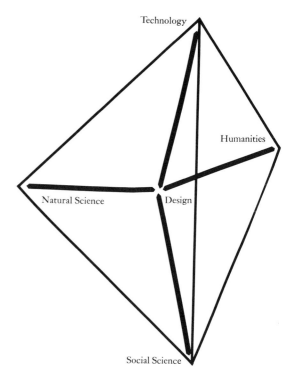

Technology

Humanities

Natural Science

Design

Social Science

"Design As Catalyst,"
diagram, 1967.

In my lifetime, Western man has been at war: militarily, cultur-ally, ideologically and economically. I have personally lived through two world wars and three revolutions: Communist, Fascist and Nazi. These have maintained a chronic disturbance, a sort of social indigestion born of fury and frustration. Banners and slo-gans have succeeded each other in confusing procession.

Abstractions like "freedom and democracy," "law and order," have never left their theoretical base to become reality in devel-oped countries in a spectacular way. Industrialization and mass-production have resulted in more food, health, machines, construction, mobility and communications in the Western world. But advantages and advances have, while sharpening ap-petites for more, left much which is essentially undone. Along with success has come disillusionment, defeatism, alienation and insecurity for the poorer societies.

An artist—who is also an architect and, by extension in scale, a planner—has to resolve the ever present dilemma of apparent contradictions. In this respect, art and science are on common ground: a paradigm described by the physicist, Gerald Holton, as the dyad of change and continuity. This contradiction I prefer to interpret as complementary opposites. Without these, man would be unable to distinguish light from dark, hot from cold, right from wrong, the ugly from the beautiful, order from chaos.

Scholars and priests, as well as politicians, have all too often contributed to the confusion. Histories—themes of values and ethics—are often ignored, more often misrepresented and more often still, conveniently forgotten.

Change, in a fundamental sense, is not recognized and cultural continuity has been interrupted. Without a proper measure of both security and sufficiency, continuity cannot operate, and so-

From a lecture, "Values and Ethics in the Design and Planning Profes-sions," given at the State University of New York at Buffalo, School of Architecture and Environmental Design, November 7, 1977; published in *Crit 4* (Association of Student Chapters, AIA), Fall 1978.

ciety loses moral strength and clear purpose. More of the same, only bigger and better, has become a most dangerous threat for even the most successful and privileged. Indeed the whole species is now endangered by gluttony running riot. Greed may destroy mankind in the long run.

While business flourishes, it manufactures religious, political, economic and artistic dogmas. Protagonists become myth makers and myth keepers. Their ill-conceived opportunistic answers cannot resolve new problems which have no precedent. Complexity of the modern world is not susceptible to change through obsolete intellectual logic or questionable artistic insights and improvisations. None of these is likely to lead to essential change and continuity nor does historical analysis lead to instant remedy.

There is growing a body of expertise which can provide a temporary answer to a complex detail of a specialized kind—but which misses the implications of the complexities of the whole. Both the wood and tree have grown bigger surprisingly fast. Joyce Milton, interested in environmental problems, writes in the *Nation*, "and the public comes to suspect that the experts are not so neutral after all, that it is being allowed to read only about findings whose aim is to convince people . . . loose prophecies of anti-science back-lash could turn out to be self-fulfilling."[14] In times of confusion and uncertainty, ignorance about complex events increases. Scientism, historicism, aestheticism, simplicism and piousness flourish.

In these times, any group of even excellent professionals, however highly motivated, educated and trained, must find it extremely difficult to promote their special interest and to practice what they preach. Preliminary questions, which must precede rational action or speculation, remain unanswered. I offer a few examples: what are the issues and priorities; to whom do we address ourselves; for whose good; by what means; in which time frame; at what scale, for what reward; who is responsible; to whom do we answer; from whom do we learn? These are simplistic questions, but they may serve to shift emphasis from simplistic answers and lead to sophisticated questions addressed to the complexities of our situations.

Perhaps the priorities are not only professional but educational. These must include a careful scrutiny of current practices.

Traditionally, all enquiry of the highest order was the province of academics. Studies were removed from political or market pressures. My experience as both practitioner and pedagogue suggests, however, that this is no longer generally true, but exists only in rare pockets of excellence that come into being almost by accident. Such examples of excellence in devotion and performance operate on two levels: scientifically based or artistically conceived. Both methods have developed the ability to integrate and to involve other disciplines—a catalytic function, rather than that of separation and specialization. Architecture, and by extension urban design and regional planning, are potentially catalytic and, therefore, important ingredients in the integrating process.

At the intersection of all intellectual vectors of forces lie the arts and sciences of creating form and making order manifest, comprehensible and acceptable. These include philosophy, mathematics, humanities, science, technologies and sociology in the university framework. Within this framework design as an educational tool can be enriched wherever it operates if new knowledge is passed to it from other interests and disciplines. Design in its turn can give form and induce order even in the greatest complexes. Its mission is to give greater scope and depth to the order-making process. It should eventually influence directly the decision making process instead of only providing the scenic backdrop for action or decoration for transient value. The professional potential must be vastly expanded before it can claim to help expand human potential through its values and ethics.

From the great earlier pioneers and prophets, we learned the indivisibility of design. A new conceptual environmental model of the biologist Patrick Geddes and the later Garden City planners made architecture embrace the natural phenomena and respect the social consequences in a new amalgam of art and science. We are still striving to make sociology both an art and a science. We are learning that architecture is equally difficult to define. We desire to educate well-grounded individuals, capable of intellectual rational approaches to problems, while providing opportunities for individuals possessing other gifts to exercise their insight and creative ability toward a common purpose. Evidence already exists that the line between intelligence and intuition is not easily drawn nor can we reasonably measure the effectiveness of either in action.

Appropriate action in a world of change inevitably must produce more options or choices at many social, economic and quality levels. At the highest level, enquiry and insight apply themselves to problems of larger frameworks and longer runs; at the lowest level, to fashions and fads—the transient, topical, seasonal, commercial and whimsical. The latter can hardly qualify as a professional activity directed to quality and public good.

Art, undeniably, is fashionable. Genius is hailed, announced and appointed by self-appointed king-makers. Architectural stars and masterpieces usually are presented more rarely. However, picture printing is getting cheaper and trash is presented more often.

We are faced with the ever-present realities of replacement of some of man's best and even greatest creations as the result of either war devastation, obsolescence, or decay. Furthermore, we now face the harsh new reality of population growth requiring new facilities and funding. The latter finds its grimmest expression in urban pressures where most employment is sought and where humanity now congregates and dominates cultural events. Unfortunately, the instant city and the master plan myths still prevail. Have you seen Albany Mall from the air, or visited the public housing in Berlin? The former is redundant extravagance; the latter is monstrously inhuman. Architecture as a whole appears to be degraded to the role of scenery, status symbols of corporate or individual's monuments. There is little visible difference between self-promoting and enriching business and their political brothers under the skin when it comes to memorializing. Cathedrals of commerce soar above churches. The latest skyscraper of the third largest bank is an exhibitionist extravaganza in New York which already has acres of unrented space in earlier "masterpieces."[15]

The architectural profession is hardly a social service for the public good. It has become very private practice indeed, but its products are all too visible in the public realm. They are monuments to private interest and profit. Public housing is negligible in quantity and with few exceptions, contemptible in quality. People moving uneasily like traffic in their shadow are indeed traffic themselves on foot or in car. They must keep moving; there are rarely places to rest. People-places open to all are at a premium. Planners tend not to identify with real people but transform them into classifications and statistical numbers. Housing projects in our great cities are human silos.

In a professional school offering a time-package, learning process, there is a new dilemma as a result of greater complexity of subject matter: the difference in capacities, skills, talents in every class are widespread. Exercises in design reveal the differences. It would be personally and professionally healthy to recognize as an essential part of the educational process a stage-by-stage evaluation and to design a system of honorable discharge, with a degree suited to individuals with certain skills, perhaps in trade schools, rather than professional schools. Several such hurdles would gradually establish group work mutually satisfactory among peers and avoid frustration and inhibition. It would help to eliminate the promotion, at great expense, of the merely facile or glib.

The advantages of professional degrees are proving a myth either for employment or as status symbols. Communication systems and the private car have been socially divisive and culturally degrading. Suburbia with television has mass-produced and down-graded taste. The symbols of material success—commercially produced and relentlessly sold—have overwhelmed education in influence on the individual and have polarized democratic society. Culture lies in fragments.

In the final analysis, we are running out of time, resources and manageable numbers of our species. Can we devise ways of conserving both natural and man-made habitats? These dilemmas lie at the very basis of our present condition of uncertainty. Yet one may, if one applies Socratic questioning, find solutions. I cannot even imagine the things that students will know or the actions which they may take in the future. Time has become a factor in all situations including those which may concern both architects and planners. We must put some limits to gradualism; some actions cannot brook delay.

CHRONOLOGY

1900	Born October 8, near Grozny in the Chechen region of the Northern Caucasus.
1910	Enters Peterboro Lodge (preparatory school), London, for British education and graduates in four years.
1914	Enters Harrow School.
1917	Graduates from Harrow with honors entrance to Trinity College, Cambridge; not taken due to the Russian Revolution.
	Gazetted briefly into the British Army as interpreter for General Maynard in Murmansk on the Eastern Front; discharged due to his Russian origins.
1918	Attached to the editorial staff of Amalgamated Press in London.
	In the following years, develops a taste for jazz and becomes well-known in London as a ballroom dancer, winning several international competitions; writes and edits *The Dancing World* magazine and continues painting.
1921	Visits Berlin briefly to meet mother and father, who arrive safely from Moscow.
1922	Sails for Argentina to a friend's *estancia*; later becomes a partner in a dance hall enterprise in Buenos Aires.
1924	Returns to London, where his father dies in the same year; he changes his surname from Issakovitch to Chermayeff after a milk uncle.
	Hired as a designer by Ernest Williams, Ltd., a decorating firm in London.
1926	Introduced to the playwright Frederick Lonsdale and to the actor and director Gerald du Murier, for whom he designed several sets; makes the acquaintance of George Bernard Shaw.

1928   Joins the London furnishing studio of Waring and Gillow to develop their modern department; designs Waring's exhibition "Modern Furnishing" (with some sections by the French designer Paul Follot), which opens in November as the first exhibition in Britain of modern furniture and decoration.

Marries Barbara Maitland May and becomes a naturalized British citizen.

In the next several years, travels extensively on the Continent for Waring and Gillow, meeting many principals of the modern movement, including Erich Mendelsohn in Berlin, where the Chermayeffs are periodic guests at Mendelsohn's new house on Rupenhorn, completed in 1929.

1929   Receives a large number of interior commissions through Waring and Gillow, including portions of the French liner *l'Atlantique* (in collaboration with Paul Follot) and Claridge's Hotel in London.

Profoundly influenced by his acquaintance with Eric Gill; begins lifelong friendships with the circle of emerging contemporary artists in Britain, including Henry Moore, Ben Nicholson, John Piper, John Skeaping, Barbara Hepworth, and Eric Ravilious.

1930   Completes a renovation of his house at St. John's Wood in London, a virtual catalogue of new materials and furnishings.

Founds the 20th Century Group with Raymond McGrath, Wells Coates, and Mansfield Forbes.

Moves his practice to a renovated office in the "Pantheon," Oxford Street, London.

Completes the Cambridge Theatre interior in London, one of the first modern theatres in Britain; opens on September 8 with a revue, "Charlot's Masquerade," starring Beatrice Lillie, with some of the sets by Chermayeff.

1931   Begins development of a series of furnishing proto-
        types which continues over the next several years (some-
        times in collaboration with designers on the Continent
        such as Walter Knoll in Stuttgart and Franz Schuster in
        Vienna). Best known were chairs and unit furniture
        manufactured by Plan, Ltd., and Pel, Ltd., London.
        Also included were lighting fixtures manufactured by
        Best and Lloyd, Ltd., London, and clocks manufac-
        tured by Garrard Clocks, Ltd., London.

        Participates in the organization of an experimental de-
        sign school, the *Académie Européenne Méditerranée*, at
        Cavaliere in the south of France: a collaborative effort
        between Theodore Wijdeveld, Erich Mendelsohn, and
        Chermayeff, architects; Amedee Ozenfant, painter;
        Paul Bonifas, ceramist; Pablo Gargallo, sculptor; Eric
        Gill, sculptor and typographer; Paul Hindemith, composer.

1932   Completes a number of studios for the new BBC in
        London as one of three modern designers (with Ray-
        mond McGrath and Wells Coates). While working on
        BBC becomes an acquaintance of several life-long
        mentors involved in left politics, including Bertrand
        Russell, J. Desmond Bernal, Alfred Bacharach, J. B. S.
        Haldane, and Julian Huxley.

        Completes renovation of studio for Anthony Gibbons
        Grinling in London.

        Site of the *Académie Européenne Méditerranée* in south
        of France is destroyed by fire; project abandoned.

1933   Develops the "Kernal" House prototype as system for
        low-rise, linear housing; executes one "Kernal" as the
        "Week End House" exhibited in the exhibition "British
        Industrial Art in Relation to the Home" at Dorland Hall
        in London; later shown in the exhibition "Modern Liv-
        ing" at Whiteley's in London.

        Designs the first plastic radio cabinetry in England, for
        E. K. Cole, Ltd.; by 1940 his Ekco Model 74 sold over
        120,000 copies.

Executes the interiors of the BBC in Birmingham, his first private house, the Shann House, Rugby, and the Elmhurst Flat, Upper Brook Street, London.

Delivers key address, "New Materials and New Methods," to the Royal Institute of British Architects, attacking the "modernism" of style instead of method; made a Fellow in the RIBA; participates in founding the MARS Group, London.

Erich Mendelsohn leaves Berlin in March and in June joins Chermayeff practice in London as partner.

1934   Enters the winning scheme in the competition for an Entertainment Hall at Bexhill in Sussex (with Erich Mendelsohn). Both architects receive the commission in spite of nationalistic attacks on their "foreign origins."

Receives commendation for his "working class housing" entry in the competition sponsored by the Cement Marketing Company and won by Tecton.

Objects (with twelve other exhibitors) to the quality of and the abundance of "sham" modernism in the exhibition "Contemporary Industrial Design in Relation to the Home" held at Dorland Hall in London.

1935   Co-authors with J. M. Richards, "A Hundred Years Ahead," a controversial New Year's prediction concerning the future of design and environment in the following century, 1935–2035, published in *The Architects' Journal*.

Delivers inaugural address in London to the newly founded student's section of the Architects and Technicians Organization in London; raises the argument for a social basis for architectural education.

Completes the Nimmo House at Chalfont, St. Giles, in Buckinghamshire (with Erich Mendelsohn).

Prepares proposals for a hotel complex at Southsea, in Portsmouth, and for large-scale redevelopment of the old White City Exhibition Grounds in London (with Erich Mendelsohn). The latter contained alternative proposals for housing, an exhibition hall to replace Olympia, and related facilities.

Completes the Entertainment Pavilion at Bexhill opened by the Duke and Duchess of York, December 12.

1936   Completes Cohen House in Chelsea in London (with Erich Mendelsohn); also prepares proposals for houses at the Frinton Park Estate in Essex, and at Dorney in Windsor.

Begins fight to gain design approval of his own house at Halland in Sussex, which was not granted by the Local Rural Council due to its modern idiom; approval is granted by the Ministry of Health in 1937.

Designs a model music room for the piano exhibition at Dorland Hall in London; included is a prototype piano executed by Steinway and Whiteley's.

Erich Mendelsohn initiates a practice in Israel (then Palestine); partnership with Chermayeff is dissolved.

1937   Completes an office building for W. & A. Gilbey, Ltd., in Camdentown in London and renovation of the Heywood-Lonsdale Flat on Connaught Place in London.

Represented in the Royal Academy exhibition "British Architecture"; receives his first extensive notice in the United States in the exhibition "Modern Architecture in England" at the Museum of Modern Art in New York.

Collaborates in organization and publication of the "Circle" group in London with J. Leslie Martin, Ben Nicholson, Naum Gabo, and others.

1938   Completes the laboratory building for Imperial Chemical Industries, at Blakely in Manchester, and his own house, "Bentley Wood" at Halland in Sussex.

1939   "Lights Out Over Europe" closes the Chermayeff

office in London; joins growing professional activism in relation to civilian defense in Britain and designs (with many others) refugee rehousing for the Ministry of Defense.

Publishes *Plan for Air Raid Precaution: A Practical Policy* which outlined architectural measures for preparing shelters against civilian casualties from bombardment.

1940   Attempts to enlist, as England enters the war, but is rejected. Leaves "Bentley Wood" with family, auctioning off the furnishings to friends; sails from Liverpool to Montreal to await an entry visa to the United States.

Immigrates with his family to the United States from Canada, staying for several months with Walter and Ise Gropius in Lincoln, Massachusetts.

Lectures to several universities and organizations on the East Coast and is introduced to many of the key figures in the modern movement in the United States.

1941   Buys a Ford convertible in April and leaves the East Coast on a cross-country tour, eventually settling in San Francisco.

Begins independent practice sharing office space with Ernest Born; gives a lecture course at the San Francisco Museum of Art.

Develops proposals for post-graduate environmental programs at Stanford University and for the University of California at Berkeley; also develops proposals for expanding the environmental programs of the Pacific Northwest Regional Planning Commission.

Begins affiliations with progressive alternative professional organizations; supports formation of TELESIS Environmental Research Group on the West Coast.

1942   Completes the Mayhew House at Piedmont (Oakland) in California for the architect Clarence Mayhew; and the Horn House at Redwood (Marin County) in California.

Accepts an appointment as chairman of the Department of Art at Brooklyn College and moves to New York City in February.

Attends the Chicago Institute of Design summer course at Samonauk in Illinois, studying the teaching methods of Lazlo Moholy-Nagy, an old colleague from London.

Begins revolutionizing the Brooklyn College Program, changing the name to "Department of Design," and organizing a radically new liberal arts design curriculum; devotes almost full time to teaching.

1943   Passes NCARB examination in New York to practice architecture in the United States and joins the American Institute of Architects.

Initiates an experimental studio study at Brooklyn College on preschool education, integrating design and social science considerations.

Develops prototype proposals for "Park Type" apartments as alternatives to traditional high-rise living (with the assistance of Peter Blake, Abel Sorenson, Norman Fletcher, and Henry Hebblen), sponsored by *Architectural Forum* and exhibited at The Architectural League of New York partially as a critical response to the design for Stuyvesant Town in Manhattan.

1944   Defends the Brooklyn College curriculum against charges of pro-communist and anarchist sympathies; the curriculum is reviewed by the Board of Higher Education of New York City and eventually receives clearance.

Designs the exhibition "Design For Use" at the Museum of Modern Art in New York.

Founds the American Society of Planners and Architects with Walter Gropius, George Howe, Joseph Hudnut, Louis Kahn, Oscar Stonorov, and others.

1945   Designs hypothetical neighborhood plan and apartments for the exhibition "Tomorrow's Small House" at the Museum of Modern Art in New York.

Continues extensive activities on behalf of alternative professional organizations, including the American branch of the International Congress of Modern Architecture (CIAM), the architects' section of the National Council on American-Soviet Friendship, and the Federation of Architects, Engineers, Chemists and Technicians.

Begins experimental community design studio at Brooklyn College.

Purchases summer cottage in Truro, Massachusetts; begins a series of additions and renovations which extends over three decades.

1946   Designs renovation for an architectural office in New York shared with Conrad Wachsmann.

Assumes presidency of the Chicago Institute of Design after the death of Lazlo Moholy-Nagy in November; moves from New York to Chicago.

1947   Begins implementation of changes in the Chicago curriculum, strengthening architectural studies under the general heading of "environmental design"; continues teaching as principal activity, closing the office in New York.

Receives honorary degree from MacMurray College in Illinois.

Begins a period of intense painting activity, contributing to the Chicago School over the following several years; exhibits extensively at the Art Institute of Chicago and elsewhere.

Awarded prize for "New York No. 2" at American Artists Annual held at the Art Institute of Chicago.

1948   Continues small-scale design activity, including completion of the Ciro store interior in San Francisco (in association with Raphael Soriano), and advertising design for The Miller Company.

Develops the new curriculum at the Chicago Institute of Design, including an architectural studies option and a new emphasis on social purpose in design.

Invited to show at the "Réalités Nouvelles" exhibition in Paris.

1949   Designs a proposal for addition to the Chicago Institute of Design, North Dearborn Street; designs the exhibition "Chicago Plans" for the Chicago Planning Commission.

Delivers the seminal talk "Architecture: Anonymity and Autonomy" at Harvard University, which begins to outline the widening ideological differences between Chermayeff and many of his modernist colleagues; participates in the Cultural and Scientific Conference for World Peace in New York, sponsored by the Council of the Arts, Sciences, and Professions.

1950   Completes office renovation for British Railways at Rockefeller Center in New York (in association with Ketchum, Gina, and Sharp); begins designing fabric patterns for L. Anton Maix, New York, extending over period of several years.

Implements incorporation of Chicago Institute of Design with the Illinois Institute of Technology, forced by financial crisis resulting from post-veteran decline in student enrollments.

1951   Exhibited in a one-man show of paintings, drawings, and textiles at the Baldwin Kingrey Gallery, Chicago.

Awarded prize in the Chicago Artists Show of the Art Institute of Chicago, later exhibited at the Whitney Annual and the Metropolitan Museum of Art; participates in the CIAM 8 meeting at Hoddesdon in England during July.

Resigns the presidency of the Chicago Institute of Design after disagreements with Illinois Institute of Technology over financial and other controls; moves to Cambridge, Massachusetts, and is appointed visiting lecturer at Massachusetts Institute of Technology.

1952   Opens architectural office in Cambridge in partnership with Heywood Cutting, a former student at the Chicago Institute of Design.

Initiates the "solar skyscraper" project at MIT within an advanced architectural design studio.

Exhibits in one-man show at the Design Forum in Providence, Rhode Island.

Designs the Payson House at Portland, Maine.

Designs a painting studio for himself at Truro; first of a series of experiments with structure and form using the traditional local wood frame construction.

Appointed professor of architecture at Harvard University, as Walter Gropius and Joseph Hudnut retire and José Luis Sert becomes dean, with Nathan Pusey as new president.

1953   Begins formulation of the first-year interdisciplinary "environmental design" curriculum at Harvard for students beginning in architecture, landscape architecture, and planning; also develops proposals for advanced research and for a Ph.D. program in environmental design.

Develops the "Tile House" prototypes for continuous low-rise patio housing, the first of a long series of housing design studies.

1954   Designs the Sigerson and Wilkinson houses at Truro, Massachusetts; both are further explorations with new adaptations of local wood frame construction; also designs office and printshop for *The Cape Codder* at Orleans, Massachusetts, using a similar idiom.

Exhibits in one-man show at the Behn-Moore Gallery in Cambridge.

Resigns from the American Institute of Architects, questioning professional commitments in general and the lack of initiative toward architectural research in particular.

Attempts to initiate collaboration with developers on several large-scale projects, including a housing proposal for the Shady Hill Estate in Cambridge owned by Harvard University and the Diamond K Ranch holdings near Sacramento in California.

1955   Completes the first full sequence of the Harvard first-year interdisciplinary curriculum, with urban neighborhood and housing studies as a primary focus.

Develops furnishing prototype proposals for Polstermoblefabrik Eugen Smith in Darmstadt, West Germany.

1956   Designs the O'Connor House at Truro, Massachusetts; develops design proposals for a boathouse for the Harvard Yacht Club in Cambridge (in collaboration with Peter Chermayeff).

Produces the first versions of the Harvard Urban Family House with students from the Graduate School of Design.

Begins active campaign to publicize the patio-type house as an alternative to the detached suburban house, in an attempt to interest the general public and developers.

1957   Dissolves the architectural practice in Cambridge with Heywood Cutting.

Develops design proposals for a cluster of patio-type houses on Bowdoin Street in Cambridge for a local developer.

Presents a Great Issues Course at Dartmouth College entitled "Design and Transition: Architecture and Planning Purpose Examined in the Light of Accelerating Events"—a comprehensive critique of United States culture and professional committments in the fifties.

1958   Attempts to implement a Ph.D. and advanced research program in design at Harvard after approval is granted by faculty of the Graduate School of Design and by the university administration.

1959   Receives a grant from the Harvard-MIT Joint Center for Urban Studies for further development of the Harvard Urban Family House research toward completion of a book eventually published as *Community and Privacy*.

Begins a collaboration with Christopher Alexander, a Ph.D. student, on development of a computer program for correlation of design and social science variables related to patio cluster housing.

Participates in organization of the third Harvard Urban Design Conference; delivers a talk, "The Shape of Quality," stressing physical and social networks of communication as the primary structural basis for urban-scale form.

Begins active participation in the fight for establishment of the Cape Cod National Seashore; approved by Act of Congress in the following year.

Designs competition entry for the Franklin Delano Roosevelt Memorial (with Peter Chermayeff, Aram Mardirosian, and Robert Reynolds, students from the Graduate School of Design).

1961   Begins collaboration with Peter Chermayeff on the graphics and design for *Community and Privacy*.

Delivers the talk "The Shape of Privacy" at Harvard University, further elaborating his critique of the culture of housing in the United States.

1962   Resigns professorship at Harvard, accepting an invitation to teach at the Yale University School of Arts and Architecture under Paul Rudolph, the newly appointed dean.

Initiates a graduate program in environmental design at Yale, publishing the first studio document, "A New Urbanity," which explores relationships between urban form and its communications infrastructure; a number of such studies evolve at Yale over the following several years.

1963   Designs his own house on Lincoln Street in New Haven; based on principles explored earlier in the Harvard Urban House Project.

Publishes *Community and Privacy* (with Christopher Alexander); begins extensive lecture schedule lasting over next several years.

Appointed Visiting Critic at Washington University in St. Louis, where urban design explorations are continued.

1964   Begins development of proposals for advanced environmental studies at Yale extending over the next several years.

Receives honorary degrees from Washington University in St. Louis; receives honorary membership in the Sociedad Colombiana de Arquitectos in Bogotá, Colombia.

Embarks on an extensive lecture tour in England in March, addressing contemporary problems of industrialization and urbanity.

Participates on the annual *Progressive Architecture* design awards jury, which refuses to grant awards to the category of the single-family house in an attempt to reinforce other priorities and concerns within the architecture profession.

1965   Receives a grant from the Twentieth Century Fund to study the formation of urban place; begins formal development of material eventually published in *Shape of Community*.

Organizes an advanced seminar at Yale toward formalization of a dialectical theory of urban organization, subsequently labeled the "Yale Model."

1966   Receives a grant from the United States National Bureau of Standards for further development of the "Yale Model"; invites the collaboration of Alexander

Tzonis, a former Yale student, and completes a second advanced seminar.

1967   Develops proposals for infill housing on Wooster Square in New Haven for the New Haven Redevelopment Authority (in association with Cambridge Seven Associates, Inc.).

Publishes the book *Advanced Studies in Urban Environments*, summarizing progress on the "Yale Model" (with Alexander Tzonis).

1968   Travels to Italy to address the "14th Triennale di Milano" on "Formal and Structural Changes in Human Settlements"; program cancelled due to student strikes and political protest.

Participates in organizing protest against the State Street highway project in New Haven.

1969   Develops the "Urban Yardstick" project with Yale students as an exploration toward measuring functional characteristics of urban place.

Retires from Yale as professor emeritus in June.

Invited to visit India as an advisor on means of improving the teaching of architecture and design under a grant from the John D. Rockefeller III Fund.

1970   Completes two-month study in India, and a report, "Design of the Physical Environment in India: Professional Standards and Education."

1971   Travels to the Far East to deliver the A. S. Hook Memorial Lecture at the Royal Australian Institute of Architects Centenary Convention in Sydney; also addresses the congress of the Australian Architectural Students Association in Auckland, New Zealand.

Publishes *Shape of Community* (with Alexander Tzonis); begins extensive lecture activity, which will last over the following years.

1972   Completes renovations and additions to house at Truro; moves from New Haven to Cape Cod.

1973   Receives the gold medal from the Royal Canadian In-
        stitute of Architecture in June in Montreal.

        Exhibits in a one-man show at the Cherrystone Gallery
        in Wellfleet, Massachusetts; publishes *Verse of Anger
        and Affection*.

1974   Delivers the Twelfth Annual Gropius Lecture at Har-
        vard University, entitled "Institutions, Priorities, Rev-
        olutions."

        Conducts a graduate seminar on contemporary issues
        in architecture at Harvard University.

1975   Withdraws substantially from public life in this and
        following several years; begins a new period of intense
        painting activity.

        Continues work over the next several years toward the
        organization of a personal archive at the Avery Ar-
        chitectural Library at Columbia University and toward
        the organization of the Chicago Institute of Design ar-
        chive within the Bauhaus Archiv in Berlin.

1977   Exhibits in a one-man show at the Wolcott Library in
        Litchfield, Massachusetts.

1979   Exhibits in one-man shows at the Kendall Gallery in
        Wellfleet, Massachusetts, and at the New Art Centre in
        London.

1980   Accepts visiting professorship at the Ohio State Uni-
        versity, where he also receives an honorary degree.

        Receives the American Institute of Architects Associa-
        tion of Collegiate Schools of Architecture Award for
        Excellence in Architectural Education.

        Receives the Sir Misha Black Medal of the Royal Soci-
        ety of Industrial Artists and Designers for his distin-
        guished service to design.

PLATES

Office and furnishings
for Ambrose Wilson,
London, 1929.

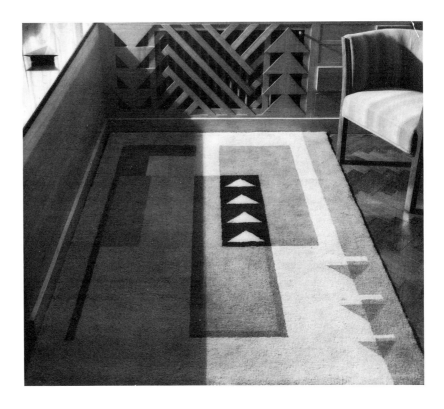

Cambridge Theatre
interior, London, 1930.
Safety curtain also
designed by
Chermayeff.

Cambridge Theatre interior, London, 1930. Upper circle lobby.

Cambridge Theatre,
London, 1930. Program
cover design for opening
night.

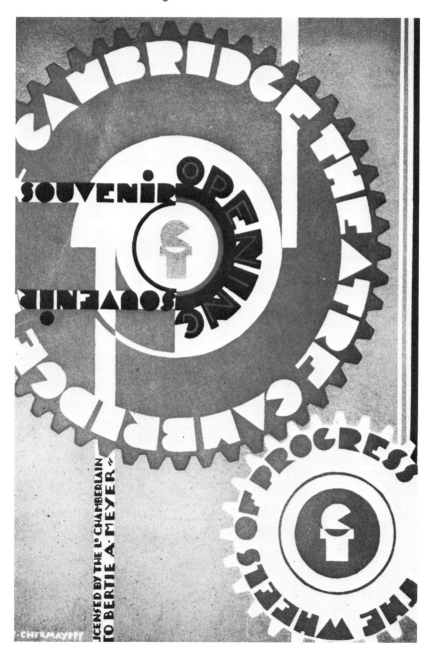

Chermayeff Flat, St. John's Wood, London, 1930. Living and dining rooms. Most furnishings designed by Chermayeff for Waring and Gillow, London.

Nesting chairs designed
for Pel, Ltd., 1932;
armchair for Plan, Ltd.,
1933; in Entertainment
Hall, Bexhill, Sussex,
1935 (in partnership
with Erich Mendelsohn).

Shann House, Rugby,
1933. Terrace and
balcony detail.

BBC Broadcasting
House, Birmingham,
1933. Small studio.

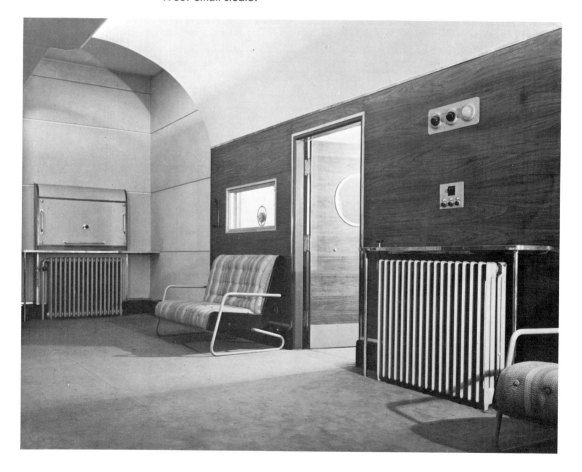

W and B Ltd., wholesale
showrooms, London,
1934. Tubular steel
chairs designed by
Chermayeff for Pel,
Ltd., London.

Nimmo House,
Chalfont, St. Giles,
Buckinghamshire, 1935
(in partnership with Erich
Mendelsohn). South
terrace.

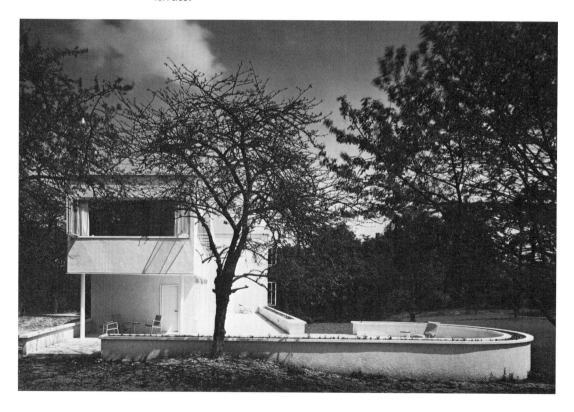

Entertainment Hall,
Bexhill, Sussex, 1935 (in
partnership with Erich
Mendelsohn). Main
staircase and terrace.

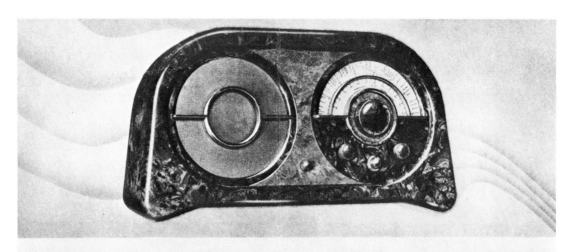

EIGHT-STAGE SUPERHET

This new 'Clear-cut reality' receiver gives tonal reproduction as true as a tuning fork and incorporates every modern technical feature. It is housed in a most striking cabinet of magnificent design.

Eight-stage superhet circuit with band-pass tuning (for A.C. Mains).

New type 'Clear-cut reality' moving coil speaker with extra large and efficient output transformer.

Station pre-selector and automatic noise suppressor.

Magnificent moulded cabinet in new walnut shade or black with chromium-plated fittings.

Fully delayed quiet automatic volume control (amplified).

Large size station scale with names and wavelengths.

Continuously variable tone control.

Light-beam and shadow station indicator.

Tone-compensated volume control.

Gramophone pick-up sockets with switch.

External speaker sockets.

Internal speaker switch.

Latest type valves : Octode, H.F. pentode, double diode, triode, L.F. pentode and full-wave rectifier.

Output 3 watts.

Dimensions : 22″ x 12″ x 9½″.

MODEL AC86

12½ Gns.

Walnut Finish.

Initial payment of £1/2/6 and 12 monthly payments of £1/2/6

Black and Chromium 10/6 extra.

MODEL B86 — EIGHT-STAGE BATTERY SUPERHET. Battery version of model AC86, incorporating Q.P.P. output and a valve combination comprising :— Triode pentode, H.F. pentode, double-diode-triode and double pentode. *H.P. Terms: Initial payment of £1/1/0 and 12 monthly payments of £1/1/0.* Black and Chromium 10/6 extra.   Walnut Finish.

11½ Gns.

(without batteries)

Advertisement for Ekco
Radio Model AC86,
designed for E. K. Cole,
Ltd., London, 1935.

Cohen House, Chelsea,
London, 1936 (in
partnership with Erich
Mendelsohn).

Heywood-Lonsdale Flat,
Marble Arch, London,
1937. Furnishings by
Chermayeff, including
chairs designed for Plan,
Ltd., London, and piano
designed for Bechstein,
London.

Office building for W.
and A. Gilbey, Ltd.,
London, 1937.

Chermayeff House,
"Bentley Wood,"
Halland, Sussex, 1938.

Chermayeff House,
"Bentley Wood,"
Halland, Sussex, 1938.
Night view toward
terrace. Chairs designed
for Pel, Ltd., London.

Dyestuffs laboratory,
Imperial Chemical
Industries, Blakely,
Manchester, 1938.

Dyestuffs laboratory,
Imperial Chemical
Industries, Blakely,
Manchester, 1938.
Typical laboratory
module.

Mayhew House,
Piedmont (Oakland),
California, 1942 (in
collaboration with
Clarence Mayhew).

Horn House, Redwood,
Marin County,
California, 1942.

"Conference of Great Powers," oil on homosote (48″ × 48″), 1947. From the collection of Peter Chermayeff.

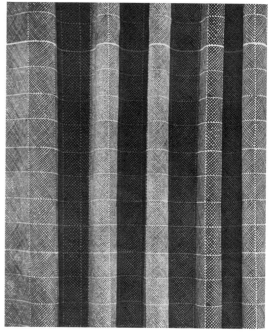

"Cross Hatch" fabric designed for Maix Fabrics, New York, 1950.

Payson House, Portland,
Maine, 1952.

Payson House, Portland,
Maine, 1952.

Chermayeff Studio,
Truro, Massachusetts,
1952.

Wilkinson House, Truro,
Massachusetts, 1954.

O'Connor House, Truro,
Massachusetts, 1956.

Harvard Urban Family
House Project, 1957.

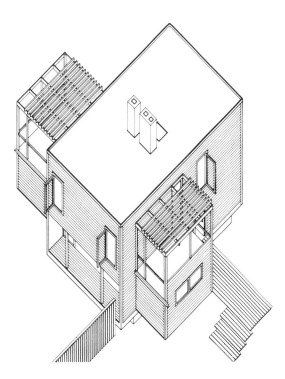

Chermayeff House, New
Haven, Connecticut,
1963.

NOTES

INTRODUCTION

1. "The Technique of Architecture from an Educator's Point of View," *The Boston Society of Architects Record* XXXVII(November 1951). This talk demonstrates the continuing affinity to the Lewis critique, including the quotation, "Architects! Where is your vortex?"

2. Wyndham Lewis, *The Caliph's Design. Architects! Where is your Vortex?* (London: The Egoist, 1919), p. 7.

3. Chermayeff followed the early writings of Lewis Mumford, another admirer of Geddes, and his friendship with Andrew Messer also furthered his appreciation for Geddes. Messer was the Chief Medical Officer of Health to the Newburn District Council, Northumberland, where he was very active in promoting housing reform, with heavy influence of Geddes' philosophy.

4. Eric Gill, *Beauty Looks After Herself* (London: Sheed & Ward, 1933), pp. 126, 127, 134.

5. For a concise history of this movement, see Gary Werskey, *The Visible College* (New York: Holt, Rinehardt and Winston, 1978).

6. J. D. Bernal, *The Social Function of Science* (London: Routledge & Kegan Paul, Ltd., 1939), p. 411.

7. See in particular "The Architectural Student: Training for What?" *Focus 4* (Summer 1939), pp. 96–101.

8. Noel Carrington, *Industrial Design in Britain* (London: George Allen & Unwin, 1976), p. 139.

9. See Chermayeff references in Gavin Stamp, ed., *Britain in the Thirties A.D. Profite 24* (London: Architectural Design, 1980). The current politicization of the history of the thirties in Britain is described in Stephen Games, "30's is a dangerous age," *The Guardian* (December 14, 1977), p. 9.

10. A summary of the political activity of this period is contained in Anthony Jackson, *The Politics of Architecture: A History of Modern Architecture in Britain* (Toronto: University of Toronto Press, 1970).

11. Serge Chermayeff and J. M. Richards, "A Hundred Years Ahead: Forecasting the Coming Century," *The Architects' Journal* LXXXI (January 10, 1935), pp. 79–86. For references to the critical reaction, see bibliography. Hélène Lipstadt has undertaken an analysis of the Chermayeff and Richards article, to be published as "Parody and Polemic in the Battle for British Modernism: 1935," in the *Oxford Art Journal*, Fall 1982.

12. Serge Chermayeff and J. M. Richards, letter to the editor, *The Architects' Journal* LXXXI(January 31, 1935), pp. 189–190.

13. J. B. S. Haldane, *A.R.P.* (London: Victor Gollancz, Ltd., 1938). Serge Chermayeff, *Plan for Air Raid Precaution: A Practical Policy* (London: Frederick Muller, Ltd., 1939).

14. "Finsbury Borough Council A.R.P. Shelters. Report on suggested signposting of Shelters," 1939. Serge Chermayeff Archive, Avery Library, Columbia University. TECTON's book on ARP, also published in 1939, deals extensively with their plan for the Borough of Finsbury: TECTON, architects, *Planned A.R.P.* (London: The Architectural Press, 1939).

15. "Telesis: The Birth of a Group," *Pencil Points* XXIII(July 1942), pp. 27–28.

16. "Activities," *Task* V(Spring 1944), p. 36.

17. Miscellaneous material on the American Chapter of the International Congress for Modern Architecture (CIAM) and on the American Society of Planners and Architects (ASPA) may be found with the Chermayeff Archive of Papers from the American Society of Planners and Architects, Widener Library, Harvard University.

18. See "National Council of Soviet-American Friendship" and "Committee of the Arts, Sciences and Professions," Serge Chermayeff Archive, Avery Library, Columbia University.

19. *The New York Times* provided extensive reportage on the conference and its aftermath. See in particular "Panel Discussions of the Cultural Delegates Cover a Wide Range of Subjects," *The New York Times* (March 27, 1949), p. 44.

20. "Task Activities," *Task* IV(1943), p. 49.

21. Brief mention of Chermayeff's efforts is made in Martin Duberman, *Black Mountain. An Exploration in Community* (New York: E. P. Dutton & Co., Inc., 1972), p. 205. Russell stayed with the Chermayeffs on East 21st Street while in New York.

22. Much of the Brooklyn College controversy over the next two years centered around reportage and editorials in the *Brooklyn Eagle*. It is also documented in *The New York Times* and elsewhere. See clippings under "Brooklyn College," Serge Chermayeff Archive, Avery Library, Columbia University.

23. The harassment of Chermayeff over his Brooklyn College appointment and later in relation to his curriculum reform must be viewed in the context of the repression waged by the Rapp-Condert Committee, created within the New York State Legislature in 1941, which targeted leftists teaching in Brooklyn College and the City College of New York.

24. Victor S. Navasky, *Naming Names* (New York: Viking Press, 1980), p. 47. Navasky analyzes the moral dilemmas of the Hollywood blacklisting. Similar dilemmas existed for architects, although less public, representing a far less pervasive crisis within the profession.

25. Of special interest in relation to the AIA position was a speech made by Carl Koch at the 1947 AIA national convention in Grand Rapids: Carl Koch, "What is the Attitude of the Young Practitioner toward the Profession?", *AIA Journal* VII(June 1947), pp. 264–269. For further discussion of the housing issue, see Richard Plunz, "The Institutionalization of Housing Form in New York City, 1920–1950," in Richard Plunz, ed., *Housing Form and Public Policy in the United States* (New York: Praeger Publishers, 1980).

26. Memorandum from Vernon DeMars dated March 31, 1952, under "National Council of Soviet-American Friendship," Serge Chermayeff Archive, Avery Library, Columbia University.

27. The conference provided an anti-McCarthy rallying point and received widespread publicity. A number of its participants were blacklisted.

28. Sir Giles Gilbert Scott, "The Inaugural Address," *The RIBA Journal* XLI(November 11, 1933), pp. 7, 10. Serge Chermayeff, "New Materials and New Methods," *The RIBA Journal* XLI(December 23, 1933), pp. 166, 179.

29. Serge Chermayeff, "An Explosive Revolution," *The Architectural Review* CLXVI(November 1979), p. 309.

30. Chermayeff's patrons are among numerous topics discussed with the author in taped interviews between 1975 and 1980.

31. "Creditor's Meeting," *The Times* (June 24, 1939), p. 39.

32. The displacement from Britain to the United States appears to have been difficult. See Rebecca West, "The First Fortnight," *Ladies' Home Journal* LVII(January 1940), p. 68.

33. "A Summary of Report on Contemporary Planning, Architecture, Design and Design Education," 1941; and "Outline for a Planning and Design Department in a Western University," 1941. Serge Chermayeff Archive, Avery Library, Columbia University.

34. Chermayeff's ire in relation to the AIA increased when Ralph Walker became president in 1949. See "The Profession of Architecture," a talk given at the Institute of Design, Chicago, dated November 2, 1950. Serge Chermayeff Archive, Avery Library, Columbia University.

35. Chermayeff describes the Harvard first-year curriculum in detail in an interview with Richard Plunz dated October 11, 1975.

36. For example, see Christopher Alexander, "The Pattern of Streets," *American Institute of Planners Journal* XXXII(September 1966), pp. 273–278. Chermayeff disapproved of aspects of direction taken by Alexander after their collaboration, a notable example being this study. See Chermayeff's copy, with notation, in the Serge Chermayeff Archive, Avery Library, Columbia University.

37. Charles Jencks, "The Architect in an Overpopulated World," *Connection No. 1*, Harvard University Graduate School of Design (1963), pp. 21–23.

38. Alan Colquhoun, book review, *Architectural Association Journal* LXXIX(December 1963), p. 166.

39. Allan Temko, "Things are getting too Crowded, too Mechanized, and too Noisy," *The New York Times Book Review* (October 13, 1963), p. 6.

40. *Search for a New Urbanity* (New Haven: Yale University School of Arts and Architecture, 1962).

41. W. Mitchell, ed., *Synopsis of Conclusions and Record of Process. The Chermayeff Studio. Autumn, 1968–69* (New Haven: Yale University School of Arts and Architecture, January 1969).

42. Rothafel claimed to have discovered the idea from a sunset or through a dream, but he and his design team did visit new London theaters in 1931, less than a year after the Cambridge Theatre opened, making it the most likely real source. A telephone conversation on February 17, 1982, with Donald Desky, the only participant in the European visit still alive, confirmed the visit to London, but he was unable to recall the itinerary. See David Loth, *The City Within A City* (New York: William Morrow & Company, 1966), p. 81; Walter H. Kilham, Jr., *Raymond Hood, Architect* (New York: Architectural Book Publishing Co., Inc., 1973), p. 139.

43. Interesting evaluations of the technical innovation at both Bexhill and Gilbey House are the Building Research Station Notes, nos. D781 and D814, both published in July 1962.

44. Some of Chermayeff's furnishings, especially chairs, were adapted from production on the Continent and are therefore of complex attribution. Some research has been initiated on this general problem. See Dennis Sharp, Tim Benton, and Barbie Campbell Cole, *Pel and Tubular Steel Furniture of the Thirties* (London: The Architectural Association, 1977).

45. The academy, initiated by Wijdeveld, was to be located near Cap Nègre between Cannes and Marseilles. Unfortunately, the site was destroyed by fire in 1933 and the venture failed. The Academy prospectus is included under "European Mediterranean Academy," Serge Chermayeff Archive, Avery Library, Columbia University.

46. Philip James, *Henry Moore on Sculpture* (London: MacDonald and Company, 1966), p. 99.

47. Charles Reilly, "Professor Reilly Speaking," *The Architects' Journal* LXXXVIII(September 22, 1938), p. 479. Even at this late date, Reilly's praise of the Chermayeff House brought fascistic response, as the subsequent letters to the editor of *The Architects' Journal* show.

48. Leonardo Benevolo, *History of Modern Architecture*, 2 vols. (Cambridge, Mass.: MIT Press, 1971), p. 588.

49. John Summerson, "Introduction," in Trevor Dannatt, *Modern Architecture in Britain* (London: Batsford, 1959), p. 17.

50. Hugh Casson, "Good Building and Bad Theatre," *Night and Day* (September 9, 1937), p. 27.

51. See Ellen Perry Berkeley, "Mathematics at Yale," *Architectural Forum* CXXXIII(July/August 1970), pp. 63–65; "Mathematics at Yale: Readers Respond," *Architectural Forum* CXXXIII(October 1970), pp. 64–66.

PART I

1. Aldous Huxley, *Point Counter Point* (New York: Doubleday and Company, Inc., 1928), p. 162.

2. An apparent to himself as a Maskelyn or magician in disguise, performing to an audience of Devants, or those who would anticipate his act. *The Oxford English Dictionary.*

3. Oscar Wilde, *The Picture of Dorian Grey* (New York: Modern Library, 1926), p. viii.

4. One of Julian Huxley's first efforts as science reporter for the BBC was to organize a lecture series called "Scientific Research and Social Needs" (October 1933–January 1934). Two of the lectures he gave touched on the theme of tradition and prejudice: "Building and Shelter," *The Listener* X(October 25, 1933), pp. 617–620; "How Science Looks After Our Clothes," *The Listener* X(November 1, 1933), pp. 649–651.

5. Oscar Wilde, *The Picture of Dorian Grey* (New York: Modern Library, 1926), p. vii.

6. P. Morton Shand, "Alvar Aalto: A Psychological Architect," *The Listener* X(November 15, 1933), p. 742.

7. "Map of Contemporary Architecture in America—By Living Architects," *Twice A Year* 2(Spring–Summer 1939), map follows p. 108.

8. The National Council of Arts, Sciences and Professions was a broad alliance of intellectuals which was particularly active in combatting McCarthyism. Chermayeff became an active sponsor. See "National Council of Arts, Sciences and Professions," Serge Chermayeff Archive, Avery Library, Columbia University, New York.

9. "A City Shows How to Fight Decay," *Life* XL(March 12, 1956), pp. 62–63.

10. *The First Two Years: 1959–1961* (Cambridge, Mass.: The Joint Center for Urban Studies of the Massachusetts Institute of Technology and Harvard University, April 1961) mentions Whiting's association with the center. There is no official record of the luncheon.

11. See mimeographed text, "Through the Vanishing Point," by Marshall McLuhan, dated May 1, 1961, in the Serge Chermayeff Archive, Avery Architectural Library.

12. E. H. Gombrich, *Art and Illusion: A Study in the Psychology of Pictorial Representation*, A. W. Mellon Lectures in Fine Arts (New York: Pantheon Books, 1960), p. 376.

13. J. Z. Young, "Doubt and Certainty in Science," Reith Lectures, The BBC, 1950; published as *Doubt and Certainty in Science: A Biologist's Reflections on the Brain* (Oxford: Oxford University Press, 1951), p. 160.

14. "Life Presents in Collaboration with the *Architectural Forum* Eight Houses for Modern Living," *Life* V(September 26, 1938), pp. 45–67.

15. Roderick Seidenberg, *Post Historic Man: an Inquiry* (Chapel Hill, N.C.: University of North Carolina Press, 1950).

16. Max Born, Evangelical Academy, Kloster Loccum, February 1953; quoted by Serge Chermayeff and Alexander Tzonis, *Shape of Community: Realization of Human Potential* (Baltimore: Penguin Books, Ltd., 1971), p. 9.

17. United States, Department of Housing and Urban Development, *Conference on New Approaches to Urban Transportation*, Washington, D.C., November 27, 1967. Charles M. Haar was deputy assistant secretary for metropolitan development, U.S. Department of Housing and Urban Development and author of *Law and Land: Anglo-American Planning Practice* (1964).

18. Tom Wicker, "The Highway Juggernaut," *The New York Times*, January 10, 1971, Sect. IV, p. 15.

19. Tom Wicker, "In the Nation: No Expo for the Centennial," *The New York Times*, March 19, 1970, p. 46; Ada Louise Huxtable, "Whither World Fairs?" *The New York Times*, March 29, 1970, Sect. II, p. 29; Jack Shepherd, "Polis for '76," *Look* XXXV(January 12, 1971), pp. 43–44; "Speedy Train Net Proposed for '76," *The New York Times*, July 18, 1971, p. 24.

20. The Nature Conservancy for the Study Conference, *The Countryside in 1970: Proceedings of the Study Conference* (London: Her Majesty's Stationery Office, 1964); Secretary, Standing Committee, "Review for the Third Conference: 'The Countryside in 1970'," 1970.

21. Probably this refers to an ecological study, "Man in the Living Environment (1971)," prepared for presentation to the United Nations Conference on the Human Environment, Stockholm, 1972. See Bayard Webster, "Supplies of Vital Phosphorous Found in Peril in Ecology Study," *The New York Times*, October 17, 1971, p. 76.

22. Loren Eiseley, "The Winter of Man," *The New York Times*, January 16, 1972, Sect. 4, p. 15.

23. Reference to Chermayeff's receipt of the Second Annual Sir Misha Black Memorial Medal. See "Escapist Architecture," *The Architects' Journal* CLXXII(October 22, 1980), p. 782.

24. Joan Robinson, *Aspects of Development and Underdevelopment* (London: Cambridge University Press, 1979), pp. 7–8.

25. Heinz Von Foerster, introduction to Serge Chermayeff and Alexander Tzonis, *Shape of Community*, p. xix.

26. Wilfred Owen, "Transition to an Urban Planet," *Bulletin of the Atomic Scientists* XXXV(November 1979), p. 12.

27. "People," *World Press Review* XVII(August 1980).

28. J. M. Richards, "Style Was a Dirty Word," *The Architectural Review* CLXVI(November 1979), p. 301.

29. John Kenneth Galbraith, *Economics and Public Purpose* (Boston: Houghton Mifflin Company, 1973), pp. 67–70.

30. Anatoly Kuznetsov, *Babi Yar: A Documentary Novel*, trans. Jacob Guralsky (New York: The Dial Press, 1967), p. 202.

PART II

1. For a brief description, see Raymond McGrath, "Mansfield D. Forbes, An Intimate Appreciation by Raymond McGrath," *The Architectural Review* LXXIX(April 1936), pp. 173–176.

2. The source of quotation is unidentified, but Cripps discusses similar ideas in "The Ultimate Aims of the Labour Party," *The Listener* X(December 6, 1933), pp. 871–872.

3. Ibid.

4. Air Raid Precaution Shelter. See Serge Chermayeff, *Plan for Air Raid Precaution: A Practical Policy* (London: Frederick Muller, Ltd., 1939).

5. The economic crisis of 1938 forced the closing of the Chermayeff office. See "Creditor's Meeting," *The Times*, June 24, 1939, p. 39.

6. Four issues of *Focus* were published in 1938–1939 by Percy Lund Humphries & Co. Ltd., London, seemingly at the initiative of the "second generation" British Moderns.

7. "Destruction and Reconstruction," *The Architectural Review* XC(July 1941), entire issue.

8. "Post-War Pattern," *The Architectural Forum* LXXIV (May 1941), pp. 309–310; "Post-War Pattern, No. 1: Planning," *The Architectural Forum* LXXV(September 1941); "Post-War Pattern, No. 2: Standardization," *The Architectural Forum* LXXV(November 1941), pp. 353–364.

9. Tom Harrisson edited *Mass-observation* (1937–1947) and has written such books as *Savage Civilization* (1937) and the *World Within: A Borneo Study* (1959).

10. Lancelot Hogben, *Science for the Citizen* (London: George Allen and Unwin, Ltd., 1938); Hogben was a major proponent of scientific humanism and an acquaintance of Chermayeff's.

11. Refers to the October 18, 1950, session in a series, "Forum for Modern Living," held at the New York Architectural League. The topic was "Must Our Architecture Be Sterile?", with Wallace K. Harrison as keynote speaker. The series was reported in "Architectural League Plans Series on Arts," *The Architectural Record* CVIII(October 1950), p. 13; "Forum at League," *Progressive Architecture* XXXI(November 1950), p. 12.

12. Refers to the October 11, 1950, session, "Can the Arts Work To-

gether?", with Joseph Hudnut as keynote speaker. The session was reported in "Strictly Functional House Held Unlivable; Designers Urged to Borrow from Past," *The New York Times*, October 13, 1950, p. 32.

13. "President Walker Reveals Introduction to His New Book on Collectivism vs. Individualism at Our September Meeting," *Bulletin. Chicago Chapter. American Institute of Architects* (October 1950), p. 6.

14. Charles Dana Loomis, letter to the editor, *American Institute of Architects Journal* XIV(October 1950), pp. 187–188.

15. William H. Scheick, "What Is BRAB and Why?" *American Institute of Architects Journal* XIV(October 1950), pp. 162–165.

16. "Skidmore, Owings, and Merrill, architects, U.S.A.," *Museum of Modern Art Bulletin* XVIII(Fall 1950), entire issue; Aline R. Loucheim, "Architecture of and for Our Day," *The New York Times*, September 24, 1950, Sect. II, p. 9.

17. Hogben, *Science for the Citizen*.

18. H. G. Wells, *Fate of Homo Sapiens* (London: Secker and Warburg, 1939); published in United States as *Fate of Man* (New York: Alliance Book Corp./Longmans, Green and Company, 1939).

19. Sigfried Giedion, *A Decade of Contemporary Architecture* (Zurich: Editions Girsberger, 1954), pp. 44–45; Congrès Internationaux d'Architecture Moderne, *Documents 7: Bergamo, 1949* (Nendeln: Kraus Reprint, 1979).

20. Eric Gill, *Beauty Looks After Herself* (London: Sheed and Ward, 1933).

21. H. J. Muller, "Science for Humanity," *Bulletin of the Atomic Scientists* XV(April 1959), p. 146.

22. A. M. Dalq, "Form and Modern Embryology," in *Aspects of Form*, edited by Lancelot Law Whyte (London: Lund Humphries and Co., Ltd., 1951), p. 91; also quoted by Lancelot Law Whyte, *Accent on Form* (New York: Harper and Brothers Publishers, 1954), p. vi.

23. Lancelot Law Whyte, *Accent on Form: An Anticipation of the Science of Tomorrow* (New York: Harper and Brothers, 1954), pp. 66–67.

24. Apparently this talk, which remains unidentified, was probably given by Rudolph just prior to Chermayeff's lecture.

25. "Two Scientists Question Value of Space and Missile Program," *The New York Times*, March 21, 1959, p. 2; "I.B.M. Deplores Remark," *The New York Times*, March 22, 1959, p. 29.

26. Walter McQuade, "Architecture," *The Nation* CXCIV(March 17, 1962), pp. 241–242.

27. The source of the quotation is unidentified, but Allen discussed similar ideas in "The Training and Education of Architects," *The Architectural Record* CXXXIII(April 1963), pp. 173–176; "Observations in America," *The Architectural Association Journal* LXXIX(September–October 1963), pp. 68–77; "The Education of Architects," *RIBA Jour-*

nal LXXI(May 1964), pp. 210–219. Allen traveled in the United States and Canada during the winter of 1963.

28. *Time* magazine covers depicted such architects as Richard Buckminster Fuller (January 10, 1964), Minoru Yamasaki (January 18, 1963), Edward D. Stone (March 31, 1958), and Eero Saarinen (July 2, 1956).

29. The architect Clarence Mayhew and his wife asked Chermayeff to design their house in Piedmont, California, a suburb of Oakland. It was completed in 1942.

30. Howe's talk was given to the first meeting of the American Society of Planners and Architects, held on January 27, 1945, in New York City. The talk was published as "Master Plans for Master Politicians," *Magazine of Art* XXXIX(February 1946), pp. 66–68; and as "Piani Maestri per i maestri della politica," *Metron* XXV(1948), pp. 12–15. The original manuscript is in the Chermayeff Archive of Papers from the American Society of Planners and Architects, Widener Library, Harvard University, Cambridge, Massachusetts.

31. "The Mind of Louis Kahn," *The Architectural Forum* CXXXVII (July/August 1972), pp. 42–89; this issue was announced in *The Architectural Forum* CXXXVI(April 1972), pp. 77–80.

32. Apparently, this refers to Beinecke Rare Book Library designed by Gordon Bunshaft of Skidmore, Owings & Merrill.

33. A description of the fire at the A & A may be found in Joseph Lelyveld, "After Fire, Yale Smolders," *The New York Times*, June 27, 1969, p. 39.

34. Gabriel de Mortillet, an eminent nineteenth-century French archaeologist, founded the magazine *Indicateur de l'archaeologie* (1872–1874); edited *Matériaux pour l'histoire et vie naturelle de l'homme* and wrote such books as *le Préhistorique, antiquité de l'homme* (1883), and *Formation de la nation francaise; textes—linguistique; palenthologie—anthropologie* (1897).

35. Colin Renfrew is a British archaeologist and the author of such books as *Before Civilization* (1973); *The Emergence of Civilization* (1972).

36. Howe, A.S.P.A. speech. See note 30.

37. "Planning Man's Physical Environment: Princeton University Bicentennial Conference Series 2 Conference 5" (Princeton, N.J.: Princeton University, 1946); the conference was described in *The Architectural Forum* LXXXVI(April 1947), pp. 12–14.

38. Reyner Banham, *Los Angeles: The Architecture of Four Ecologies* (New York: Harper and Row, 1971).

39. James D. Edmonds, Jr., "The Tree of Science: Beautiful Blossoms But Bitter Fruits," *Bulletin of the Atomic Scientists* XXX(February 1974), pp. 25–26.

40. Samuel H. Day, Jr., "A Statement of Purpose," *The Bulletin of the Atomic Scientists* XXX(April 1974), pp. 2–3.

41. John Kenneth Galbraith, *Economics and Public Purpose* (Boston: Houghton Mifflin Company, 1973), p. 145.

42. Gunnar Myrdal, *Against the Stream* (New York: Pantheon Books, 1973), pp. 267–268.

43. Walter Gropius, letter to students, January 14, 1964; quoted by Serge Chermayeff and Alexander Tzonis, *Shape of Community: Realization of Human Potential* (Baltimore: Penguin Books, Ltd., 1971), p. xxiv.

44. Eric Gill, *Beauty Looks After Herself* (London: Sheed and Ward, 1933).

PART III

1. Aldous Huxley, *Point Counter Point* (New York: Doubleday and Company, Inc.), p. 162.

2. The Armour Institute of Technology became the Illinois Institute of Technology. Mies van der Rohe became the director in 1938.

3. Philip Johnson, "The Seven Crutches of Modern Architecture," *Perspecta* 3(1955), pp. 40–45.

4. Mies's glass skyscraper projects can be found in L. Hilberseimer, *Mies van der Rohe* (Chicago: Paul Theobald and Company, 1956), pp. 25–27.

5. An apparent reference by Johnson to a Chermayeff comment about the Glass House, edited out of the published version of Johnson's talk.

6. Albert Szabo was Chermayeff's assistant in the design studio.

7. "Education and Architecture," *The Architectural Forum* CXX(January 1964), p. 63.

8. Serge Chermayeff, letter to the editor, *The Architectural Forum* CXX(February 1964), p. 64.

9. Ibid.

10. Ibid.

11. Mayor's Task Force, William S. Paley, chairman, "The Threatened City: A Report on the Design of the City of New York," February 7, 1967. Steven V. Roberts, "Report Urges Drastic Changes in City's Approach to Planning," *The New York Times*, February 8, 1967, p. 33; "The Design of the City," *The New York Times*, February 13, 1967, p. 32; Philip C. Johnson, I. M. Pei, Jaquelin Robertson, Robert A. M. Stern, letter to the editor, *The New York Times*, February 17, 1967, p. 36.

12. Eric Gill, *Beauty Looks After Herself* (London: Sheed and Ward, 1933).

13. Donald W. Buchanan was affiliated with the National Film Board of Canada and the National Gallery of Canada in the 1940s. Chermayeff discussed a number of projects with him, none of which seem to have

materialized. See "D. W. Buchanan," Serge Chermayeff Archive, Avery Library, Columbia University, New York.

14. Joyce Milton, "Genetic Roulette," *The Nation* CCXXV(October 15, 1977), p. 365.

15. Apparently, this refers to the Citicorp Building designed by Hugh Stubbins.

BIBLIOGRAPHY

The bibliography for architectural and other design projects has been substantially abridged to include only the most complete sources, with elimination of most duplicate information.

ARCHITECTURAL PROJECTS: GENERAL BUILDING

Proposal for a hotel complex at Southsea, Isle of Wight (in partnership with Erich Mendelsohn), 1935.

Martin, J. L.; Nicholson, Ben; and Gabo, N. *Circle: International Survey of Constructive Art*. London: Farber and Farber, Ltd., 1937; Section 3, Plates 11, 12.

Whittick, Arnold. *Eric Mendelsohn*. London: Leonard Hill Books, Ltd., 1956; pp. 102, 107; Plates 33A, 33B.

Zevi, Bruno. *Erich Mendelsohn. Opera Completa*. Milan: Etwas Compass, 1970; pp. 231–233.

De La Warr Pavilion, Bexhill, Brighton (in partnership with Erich Mendelsohn), 1935.

The Architect and Building News CXXXVII(February 2, 1934), pp. 161–164; (February 9, 1934), p. 196; CLXIV(December 20, 1935), "The Architect's Portfolio," no. 322, follows p. 352; (December 27, 1935), "The Architect's Portfolio," no. 323, follows p. 372.

The Architects' Journal LXXIX(February 8, 1934), pp. 197, 205–206, 213–217; LXXXII(December 12, 1935), pp. 865–866, 873–885; (December 19, 1935), pp. 917–918; (December 26, 1935), pp. 957–960.

De La Warr, Lord. "Letters from Readers: Alien Architects Invade Britain." *The Architects' Journal* LXXIX(February 15, 1934), p. 244.

Heath, Walter. "Letters from Readers: Alien Architects Invade Britain." *The Architects' Journal* LXXIX(February 15, 1934), p. 244.

Bridgewater, D. L. "Letters from Readers: Alien Architects Invade Britain." *The Architects' Journal* LXXIX (February 22, 1934), p. 278.

Burford, James. "Letters from Readers: Alien Architects Invade Britain." *The Architects' Journal* LXXIX(February 22, 1934), pp. 278–279.

Griggs, H. S. Brock. "Letters from Readers: Alien Architects Invade Britain." *The Architects' Journal* LXXIX(February 22, 1934), p. 278.

De La Warr, Lord. "Letters from Readers: The Bexhill Competition." *The Architects' Journal* LXXIX(March 8, 1934), p. 351.

Helsby, C.; Hamann, C. W.; Samuely, F. J. "Welded Structural Steelwork for Entertainment Hall, Bexhill, Sussex." *The Welder* X(April

1935), pp. 529–533; (May 1935), pp. 559–565; XI(October 1935), pp. 716–722; (November 1935), pp. 751–759; (December 1935), pp. 783–789.

Architectural Design and Construction VI(January 1936), pp. 90–93.

Cinema and Theatre Construction XIV(January 1936), pp. 35–38.

Quigley, Hugh. "Bexhill and its Pavillion." *Design for Today* IV(February 1936), pp. 49–54.

Chermayeff, Serge (pseud. Peter Maitland). "Leisure at the Seaside IV: The Architect." *The Architectural Review* LXXX(July 1936), pp. 19, 21–28, 50; Plate iii.

The Architectural Review LXXXIV(December 1938), p. 309.

L'architecture d'aujourd'hui VII (October 1936), pp. 45–53.

Lubetkin, B. "Modern Architecture in England." *American Architect and Architecture* CL(February 1937), pp. 31–33.

The Architectural Record LXXXI(March 1937), pp. 1, 15–16.

Hitchcock, Henry-Russell. *Modern Architecture in England.* New York: The Museum of Modern Art, 1937; pp. 30, 37, 40; Plate 42.

Buildings of Britain: Yesterday, Today, and Tomorrow. New York: The British Information Service, 1946; p. 77.

Hamlin, Talbot. *Forms and Functions of Twentieth Century Architecture.* 3 vols. New York: Columbia University Press, 1952; II:254.

Whittick, Arnold. *Eric Mendelsohn.* London: Leonard Hill Books, Ltd., 1956; pp. 99–102; Plates 30, 32.

Joedicke, Jurgen. *Geschichte der Modernen Architektur.* Stuttgart: Verlag Gerd Hatje, 1958; pp. 158–159.

Buildings Research Station Notes, no. D781. *Long Term Durability of Buildings XIV: The De La Warr Pavillion, Bexhill-on-Sea, Sussex.* Garston, Watford, Hertshire: Department of Scientific and Industrial Research, July 1962.

Jackson, Anthony. *The Politics of Architecture.* Toronto: University of Toronto Press, 1970; pp. 56–57, 104–106.

Benton, Charlotte, and Benton, Tim. "De La Warr Pavillion, Bexhill-on-Sea." *Summer School Booklet A305 History of Architecture and Design, 1890–1939.* London: The Open University, 1976; pp. 5–21.

Benton, Tim, "The De La Warr Pavillion. A Type for the 1930's." In *Leisure in the Twentieth Century. Fourteen Papers Given at the 2nd Conference on 20th Century Design History.* London: Design Council Publications, 1977; pp. 72–80.

Office building for W. & A. Gilbey, Ltd., Camdentown, London, 1937.

The Architects' Journal LXXXVI(July 15, 1937), pp. 98–108; (May 19, 1938), pp. 849–851; CLXXII(October 15, 1980), p. 738.

The Architect and Building News CLI(July 30, 1937), pp. 149–154.

The Architectural Review LXXXII (July 1937), pp. 11–22; LXXXIV (September 1938), p. 134.

"The Building that Stands on Cork." *Ferroconcrete* (July 1937), reprint.

Martin, J. L.; Nicholson, Ben; and Gabo, N. *Circle: International Survey of Constructive Art.* London: Farber and Farber, Ltd., 1937; Section 3, Plates 9, 10.

Architecture Illustrated XVI(February 1938), p. 51.

McCallum, Ian. *Pocket Guide to Modern Buildings in London.* London: The Architectural Press, 1951; pp. 23–25, 27.

Building Research Station Notes, no. D814. *Long Term Durability of Buildings XV: The Offices of Messrs. W. and A. Gilbey, Ltd., Gilbey House, Oval Road, London W. 1.* Garston, Watford, Hertshire: Department of Scientific and Industrial Research, July 1962.

Thirties. British Art and Design Before the War. London: Arts Council of Great Britain, 1979; p. 196.

Laboratory building for Imperial Chemical Industries, Blakely, Manchester, 1938.

The Architect and Building News CLIII(January 21, 1938), pp. 92–94.

The Builder CLIV(March 4, 1938), p. 451.

RIBA Journal XLV(March 7, 1938), p. 45.

The Architectural Review LXXXIII(March 1938), pp. 117–126; LXXXIV(August 1938), p. 83.

The Architects' Journal LXXXVII(March 24, 1938), pp. 507–511; LXXXVIII (October 6, 1938), pp. 571–572; (October 20, 1938), pp. 647–648.

Progressive Architecture XXX(January 1949), pp. 59–65.

Imperial Chemical Industries Limited. *The New Research Laboratories.* Manchester: 1938.

Offices and plant for *The Cape Codder*, Orleans, Massachusetts, 1954.

The Architectural Forum CII(May 1955), pp. 156–157.

"The Architect's Eye." *Cooper Union Museum Chronicle* III(September 1962), p. 45.

Competition entry for Franklin Delano Roosevelt Memorial (in association with Peter Chermayeff, Aram Mardirosiam, Robert Reynolds), 1960.

Creighton, Thomas H. *The Architecture of Monuments.* New York: Reinhold Publishing Corporation, 1961; p. 133.

ARCHITECTURAL PROJECTS: GENERAL INTERIORS

Office for Ambrose Wilson, Ltd., Vauxhall Bridge Road, London, 1929.

Design in Industry Quarterly Journal, no. 10 (December 1929), second photo following p. 14.

Decorative Art Yearbook 1930. London: The Studio, 1930; p. 88.

The Architectural Review LXVIII(July 1930), p. 40.

Design in Industry, no. 1 (new series) (Spring 1932), p. 9.

Chermayeff office, Pantheon, Oxford Street, London, 1930.

The Architectural Review LXVIII(July 1930), p. 36.

Dressmaker's showroom (unidentified client), London, 1930.

Decorative Art Yearbook 1930. London: The Studio, 1930; p. 89.

Cambridge Theatre, Seven Dials (in association with Wimperis, Simpson and Guthrie, architects), London, 1930.

The Architect and Building News CXXIV(October 10, 1930), pp. 484, 491–496, 508; CXXV(January 9, 1931), pp. 76–77.

The Architectural Review LXVIII(October 1930), pp. 159–164; LXIX (May 1931), pp. 181–182.

The Architects' Journal LXXII(October 8, 1930), pp. 539–542.

Creative Art VII(November 1930), p. 383.

Architecture Illustrated II(April 1931), pp. 119–129.

Moderne Bauformen XXX(May 1931), pp. 208, 217–224.

Architectural Design and Construction II(June 1932), p. 325.

Whittick, Arnold. *European Architecture in the Twentieth Century*. London: Crosby, Lockwood, and Sons, Ltd., 1953; pp. 172–173, plate LXXXV.

Sharp, Dennis. *The Picture Palace*. London: Hugh Evelyn, Ltd., 1969; p. 172.

Howard, Diana. *London Theatres and Music Halls, 1850–1950*. London: The Library Association, 1970; Entry 125.

Thirties. British Art and Design Before the War. London: Arts Council of Great Britain, 1979; p. 272.

Interiors for the ship *l'Atlantique* (in association with Paul Follot), 1931.

Guardian, G. B. "La decoration de l'Atlantique." *Beaux Arts* XI(October 1931), p. 11.

Chavance, R. "Le Paquebot l'Atlantique et les beaux métiers." *Art et Decoration* LX(November 1931), pp. 153–164.

Competition entry for exhibition booth for Venesta Plywood Corporation, Building Trades Exhibition, Olympia, London, 1931.
The Architect and Building News CXXV(March 13, 1931), p. 376.

Office for a dermatologist (unidentified client), London, 1931.
Architectural Review LXXII(July 1932), p. 33.
Design for Today III(June 1935), p. 228.

Interiors for the BBC Broadcasting House, London (entire eighth floor and third floor talk studio), 1932.
The Architect and Building News CXXX(May 20, 1932), pp. 258–266; CXXXII(October 14, 1932), "The Architect's Portfolio, no. 188," follows p. 44; (October 21, 1932), "The Architect's Portfolio, no. 189," follows p. 76.
The Architects' Journal LXXV(May 25, 1932), pp. 689–693.
The Architectural Review LXXII(August 1932), pp. 53–56, 64–65, 68–70, 72, plates V, VI; LXXIII(March 1933), pp. 133–135; LXXXIII(May 1938), p. 256.
Country Life LXXI(May 28, 1932), pp. 596–603.
Design for Today I(May 1932), pp. 26, 28; II(November 1934), p. 421.
The British Broadcasting Corporation. *Broadcasting House.* London: 1932. Booklet.
MacCarthy, Fiona. *All Things Bright and Beautiful.* London: Allen and Unwin, 1972; plate 110.

Interiors for the BBC Broadcasting House, Birmingham, 1933.
The Architects' Journal LXXIX(February 22, 1934), pp. 268, 280–286.
The Architectural Review LXXV(February 1934), p. 72; (March 1934), pp. 106, 108.
The Architectural Forum LXIV(June 1936), p. 486.

W. B. Corset Showroom, Regent Street, London, 1934.
The Architectural Review LXXV(March 1934), pp. 79–81.
Design for Today II(April 1934), pp. 136–137.
W. B. Corset Showrooms. London: Maddox House, January 1936. Advertising brochure.

Ciro Jewelry Store, Old Bond Street, London, 1938.
The Architect and Building News CLVI(November 4, 1938), pp. 128–129.

Renovation of interior, Ciro of Bond Street, Jewelers, San Francisco (in partnership with Raphael Soriano), 1942.
The Architectural Forum LXXXVIII(May 1948), p. 128.

The Architect and Building News CXCVI(August 5, 1949), supplement, pages following p. 138.

Renovation of Chermayeff office, East 37th Street, New York City (in partnership with Conrad Wachsmann), 1946.

Interiors CVI(February 1947), pp. 83–86.

Office for British Railways Inc., Rockefeller Center, New York City (in association with Ketchum, Gina and Sharp), 1950.

Progressive Architecture XXXI(June 1950), pp. 84–86.

ARCHITECTURAL PROJECTS: HOUSES AND HOUSING

Proposal for Chermayeff House, Puttenham, Surrey, 1932.

The Architectural Review LXXII(November 1932), pp. 214–215.

Chermayeff, Serge. *Book on Colour.* London: Nobel Chemical Finishes, January 1936.

Proposal for a pool house (unidentified client), circa 1932.

Chermayeff, Serge. *Book on Colour.* London: Nobel Chemical Finishes, January 1936.

"Kernal" House prototype and furnishings, 1933.

The Architects' Journal LXXVII(July 29, 1933), pp. 868–870; LXXVIII (July 6, 1933), p. 14; (November 30, 1933), pp. 691–695.

The Architectural Review LXXIV(July 1933), pp. 20–21; LXXVI(September 1934), p. 105.

Design for Today I(July 1933), pp. 94–95; II(February 1934), p. 59.

Decorative Art Yearbook 1934. London: The Studio, 1934; p. 53.

The Exhibition of British Industrial Art in Relation to the Home (catalogue). London: Dorland Hall, 1933; pp. 22–24.

Summerson, John, and Williams-Ellis, Clough. *Architecture Here and Now.* London: Thomas Nelson and Son, Ltd., 1934; p. 44.

Shann House, Rugby, 1934.

The Architects' Journal LXXIX(April 19, 1934), pp. 564–565; (April 26, 1934), pp. 605–606; (May 10, 1934), pp. 685–688.

The Architectural Review LXXV(June 1934), p. 221.

Architectural Design and Construction IV(October 1934), pp. 19–20.

Decorative Art Yearbook 1936. London: The Studio, 1936; p. 26.

McGrath, Raymond. *Twentieth Century Houses.* London: Faber and Faber, 1934; pp. 102–103.

Yorke, F. R. S. *The Modern House.* London: The Architectural Press, 1934; pp. 164–165.

Competition entry for workers' flats, Cement Marketing Company, 1935.

The Architects' Journal LXXXI(March 28, 1935), pp. 482–485.

Denby, Elizabeth. "Competition for Workingmen's Flats: the Designs Reviewed." *The Architects' Journal* LXXXI(March 21, 1935), pp. 438–440.

Cement Marketing Company, Ltd. *Working-Class Residential Flats in Reinforced Concrete.* London: 1937; pp. 32–35.

Proposal for Chiswick Apartments, London (in partnership with Erich Mendelsohn), 1935.

Zevi, Bruno. *Erich Mendelsohn. Opera Completa.* Milan: Etwas Compass, 1970; p. 227.

Nimmo House, Chalfont, St. Giles, Buckinghamshire (in partnership with Erich Mendelsohn), 1935.

The Architectural Review LXXVIII(November 1935), pp. 174–178; LXXX(December 1936), p. 299–301, 317; LXXXII(December 1937), p. 250.

The Architects' Journal LXXXIII(January 2, 1936), pp. 9–14.

Decorative Art Yearbook 1936. London: The Studio, 1936; pp. 16–17, 36, 38, 46, 76, 79.

Revista de Arquitectura (January 1937), pp. 14–22.

Abercrombie, Patrick, ed. *The Book of the Modern House,* with text by Oliver Hill and G. A. Jellicoe. London: Hodder and Stoughton, 1939; pp. 209, 218, 232–233, 246–247.

Whittick, Arnold. *Eric Mendelsohn.* London: Leonard Hill Books, Ltd., 1956; p. 99.

Proposal for redevelopment of the White City Exhibition Grounds, London (in partnership with Erich Mendelsohn), 1935.

Towndrow, F. E. "A Scheme of National Importance." *Architectural Design and Construction* V(April 1935), pp. 192–199.

The Architectural Review LXXIX(April 1936), plate ii, follows p. 164.

Astragal (pseud.). "Notes and Comments." *The Architects' Journal* XC(July 27, 1939), p. 128.

Whittick, Arnold. *Eric Mendelsohn.* London: Leonard Hill Books, Ltd., 1956; pp. 102–106; plates 33c, 34a, 34b.

Zevi, Bruno. *Erich Mendelsohn. Opera Completa.* Milan: Etwas Compass, 1970; p. 226.

Proposal for a house, Frinton Park Estate, Essex (in partnership with Erich Mendelsohn), 1936.

The Architects' Journal LXXXIV(October 1, 1936), p. 461.

Architectural Design and Construction VII(August 1937), p. 387.

Carter, Ella. *Seaside Houses and Bungalows*. London: Country Life Ltd., 1937; p. 40.

Gould, Jeremy. *Modern Houses in Britain, 1919–1939*. Architectural History Monographs No. 1. London: Society of Architectural Historians of Great Britain, 1977; p. 31.

Proposal for a house (unidentified client), Dorney, Windsor, 1936.

Architectural Design and Construction VII(August 1937), p. 388.

Cohen House, Church Street, Chelsea, London (in partnership with Erich Mendelsohn), 1936.

The Architects' Journal LXXXIV(December 24, 1936), pp. 872–874; LXXXVII(June 2, 1938), pp. 945–946; (June 9, 1938), p. 985–986; (June 16, 1938), pp. 1025–1026; (June 23, 1938), pp. 1065–1066.

The Architectural Review LXXX(December 1936), pp. 254–255.

Abercrombie, Patrick, ed. *The Book of the Modern House*. London: Hodder and Stoughton, 1939; pp. 94–95.

Yorke, F. R. S. *The Modern House in England*, 2nd ed. London: The Architectural Press, 1944; pp. 32–33, plate facing p. 20.

Chermayeff House, "Bentley Wood," near Halland, Sussex, 1938.

The Architects' Journal LXXXV(February 18, 1937), p. 293; LXXXIX (February 16, 1939), pp. 293–300; (March 2, 1939), pp. 371–372; (March 9, 1939), pp. 411–412; (March 23, 1939), pp. 491–492; (March 30, 1939), pp. 531–532.

Astragal (pseud.). "Notes and Comments." *The Architects' Journal* LXXXV(February 11, 1937), p. 255; (March 11, 1937), p. 414.

Reilly, C. H. "Professor Reilly Speaking." *The Architects' Journal* LXXXVIII(September 22, 1938), p. 479; (October 20, 1938), pp. 637–638.

Aylwin, G. Maxwell. "Letters from Readers: Professor Reilly and the Architect's House." *The Architects' Journal* LXXXVIII(September 29, 1938), p. 529.

Sampson, R. W. "Letters from Readers." *The Architects' Journal* LXXXVIII(October 13, 1938), p. 608.

The Times (London), March 2, 1937, p. 13e.

The Architectural Review LXXXIII(April 1938), p. 198; LXXXV(February 1939), pp. 61–78.

Bareham, Peter. "Letter to the Editor: Time and Chermayeff." *The Architectural Review* CXXVII (June 1960), p. 370.

Knobel, Lance. "The Tragedy of Bentley Wood." *The Architectural Review* CLXVI(November 1979), pp. 310–311.

Hussey, Christopher. "A Modern Country House." *Country Life* LXXXVIII(October 26, 1940), pp. 368–371; (November 2, 1940), pp. 390–393.

Myerscough, Walker. "The Reasons for this House. . . ." *The Ideal Home* (May 1939), pp. 384–388.

Construzioni Casabella XIII(December 1940), pp. 39–41.

Interiors CIX(July 1950), pp. 80–83.

"What Kind of House?" *The Listener* XVII(March 8, 1937), pp. 444–445.

Tunnard, Christopher. *Gardens in the Modern Landscape*. London: The Architectural Press, 1938; pp. 68, 76.

Richards, J. M. *An Introduction to Modern Architecture*. London: Penguin Books, Ltd., 1940; pp. 114–115, plate 29.

Yorke, F. R. S. *The Modern House*. London: The Architectural Press, 1944; pp. 82–84.

Kassler, Elizabeth B. *Modern Gardens and the Landscape*. New York: Museum of Modern Art, 1964; p. 84.

James, Philip. *Henry Moore on Sculpture*. London: MacDonald and Co., 1966; p. 98, plate 25, pp. 99, 101.

Mayhew House, Oakland, California (in association with Clarence Mayhew), 1942.

The Architectural Forum LXXXIV(June 1946), pp. 117–123.

House and Garden XCI(May 1947), pp. 96–99, 181.

The Architectural Review CII(July 1947), pp. 43–45.

Creighton, Thomas H. *Homes*. New York: Reinhold, 1947; pp. 160–161.

Fisker, Kay. "Den Funktionelle Tradition. Spredte Indtryk af Amerikansk Arkitektur." *Arkitekten* LII(May–June 1950), pp. 90–91.

Amerikanische Architektur seit 1947. Stuttgart: G. Hatje, 1951; p. 32.

Lohse, Richard; Schader, Jacques; and Zietzschmann, Ernst. *L'Architecture Internationale de Demain*. Rochecorbon, France: Les Editions Charles Gay, 1954; pp. 124–127.

Macintosh, Duncan. *The Modern Courtyard House*. London: The Architectural Association. Paper no. 9, 1973; p. 16.

Horn House, Redwood (Marin County), California, 1942.

The Architectural Forum LXXXVI(January 1947), pp. 72–75.

The Architectural Review CII(July 1947), pp. 45–46.

Interiors CVII(September 1947), pp. 82–83.

The Architect and Building News CXCVI(July 1, 1949), supplement, pages follow p. 16; (July 8, 1949), pages follow p. 36.

Amerikanische Architektur seit 1947. Stuttgart: G. Hatje, 1951; pp. 26–27.

Proposal for "Park Type" apartments (in association with Peter Blake, Abel Sorenson, Norman Fletcher, Henry Hebblen), 1943.

The Architectural Forum LXXVIII(May 1943), pp. 138–145; LXXIX (July 1943), p. 39.

Abel, Joseph H., and Severud, Fred. *Apartment Houses*. New York: Reinhold, 1947; pp. 63–66.

Hamlin, Talbot. *Forms and Functions of Twentieth Century Architecture*. 3 vols. New York: Columbia University Press, 1952; III:75.

Proposal for prototype apartments in a hypothetical neighborhood, Museum of Modern Art (in association with Vernon DeMars and Susanne Wasson-Tucker), 1945.

The Museum of Modern Art. *Tomorrow's Small House* (catalogue). New York, 1945; pp. 3, 19–20.

Chermayeff Studio, Truro, Massachusetts, 1952. Guest house addition, 1957.

House and Home VI(July 1954), pp. 121, 124.

Bauen und Wohnen XI(March 1956), p. 98.

Revista Informes de la Construction No. 90 (April 1957).

The Architectural Record CXXVIII(November 1960), pp. 168–170.

"The Architect's Eye." *Cooper Union Museum Chronicle* III(September 1962), p. 44.

House and Garden (London) XXII(May 1967), pp. 84–85.

Kaspar, Karl. *Vacation Houses. An International Survey*. New York: Frederick A. Praeger, 1967; pp. 30–31.

Payson House, Portland, Maine, 1952.

House and Home III(January 1953), pp. 108–115.

The Architects' Journal CXVII(April 9, 1953), p. 458.

The Architectural Review CXV(June 1954), pp. 370–374.

The Architect and Building News CCVII(April 14, 1955), supplement, pages follow p. 30; (April 21, 1955), pages follow p. 30.

Hoffman, Kurt. *Neue Einfamilienhaüser*. Stuttgart: Julius Hoffmann Verlag, 1955; pp. 84–85.

Sigerson Cottage, Truro, Massachusetts, 1954.

House and Home VI(July 1954), p. 123.

Revista Informes de la Construction No. 90 (April 1957).

"The Architect's Eye." *Cooper Union Museum Chronicle* III(September 1962), p. 44.

Wilkinson Cottage, Truro, Massachusetts, 1954.

House and Home VI(July 1954), pp. 120–125.

Bauen und Wohnen XI(March 1956), pp. 96–97.

Revista Informes de la Construction No. 90 (April 1957).

"The Second House." *Time* LXXX(August 17, 1962), pp. 44–46.

"The Architect's Eye." *Cooper Union Museum Chronicle* III(September 1962), pp. 44–45.

Barran, Fritz R. *Ferienhauser*. Stuttgart: Julius Hoffmann Verlag, 1961; pp. 52–53.

O'Connor House, Truro, Massachusetts, 1956.

"Late American on Cape Cod." *New York Times Magazine* (September 29, 1957), pp. 50–51.

Barran, Fritz R. *Ferienhauser*. Stuttgart: Julius Hoffmann Verlag, 1961; p. 63.

Chermayeff, Ivan. *Observations on American Architecture*. New York: Viking Press, 1972; p. 136.

Harvard Urban Family Houses, 1956–1960.

Press release, Harvard University, Graduate School of Design, to Sunday papers of February 24, 1957; Serge Chermayeff Archive, Avery Library.

The Boston Sunday Herald (February 24, 1957), p. 54.

Foell, Earl. "Harvard Professor Twins Privacy and Quiet in House for Urban Living." *Christian Science Monitor* (February 25, 1957), p. 6.

The Architectural Record CXXI(March 1957), p. 404.

New York Herald Tribune, March 10, 1957.

The New York Times (March 10, 1957), Sect. 2, pp. 1, 4.

"The Patio House." *Harvard Alumni Bulletin* (March 16, 1957), pp. 464–465.

Post (Houston, Texas), April 1, 1957.

Interiors CXVI(July 1957), p. 16.

The American City LXXII(July 1957), p. 200.

Topeka Kansas State Journal, September 5, 1957.

Springer, John L. "Revolution in City Living: The 'Walled House'." *This Week Magazine* (September 1, 1957), cover, pp. 8–9.

House and Home XII(October 1957), pp. 140–140A.

Rowntree, Diana. *The Guardian* (April 29, 1964), p. 9.

Schoenauer, Norbert, and Seeman, Stanley. *The Court Garden House*. Montreal: McGill University Press, 1962; pp. 88–89.

Macintosh, Duncan. *The Modern Courtyard House*. London: The Architectural Association, Paper no. 9, 1973; pp. 17–19.

Chermayeff House, Lincoln Street, New Haven, Connecticut, 1962.

Architectural Design XXXIII(October 1963), pp. 494–495.

O'Brien, George. "Designed for Privacy." *The New York Times Magazine* (September 13, 1964), pp. 117–119.

Proa CLXIX(February 1965), p. 12.

Arkkitehti—Arkitekten No. 7-8 (1966), pp. 100–101.

Baumeister LXIV(May 1967), pp. 604–608.

Gas + Architektur, no. 20 (1968), pp. 12–17.

Metz, Don, and Noga, Yuji. *New Architecture in New Haven.* Cambridge: MIT Press, 1966; pp. 46–47.

Hoffmann, Hubert. *One Family Housing: Solutions to an Urban Dilemma.* London: Thames and Hudson, 1967; pp. 147–149.

Macintosh, Duncan. *The Modern Courtyard House.* London: The Architectural Association, Paper no. 9, 1973; pp. 17–19.

ARCHITECTURAL PROJECTS: HOUSE INTERIORS

Chermayeff House, Abbey Road, St. John's Wood, London, 1930.

Decorative Art Yearbook 1929. London: The Studio, 1929; p. 115.

The Architectural Review LXVII(May 1930), pp. 270–272, 288–289, 292; LXXI(February 1932), p. 74; LXXII(October 1932), p. 154.

Creative Art VII(August 1930), pp. 144–145.

The Studio (London) C(August 1930), pp. 144–145.

Decorative Art Yearbook 1931. London: The Studio, 1930; pp. 74–108.

Aloi, Roberto. *L'Arredamento Moderno.* 6 vols. Milan: U. Hoepli, 1934; I:Plate 547.

Hoffmann, Herbert. *Die Neue Raumkunst in Europa und Amerika.* Stuttgart: J. Hoffmann Verlag, 1930; pp. 92–93.

Interiors at Bath House, Piccadilly, London, for Lady Ludlow, 1930.

Causey, Andrew. *Paul Nash.* Oxford: Clarendon Press, 1980; p. 237.

Flat (unidentified client), Gloucester Square, London, 1931.

The Studio (London) IV(July 1932), pp. 48–49.

Studio for Anthony Gibbons, Grinling, Swan Street, Chelsea, London, 1932.

London Studio 5 or *Studio 105* (May 1933), pp. 312–313.

Patmore, Derek. *Color Schemes and Modern Furnishing.* London: The Studio, 1945; p. 23; Plate 21.

Elmhurst Flat, Upper Brook Street, London, 1934.

Architecture Illustrated IX(December 1934), pp. 196–198.

The Architectural Review LXXVII(May 1935), pp. 223–226.

London Studio 9 or *Studio 109* (May 1935), pp. 269–271.

Decorative Art Yearbook 1936. London: The Studio, 1936; p. 51.

The Studio (London) CXXI(January 1941), p. 19.

Heywood-Lonsdale Flat, Connaught Place, London, 1937.

The Architectural Review LXXXII(December 1937), pp. 261–268.

Interiors CVI(December 1946), pp. 102–109.

Abercrombie, Patrick, ed. *The Book of the Modern House.* London: Hodder and Stoughton, 1939; p. 370.

Aloi, Roberto. *L'Arredamento Moderno.* 6 vols. Milan: U. Hoepli, 1934; II:Plates 580, 738; III:Plates 461, 664.

Chermayeff Cottage (and later additions), Truro, Massachusetts, 1944–1972.

The Architectural Record CXXVIII(November 1960), pp. 168–170.

Kaspar, Karl. *Vacation Houses. An International Survey.* New York: Frederick A. Praeger, 1967; pp. 30–31.

ARCHITECTURAL PROJECTS: MISCELLANEOUS FURNISHINGS

Interiors and furnishings (unidentified), Waring and Gillow, London, 1928–1930.

Decorative Art Yearbook 1929. London: The Studio, 1929; p. 118.

Yerbury, F. R. *Small English Houses.* London: Victor Gollancz, Ltd., 1929; Plate CXXXVI.

Decorative Art Yearbook 1930. London: The Studio, 1930; pp. 59–62, 88, 91, 98.

The Architectural Review LXVII(May 1930), p. 298; LXIX(April 1931), p. 146; LXXI(March 1932), p. 113; (April 1932), p. 164; LXXII(October 1932), pp. 151, 154; LXXV(February 1934), p. 70.

Decorative Art Yearbook 1931. London: The Studio, 1930; p. 91.

The American Federation of Arts. *Decorative Metalwork and Cotton Textiles.* New York, 1930–1931; Illustration no. 41. Catalogue of the Third International Exhibition of Contemporary Industrial Art.

Rogers, J. C. *Modern English Furniture.* London: Country Life, 1930; pp. 30, 32, 59–60, 92, 95, 129.

Sharp, Dennis; Benton, Tim; and Cole, Barbie Campbell. *Pel and Tubular Steel Furniture of the Thirties.* London: The Architectural Association, 1977.

Thirties. British Art and Design Before the War. London: Arts Council of Great Britian, 1979; p. 148.

Carpets manufactured by Wilton Royal Carpet Factory, Ltd., 1929–1936.

Smithells, Roger, and Woods, S. John. *The Modern Home.* Essex: F. Lewis Limited, 1936; p. 96.

Mendes, Valerie. "Carpets and Furnishing Textiles." In *Thirties. British Art and Design Before the War.* London: Arts Council of Great Britain, 1979; pp. 87, 147.

Miscellaneous furnishing, BBC Broadcasting House, London, 1932.

The Architect and Building News CXXXII(October 14, 1932), "Architects' Portfolio no. 188" follows p. 44.

The Architectural Review LXXII(August 1932), pp. 65, 68, 70, 72; (December 1932), p. 302.

Design For Today II(November 1934), p. 421.

Boumphrey, G. M. "Nationality in Easy Chairs." *Design For Today* I(May 1932), pp. 26, 28.

MacCarthy, Fiona. *All Things Bright and Beautiful.* London: Allen and Unwin, Ltd., 1972; Plate 110.

Thirties. British Art and Design Before the War. London: Arts Council of Great Britain, 1979; p. 148.

Nesting armchair with steel frame, Model R.P.7 for Pel, Ltd., 1932.

The Architectural Review LXXVIII(December 1935), p. 261.

Read, Herbert. *Art and Industry: The Principles of Industrial Design.* London: Farber and Farber, Ltd., 1934; p. 79.

MacCarthy, Fiona. *All Things Bright and Beautiful.* London: Allen and Unwin, Ltd., 1972; Plate 108.

Sharp, Dennis; Benton, Tim; and Cole, Barbie Campbell. *Pel and Tubular Steel Furniture of the Thirties.* London: The Architectural Association, 1977.

Bakelite Radio Cabinets for Ekco, E. K. Cole, Ltd., London, 1933–1935.

Design For Today I(October 1933), p. 239. (Model 74)

Chermayeff, Serge. Letter to the editor. *Design For Today* I(November 1933), p. 282. (Model 74)

Littman, Frederic H. "The Evolution of the Wireless Receiver and Its Use in the Home." *Design For Today* IV(March 1936), p. 97. (Model AC 86)

Decorative Art Yearbook 1934. London: The Studio, 1934; p. 126. (Model 64)

The Architectural Review LXXVIII(December 1935), p. 282. (Model AC 86)

Pevsner, Nikolaus. "Broadcasting Comes of Age." *The Architectural Review* LXXXVII(May 1940), p. 190. (Model 74)

Trend in Design of Everyday Things II(Summer 1936), p. 83. Quarterly of the Design and Industries Association. (Model 74 and Model AC 86)

Cames, Stephen. "Wireless Workshop." *The Listener* XCVIII(March 30, 1978), p. 414. (Model 74)

Pevsner, Nikolaus. *An Enquiry into Industrial Art in England.* Cambridge: Cambridge University Press, 1937; pp. 104–106, 199. (Model 74)

Armchair with wooden frame and detachable upholstery, Model W-5 for Plan, Ltd., 1933.

The Architectural Review LXXIV(July 1933), p. 30; (August 1933), p. 72; LXXVIII(December 1935), p. 265.

Design For Today II(December 1934), pp. 454–455.

Bentwood straight chair for Plan, Ltd., 1933.

The Architectural Review LXXIV(August 1933), p. 72.

Unit furniture in wood for Plan, Ltd. (adapted from designs by Franz Schuster), 1933.

The Architectural Review LXXIV(July 1933), p. 28; LXXVIII(December 1935), p. 272; LXXX(November 1936), p. 229.

The Architects' Journal LXXVIII(July 6, 1933), pp. 26–27.

Chermayeff, Serge. "Letters from Readers: Plan Furniture." *The Architects' Journal* LXXVIII(July 6, 1933), p. 12.

Design For Today II(July 1933), pp. 94–95; (April 1934), p. 144; (October 1934), pp. 378–379; (December 1934), pp. 454–455, 459.

Decorative Art Yearbook 1936. London: The Studio, 1936; p. 89.

Read, Herbert. *Art and Industry: The Principles of Industrial Design.* London: Farber and Farber, Ltd., 1934; pp. 86–87.

Pevsner, Nikolaus. *An Enquiry into Industrial Art in England.* Cambridge: Cambridge University Press, 1937; pp. 37, 41.

Lamps and brackets, Bestlite Models 29532, 29893, Best and Lloyd, Ltd., 1933.

The Architectural Review LXXVIII(December 1935), p. 231.

Pevsner, Nikolaus. *An Enquiry into Industrial Art in England.* Cambridge: Cambridge University Press, 1937; p. 29.

Thirties. British Art and Design Before the War. London: Arts Council of Great Britain, 1979; p. 233.

Armchair with tubular steel frame, Model M-7 for Plan, Ltd., 1934.

Read, Herbert. *Art and Industry: The Principles of Industrial Design.* London: Farber and Farber, Ltd., 1934; p. 106.

The Architectural Review LXXVIII(December 1935), p. 261.

Armchair with tubular steel frame, Model M-11 for Plan, Ltd., 1934.

The Architectural Review LXXVIII(December 1935), p. 262.

Clocks manufactured by Garrard Clocks Ltd., London, 1934.

Exhibition of British Art in Industry. London: Royal Academy of Arts, 1935; pp. 72–73.

Pianos with harp by Steinway and cabinetry by Whiteley's (and possibly other manufacturers), 1935–1937.

The Builder CLI(September 18, 1936), p. 518; (September 25, 1936), p. 571.

The Architectural Review LXXXII (December 1937), p. 261.

Abercrombie, Patrick, ed. *The Book of the Modern House.* London: Hudder and Stoughton, 1939; p. 376.

Fabrics manufactured by L. Anton Maix, New York, 1950–1955.

"New Patterns Shown by Fabric Designers." *The New York Times* (April 22, 1950), Sect. 12, p. 3.

Pepis, Betty. "Patterns for Prints." *The New York Times Magazine* (May 28, 1950), pp. 38–39.

Current Design: A Quarterly Survey (Spring 1951), Plate: "Fabrics 14." Published by the Department of Design in Industry, Institute of Contemporary Art, Boston.

Industrial Design II(December 1955), p. 66.

Unidentified interiors and furnishings.

Decorative Art Yearbook 1932. London: The Studio, 1932; p. 32.

Aloi, Roberto. *L'Arredamento Moderno.* 6 vols. Milan: U. Hoepli, 1934; I:Plates 399, 642.

Smithells, Roger, and Woods, S. John. *The Modern Home.* Essex: F. Lewis Limited, 1936; p. 66.

EXHIBITION DESIGNS

Interiors and furnishings for the exhibition "Modern Furnishings," Waring and Gillow, London (in association with Paul Follot), 1928.

Robertson, Howard. "Modern Art in Decoration and Furnishing." *The Architect and Building News* CXX(November 30, 1928), pp. 693–697.

The Architects' Journal LXVIII(December 26, 1928), p. 918; LXXIV (November 4, 1931), p. 606.

Rogers, J. C. "Modern Decoration at Warings." *Design in Industry Quarterly Journal* (December 1928), pp. 4–6; see also p. 3.

The Architectural Review LXV(January 1929), p. 51; LXVIII(December 1930), p. 266; LXXII(October 1932), pp. 148, 151.

Decorative Art Yearbook 1929. London: The Studio, 1929; pp. 101–115.

Wainwright, Shirley B. "The Waring Exhibition." *Creative Art* IV(February 1929), pp. 131–135.

The Cabinet Maker (June 28, 1930), p. 735.

Rogers, J. C. *Modern English Furniture.* London: Country Life, 1930; pp. 24, 26, 30, 52, 76–77.

Battersby, Martin. *The Decorative Twenties.* New York: Walker and Company, 1969; p. 164.

Model "Week End House" for the exhibition "British Industrial Art in Relation to the Home," Dorland Hall, London, 1933.

See " 'Kernal' House prototype" entry under "Architectural Projects: Houses and Housing."

Ground floor exhibit space for the exhibition "British Industrial Art in Relation to the Home," Dorland Hall, London (in collaboration with Wells Coates), 1933.

Design For Today I(June 1933), p. 74; (August 1933), p. 139.

Model exercise court for the exhibition of "British Industrial Art in Relation to the Home," Dorland Hall, London (in association with Oliver Hill), 1933.

The Architects' Journal LXXVII(June 29, 1933), p. 866.

The Architectural Review LXXIV(July 1933), p. 24.

Exhibition "Modern Living" for Whiteley's, London (including model "Week End House"), 1933.

For "Model 'Week End House' " entries see " 'Kernal' House prototype" entry under "Architectural Projects: Houses and Housing."

The Architects' Journal LXXVIII(November 30, 1933), pp. 691–695.

Astragal (pseud.). "Review of the Year." *The Architects' Journal* LXXIX(January 11, 1934), p. 93.

Design For Today I(November 1933), p. 285; (December 1933), p. 322; II(January 1934), pp. 32–33; (February 1934), p. 59.

The Architectural Review LXXVI(September 1934), p. 105.

Joel, David. *The Adventure of British Furniture, 1851-1951.* London: Ernest Benn, Ltd., 1953; p. 117.

Model living room for the exhibition "Contemporary Industrial Design in the Home," Dorland Hall, London, 1934.

Bertram, Anthony, et al. "Letters from Readers: The Dorland Hall Exhibition." *The Architects' Journal* LXXX(November 1, 1934), p. 641.

Frost, A. E. "The Exhibition of Contemporary Industrial Design in the Home." *The Architects' Journal* LXXX(November 1, 1934), pp. 642–644.

Frost, A. E. "The Contemporary Industrial Design Exhibition." *Design For Today* II(November 1934), p. 425.

Bertram, Anthony. "Contemporary Industrial Design. The Dorland Hall Exhibition." *Design For Today* II(December 1934), p. 451.

Music room with piano for the piano exhibition, Dorland Hall, London, 1936.

The Builder CLI(September 18, 1936), p. 518; (September 25, 1936), p. 571.

The Architectural Review LXXX(October 1936), p. 185.

Exhibition of "Park Type" apartments, The Architectural League, New York, 1943.

See "Proposal for 'Park Type' apartments" entry under "Architectural Projects: Houses and Housing."

"Design for Use" exhibition at the Museum of Modern Art, New York, 1944.

The Architectural Forum LXXXI(July 1944), p. 4.

The Museum of Modern Art. *Art in Progress.* New York, 1944; pp. 190–201.

Jewell, Edward Alden. "Another Milestone." *The New York Times* (May 28, 1944), Sect. II, p. 8.

Press Release. "Museum of Modern Art to Celebrate Fifteenth Anniversary with Large Exhibition of Art in Progress," Sarah Newmeyer, publicity director.

"Notes on the Industrial Design Exhibition, May, 1944," Museum of Modern Art, January 17, 1944.

Little, Helen. "Modern Museum Opens Art in Progress Show." *Retailing Home Furnishings* XVI(May 29, 1944), pp. 1, 25.

Plastics (July 1944), pp. 18–19.

Lohse, Richard P. *New Design in Exhibitions.* New York: Praeger Publishers, 1954; pp. 180–181.

Gardner, James, and Miller, Caroline. *Exhibition and Display.* London: B. T. Batsford, Ltd., 1960; p. 44.

Hypothetical neighborhood and prototype apartments in "Tomorrow's Small House" exhibition, Museum of Modern Art, New York, 1945.

The Museum of Modern Art. *Tomorrow's Small House* (catalogue). New York, 1945; pp. 3, 19–20.

"Chicago Plans" exhibition for the Chicago City Planning Commission, City Hall, Chicago, 1949.

Lohse, Richard P. *New Design in Exhibitions.* New York: Praeger Publishers, 1954; pp. 182–187.

Franck, Klaus. *Exhibitions.* London: The Architectural Press, 1961; p. 47.

ACADEMIC PROJECTS

Children's Center Project, Brooklyn College Department of Design, 1943.

A Children's Center or Nursery School. Revere's Part in Better Living No. 20. New York: Revere Copper and Brass Company, 1944.

Plan for the Brooklyn College Community, Brooklyn College Department of Design, 1947.

"A Brooklyn College Plan." Typed text for project report, January 1947. (Serge Chermayeff Archive, Avery Library, Columbia University).

Harvard Urban Family House Project, Harvard University Graduate School of Design, 1956–1960.

See entry under "Architectural Projects: Houses and Housing."

"New Urbanity" Project, Yale University School of Arts and Architecture, 1963.

"Search for a New Urbanity." *Ekistics* XVI(November 1963), pp. 301–305.

Critical reaction to "Search for a New Urbanity." Tzonis, Alexander. "Search for a New Urbanity: Commentary." *Ekistics* XVI(November 1963), p. 306.

New Haven Redevelopment Study, Yale University School of Arts and Architecture, 1964.

Drogan, Marc. "Space for Improvement." *New Haven Register Sunday Pictorial* (May 17, 1964), p. 4.

"Yale Model," Yale University School of Arts and Architecture, 1966–1967.

With Alexander Tzonis. *Advanced Studies in Urban Environments.* New Haven: Yale University, 1967. Report for the Institute for Applied Technology, U.S. Bureau of Standards.

With Alexander Tzonis. *Shape of Community. Realization of Human Potential.* Baltimore: Penguin Books, 1971.

"Urban Yardstick" Project, Yale University School of Arts and Architecture, 1968.

W. Mitchell, ed. *Synopsis of Conclusions and Record of Process. The Chermayeff Studio. Autumn, 1968–69* (photostated booklet). New Haven: Yale University School of Arts and Architecture. January, 1969.

VISUAL ARTS

Miscellaneous reviews and catalogue entries, 1946–1979.

Interiors CVI(November 1946), cover.

58th Annual Exhibition of American Paintings and Sculpture. Abstract and Surrealist Art. Chicago: The Art Institute of Chicago, 1947.

Riley, Maude Kemper. "Art is Everywhere." Letter to the editor. *Progressive Architecture* XXVIII(December 1947), pp. 8–10.

Realities Nouvelles. Paris: Salon des Realities Nouvelles, 1948.

52nd Annual Exhibition. Artists of Chicago and Vicinity. Chicago: The Art Institute of Chicago, 1948.

Contemporary American Painting. 1949. Urbana, Illinois: University of Illinois, 1949.

53rd Annual Exhibition. Artists of Chicago and Vicinity. Chicago: The Art Institute of Chicago, 1949.

Contemporary American Painting. 1950. Urbana, Illinois: University of Illinois, 1950.

54th Annual Exhibition. Artists of Chicago and Vicinity. Chicago: The Art Institute of Chicago, 1950.

American Painting Today. New York: Metropolitan Museum of Art, 1950.

The Chicago Art Institute Scrapbook. Chicago: The Art Institute of Chicago, 1951.

Bulliet, C. J. "Exhibition of Drawings and Paintings at Baldwin-Kingery Gallery, Chicago." *The Art Digest* XXV(February 1, 1951), p. 12.

1951 Annual Exhibition of Contemporary American Painting. New York: The Whitney Museum of Art, 1951.

60th Annual American Exhibition. Chicago: The Art Institute of Chicago, 1951.

"La Peintre Abstraite aux U.S.A." *Art d'Aujourd'hui* II(June 1951).

Seuphor, Michel. "Paris New York 1951." In Motherwell, Robert, and Reinhardt, Ad. *Modern Artists in America.* New York: Wittenborn Schultz Inc., 1951.

Contemporary Drawings from 12 Countries. Chicago: The Art Institute of Chicago, 1952.

61st American Exhibition. Paintings and Sculpture. Chicago: The Art Institute of Chicago, 1954.

"Abstracts on Display at Behn Moore." *The Harvard Crimson* (January 11, 1955).

"Art Exhibition, Behn Moore Gallery." *Christian Science Monitor* (February 4, 1955).

Cochran, Betsy, and Hobbs, Gwen. "A Reflective Serge Chermayeff Shows His Paintings—Writes His Grandchildren." *The Cape Codder* (July 26, 1973), Sect. II, p. 2.

Cochran, Betsy. "The New Chermayeff Exhibit." *The Cape Codder* (July 17, 1979), pp. 4–5.

PUBLISHED ARTICLES AND TALKS

"Modernism. 1880–1930. Phases of Furnishing Fashion." *The Cabinet Maker* (June 28, 1930), pp. 734–735.

"German Furniture. Notes on the Exhibition at Leipzig. . ." *The Cabinet Maker* (March 28, 1931), p. 789.

"Contemporary Decoration." Letter to the editor. *The Architects' Journal* LXXIII(April 1, 1931), p. 486.

"A New Spirit and Idealism." *The Architects' Journal* LXXIV(November 4, 1931), pp. 619–620; excerpts from a talk at Heal and Sons, London, October 26, 1931.

"Film Shots in Germany with Notes on the Film." *The Architectural Review* LXX(November 1931), pp. 131–133.

"Review of the Daily Express Building, Ellis and Clarke, Architects." *The Architectural Review* LXXII(July 1932), pp. 3–30.

"Away with Sentiment, Snobbery and Stupidity." *The Listener* VIII(September 21, 1932), pp. 393–395, 420. Talk broadcast on BBC, September 14, 1932.

"The Modern Approach to Architecture and its Equipment." *The Architects' Journal* LXXVII(March 8, 1933), pp. 337–400. Talk to West Yorkshire Society of Architects, March 2, 1933. Synopsis and excerpt of talk in *The Builder* CLVI(April 7, 1933), p. 589.

"Design Demonstrated in the Exhibition of British Industrial Art." *Design for Today* I(July 1933), p. 92.

"Thoughts on Modern Architecture. A Review by Serge Chermayeff." *Review of the Architecture of a New Era* (London: D. Archer, 1933) by R. A. Duncan. *The RIBA Journal* XL(July 8, 1933), p. 689.

"The Grammar of Groundwork." *The Architectural Review* LXXIV(October, 1933), pp. 147–148, 153–154.

"New Materials and New Methods." *The RIBA Journal* XLI(December 23, 1933), pp. 165–179. Talk and discussion, RIBA general meeting, December 18, 1933. Excerpts from talk in *The Architects' Journal* LXXVIII(December 21, 1933), pp. 784, 786. Excerpts from talk with summary of discussion in *The Builder* CVL(December 22, 1933), pp. 984–985.

Critical reaction to "New Materials and New Methods" in "The News of the Week." *The Architect and Building News* CXXXVI(December 22, 1933), p. 325; "Minutes of the Third General Meeting of 1933–34." *The RIBA Journal* XLI(December 23, 1933), p. 208; Percival M. Fraser. Letter to the editor. *The RIBA Journal* XLI(January 27, 1934), pp. 313–314; Edwin S. Hartley. Letter to the editor. *The RIBA Journal* XLI(February 10, 1934), pp. 371–372; Serge Chermayeff. Letter to the editor. *The RIBA Journal* XLI(February 10, 1934), p. 371.

With J. M. Richards. "A Hundred Years Ahead: Forecasting the Coming Century." *The Architects' Journal* LXXXI(January 10, 1935), pp. 79–86.

Critical reaction to "A Hundred Years Ahead: Forecasting the Coming Century" in A. K. Chesterton. Letter to the editor. *The Architects' Journal* LXXXI(January 17, 1935), p. 120; Keith Aitken. Letter to the editor. *The Architects' Journal* LXXXI(January 24, 1935), p. 159–160; A. Croft. Letter to the editor. *The Architects' Journal* LXXXI(January

24, 1935), p. 159; Anti-Fascist (pseud.). Letter to the editor. *The Architects' Journal* LXXXI(January 31, 1935), p. 188; A. K. Chesterton. Letter to the editor. *The Architects' Journal* LXXXI(January 31, 1935), p. 188; D. V. W. P. Letter to the editor. *The Architects' Journal* LXXXI (January 31, 1935), pp. 188–189; J. H. Madge. Letter to the editor. *The Architects' Journal* LXXXI(January 31, 1935), p. 189; Progressive Architect (pseud.). Letter to the editor. *The Architects' Journal* LXXXI (January 31, 1935), p. 189; F. Wickham. Letter to the editor. *The Architects' Journal* LXXXI(January 31, 1935), p. 189; Editorial note. *The Architects' Journal* LXXXI(January 31, 1935), p. 189; Serge Chermayeff and J. M. Richards. Letter to the editor. *The Architects' Journal* LXXXI(January 31, 1935), pp. 189–190; J47845 (pseud.). Letter to the editor. *The Architects' Journal* LXXXI(February 7, 1935), p. 225; Cyril Adler. Letter to the editor. *The Architects' Journal* LXXXI(February 14, 1935), pp. 263–264; A. K. Chesterton. Letter to the editor. *The Architects' Journal* LXXXI(February 14, 1935), p. 264; H. T. Brock Griggs. Letter to the editor. *The Architects' Journal* LXXXI(February 14, 1935), p. 264; James Macquedy. Letter to the editor. *The Architects' Journal* LXXXI(February 14, 1935), p. 264; Robert Townsend. Letter to the editor. *The Architects' Journal* LXXXI(February 14, 1935), p. 264; Editorial note. *The Architects' Journal* LXXXI(February 14, 1935), p. 264; Quote from *The Weekly Sentinel* (Hanley). *The Architects' Journal* LXXXI(February 21, 1935), p. 294.

"The Architect and the World Today." *The Architects' Journal* LXXXI(March 21, 1935), pp. 435–436. Talk to the students section of the Architects and Technicians Organization, London, March 18, 1935.

"Remodeling a Flat." *The Studio* (London) IX(May 1935), pp. 269–271.

"The Architect's Duty to the Modern World." *The Builder* CL(January 24, 1936), p. 205. Excerpts from talk to the Manchester Society of Architects, January 8, 1936.

Review of *Specification 1936* (London: The Architectural Press, 1936), F. R. S. Yorke, ed. *The Architectural Review* LXXIX(March 1936), p. 138.

Letter to the editor. *The Architects' Journal* LXXXIII(April 23, 1936), pp. 616–617.

Peter Maitland (Chermayeff pseud.). "Leisure at the Seaside: IV. The Architect." *The Architectural Review* LXXX(July 1936), pp. 18–28.

"Modern Art and Architecture." *The RIBA Journal* XLIV(January 9, 1937), p. 209. Summary of remarks made by Serge Chermayeff at a RIBA general meeting, December 9, 1936, following talks by L. Moholy-Nagy, N. Gabo, Eileen Holding, and Herbert Read.

"Whither the English House? A Discussion." *Architectural Design and Construction* VII(August 1937), pp. 370–372. Invited exchange between Serge Chermayeff, Baillie Scott, and Naseby Adams.

"Circulation: Design: Display: The Architect at the Exhibition." *The Architectural Review* LXXXII(September 1937), pp. 91–104.

"Reinforced Concrete." *News Chronicle* (March 24, 1938), p. 19.

"The Architect's Place and Purpose in Modern Society." *Northern Architectural Students' Association Journal* III(February 1939), pp. 21–22.

"Windows in Germany." Review of *Glas und Fenster* (Berlin: Bauwelt-Verlag, 1939) by Otto Volker. *The RIBA Journal* XLVI(May 8, 1939), pp. 684–685.

"The Architectural Student: Training for What?" *The Builder* XV(June 2, 1939), pp. 1045–1046. Excerpts from talk and discussion, The Architectural Association, London, May 23, 1939. Complete text including discussion with Henry Morris and J. D. Bernal in *Focus 4* (Summer 1939), pp. 96–101.

Review of *The Flat Book* (London: Percy Lund, Humphries and Co., Ltd., 1939) by J. L. Martin and Sadie Speight. *Focus 4* (Summer 1939), pp. 80–81.

"Architects and the Air Raid Precaution." *Pencil Points* XXI(November 1940), special supplement.

"Architecture and a New World." *Arts and Architecture* LVIII(May 1941), pp. 18–19, 38, 40.

"Implications of Air Raid Precaution." *Pencil Points* XXII(July 1941), pp. 489–490.

"Air Raid Precaution (ARP) and our Office of Civilian Defense." *Pencil Points* XXII(September 1941), pp. 591–593.

"A Reply." *Pencil Points* XXII(October 1941), p. 656.

"Is High Explosive the Greatest Danger?" *Pencil Points* XXII(November 1941), pp. 725–726.

Review of *Civil Air Defense* (New York: McGraw-Hill, 1941) by Lieutenant Colonel Augustin M. Prentiss. *Pencil Points* XXII(December 1941), p. 10.

"Textbooks and Actuality." *Pencil Points* XXII(December 1941), pp. 777–778.

"San Francisco Blackout." *Pencil Points* XXIII(January 1942), pp. 27–28.

"Telesis: The Birth of a Group." *Pencil Points* XXIII(July 1942), pp. 45–48.

"The Necessity of a Second Front." *Observer-Kaleidoscope*, Brooklyn College, October 21, 1942.

"Prof. Chermayeff Clarifies Position on Second Front." Letter to the editor. *Brooklyn College Vanguard*, November 20, 1942, p. 4.

"Planning: Urns or Urbanism." *Progressive Architecture* XXIV(February 1943), pp. 72–76.

"Future Possibilities of Multiple Dwellings." In Paul Zucker, ed., *New Architecture and City Planning*. New York: Philosophical Library, 1944; pp. 278–289.

"The House in its Neighborhood." *Tomorrow's Small House*. New York: Museum of Modern Art, 1944; pp. 18–19.

"Art and the Industrial Designer." *Magazine of Art* XXXVIII(February 1945), pp. 50–53.

"Mondrian of the Perfectionists." *Art News* XLIV (March 15, 1945), pp. 14–16. Review of exhibition at the Museum of Modern Art, New York. Also published as "Mondrian y si Perfecionismo." *Revista de Arquitectura* XXXII(January 1947), pp. 35–39.

"Chemical Research Laboratory." *Proceedings. American-Soviet Building Conference*. New York: Architects Committee of the National Council of American-Soviet Friendship, 1945; pp. 134–136. Talk given to Industrial Buildings Panel, American-Soviet Building Conference, May 5, 1945.

"Structure and the Esthetic Experience." *Magazine of Art* XXXIX(May 1946), pp. 190–194.

"Education for Modern Design." *College Art Journal* VI(Spring 1947), pp. 219–221. Inaugural address to Chicago Institute of Design, February 4, 1947.

"Cultural Delinquency and How to Prevent its Spread." *California Arts and Architecture* LXIV(August 1947), pp. 28, 51–52. Talk to Western Art Association, April 30, 1947.

"Naum Gabo." *Magazine of Art* XLI(February 1948), pp. 56–59. Review of the exhibition at the Museum of Modern Art, New York, 1948.

"Painting Toward Architecture." *California Arts and Architecture* LXV(June 1948), pp. 24–31. Review of the Miller Company collection of painting and sculpture, Meriden, Connecticut.

Introduction to the "Case-Study House" issue. *Interiors* CVII(September 1948), pp. 96–119.

"Institute of Design Integrates Art, Technology and Science." *Interiors* CVIII(September 1948), pp. 142–151.

"The Institute of Design—a Laboratory for a New Education." *Interiors* CVIII(October 1948), pp. 134–140.

"Architecture at the Institute of Design." *Interiors* CVIII(November 1948), pp. 118–125.

Comments After Judging 735 Entries to the Annual Exhibition of Design in Chicago Printing (pamphlet). Chicago: The Society of Typographic Arts, 1948. Also published in Hans Wingler. *The Bauhaus*. Cambridge: MIT Press, 1969; p. 205.

Introduction to exhibition catalogue. *Exhibition of Designs by Will Burton*. Chicago: The Art Director's Club of Chicago, 1949.

Chicago Plans (exhibition brochure). Chicago: Chicago Planning Commission, 1949.

"Architecture at the Chicago Institute of Design." *L'Architecture d'Aujourd'hui* XX(February 1950), pp. 50–68.

"Theatre Planning: A Symposium." *Educational Theatre Journal* II(March 1950), pp. 1–8. Written exchange with Norman Bel Geddes, Edward C. Cole, Arch Lauterer, and Stanley McCandless.

Ludwig Mies van der Rohe, Serge Chermayeff, Walter Gropius. Three Addresses at the Blackstone Hotel, April 17, 1950 on the Occasion of the Addition of the Institute of Design to Illinois Institute of Technology. Chicago: Illinois Institute of Technology, 1950.

"The Social Aspects of Art." In Julien Harris, ed. *The Humanities: An Appraisal.* Madison: University of Wisconsin Press, 1950; pp. 140–142.

"Design Demonstrated." *Furniture Forum* II(April 1951). Introduction.

"A Symposium on How to Combine Architecture, Painting and Sculpture." *Interiors* CX(May 1951), pp. 100–105. Discussion includes remarks by Serge Chermayeff.

"The Technique of Architecture from an Educator's Point of View." *The Boston Society of Architects Record* XXXVII(November 1951). Excerpts from talk to Boston Society of Architects, October 9, 1951.

"Education of Architects." *Perspective 1951.* The Manitoba Association of Architects, Students Architectural Society, 1951.

"The Gropius Symposium." *Arts and Architecture* LXIX (May 1952), pp. 27–31; 36–38. Discussion with Gyorgy Kepes, Pietro Belluschi, Walter Gropius, and Charles Burchard at the American Academy of Sciences, Boston, January 31, 1952.

"Chermayeff Seems to Prefer 57th Street on 57th Street." *The Cape Codder*, June 12, 1952, p. 6. Review of opening of Mayo Galleries, Orleans, Massachusetts.

"The Art of Presentation." *American Society of Planning Officials Yearbook* (1952), pp. 22–25. Talk to National Planning Conference, American Society of Planning Officials, Boston, October 13, 1952.

"History of Thin Concrete Shells." Clipping from unidentified publication in Serge Chermayeff Archive, Avery Library, Columbia University.

"Der Verantwortung des Gestalters." *Der Aufbau* X(February/March 1955), pp. 68–70.

"The Shell Game." Letter to the editor. *The Architectural Form* CIX (July 1958), pp. 54, 56.

"Transportation as a Builder of Cities." *Planning for Urban Transportation.* Ithaca, New York: Cornell University Department of City and Regional Planning, 1959. Talk given to Second Annual Spring Conference of the Organization of Cornell Planners, Ithaca, March 20, 1950.

"A Star is Sought—Some Disturbing Remarks on the Propensity to Create Architectural Heroes." *The Architectural Forum* CXI(August 1959), p. 174.

"The Shape of Quality." *Architecture Plus* No. 2 (1959–1960), pp. 16–23. Talk at Texas A&M University, Department of Architecture, March 17, 1959.

"The New Nomads." *The Traffic Quarterly* XIV(April 1960), pp. 189–198.

"Statement of Serge Chermayeff, Professor of City Planning, Harvard University." *Cape Cod National Seashore Park Hearing of the Committee on Interior and Insular Affairs, U.S. Senate, Eighty-Sixth Congress.* Washington, D.C.: Government Printing Office, June 21, 1960; pp. 357–359.

"Statement of Serge Chermayeff, Professor of Architecture Harvard University." *Cape Cod National Seashore Park Hearings, Eighty-Sixth Congress.* Washington, D.C.: Government Printing Office, December 16, 1960; pp. 101–110.

"Design of the Automobile." *Canadian Art* XIX(January 1962), pp. 20–23.

Frederick Sherman. "Our Architects Get the Point." *Miami Herald,* January 28, 1962, pp. 5–6. Summary of talk given at Florida South Chapter, American Institute of Architects, January 27, 1962.

"Mobility and Urban Design." *Program*, Columbia University School of Architecture (Spring 1962), pp. 3–12.

"The Hub of the Matter." Review of *The Turning Point of Building; Structure and Design* (New York: Reinhold Publishing Corp., 1961) by Conrad Wachsmann. *Progressive Architecture* XLIII(May 1962), pp. 196, 202, 208, 212.

"The Designer's Dilemma." *Yale Reports*, No. 255 (May 20, 1962).

Review of *Architecture and the Esthetics of Plenty* (New York: Columbia University Press, 1961) by James Marston Fitch. *Scientific American* (June 1962), pp. 183–187.

"The Designer's Dilemma." Edward J. Zagorski, ed. *Serge Chermayeff, Heinz von Foerster, Ralph Caplan, Sibyl Moholy-Nagy: A Panel Discussion.* Chicago: Industrial Design Education Association, 1962. Talk to the annual meeting of the Industrial Design Education Association, University of Illinois, March 17, 1962.

Review of *Guide to Modern Architecture* (London: The Architectural Press, 1962) by Reyner Banham. *The Architectural Forum* CXVIII(March 1963), p. 145.

"Search for a New Urbanity." *Ekistics* XVI(November 1963), pp. 301–305.

Critical reaction to "Search for a New Urbanity." Alexander Tzonis. "Search for a New Urbanity: Commentary." *Ekistics* XVI(November 1963), p. 306.

"Let Us Not Make Shapes: Let Us Solve Problems." *Four Great Makers of Modern Architecture.* New York: Columbia University, 1963. Talk at Columbia University School of Architecture, April 13, 1961.

"From the Other End of the Spectrum: Some Thoughts on the Architectural Condition." *Yale Reports*, No. 309 (January 19, 1964).

"Education and Architecture." Letter to the editor. *The Architectural Forum* CXX(February 1964), p. 40.

"From the Other End of the Spectrum." *Image 2*, University of Texas School of Architecture (May 1964). Talk given at the University of Texas School of Architecture, March 1963.

"Private Affluence and Public Squalor." *Punch* CCXLVI(June 17, 1964), pp. 880–883.

"The Architectural Condition." *The Architectural Association Journal* LXXX(July/August 1964), pp. 45–50. Talk and discussion, The Architectural Association, London, April 29, 1964. Also published as "La Prosperidad Privada y la Desidia Publica." *Proa: Urbanisme Arquitectura Industriel* CLXIX(February 1965), pp. 30, 32, 34.

"Jury Discussion." *Progressive Architecture* XLVI(January 1965), pp. 126, 168–170. Comments on entries to 1964 Progressive Architecture Annual Awards Competition.

"Architecture and the Computer." *Architecture and the Computer*. The Boston Architectural Center, 1965, pp. 21–22, 44, 48–49, 50–51. Talk and discussion, The Boston Architectural Center, December 5, 1964. Excerpts also appear in "Foot-dragging?" *Architectural And Engineering News* VII(March 1965), p. 96.

Review of *Architecture and the Computer*. Bernard P. Spring. "Review: Concerning Computers." *AIA Journal* XLV(May 1966), pp. 87–88.

"A Dilemma of Our Times." *Basis* I, Auburn University School of Architecture and the Arts (Spring 1965), pp. 7–10. Talk given at "Eyes West 1963" Conference, Monterey, California, September 14, 1963.

"Random Thoughts on the Architectural Condition." Marcus Whiffen, ed. *The History, Theory and Criticism of Architecture: Papers from the 1964 AIA-ACSA Teacher Seminar*. Cambridge: The MIT Press, 1965; pp. 23–36. Talk given at AIA-ACSA Teacher Seminar, Cranbrook Academy, June 9, 1964.

Critical Reaction to "Random Thoughts on the Architectural Condition." Donlyn Lyndon. "Cranbrook, 1964." *Journal of Architectural Education* XIX(September 1964), pp. 26–28; Marcus Whiffen, ed. "History, Theory and Criticism, The 1964 AIA-ACSA Teacher Seminar." *AIA Journal* XLII(November 1964), pp. 29–40.

"Urban Playboys." Letter to the editor. *The Architectural Forum* CXXIV(April 1966), p. 91.

"Environmental Design and Adaptation to Change." *Urban Exploration*. Proceedings of Conference, Florida State University, October 28–29, 1966, pp. 1–7. Talk given at Florida State University, October 29, 1966.

"Collage of Concern." *Eye: Magazine of the Yale Arts Association* No. 1 (1967), pp. 20–24.

"Design as Catalyst." *Socio-Economic Planning Sciences* I(1967), pp. 63–69. Talk at University of Illinois, Urbana, March 13, 1967.

"Urban Commitments." *Novum Organum 3*, Yale University School of Arts and Architecture (January 6, 1969).

"Physical Mobility and Social Change." *Yale Reports*, No. 501 (February 2, 1969).

"No Simple Answers." *Modulus 5*, University of Virginia School of Architecture (1969). Talk and discussion, University of Virginia School of Architecture, December 13–14, 1968.

"Mathematics at Yale: Readers Respond." Letter to the editor. *The Architectural Forum* CXXXIII(October 1970), p. 65.

"After the S.S.T.: A Look Ahead." Letter to the editor. *The New York Times*, April 15, 1971.

"Design as Catalyst." *Architecture in Australia* (August 1971), pp. 631–637. The A. S. Hook Memorial Lecture given at the Australian Institute of Architects Centenary Convention, May 22, 1971.

"The Shape of Humanism." *Arts and Society VII*, The Pennsylvania State University (1971), pp. 517–531. Talk and discussion at the Pennsylvania State University, November 17, 1970.

"On Urbanization, Broad Frameworks, and Commitment." *Printout*, The Australian Architectural Students Association (1971). Talk and discussion, the Australian Architectural Students Association Convention, May 16–23, 1971.

"Shape of Community." *Transportation*. Proceedings of the Fifth Boston Architectural Center Lecture Series (1971), pp. 7–14. Talk and discussion at Boston Architectural Center, January 27, 1971.

With Barbara Chermayeff and Sybil Perry. "Running Amok in Paradise." Letter to the editor. *The Cape Codder*, May 24, 1973, Sect. 2, p. 2.

"Some Journeys in Search of Questions." Sammuel P. Snow, ed. *The Place of Planning*. Auburn, Alabama: Auburn University Graduate School, November, 1973; pp. 55–64.

"The Shape of Humanism." Gregory Battcock, ed. *New Ideas in Art Education*. New York: E. P. Dutton, 1973; pp. 3–10.

"Institutions, Priorities, and Revolutions." *The Future Role of Professionals in the Built Environment*. Cambridge: Harvard University, 1974. Talk at Harvard University, Graduate School of Design, May 1, 1974.

Critical reaction to "Institutions, Priorities, and Revolutions: Serge Chermayeff Assesses Role of Urban Designers." *The Harvard Gazette*, May 3, 1974.

"In Search of Questions." *The John William Lawrence Memorial Lectures. Serge Chermayeff, 1974*. New Orleans: Tulane University School of Architecture, 1974. Talk and discussion at Tulane University, New Orleans, April 19, 1974.

"Values and Ethics: The Continuity of Change." *Crit 4*, Association of Student Chapters, A.I.A. (Fall 1978), pp. 19–21. Talk given at the State

University of New York at Buffalo, School of Architecture and Environmental Design, November 7, 1977. Also published as "Values and Ethics in the Design and Planning Profession: Questions and Answers." *Spazio E Societa* No. 6 (June 1979), pp. 93–97, 114–116.

"An Explosive Revolution." *The Architectural Review* CLXVI(November 1979), p. 309.

"Thinking Before Acting." *AIA Journal* LXIX(April 1980), pp. 58–61. Talk given at Ohio State University, February 13, 1980.

"Serge Chermayeff. The Man Who Received This Year's Sir Misha Black Memorial Medal for Distinction in Design Education Reviews His Teaching Career." *Designer*, Society of Industrial Artists and Designers, London, December 1980, pp. 7–8.

BOOKS AND REPORTS

Color and its Application to Modern Building. London: Nobel Chemical Finishes, Ltd., January 1936. Booklet written and designed by Serge Chermayeff.

Critical reactions to *Color and its Application to Modern Building*: Philip Scholberg. "Review of a Booklet on Colour Prepared for Nobel Chemical Finishes, Ltd. by Serge Chermayeff." *The Architects' Journal* LXXXIII(January 23, 1936), pp. 175–176.

The New Research Laboratories. Manchester: Imperial Chemical Industries, Ltd., 1938. Booklet written and designed by Serge Chermayeff.

Plan for Air Raid Precaution: A Practical Policy. London: Frederick Muller, Ltd., 1939.

Critical reactions to *Plan for Air Raid Precaution: A Practical Policy*: Astragal (pseud.). "Notes and Comments." *The Architects' Journal* LXXXIX(February 16, 1939), p. 274; Felix J. Samuely. "Aspects of ARP." *Focus* No. 3 (Spring 1939), p. 48.

Rude and Random Rhymes. Orleans, Massachusetts: Cape Codder Printery, circa 1955. Designed by Ivan Chermayeff.

Report on Future Development of Diamond K Ranch. Cambridge, Massachusetts: Chermayeff and Cutting, Architects, circa 1955. (Serge Chermayeff Archive, Avery Library, Columbia University)

Shape of Privacy. Cambridge, Massachusetts: Harvard University Graduate School of Design, 1961.

Search for a New Urbanity. New Haven: Yale University School of Arts and Architecture, 1962. Excerpts published in "Search for a New Urbanity." *Ekistics* XVI(November 1963), pp. 301–305.

Critical reactions to *Search for a New Urbanity*: Alexander Tzonis. "Transformation of the Initial Structure." *Perspecta 12*, Yale University School of Arts and Architecture (1969), pp. 11–14; Alexander Tzonis. "Commentary." *Ekistics* XVI(November 1963), p. 306.

With Christopher Alexander. *Community and Privacy: Toward a New Architecture of Humanism.* New York: Doubleday and Company, 1963. Excerpts published in "The Future of the American City." *Current* No. 42 (October 1963), pp. 58–63.

Critical reactions to *Community and Privacy.* General reviews and articles: Charles Jencks. "The Architect in an Overpopulated World." *Connection* No. 1, Harvard University Graduate School of Design (1963), pp. 21–23; Allan Temko. "Things Are Getting Too Crowded, Too Mechanized and Too Noisy." *The New York Times Book Review* (October 13, 1963), p. 6; David B. Carlson. "Shaping a New Pattern for Urban Living." *The Architectural Forum* CXIX(December 1963), pp. 106–107; "The City." *The Architectural Record* CXXIV(December 1963), p. 42; Robert C. Weinberg. "Are We Ever Left Sufficiently to Ourselves?" *New York AIP Letter*, American Institute of Planners, New York Chapter (December 1963), pp. 18–19; Bernard Rudolfsky. "Serge Chermayeff: i mali, i pericoli, e la possible salvezza, del moderno abitare urbano." *Domus* CDX(January 1964), pp. 45–46; Jan White. "2 Architects + 1 Computer = New Design Criteria." *House and Home* XXV(January 1964), p. 112; Frederick Gutheim. "Rooms for All." *The Nation* CXCVIII(January 13, 1964), p. 54; Alan Colquhoun, *Architectural Association Journal* LXXIX(December 1963), p. 166: Lionel Brett. "Court Houses." *The Architectural Review* CXXXV(February 1964), p. 89; Wolf Von Eckhardt. *Library Journal* LXXXIX(February 1, 1964), p. 620; Kenneth Rexroth. "On Fouling up Our Nests." *Book Week* (March 8, 1964), p. 2; *American City Magazine* LXXIX(April 1964), pp. 187, 189; Daniel Perry. *AIA Journal* XLI(April 1964), p. 66; Philip Thiel. *Landscape*, Santa Fe, New Mexico (Spring 1964); *Scientific American* CCXI(July 1964), p. 136; Robert Damora. *Industrial Design* XI(December 1964), p. 28; P. A. P. Melvin. *The West African Builder and Architect* V(January-February, 1965), p. 17; David Mackay. *Contradictions in Living Environment.* London: Crosby, Lockwood and Son, Ltd., 1971, pp. 9, 69–70; Alexander Tzonis. *Towards a Non-Oppressive Environment.* Boston: I-Press, 1972, pp. 96–100; Duncan Macintosh. *The Modern Courtyard House.* London: Architectural Association Paper No. 9, 1973, pp. 18–19; Oscar Newman. *Defensible Space.* New York: Collier Books, 1973, pp. 148–155.

Newspaper reviews: "The Deadly Street." *The Nashville Tennessean,* September 29, 1963; Mel Wax. "IBM 704 Conceives a New Home Environment." *San Francisco Cronicle*, October 13, 1963; Charles Brock. "Elbowed From All Sides." *Jacksonville Journal*, October 20, 1963; Nathaniel Polster. "Scale Is the Secret of City Plan." *Savannah Morning News*, October 27, 1963; Glade Little. "Our Crowded Lives." *Sunday Gazette-Mail* (Charleston, W.Va.), November, 1963; *News and Courier* (Charleston, S.C.), December 15, 1963; *Sacramento Bee*, January 12, 1964; "An Important Book and Cape Cod's Meaning." *The Cape Codder*, February 20, 1964; Robert Wyatt. "An Architecture Needs Humanism." *Tulsa World*, February 23, 1964; "Cities Attacked." *Ed-*

monton Journal (Alberta), December 10, 1965; Diana Rowntree. "The Pace of the Race." *Guardian*, November 25, 1966; Peter Hall. "A Nightmare Overcome." *London Sunday Times*, December 11, 1966, p. 46; "Private Convenience." *The Times Literary Supplement*, December 29, 1966, p. 1201; Dirk Bolt. "Laying Siege to Suburbia." *The Canberra Times*, March 18, 1967.

Non-English language editions: *binario* No. 160 (January 1972), p. 47; *Die Tat*, Zurich XXXVII(January 11, 1972), p. 11; "Pladoyer fur humanes Bauen." *Stuttgarter Zeitung* (January 22, 1972), p. 53; *ons huis, maanblad voor de woninginrichtig* XXX(February 1972), pp. 209–210; *Suddeutsche Bauwirtschaft* XXII(1972), p. 93; *Formes Nouvelles* No. 3 (March 1972), p. 8055; *Der Staedtler-Brief* No. 21 (Summer 1972), p. 592; *Architektur und Wohnwelt* LXXX(July 1972), p. 336; *Der Deutsche Baumeister* XXXIII(July 1972), p. 543; Agnoldomenico Pica. *Domus* No. 513 (August 1972), p. 26; *Deutsches Architektenblatt* No. 18 (September 15, 1972), p. 1211; *Der Ingenieur im offentlichen Dienst* I(October 1972), p. 64; *Architectural Science Review* XVII, No. 1 (1974).

With Alexander Tzonis. *Advanced Studies in Urban Environments*. New Haven: Yale University, 1967. Report for the Institute for Applied Technology, U.S. Bureau of Standards.

W. Mitchell, ed. *Synopsis of Conclusions and Record of Process. The Chermayeff Studio. Autumn, 1968–69* (photostated booklet). New Haven: Yale University School of Arts and Architecture. January 1969.

With Alexander Tzonis. *Shape of Community. Realization of Human Potential*. Baltimore: Penguin Books, 1971.

Critical reactions: Cliff Rowe. "Good for Exercise." *The Morning Star*, January 28, 1971; George Rose. "Piazza Pie." *The New Society* XVII(April 1, 1971), p. 549; Patrick Shaffrey. "The Modern City." *The Irish Times*, June 3, 1971; "Save Our Cities." *The Times Literary Supplement* (June 4, 1971), p. 642; *The Tacoma News Tribune and Sunday Ledger*, July 18, 1971; Thomas Creighton. "Eco-relationship and Urban Design." *The Sunday Star Bulletin and Advertiser* (Honolulu), August 22, 1971, p. A-27; Karl W. Deutsch. "A Community of Ideas and an Idea of Community." *Yale Review* LXI(Autumn 1971), pp. 101–109; *Revista de Psicologia General y Aplicada* XXVI(1971), p. 185; Geoffrey Broadbent. "Hello Aquarius." *RIBA Journal* LXXVIII(January 1972), p. 36; Joseph Smucker. *American Political Science Review* LXVII(June 1973), pp. 594–595.

Verse of Anger and Affection, 1957–1973. Orleans, Massachusetts: Tompson's Printing, 1973.

Critical reactions: Orin Tovrov. "Chermayeff Verse: A New Facet to the Man." *The Cape Codder* (December 20, 1973), Sect. 2, p. 12.

UNPUBLISHED MANUSCRIPTS (Serge Chermayeff Archive, Avery Architectural Library, Columbia University)

With Paul Follot. "The Evolution of Decorative Art: its Motives, its History, and its Present Tendencies." Talk at Exhibition of Modern Furnishings at Waring and Gillow, London, 1928.

"Modern Decoration," 1929.

"Brief Statement of the 20th Century Group Beliefs," 1930.

"Artificial Light. A Few Remarks on Power, Position and Use," circa 1930.

"Furniture and Decoration," circa 1930.

"Harmony in the House," circa 1930.

"Originality vs. Plagiarism, or Alternatively, Creating vs. Copying," circa 1930.

"Private Lives—Private Lights," circa 1930.

"The Modern Approach to Furniture Design." Talk at Art Workers' Guild, London, 1932; similar talk previously given to Design and Industries Association, London, March 31, 1932.

"Modern Furniture." Talk at Victoria and Albert Museum, London, November 17, 1932.

"Unit Building." Talk at Architecture Club, London, October 26, 1933.

"Planning the Home for Modern Living." Talk at Exhibition of Contemporary Domestic Architecture in the West, 1933.

"Noise Prevention in Building," circa 1934.

"Design for Selling." Talk at Publicity Club, London, January 21, 1935.

Untitled. Talk at Marx House, February 3, 1935.

"The Architect in Society." Talk at the Harrow School, July 9, 1935.

"The Modern House." BBC television broadcast, London, December 11, 1936. (Includes discussion with John Gloag.)

Critical Reactions: Astragal (pseud.). "Notes and Comments." *The Architects' Journal* LXXXIV(December 10, 1936), p. 798; (December 17, 1936), p. 832.

"Art in Modern Architecture." BBC television broadcast, London, January 27, 1937.

"Rebuilding England." BBC television broadcast, London, April 8, 1937.

"Contemporary Architecture." Talk at the Edinburgh Architectural Association, November 4, 1938.

"Government Employment of Architects in Connection with Rearmament and Defense," 1938.

"Finsbury Borough Council A. R. P. Shelters. Report on suggested signposting of Shelters," 1939.

Untitled Luncheon Speech. Talk to the Ontario Architectural Societies, Toronto, March 11, 1940.

"Why Modern Architecture?" CBC broadcast, March 26, 1940.

"Present Position in Architecture or the Crisis in Architecture." Talk at Harvard University, Graduate School of Design, April 18, 1940; also given at Yale University, date unknown.

"Crisis in Architecture." Talk at the Museum of Fine Arts, San Francisco, September 18, 1940.

"Biographical Note," 1940.

"False Gods?" Unpublished article prepared for *Task* No. 2 (November 1941).

"Address to the Alumni Association." Talk at Columbia University Architecture Alumni Association, May 28, 1942.

"Excerpts from Report to the President of Brooklyn College," December 1942.

"A Summary of Report on Contemporary Planning, Architecture, Design and Design Education," circa 1947.

"Outline for a Planning and Design Department in a Western University." Prepared for Stanford University, circa 1947.

"Memorandum Based on a Conversation Between Mr. Jalkut, Mr. Abbott and Mr. Chermayeff, Held at the Museum of Modern Art on March 11, 1943," 1943.

"Modern Architecture in Palestine." Unidentified talk dated March 22, 1943.

"Design for Use." Text developed in relation to the exhibition at the Museum of Modern Art, New York, 1944.

"Broadcast from Union College." Radio talk, Schenectady, New York, February 25, 1945.

"Architecture, Painting and Sculpture." Talk at symposium at Hampton Institute, January 1946.

"Industry, Architecture and Design." Talk at University of Toronto, January 26, 1946.

"Report to the Board of Directors, Institute of Design, Chicago," 1947.

Review of a publication of the "American Abstract Artists," February 10, 1947.

"President's Report." Chicago Institute of Design, March 11, 1947.

"Safe at Home—or Are We?" Talk at American Designers' Institute, Chicago, January 7, 1948.

"Form in Design." Talk given in the series, "Society and Design," Chicago Institute of Design, April 22, 1948.

"Social Responsibility and the Artist." Talk at the Minneapolis School of Art, June 3, 1948.

"Are Our Houses Fit to Live In?" Talk at Home Institute Meeting, The Minneapolis Institute of Arts, March 8, 1949.

"Address to Planning and Building Panel." Talk to the Planning and Building Panel, Cultural and Scientific Conference for World Peace, New York City, March 26, 1949.

"Architecture: Anonymity and Autonomy." Harvard University, Graduate School of Design, Fogg Art Museum, April 11, 1949.

"Design in the Elementary and Secondary School Art Program." Talk at Iowa State University, May 1949.

"Fine Arts in General Education." Panel discussion (P. R. McIntosh, chairman, with H. Harvard Arnason, Arnold Blanch, C. Howard Church, Charles Parkhurst), Midwestern College Art Conference, Minneapolis and St. Paul, November 10–12, 1949.

Talk given at "Fifty Books of the Year" dinner, American Institute of Graphic Arts, New York, April 4, 1950. (Includes statements by others.)

"IIT-ID, Formal Announcement of Merger," April 17, 1950.

"The Profession of Architecture." Talk at the Institute of Design, Chicago, November 2, 1950.

Untitled text attributed to Mies van der Rohe and Serge Chermayeff, for fund raising for new Illinois Institute of Technology architecture building, 1950.

"An Approach to Redevelopment." Panel discussion, Harvard University Community Appraisal Study, Graduate School of Design, Spring 1951.

"Memorandum to Dean Sert." Harvard University, Graduate School of Design, November 3, 1953. (Includes a memorandum to the Committee on Design Research).

"Commencement Address." Rhode Island School of Design, June 12, 1954.

"The Visual Arts: Their Relationships." Transcript from a symposium (with Serge Chermayeff, Naum Gabo, Ben Shahn, James J. Sweeney, Sigfried Giedion, and Jose Luis Sert, moderator). Harvard University, Graduate School of Design, February 8, 1955.

Environmental Design Seminar transcripts. Harvard University, Graduate School of Design, dated October 1, October 15, October 22, October 27, November 5, November 12, December 3, December 17, 1954; and January 7, January 14, February 11, and April 7, 1955.

"Memo to Dean José L. Sert. Comments on Present Curricula." Harvard University, Graduate School of Design, hand dated Spring 1955.

"Environmental Design. Chermayeff Seminar." Course Outline, Harvard University, Graduate School of Design, circa 1955.

"Environmental Design. First and Second Semester." Harvard University, Graduate School of Design, circa 1955.

"Memo to Dean Sert." Harvard University, Graduate School of Design, January 1956.

Untitled transcript from NBC "Home" telecast, April 10, 1956.

"To Dean Sert." Harvard University, Graduate School of Design, April 26, 1956.

"Memo to Dean Sert, Re: General Policy of the Graduate School of Design." Harvard University, Graduate School of Design, June 8, 1956.

"Design and Transition: Architecture and Planning Purpose Examined in the Light of Accelerating Events." Talk at Dartmouth College Great Issues Course, April 22, 1957.

"Modes and Manners in Art." Talk at Brooklyn College, May 20, 1957.

Unidentified notes for television broadcast on Harvard Urban Family House Project, May 1957.

"Education for Designers." Talk at Institute of Contemporary Arts, London, July, 1957.

"Memorandum to Dean Sert." Harvard University, Graduate School of Design, December 17, 1957.

"First Year Design Curricula." Harvard University, Graduate School of Design, 1957.

"Scale, Shape, Mobility." Talk to Division of Architecture, Texas A&M University, March 17, 1959.

"Center for Urban Studies. Proposal for a Research Project at the G.S.D., Harvard," May 1959. (Labeled "2nd Draft.")

"The Urban Family House. First Report on Progress." Harvard University, October 15, 1959.

"Center for Urban Studies. Proposal for a Research Project at the G.S.D., Harvard," November 1959. (Labeled "Revision.")

"The Shape of Privacy." Talk at Harvard University, Graduate School of Design, May 9, 1961.

"The Designer's Dilemma." Talk to the Annual Spring Convocation, Yale Arts Association, April 14, 1962.

Unidentified radio interview. Minneapolis, April, 1963.

"In Search of a New Urbanity." Talk at Walker Art Institute, Minneapolis, April 1963; also given at Baltimore Museum of Fine Arts, October 1963, and University of Illinois, Chicago, November 1963.

"Some Thoughts on the Architectural Condition." Talk at University of California at Berkeley, September 18, 1963.

"No Style—Either Regional or International." Talk at Pratt Institute School of Architecture, February 20, 1964. (Partially handwritten.)

"What Should Our Environment Goals Be?" Talk to State of Connecticut Sixteenth Annual Development Conference, 1964.

"The Architect and the Future." Identified as talk given to secondary school pupils as part of a Careers Advising Seminar, 1964.

"The Computer and the Humanities." Talk at Yale University conference, January 23, 1965.

"Urban Environment Studies. A Proposal for Yale University," February 11, 1965.

"Planning Places." Proposal to 20th Century Fund, April 1965.

"Advanced Studies in Urban Design. A Proposal for a Research Grant to the Department of Architecture." Yale University, 1965.

Untitled. Talk at Louisiana State University, 1965.

"Advanced Studies in Urban Environments." Yale University, School of Art and Architecture, March 15, 1966.

"Technology and the City Matrix." Talk at Conference of National Bureau of Standards, University of California at Santa Barbara, August 24, 1966.

"Chermayeff Interview." Telecast by WGBH, Boston, in series on architectural education, March 18, 1966.

"Advanced Studies in Urban Design. Proposals for New Courses in the Department of Architecture, Yale," Fall 1966.

"Shape of the Urban Community: Humanistic Considerations." Talk at New York Academy of Sciences, October 19, 1967.

"Urban Commitments and a Theory of Design." Talk to Yale University Department of City Planning, October 1968.

"Formal and Structural Changes in Human Settlements." Undelivered talk for 14th Triennale di Milano, 1968.

"Architecture of Human Environment." Talk at Middle East Technical University, Ankara, December 19, 1969.

"Design of the Physical Environment in India—Professional Standards and Education." Report to the JDR 3rd Fund, March 31, 1970.

"The Shape of Community Revisited." Talk at Yale University, April 26, 1972.

Untitled Gold Medal acceptance speech, Royal Canadian Institute of Architects, Montreal, June 1, 1973.

Untitled notes for the conference, "The Future of Architecture," Cornell University, October 1976.

Untitled talk for ASCA Annual Meeting, San Antonio, March 1980.

"Continuity and Change. Concern and Commitment." Talk to International Design Conference, Aspen, Colorado, June 18, 1980.

"Continuities and Changes. Concerns and Commitments." Talk to Illinois Council of the American Institute of Architects Annual Convention, September 12, 1980.

"The Third Ecology." Talk given at fiftieth anniversary of the Society of Industrial Artists and Designers, London, October 10, 1980.

Untitled notes for talk to Architectural Student Chapters Annual Meeting, American Institute of Architects, Temple University, November 25, 1980.

ILLUSTRATION CREDITS

p. ii
Tomash Breuer

p. iii
Ferenc Berko

p. 8
Decorative Metalwork and Cotton Textiles, 1930

p. 12
The Architect and Building News, October 10, 1930

p. 18
Book on Colour, 1936

p. 26
The Architects' Journal, April 19, 1934

p. 32
The Architectural Review, July 1933

p. 36
Design for Today, June 1933

p. 46
The Architectural Review, March 1933

p. 56
The Architectural Review, July 1936

p. 62
Book on Colour, 1936

p. 72
Revista de Arquitectura, January 1937

p. 112
The Architectural Review, July 1937

pp. 116, 122
The Architectural Review, February 1939

p. 126
The Architectural Review, March 1938

p. 136
RIBA Journal, March 7, 1938

p. 142
House and Garden, May 1947

p. 148
The Architectural Forum, January 1947

p. 212
House and Home, July 1954

p. 300
Eye: Magazine of the Yale Arts Association, 1967

pp. 325, 327, 329, 337, 340, 341
Dell and Wainwright

pp. 330, 335, 342, 343
Herbert Felton

p. 333
Studio Sun Ltd.

p. 334
Sydney W. Newbery

p. 338
Millar & Harris

pp. 344, 345
Roger Sturtevent

p. 347 (top and bottom)
Ezra Stoller © ESTO

p. 348
Joseph W. Molitor

p. 349
Ben Schnall

p. 350
Hans Namuth

p. 351 (bottom)
Norman R. C. McGrath

INDEX